France Since 1930

France
Since
1930

Edited with an Introduction by

John E. Talbott

A NEW YORK TIMES BOOK

 *Quadrangle Books*
A NEW YORK TIMES COMPANY

Library of Congress Catalog Card Number: 77-130395
International Standard Book Number: cloth 0-8129-0254-8
paper 0-8129-6196-X

The publishers are grateful to the contributors herein for permission to reprint their articles.

Contents

3. The Fourth Republic

4. The Fifth Republic

France Since 1930

Introduction

AS RECENTLY as the mid-1950's many observers were writing of France as the new sick man of Europe. Over the preceding quarter-century, in the face of economic instability, political turmoil, and an unending succession of wars, pessimism about France's future had become an easily acquired habit. Yet a half-dozen years after the establishment of the Fifth Republic (1958), the gloomy prognostications of the fifties had virtually disappeared from the press. In the early 1960's some journalists claimed to see a "new French Revolution" at work, equal in magnitude, the phrase was meant to suggest, to the cataclysm which ended the Old Regime. If these observers had some regrets about the passing of an older France, an optimistic mood nonetheless pervaded their writing. Today no one regards France as a sick man. Whether the French have embarked on a new course, whether the changes now taking place amount to a "revolution," remain controversial questions. At any rate, recovery did not take place overnight; many of the forces whose cumulative impact some now regard as revolutionary were already at work in the darkest days of the recent past.

The following articles discuss aspects of the French experience from 1930 to our own day. These years have been as turbulent as any in the history of France since the era of the Great Revolution. But turbulence alone is probably not sufficient excuse to regard the period from 1930 to the present as an historical unit. What gives these years an underlying unity, and at the same time accounts for at least some of their turbulence, is the breakdown of an old order and the emergence of a new. To be sure, any scheme of historical periodization is always debatable. Some writers have argued that a strong and stable France never recovered from the disastrous effects of the First World War, and that the years 1914–1918 constitute the most important watershed in the history of modern France. Others have claimed that the Second World War marked such a traumatic break in the continuity of the French experience that the history of contemporary France should in fact begin in 1945.

Yet a strong case can be made that the Third Republic weathered the terrible storms of the First World War intact. The political, economic, and social system—the "old order"—which the Third Republic represented, began to crumble only with the onslaught of the depression, in the thirties. Once the wreckage of the Second World War was cleared away, the most perplexing issues France confronted were those inherited from the pre-war era. Thus the obsession of the Gaullists with the weakness of the authority of the executive, for example, cannot be understood without some knowledge of the historical experience of the thirties, which marked General Charles de Gaulle as deeply as the war years did. Finally, talk of the emergence of a "new" order of politics, society, and economics makes little sense unless one has a grasp of what the old order was like. By 1945 that order had already been substantially altered; in the early 1930's it was still pretty much intact.

In 1930 France was still predominantly a nation of small farms, small industries, and small businesses. More people made their living from the land than in any other Western European nation— in 1930 about 35 per cent of the active French population were farmers. Most were smallholders, many of whom raised only enough to support their families. Still, in good years, so abundant was agricultural production that France could not only feed its own people but export a surplus as well. But what some Frenchmen considered a healthy "balance" between industry and agriculture, others regarded as economic backwardness. The pace of industrialization in France had been slower than that of any other major industrial power. Some historians have placed the blame for this on material handicaps—on France's scarcity of coal deposits, for example. Others have argued that the psychological attitudes of the French businessman—his sense of the firm as a precious family inheritance and his consequent reluctance to undertake risks, his suspicion of outsiders with capital to invest, his acceptance of social values which disdained business activity—have had more to do with economic retardation than a lack of important material resources. Still others have cast doubts on both the psycho-sociological and the material-structural explanations for French economic backwardness; some have maintained that, except for the interwar period, the French economy has not performed as badly as some critics have suggested. In any case, just as the small peasant dominated French agriculture, so the small firm dominated French industry. In 1930, 80 per cent of French firms employed fewer than twenty workers; and only a handful employed more than five hundred. Retail trade was similarly dominated by small, family-run shops.

In this land of the little man, the schizophrenic ideology of France's Radical party exemplified the little man's outlook: in favor of equality but hankering after property and individual achievement; against social injustice but convinced that one's own bootstraps afforded the only legitimate means of social ascent; patriotic but suspicious of the government; generous in principle but made uneasy by the poor and at the same time envious of the wealthy.

The Radical party had dominated the French parliament since the turn of the century, and under the Third Republic, parliament reigned supreme. Mainly because of historical accident, parliament had acquired at the expense of the executive more power than the founders of the Third Republic had meant for it to have. No government lasted very long in such circumstances. But the political instability of the Third Republic is easy to exaggerate. In the first place, under the Third Republic a stability of ministers compensated for ministerial instability. Year after year, the same deputies kept popping up in one ministry after another, often in the same posts, thus making the development and execution of policy less subject to twists and turns than the waltz of ministries made it seem. The instability of political authority was also counterbalanced—too strongly counterbalanced, many people thought—by the highly centralized administration, whose high civil servants assured continuity in the conduct of the state's business even as the political ministers came and went.

The political machinery of the Third Republic worked very well at keeping things from getting done, which many Frenchmen considered one of the virtues of the system. The peasantry and the middle classes who dominated the Third Republic did not want the government to do a great deal, apart from maintaining order and passing a limited amount of legislation on behalf of themselves. This is not to say that social issues were ignored. Few who held positions of responsibility opposed the use of state power to alleviate the worst abuses of industrialism. But most believed that narrow limits should be set to government intervention in the economy on behalf of industrial and agricultural workers. The working class itself was too poorly organized and too underrepresented in the National Assembly to make its weight felt. Concessions came grudgingly, and France lagged behind Germany and Great Britain in passing social legislation.

To be sure, the Third Republic had shortcomings aplenty. The political system functioned well only so long as no one called upon it to do anything; social problems were in the main glossed over and economic backwardness held to be a virtue; the working class was kept at arm's length from the rest of society; the birthrate, on the decline since the middle of the nineteenth century, and the lowest of any country in Western Europe, suggested that Frenchmen had no great confidence in the future of their own society. Nevertheless, had the Third Republic been as brittle a structure as some of its critics have maintained, it is hard to see how it could have withstood the strains of the First World War. But in fact the Third Republic emerged intact, having summoned from Frenchmen the utmost in blood and treasure. In the absence of further severe trials, the system might have adjusted itself to the demands of the twentieth century. But just as recovery from the material costs of the war appeared to have been accomplished, the old order fell victim to a series of blows. The first of these was the Great Depression, to which the troubles of the 1930's were all in some way related.

Shielded by its relative economic self-sufficiency, France escaped the depression for a time. By 1932, however, the French found themselves deep in the economic doldrums. Industrial production plummeted, and scraped along for years at a level fully 20 per cent below that of 1929. Unemployment soared. While in the United States the power and the moral authority of the presidency lay ready to hand as weapons against the crisis, in France no such instrument existed. The French parliament seemed to hope for the discovery of a miracle cure. Governments succeeded each other at an accelerating rate; large sectors of an increasingly restive and worried electorate began to suspect that their representatives had chosen to deal with the crisis by turning their backs on it. Anti-parliamentary feeling ran high.

In the winter of 1933–1934 revelations began to be made about the financial manipulations of Serge Stavisky, a big-time con man who got along, it was rumored, with a little help from his friends in high places in the government and the administration, and especially in the Radical party. Right-wing leagues seized upon the Stavisky Affair to mount a demonstration against parliament which degenerated into a bloody riot. The riot, which drastically affected the politics of the 1930's, remains a controversial episode. What were the rioters' intentions? What was the nature of the organizations that took part? In the view of some, the rioters meant only to demonstrate their contempt for parliament—at the most to force the resignation of the despised Radical government (an aim which they accomplished). Others contend that the leaders of the demonstration aimed to bring down the Third Republic itself. To support this claim they point to the well-organized character of the demonstrations and to the prominent role played in them by the anti-republican leagues. But it is a long way from a well-organized demonstration to a *coup d'état*. If the leaders had a *coup* in mind, their behavior was singularly lackadaisical; among other things, they apparently made no effort to sound out the armed forces or even to secure control of strategic points in the capital.

Some historians have argued that the major participating organizations in the riot represented yet another outburst of an anti-parliamentary, nationalist, and Catholic traditionalism deeply rooted in French history. Colonel François de la Rocque and his troops, they suggest, represented a kind of boy-scout movement for grownups. Others have detected something more sinister: a manifestation of a home-grown variety of fascism. The rioters, they contend, were toughs of the radical right, whose leaders aimed to replace the Third Republic with a Hitlerian regime. Elements of both traditionalist groups and of self-styled fascist organizations took part in the Stavisky riot (to complicate matters further, so did members of the Communist party), but it would be hard to say which gave the predominant tone to the affair. Whether France narrowly averted a fascist revolution in the early 1930's remains an open and, in the end, probably unanswerable question.

At any rate, the parties of the Left believed they had barely escaped a fascist revolution. The Stavisky riot provoked counter-demonstrations against the threat of fascism and a series of arduous negotiations which ended in the formation of the Popular Front. As recently as the end of 1932, insurmountable differences had appeared to stand in the way of a coalition of Radicals, Socialists, and Communists, the three main parties of the Left. But in January 1933 the Nazis came to power in Germany. The Stavisky riots overnight transformed fascism into a domestic threat. Meanwhile, the Soviet Union subordinated hostility to the capitalist states of the West to the need for a common struggle against fascism. The change in Soviet foreign policy removed the most serious obstacle to the unity of the Left, and the French Communist party, faithful to its duty to defend "socialism in one country," abandoned its intransigent hostility to the bourgeois Third Republic and wrapped itself in the French tricolor.

The program of the Popular Front incorporated long-standing demands for reform, but the coalition itself rested on a shaky foundation. Each of the major partners had joined the Front for reasons which did not altogether square with those of its allies. The Communists were mainly interested in promoting the foreign-policy aims of the Soviet Union; the Radicals wanted to stay afloat on a leftward-running tide; only the Socialists unequivocally embraced the whole program.

Nevertheless, the Popular Front's electoral victory in May 1936 generated enormous enthusiasm and gave rise to immense hopes. Léon Blum became the first Socialist prime minister in French history, and in the mythology of the French Left the early months of 1936 took their place alongside the early months of 1848, when revolution swept Europe, as a "Springtime of the People."

The major accomplishments of the Popular Front came early. A wave of largely spontaneous strikes swept across France on the eve of Blum's assumption of office. Blum, however, managed to turn a serious embarrassment into a tool for reform. Management, angered but frightened by the workers' occupation of the factories, was brought to accede to a series of measures known as the Matignon Agreements, which granted wage increases and recognized the principle of collective bargaining and the right of workers to a paid vacation. Parliament then limited the work week to forty hours. The paid vacation in itself accomplished a small social revolution, for it meant that leisure was no longer to be exclusively the prerogative of the well-to-do. Blum later remembered the summer of 1936, when for the first time working-class families headed for the beaches and the mountains, as one of the proudest times of his life.

But the Matignon Agreements also symbolized the predicament of the Popular Front. As social reform, the forty-hour week, for example, met a long-standing demand. But the reduction in the work week also hampered efforts to increase industrial production, a prerequisite of economic recovery.

Financial stability was another prerequisite of recovery. During the election campaign the Popular Front had unwisely pledged not to devalue the franc, which was still pegged to gold at too high a price. But French goods continued to be overpriced in the world market; holders of overvalued francs continued to unload them in favor of sounder currencies; and capital continued to flee the country. In October 1936 the Blum government finally devalued the franc, but the right psychological movement for such a measure had passed.

In 1937 production continued to bump along at a level far below that of the late 1920's. In February, in the face of the government's continued economic and financial difficulties, Blum called a "pause" to social reform; in June he sought from parliament the authority to stem the flow of capital by the device of decree-laws issued by the government. The Radical-dominated Senate refused him powers granted other prime ministers in the recent past, and Blum resigned. With the fall of his government the Popular Front experiment died, and dead along with it were most of the hopes to which it had given birth.

Control of the government returned to the moderates and those members of the Radical party's conservative wing who had been in power before 1936. The *élan* having gone out of the Popular Front, the fears it had inspired among conservatives subsided somewhat, but the ideological passion aroused by the strife of the previous years lingered on. In such conditions perhaps a policy of national union against the depression or against fascism was impossible. The program of the Popular Front gave way to a policy of drift. In any event, from the mid-1930's on, foreign policy increasingly diverted the attention of the government from domestic concerns, until at last it had little time or energy for anything else. In the end the Third Republic did not give way to internal weaknesses but to the blast of war.

In 1930 France was the strongest military power on the continent. Since 1918 the main preoccupation of French foreign policy had been security from renewed German aggression. To accomplish this aim, France counted on both traditional bilateral military-defense treaties, notably with Poland and the new states of Rumania, Yugoslavia, and Czechoslovakia—the so-called "Little Entente"—and on the new concept of collective security, based on multi-lateral commitments of the membership of the League of Nations. Aristide Briand, the architect of this policy, was one of the most accomplished masters of diplomatic sleight of hand, if not the greatest diplomat, ever to occupy the Foreign Ministry. To the French Left, which regarded the League of Nations as the best hope for the maintenance of peace, Briand's policy seemed to be based squarely on a rapprochement with Germany and a reliance on collective security. To the Right, Briand's treaties appeared to have woven a web of militarily enforceable restraints around the German frontiers.

As the 1930's wore on, both the "liberal" and "conservative" aspects of this policy fell into disuse. France played its last strong hand in 1934, the year after Hitler came to power, when Louis Barthou, a veteran politician of the Right, sought to round up a grand alliance of the European powers against Germany. But an assassin's bullet put an end to Barthou and to his scheme in October of the same year. Some of Barthou's successors refused to believe that Hitler meant what he said; they convinced themselves that he was a reasonable man with reasonable demands. If some of these demands were met, they believed, surely he would stop making trouble. But each time a concession was made, Hitler raised the ante on his next move. Other French policy-makers, notably Pierre Laval, believed Mussolini might be used against Hitler. But courting one dictator did not discourage the ambitions of another. Foot-dragging in negotiations undertaken with the Soviet Union in 1935 only heightened Soviet suspicions of Western aims.

In March 1936 the military occupation of the Rhineland destroyed the bases on which French foreign policy had rested since the end of the First World War. Despite some sentiment within the French Cabinet for an immediate military riposte, the army command advised against such a move; the government, reluctant to act without the assistance of England, in the end did nothing. Hitler's gamble paid off. The German frontier was closed to invasion and the French alliance system lay in ruins, for France's eastern allies could no longer believe France would come to their aid and so moved into the Nazi orbit.

In a democracy the conduct of a coherent foreign policy requires a substantial national consensus on the government's aims. Ideological divisions within France made this task increasingly difficult. When the Spanish Civil War broke out in the summer of 1936, shortly after the Popular Front assumed office, important sectors of the Right sided with General Franco's rebellion, which received aid from Italy and Germany, while the Left supported the legal republican government. At the outset, the Blum government agreed to ship arms to Spain's loyalist forces; but under criticism from allies, domestic opponents, and from within the cabinet itself, it quickly retreated to a position of nonintervention. The decision against intervention may have sealed the fate of the Spanish Republic, as some historians have argued, but it is questionable whether French involvement in the Spanish Civil War would have discouraged Hitler, as Blum's critics have contended, for the German dictator's designs on Eastern Europe were clear. Indeed, the commitment of the French army in Spain might have played right into his hands.

Having absorbed Austria in the spring of 1938, with scarcely a murmur from the Western powers, Hitler began to turn the screws on Czechoslovakia. The Nazis backed a German separatist movement whose demands, if recognized, meant the dismemberment of the country. Despite formal obligations to assist the Czechs if they were attacked, the French government subordinated itself to the lead of England, whose prime minister, Neville Chamberlain, had publicly declared his government's lack of interest in what happened in Eastern Europe. Chamberlain and Edouard Daladier, the French premier, met Hitler in Munich in September 1938; with Mussolini looking on, they gave him pretty much what he wanted: the cession of territory which foreshadowed the end of Czechoslovakia as a viable state.

Daladier realized what had been done, but he received a hero's welcome when he returned from Munich, for the agreement meant that war had been averted. Five months later the German army occupied Czechoslovakia. Western resistance to German expansionism now stiffened. The British government hastened to guarantee Poland, the next victim on Hitler's list, from attack; France reluctantly went along. But domestic opinion on French foreign policy remained deeply divided. Marcel Déat, a renegade Socialist, declared himself unwilling to die for Danzig—a sentiment large numbers of his countrymen probably shared.

In the summer of 1939 the French and British governments sought an alliance with the Soviet Union. But Stalin could hardly have been impressed by Western steadfastness in the face of German expansionism thus far, and he chose to come to terms with Hitler instead. The stupefying news of a Nazi-Soviet nonaggression pact was made public in late August 1939. If the Western powers were to honor their declarations on Poland, war with Germany now seemed inescapable. Still, Georges Bonnet, the French foreign minister, found himself able to inquire whether Poland would be willing to commit suicide as a national entity in order to avoid war. The German army invaded Poland on September 1. Two days later, on September 3, France and Great Britain declared war on Germany.

Why did the nearly unassailable military and diplomatic position of the France of 1930 deteriorate so rapidly and so badly? In their memoirs some leading French policy-makers made themselves out to be the victims of their fainthearted British allies, but such self-serving arguments are clearly suspect. At the time many journalists remarked on the hold an almost instinctive pacifism exercised over the French people. In their view, Frenchmen were ready to go to almost any lengths to avoid a repetition of the horrors of the First World War. Some historians have emphasized the ideological divisions that cut deeply into France's sense of national unity, especially the Right's propensity to see in Hitler an ally against "bolshevism" at home and abroad. Others have blamed the failures of the thirties on a lack of political leadership. The most able members of a generation had been killed in the First World War; among the older men there was no one of the stature of a Clemenceau, who might have rallied the nation against the most discouraging odds. Still others have suggested that France was overwhelmed by circumstances not even such giants as Clemençeau could have overcome. They argue that the Third Republic simply faced too many problems, in too short a time, with too few material and psychological resources.

After a winter of silence along the Western front—the so-called "phony war"—the German army smashed into Belgium and the Low Countries on May 10, 1940, and crossed into France on May 12. Within a week, French defenses were almost completely disorganized; communications broke down; refugees clogged the roads. The ensuing weeks were a long nightmare of chaos and disaster. On June 10 the government fled from Paris to Bordeaux. A week later Paul Reynaud, the premier, resigned when the majority of his cabinet voted to ask the Germans what their conditions for an armistice might be. Even to ask such a question was to admit defeat. Marshal Philippe Pétain, the old war hero who had been brought into the government to fire resistance to the Germans, replaced Reynaud and became instead a front man for the defeatists. On June 22, barely six weeks after the German invasion had begun, French representatives signed an armistice at Compiègne, in the same railroad car where the victorious Marshal Foch had received the Germans two decades before. As the historian Gordon Wright has put it, "Never before in modern history had France been so prostrate, so stunned and broken in spirit. Defeat the French had known, in 1814, 1815, 1871. But this was far more than defeat: it was utter humiliation, almost too deep for any Frenchman to comprehend."

The war years constitute one of the most bizarre and tangled episodes in modern French history. The question of what attitude should be taken toward the invader—should one resist? should one instead sit the war out?—opened new divisions among Frenchmen. Decisions made in wartime followed their makers into the peace, establishing the careers of some men and ruining the lives of others. The era of the German Occupation remains a period which continues to trouble the consciences of many Frenchmen.

After the armistice the government moved to the resort town of Vichy. On July 10 the parliament of the Third Republic, with only eighty dissenting votes, vested full powers in Marshal Pétain, who declared himself Head of the French State and dispensed with the need to consult any representative bodies on the governance of France. Defeat had discredited the politicians, but Pétain, though a leading defeatist himself, had managed to preserve intact the legendary reputation for leadership he had acquired in the previous war. In the summer of 1940 he probably had the support of the overwhelming majority of a demoralized and bewildered people. On June 18 a former protégé of Pétain, one Brigadier General Charles de Gaulle, declared over the BBC that the war had not ended and called upon all French military personnel who wished to continue the struggle against Germany to join him in London. Very few Frenchmen heard the appeal; at the outset, even fewer joined de Gaulle. Shortly thereafter the Vichy government condemned him to death on charges of desertion. De Gaulle, however, refused to accord the government of Pétain a shred of legitimacy.

Despite their unremitting hostility, the men of the Resistance and the men of Vichy shared in common a determination to turn their backs on the political system of the Third Republic and to build a new France.

Vichy, a town where people were used to living out of suitcases, provided the perfect setting for the transient factions which made up Pétain's regime. The state administration, like the discreet and efficient management of Vichy's resort hotels, provided the one element of stability amidst the constant coming and going of the guests: patriots and idealists who believed it their duty to come to the aid of an eternal France in its hour of need; politicians who were ready to play any tune in exchange for a seat on the bandwagon; the authoritarian reactionaries in Pétain's immediate entourage, whose corporatist program, grandly referred to as the National Revolution, never got far beyond the phrase-making stage; outright collaborationists of several varieties—pre-war Fascists and recent converts, ideologues of Right and Left, most of whom were contemptuous of the Pétainists and their boy-scout schemes and preferred Paris, where the real power sat, to Vichy; well-meaning technocrats, who had nothing much to begrudge the Third Republic but its inefficiency; hired guns and social misfits whose membership in the Vichy police enabled them to draw the cloak of legality around the settling of old scores.

But the single most important actor on this crowded stage was Pierre Laval, who didn't believe in much of anything except his own considerable ability. Laval, who thought the Third Republic had slighted and thwarted him when he had been prime minister in the thirties, had pulled the wires which dropped full power into the hands of Pétain. He seemed to have thought of Hitler as just another politician, and as vice-premier of the Vichy government he sought to win a place for France as faithful second in Hitler's New Order.

In December 1940 Laval fell victim to the perpetual intrigue that surrounded Pétain and was dismissed from office. His successor, Admiral François Darlan, brought to office the intense Anglophobia of the French Navy and a tireless zeal for seeking favors from the Nazis in return for favors done. Despite Darlan's fourteen months in office, nothing much came of these efforts. In the spring of 1942, after the United States had entered the war, the more cautious elements of the Vichy regime began to fear that Darlan had stuck his neck out too far, and Laval was returned to office. The permanence of the German mastery of Europe now seemed in doubt, and Laval began to play a muted tune of his own by seeking to evade the steadily rising exactions of the Nazis whenever the opportunity presented itself. But Laval's policy did the Vichy regime little credit. It is true, for example, that he saved many French Jews from the extermination camps of the Nazis. But he did so at the price of handing over to them non-French Jews found on French territory.

Pétain's defenders have maintained that he was engaged in a double game. The Marshal, they claim, regarded the Resistance as the sword of France; he saw himself as the shield, cooperating with the Germans in order to protect an occupied France against the fate of Poland, but all the while working in secret with the Allies. But no evidence has been brought forward to support this thesis. Certainly the independence of Vichy was the sheerest illusion. If France escaped "polonization," it was not because of the efforts of Pétain and Laval, but because the Germans believed it was not to their advantage to subject France to the rule of a gauleiter. Pétain fully deserved the reputation he had established in the First World War. But when the Second War broke out he was eighty-four years old, and little remained of the brilliant military commander but a stubborn craftiness and an overweening vanity. "Old age," Charles de Gaulle wrote in his *Memoirs,* "is a shipwreck." He was writing of his former patron, and in the case of Pétain, at least, there seems little reason to dispute this judgment.

As the France of Vichy flickered on in the shadow of the conqueror, the France of the Resistance grew in strength. Drawn together by the common aim of hurling the Germans out of France, the men of the Resistance came from the most diverse backgrounds. Many had been bitter antagonists in peacetime; once the war ended, they resumed their quarrels. De Gaulle's headquarters in London had serious disagreements with the Resistance in France. Factional struggles raged within each camp.

Charles de Gaulle's political career was filled with dramatic moments, but none was finer than its beginning on June 18, 1940, when he spoke for a France which refused to accept defeat. Few French leaders have aroused such bitter hatred and such fervent admiration, and opinion on de Gaulle's career and his achievements is likely to remain divided for some time to come. As he himself once wrote, "It is not easy to write about General de Gaulle." Aloof, authoritarian, very hard to get on with, de Gaulle intentionally wrapped himself in mystery. Yet Stalin, who was a shrewd judge of men, is said to have remarked that de Gaulle was really quite simple. It is true that the Gaullism of de Gaulle rested on a few unshakable principles—above all on the insistence that France must play a role of the first importance in world affairs; that to execute this role France must be independent of the will of any other power; and, finally, that France is the sole judge of its own interests. But de Gaulle's interpretation of these principles was characterized in practice by a high degree of pragmatism and tactical flexibility. Gaullism was an historical doctrine, and what it meant depended on how de Gaulle interpreted the demands of the moment. Stridently imperialist and anti-communist in the late forties, for example, de Gaulle had become by the mid-sixties a friend of both the Third World and the Soviet Union.

As a member of de Gaulle's inner circle in London has written, wartime Gaullism above all meant resistance to the Nazis. All other considerations were to be subordinated to the aim of routing the invader from French soil. De Gaulle's refusal to speculate about the postwar era gave rise to Allied mistrust of the London-based Resistance, especially among American leaders, some of whom suspected de Gaulle of plotting to establish a fascist dictatorship of his own. Indeed, relations between the United States and the London Resistance were troubled from the beginning and went from bad to worse. American suspicions of de Gaulle were heartily reciprocated. The French leader could not bring himself to swallow America's recognition of the Vichy regime; he believed the United States and England had designs on the French Empire. Intense personal antagonism between Franklin D. Roosevelt and de Gaulle sharpened disagreements over policy; legitimate grievances piled up on both sides. On the whole, the American wartime relationship with France was neither a very successful nor a very happy episode.

De Gaulle feared the end of the war might simply mean that a friendly occupier would replace the hostile one. If the British and the Americans were to liberate France, he believed, they might also insist on governing France, at least until the nation had recovered from the effects of the war. In order to forestall this possibility, de Gaulle insisted that Frenchmen must participate in their own liberation—not as part of another nation's army but as an independent military force. The instrument of this policy was the Free French forces, which grew from the little band of men initially gathered in London and in the Empire into the divisions which participated in the Italian campaign and the landings of 1944. In de Gaulle's view, the military capability of the Free French mattered much less than their usefulness as a political and diplomatic weapon—a constant and visible reminder of the independence of France.

In France itself, tiny bands of resisters began springing up after the first shock of defeat had passed. The Communist party, anxious to overcome the blackened reputation which support of the Nazi-Soviet Pact had given it, later claimed to have been the first group to have taken up arms against the invader. Individual Communists may have done so, but there is little evidence that, as a party, the Communists contributed much to the Resistance before Germany attacked the Soviet Union in June 1941. Nevertheless, the party was well prepared to undertake a clandestine struggle, and once in the field the Communists compiled a heroic record.

Active members of the underground remained a tiny proportion of the population, for to join the Resistance was an easy commitment to avoid and a very difficult one to undertake. At the outset the disparate movements of the Resistance operated independently of each other, printing clandestine tracts, gathering intelligence, and committing acts of sabotage against German military installations and personnel. In 1942 Jean Moulin, de Gaulle's personal representative, parachuted into France in order to unify the movements under a national leadership. The Gestapo caught up with Moulin and tortured him to death in Lyons, but not before his work had been done. Under his successor, Georges Bidault, the National Council of the Resistance laid down a sweeping program for the reform of postwar France, and the scattered guerrilla bands of the Resistance were unified as the *Forces Françaises de l'Intérieur* (FFI).

In early 1943, soon after the allied landings in North Africa, de Gaulle moved his headquarters from London to Algiers, in order to operate from French territory. Admiral Darlan had turned up in North Africa, making himself available as negotiator of a cease-fire between the Vichy and Allied forces. But the deal with Darlan also involved recognition of him as the chief French authority in North Africa. The Admiral's murder, at the end of 1942, released the Americans from their commitment to this odious expedient. Still mistrustful of de Gaulle, the Allies tried to impose their own chosen leader, General Henri Giraud, upon the anti-Vichy forces. But de Gaulle pushed the politically inept Giraud aside in the space of a few months and established himself as undisputed leader of the Free French. Late in 1943 the British accorded de Gaulle full powers to re-establish the legitimate government of France once liberation had been achieved, but the Americans, still suspicious of his intentions, held off *de jure* recognition until the fall of 1944.

If the British considered de Gaulle the rightful organizer of postwar France, they did not bother to inform him of the Allied invasion of Normandy on June 6, 1944, until troops had begun to land. This deliberate oversight nearly caused an open breach between Winston Churchill and de Gaulle. Nevertheless, de Gaulle had won the major battle he had been waging since 1940: the Allied invasion forces turned over the governance of the newly liberated areas of France to Gaullist representatives. As the Germans retreated before the Allied advance, Gaullist and Communist agents raced each other into the vacuum of power created by the Nazi departure, and a struggle for control ensued until the Communist party leadership, calculating that it might come to power by legal means once the war had ended, gave way to the Gaullists. The liberation of Paris was mainly a French affair, triggered by a rising of the populace and the advance of the troops of General Jean Leclerc. On August 26, 1944, de Gaulle marched down the Champs Elysées to the wild acclaim of a people who would not have recognized his name four years before.

Skeptics have questioned whether either the Resistance or the

Free French merited the sacrifices made for them. Neither, they contend, altered the outcome of the war or shortened it by so much as a day. It is hard to dispute this judgment. But without the Resistance, and in the absence of de Gaulle, the French memories of the war would have been limited to the humiliation of the defeat and the government of Vichy, badly compromised by its dealings with the Germans. The military contribution of the Resistance may have been negligible. Its contribution to the self-regard of the French people was incalculably great.

At the moment of liberation, the burdens of history seemed to have dropped away and the future to be filled with promise. With the Germans gone, Vichy discredited, and the old politicians lying low, the heroes of the Resistance were ready to remake French democracy. So exalted a mood was impossible to sustain. As the giddiness induced by newly recovered freedoms subsided, a kind of emotional and psychological gap opened up between the Resisters, who had risked their lives for a republic *pure et dure,* and the majority of the French people, who didn't feel up to new sacrifices. The war, as Sir Denis Brogan points out, had not resolved the old problems; the burdens of history had to be taken up again.

The provisional government of General de Gaulle faced an enormous task simply repairing war damage, but this was done with considerable dispatch. The Resisters, however, considered the restoration of the productive capacity of pre-war France only a prelude to the remaking of the economy and society. First of all, they aimed to extend the principles of political democracy to economic and social life. Public control of key sectors of the economy had been a long-standing aim of the Left, and in 1946 the provisional government moved swiftly to nationalize coal mines, the electricity and gas industries, transportation facilities, and certain banks and insurance companies.

The outstanding accomplishment of this period, however, and one of the most far-reaching undertakings in the history of postwar France, was the adoption of a system of economic planning. Under the leadership of Jean Monnet, the first plan, drawn up to cover a five-year period, established guidelines for investment in the re-equipment and modernization of industry. The economic and financial staff of the plan, a lean and efficient organization by the usual bureaucratic standards, drew on the advice of representatives of government, industry, and labor. The plan had no legal coercive authority; it could only make recommendations. Still, the Monnet Plan converted some of the most skeptical defenders of the free market into believers in planning. Industrial production reached pre-war levels by 1951; shortly thereafter France crossed the threshold of a growth rate not experienced for a century.

Postwar French politics provided a less happy story. In a referendum of October 1945, voters overwhelmingly rejected the idea of a return to the Third Republic; the same month they elected a constituent assembly charged with preparing a new constitution for France. Leading pre-war politicians of the right and center had been discredited by their association with Vichy. The parties of the Left, whom voters identified with the Resistance, dominated the constituent assembly. The Communists won the most seats, followed closely by the Socialists. But the major surprise of the election was the success of the new Christian Democratic party, the *Mouvement républicain populaire* (MRP), whose liberal Catholicism represented an old but hitherto distinctly minor force in French politics.

Charles de Gaulle became head of a government composed of Communists, Socialists, and Popular Republicans, an arrangement known as "Tripartism" that became increasingly unworkable once the chill of the Cold War set in. Everyone in the constituent assembly agreed on the desirability of a republican form of government, but serious disagreement existed on how power should be distributed within the republican system. The assembly had two distinct alternatives before it. De Gaulle wanted a presidential regime in which the naming of ministers and the initiative in policy-making rested in the hands of the chief executive. The Left favored a parliamentary regime purified of the old abuses. When de Gaulle saw that he had little chance of getting his way, he seized upon the first pretext he could find to resign, convinced that his views would eventually prevail. Perhaps he expected to be recalled immediately; perhaps he saw that French democracy was in for difficult times, and withdrew from politics in order to hold himself ready for the crisis which would return him to power. Whatever his expectations, he remained out of power for the next dozen years.

With de Gaulle out of the way, the constituent assembly chose a parliamentary regime. But the three main parties disagreed on how parliament should be organized. The Communists wanted an all-powerful, one-house legislature. Citing the precedent of the Revolutionary Convention, they claimed that such an assembly would be more responsive to the demands of the people than a two-house parliament. The Socialists reluctantly went along. But the majority of the electorate, fearful that a Communist-dominated unicameral legislature would open the way to a Communist seizure of power, rejected a constitutional draft that embodied this scheme.

Voters then returned a new constituent assembly in which the MRP emerged as the largest party. The only solution open to this new and more conservative assembly seemed to be a return to something on the order of the Third Republic. Various stabilizing devices were installed in the new constitutional draft in the hope of avoiding the governmental gyrations of the Third Republic. In an almost total absence of enthusiasm the voters, who had now been called to the polls four times in less than a year, approved this draft and the Fourth Republic was born.

As Jacques Fauvet's article, "Tragic Circus—France's Parliament," shows, long-standing habits prevailed against the gadgets built into the constitution. By 1947 Frenchmen discovered they had wound up with a regime much like the Third Republic after all, and the aversion of their representatives to the old system soon seemed about as ingenuous as Br'er Rabbit's distaste for the briar patch.

Governmental instability seemed to have passed from the Third Republic to the Fourth like some hereditary affliction. The revolving-door governments in the Palais Bourbon seemed remote from the concerns of ordinary Frenchmen, struggling to make ends meet against a runaway inflation. But if parliament seemed a "tragic circus," the appearance of government instability could be as misleading as it had been under the Third Republic. The regime was strong enough to meet a serious challenge from the extreme Left, in the form of the potentially insurrectionary strikes of the winter of 1947, and wily enough to head off a challenge from the extreme Right, in the form of General de Gaulle's *Rassemblement du peuple français*. By 1952 the government of Antoine Pinay had mastered inflation (or had been lucky enough to come to power when the trend had run its course), and the economy was once again beginning to show the vigor it sustained without let-up for more than a decade. Like its predecessor, the Fourth Republic did not collapse from internal weaknesses; it was to be a casualty of another war.

The Second World War, by loosening the grip of the major European powers on the lands they ruled in Asia and Africa, opened the way for the anti-colonialist revolutions that have dominated the history of our own times. Some of the Frenchmen who had served in the Empire during the war had sensed that the reassertion of the old system of direct rule in the face of nationalist demands for autonomy might provoke troubles with which France was not prepared to deal. This view was reflected in the constitution of the Fourth Republic, which provided for the reorganization of the Empire into a "Federal Union" whose members were to be largely autonomous. But the pace of events outran this scheme.

In September 1945, as the short-lived Japanese domination of Southeast Asia came to an end, Ho Chi Minh proclaimed the independence of Vietnam. France wavered between two sharply different reactions to this challenge to the reassertion of its rule in Indochina. General Leclerc, the French military commander on the scene, favored a negotiated accord, to the point of pronouncing the word "independence," if necessary, prior to a French re-occupation of Vietnam. But Leclerc was the subordinate of the High Commissioner, Admiral Thierry d'Argenlieu, a monk turned sailor and one of the more bizarre figures to have rallied to General de Gaulle. D'Argenlieu favored the military reoccupation of Vietnam first, with talks to come later, if at all. Paris appeared to want to avoid a head-on clash with the forces of Ho Chi Minh, but it was unable to control d'Argenlieu's actions. In the end the government chose to attempt to put down the revolution instead of seeking a negotiated settlement which might have left France with influence in Indochina and avoided the tragedy which ensued.

The army, short of equipment and personnel, found itself engaged in a war it had not been trained to fight. The aims of French policy in Indochina were never clearly defined. Each government seemed less eager to prosecute the war than to unload it on its successor. As the fighting dragged on, some high official would occasionally declare that he could see light at the end of the tunnel. Then came the defeat at Dien Bien Phu, in May 1954, and it became apparent overnight that France had lost not only a battle but the war.

Four years earlier Pierre Mendès-France, leader of the reformist wing of the Radical party, had warned parliament that the country had to be told the truth about the painful choices before it in Indochina. After Dien Bien Phu, when there were no longer any choices to be made, Mendès-France was called upon to extricate France from the war. He not only negotiated an armistice in Indochina; he also took important steps toward granting independence to the North African colonies of Tunisia and Morocco.

Mendès-France and the young reformers gathered around him intended the settlement of the Indochina war to be the prelude to sweeping economic and social reform at home. But the bitter struggle over the European Defense Community distracted their attention. The EDC, a plan for the formation of a multi-national army, divided the center parties internally and squeezed adherents of the plan between the Gaullist Right, which charged that such a force would divest France of its sovereignty and put Europe under American domination, and the Communist Left, which regarded a European army as a threat to the security of the Soviet Union. Mendès-France managed to shelve the EDC, but in January 1955 he was driven from office before his reform program had made much advance. Aside from de Gaulle, Mendès-France was probably the most able political leader to have emerged in France since the end of World War I, but he was not popular in parliament, and his government lasted only seven months.

If most Frenchmen were glad to be rid of the war in Southeast Asia, the Indochina settlement did not make everyone happy. The extreme Right, nostalgic for the grandeur of Empire, complained of a sellout. The army resented having been made to swallow one more defeat, and this proved to be much more dangerous than the noisy posturing of the Right. Many career officers had scarcely set foot in France for more than fifteen years, and they had long since begun to feel intellectually and emotionally isolated from their countrymen. Some of the army's best units had been sacrificed in Indochina; these losses seemed pointless, and the abandonment of the Vietnamese who had fought alongside the French seemed dishonorable. At home, nobody appeared to care. Officers who had discovered the writings of Mao Tse-tung in Vietnamese prison camps began to think they had found a magic formula which the French army could employ in a future encounter with guerrillas . . . and against the moral rot at home.

Their opportunity came sooner than anyone expected. In the early morning of November 1, 1954, terrorist activity signalled the beginning of a revolt against French rule in Algeria and of a war that dragged on for nearly eight years. Mendès-France had negotiated the beginning of an end to French rule in Morocco and Tunisia. But Algeria was not just another French colony. More than a million settlers of European origin lived there. Many of them had ancestors who had come to Algeria a century before, and most were determined to stay. The Nobel prizewinner Albert Camus, born and reared in Algiers, remarked that if it came to choosing between justice and his mother, he would choose his mother. Therein the tragedy lay.

At the outset of the rebellion, most metropolitan Frenchmen believed Algeria was French, as their schoolbooks had taught them, but they were not prepared to go to any lengths to maintain French rule. In the elections of January 1956, the platform of the victorious leftist coalition called for a negotiated settlement of the war. But the diehard, or "ultra," faction of French settlers in Algeria fiercely opposed any negotiation with the rebels, and the government of Guy Mollet, the Socialist premier, gave in to the pressure of the ultras and their sympathizers in France. Conscripts were sent to join the professional army in the hunt for guerrilla bands; soon France had committed more than 400,000 troops to Algeria. The ultras in Algiers replied to terrorist tactics with terrorism of their own. Army officers convinced themselves that torture was a justifiable weapon to use in such a war. As city and countryside both deteriorated into a state of general insecurity, the army accumulated more and more power until it had become the real ruler of Algeria. To concentrate so much authority over civilian affairs in the hands of army officers who had lost all respect for the regime was asking for trouble. For a time, what went on in Algiers became more important politically than what happened in Paris.

For a medium-sized city, Algiers had more than its share of plotters: competing factions of ultra settlers, some of whom toyed with fascist ideas and all of whom were determined to keep Algeria French; Gaullists who saw in the Algerian affair a means of bringing de Gaulle back to power; army officers bent on avoiding another humiliating defeat and who belonged to both the Gaullist and ultra camps.

The government of Felix Gaillard fell on April 15, 1958, opening a parliamentary crisis which gave the plotters a chance to act. Rumors circulated that a new government would seek to negotiate a settlement with the rebels. In early May the military high command in Algiers threatened in scarcely veiled terms to disobey any government that opened negotiations. On May 13 ultra leaders, with the connivance of key regimental commanders in Algiers, seized government buildings and set up a "Committee of Public Safety" to take over civil powers from the legal government. The Gaullist plotters managed to elbow the ultra and army leaders aside and to use the Algiers Committee as a public platform from which to appeal for the return of de Gaulle. The Gaullists apparently acted without the knowledge of de Gaulle, but once the wheels had been set in motion he was kept informed of developments.

While rumors flew that paratroopers were about to descend on Paris (plans for such a move were indeed afoot), de Gaulle let it be known that he would accept the responsibility of government, but only if it were legally invested. The moderates and some elements of the Left swung round behind de Gaulle when they began to fear they might have a civil war on their hands if they did not. Many of the army leaders and ultras were bitterly anti-Gaullist, but they persuaded themselves that only de Gaulle could keep Algeria French. The General did not yet disabuse them of this notion. On June 1, 1958, by a vote of 329 to 224, he became the last prime minister of the Fourth Republic. Three weeks earlier, he probably would not have received a hundred votes.

De Gaulle must have savored the ironies of the situation in which he now found himself: an aging army officer, hero of a previous war, called upon as a savior in a time of national crisis, and voted full powers by a parliament once dominated by a coalition of the Left. Pétain had played the same role in 1940.

The settlers had appealed to de Gaulle because they believed he would keep Algeria French. Most of them had no political aims beyond this. But de Gaulle considered France's inability to resolve a long colonial war merely a symptom of fundamental domestic weaknesses, especially of the feebleness of the state. He did not mean to allow the Algerian tail to go on wagging the metropolitan dog. In any event, no solution to the Algerian question could be found until the crisis of governmental authority had been surmounted in France.

The constitution of the Fifth Republic, drafted in the summer of 1958, was an attempt to codify de Gaulle's views on the problem of governing France. The theme he had most often sounded since 1946 had been the need to endow France with a strong executive authority. Unlike the constitution of the Fourth Republic, which ended as an attempt to correct the flaws in the political system of the Third, the constitution of the Fifth Republic sought to turn republican institutions in a new direction.

The constitution provided for a president and a parliament, just as earlier constitutions had done, but this time the balance of power was clearly tilted in favor of the president, who now had the authority to choose his own ministers. Most important, the president chose the prime minister. Thus the making of a government rested completely with the head of state; the prime minister no longer received his mandate to govern from parliament. The respective responsibilities of the president and the prime minister within the two-headed executive were not very clearly defined, and this was a possible source of conflict. Under the first two presidents of the Fifth Republic, however, serious conflicts have not arisen. Thus far the president has laid down the main lines of policy and the prime minister has been an executor, carrying on the day-to-day business of government.

The Algerian War dragged on nearly as long after de Gaulle came to power as it had lasted under the Fourth Republic. The General had always regarded secretiveness and surprise as weapons no less important in diplomacy than in warfare. He managed to retain considerable room for maneuver in the Algerian affair by keeping everyone guessing about his intentions. But he revealed the drift of his Algerian policy in a speech of September 1959, when he announced that the French could choose among three options: integration of the Muslim population into France (the ultra solution); complete independence (a solution, de Gaulle charged, which would lead a war-torn and underdeveloped country to disaster); and a form of cooperative association between Algeria and France which would leave Algeria virtually autonomous (the solution which de Gaulle himself favored).

Despite this speech, de Gaulle's Algerian policy followed a tortuous path—now appearing to twist in the direction of a "French Algeria," in order to appease dissident and still powerful elements in the army, now veering toward a negotiated settlement. Some of de Gaulle's critics have charged that all this twisting and turning unnecessarily prolonged the war, that he could have arrived at a negotiated settlement much sooner had he bent all his efforts in this direction. But his defenders have maintained that such a straightforward course was out of the question until de Gaulle had surmounted the threat to his regime from the diehards —the very groups that had brought him to power.

As the war dragged on, it raised deeply troubling moral and political issues which came to dominate French public life. The attempt to crush the rebellion militarily, and the methods employed by the Army—especially the use of torture—caused opponents of the war to fear that the Algerian experience was rotting away the moral fiber of the nation. The student Left and leading French intellectuals mounted demonstrations and published exposés and petitions against the war; the government countered with police batons and the seizure of anti-war literature. In the meantime, ultra settlers and diehard army officers rightly sensed that the ground was giving way beneath their feet, and they sought to repeat their success of May 13, 1958—the imposition of the will of Algiers on Paris—and this time to dislodge de Gaulle from power. But these efforts failed miserably. The attempted *putsch* of April 1961, a ludicrous flop, ended the army's threat to the regime. In desperation the diehards went underground, and in the OAS, or Secret Army Organization, embarked on a campaign of vengeance and terror which the government mercilessly put down. At the same time, de Gaulle had maneuvered steadily toward a negotiated settlement with the FLN, as the Algerian liberation front was called. In March 1962 the Evian accords brought a cease-fire, and on the following July 1 Algeria became independent.

Some deputies grumbled about de Gaulle's machiavellian methods, but parliament did not seek to intervene in his handling of the Algerian problem. The president feared that once a settlement had been reached, however, the deputies would seek to re-assert the power they had enjoyed under the Third and Fourth Republics. The Algerian crisis had already transformed the office of the presidency from the arbitrator of the constitution of 1958 into an advocate of his own policies, similar in this respect to the American presidency. De Gaulle wished further to strengthen the executive by having the president elected by the direct vote of all the people. But among the deputies such an idea aroused historical memories of enemies of republican government. De Gaulle bided his time until an attempt on his life provided him with a dramatic opportunity to raise the question of his "succession" and to call for a referendum approving the election of the president by universal suffrage. This move, and the dubious constitutional procedures by means of which de Gaulle sought to get his way, raised a storm of opposition, but the president prevailed.

In 1962 France was at peace after twenty-three years of war. Many people doubt whether anyone but de Gaulle could have mastered the Algerian crisis. If they are correct, the demise of the Fourth Republic is perhaps a cheap price to have paid. Still, the Gaullists have been inclined to exaggerate the weaknesses of the regime they succeeded (and for whose downfall they themselves bear some of the blame), and to claim more credit for improvements in the well-being of Frenchmen than they deserve. Whatever their claims, the economic prosperity of the 1960's was a legacy of the unlamented Fourth Republic. The evolution of economy and society under the Fifth Republic has been pretty much a continuation of earlier trends.

After all the years of stagnation, rapid economic growth was news; change was what got reported in the newspapers. But in the late 1960's one could still find old people in France who believed the earth is flat and who had never traveled more than a few miles from the village in which they were born. Of course they might live down the road from teen-agers who dressed in the latest left-bank fashions. As John Ardagh has remarked, contrasts between the old and the new were sharper in France than in almost any other Western nation.

A static France dwelled in the shadow of the dynamic France which got most of the attention in the press. The Northeast, from just south of Paris to the Belgian frontier, constituted less than one-fifth of French territory and contained something over a third of its population, but it possessed more than half the productive capacity of the nation. France south of the Loire, especially toward the southwest, remained an area of poor and inefficient farms, and in that respect bore some resemblance to southern Italy. In addition to the persistence of geographical contrasts between poverty and progress, a sharply uneven distribution of wealth persisted among social classes. In 1971, for example, some postal workers in Paris had to make do on less than $200 a month; and some old-age pensions remained pitifully small. The venerable French custom of tax-dodging continued to make it hard for the state to tap existing sources of wealth for public purposes.

Like their American contemporaries, Frenchmen spent a great deal on individual consumption and scrimped on social investment. Thus the boom economy of the fifties and early sixties had not been an entirely unmixed blessing. The automobile, symbol of the consumer society, threatened to devour Paris. The telephone was a public scandal. A housing shortage put a strain on pocketbooks, marriages, and in-laws. Mass transportation facilities in the Paris region were inadequate, and hospitals were crammed with more patients than they had been designed to care for. It is true that the government was struggling to surmount these problems; some imaginative solutions had been laid down on paper. But the telephone system, for example, had suffered from decades of neglect;

French technicians have nearly all they can do to keep over-strained facilities from deteriorating still further. But the decay of an aging economic infrastructure is a problem common to all advanced industrial societies. It would be hard to contend that the Fifth Republic's efforts to combat the decay have been markedly less energetic than those of any other industrial power.

In the early 1960's the opposition did not make much headway in pinning the blame for the diffuse aggravations of day-to-day existence on the Gaullists. The end of the Algerian War left a kind of vacuum in French political life. The atrophy of parliament, the government's stinginess with radio and television time on the state-controlled networks, the divisions of the Left, and de Gaulle's lofty disdain for his opponents made it hard to find a vulnerable spot at which to strike at the regime. Beyond the "political class"— the professional politicians, party activists, and politically engaged intellectuals—most people were content to leave things up to de Gaulle, whose own main concerns, defense and foreign policy, were remote from those of the citizenry at large. This mood of public indifference to politics was widely commented on in the press, and dozens of theories were contrived to explain it. Nonetheless, slippages in the popularity of the president and of his regime began to appear: de Gaulle himself was unexpectedly forced into a runoff ballot in his campaign for re-election to the presidency in 1965; and the Gaullists were reduced to the slimmest of majorities in the parliamentary elections of 1967.

Still, as the tenth anniversary of the founding of the Fifth Republic approached, published assessments of the regime's first decade were on the whole favorable. Then France suddenly plunged into a grave social and political crisis, and for a few days the Fifth Republic appeared to be on the verge of collapse. Less than a revolution, more than a series of riots, what happened in France in the spring of 1968 is simply referred to as "the events of May." The events came as a surprise to the most seasoned and well-informed observers. As if to make up for being caught unaware, students of French society flooded bookstores with accounts of why everything had happened and what everything meant almost before the tear gas had settled. Historians of the events of May already have a mountain of information to mine. But some of the literature is more a manifestation of the crisis than an explanation of it; the whole story of what was a very complicated episode is still far from known. But at least an outline of the crisis can be sketched in here.

In a year that witnessed violent outbreaks of student discontent from Tokyo through Berkeley and New York to Berlin, perhaps it is not surprising that Paris had its own student rising. French university students had plenty of grievances. The demographic tidal wave had washed over the universities, leaving them overcrowded, understaffed, and underequipped. Enrollments increased tenfold in the thirty years between 1938 and 1968; in the five years between 1962 and 1967 alone, they more than doubled. The students charged that, aside from the problems sheer numbers created, the curriculum, modes of instruction, and the examination system were antiquated, insensitive, and unresponsive to their needs.

These educational grievances were articulated in a highly politicized milieu. On the Left, leadership of student activism had passed from the Communist party to Maoist and Trotskyite splinter groups, whose tactical adroitness and lack of scruples compensated for their small numbers. Educational grievances and radical political activism came together at the University of Nanterre, a new and cheerless campus located in an industrial slum on the outskirts of Paris. The activists provoked confrontations with the authorities over everything from dormitory regulations to the war in Vietnam, but for a year prior to 1968 run-ins between students and the police had been confined to Nanterre.

On May 3 the trouble spread to Paris. University officials called in police to clear the courtyard of the Sorbonne of demonstrators who had gathered to protest disciplinary proceedings against student leaders. The students left without incident, but the police then proceeded to herd them into police vans in order to undertake a "routine identity check." This proved a serious blunder. Latecomers believed their comrades had been arrested; scuffling broke out between themselves and the police. Exchanges of rocks and tear gas soon engulfed the Latin Quarter. The Sorbonne was closed down. On successive nights police and students engaged in running battles. The behavior of the police, who took to roughing up nearly everyone they encountered in the neighborhood, initially rallied public sympathy to the side of the students. A week after the incident at the Sorbonne, barricades sprang up in the streets, calling to mind the Parisian revolutions of the nineteenth century— only this time radio reporters on the scene carried the battle to the entire nation.

The crisis, limited thus far to an especially serious form of student rioting, suddenly deepened and broadened over the weekend of May 10-12. Prime Minister Georges Pompidou returned from a state visit to Afghanistan prepared to reopen the Sorbonne, in the hope that such a gesture would put an end to disorder. Pompidou's critics claim that this conciliatory move transformed the student riots into a nationwide social crisis. Had the government employed the army against the students, they contend, further trouble would have been averted. Instead the workers, thinking they too might have something to gain from seizing the government by the throat, went on strike. Pompidou's defenders claim the conciliatory gesture avoided the possibility of bloodshed and won the government time to recover its poise, a policy which paid off in the elections of June.

At any rate, a movement that began as a wildcat strike spread quickly, as disciplined trade-union members joined in. Throughout the country, workers occupied their factories. The historical precedent everyone thought of this time was the summer of 1936. But the strikes of 1968 were more widespread than those of 1936. Eventually, between 6.5 and 7 million Frenchmen (not 9 to 10 million, as reported at the time) walked off their jobs. The French economy was brought to a virtual standstill. The workers' movement was potentially a much greater threat to the government than the agitation of the students. But the strikes lacked the revolutionary *élan* of those of 1936. Despite the effort of student activists to forge an alliance with the workers, the majority of strikers remained aloof, sensitive to generational and cultural differences, suspicious of the students' motives and endurance, and alarmed by the rhetoric of some of the student leaders.

De Gaulle himself, imperturbable in crisis after crisis, now seemed to have lost his grip. Having flown off in the midst of the events on a state visit to Rumania, he suddenly returned, appeared on television, and said something vague about a referendum. But the medium that had served him so well in the past turned against him; viewers saw not the commanding presence of earlier times, but a tired old man. Some of the worst rioting followed the speech.

On May 25 Pompidou managed to bring the government, employers, and trade-union leaders together for an agreement which accorded substantial wage increases and improvements in certain welfare benefits. The government hoped acceptance of this accord would lead to a return to work that would leave the students isolated. But rank-and-file union members rejected it. The strikes continued; student rioting worsened; and the parliamentary opposition began to talk openly of a successor to de Gaulle.

An industrial society brought to a standstill made a disquieting spectacle. To be sure, there was something greatly appealing in the lyricism of the wall posters and slogans plastered up and scrawled everywhere in the Latin Quarter; the calls for putting "imagination in power" seemed to insist that revolution could wear a gentle face. But the suddenness and unexpectedness of the crisis, the breakdown of order, the ineptitude of a government which had always prided itself on its toughness and efficiency, also provoked widespread fear and uneasiness.

On May 29 de Gaulle suddenly disappeared. Rumors circulated that he had packed his bags and gone off to his country house to write the remaining volumes of his memoirs: this time, many thought, he was finished. In reality he had flown to Baden-Baden to confer with General Jacques Massu, commander of French forces in West Germany, apparently in order to assure himself of the loyalty of the army. Exactly what they talked about remains unknown, but de Gaulle returned to Paris and on May 30 made a tough new speech in which he cast aside his earlier proposal for a referendum, dissolved the national assembly, and scheduled new elections. He seemed to have recovered the old magic. The dissolution of the assembly pulled the rug out from under the Opposition leaders, the strikers began to return to work, and by mid-June the student activists had isolated themselves from a society by now grown weary of disorder.

The Right turned out to be the chief beneficiary of the specter of revolution. In the election campaign the Gaullists followed the

General's lead in heaping blame for the events on the Communists. Some observers have contended that, at the height of the crisis, the Communists flirted with the idea of bringing down the regime; others have argued that the party, dismayed and frightened by the undisciplined behavior of the student leftists, remained the General's staunchest ally throughout the events. Clearly, the Communists were not the driving force behind the events of May. Whether or not the voters swallowed the government's line, they returned a huge Gaullist majority to the assembly. For the first time in French history a single party controlled parliament. Yet Pompidou, who had emerged as the most resourceful and steady-nerved member of the government, and who managed the successful election campaign, was dismissed from his post as prime minister. He and de Gaulle had clashed over how the crisis should be met; gratitude for services rendered had never been one of the General's virtues.

The causes of the Great Revolution of 1789 continue to provoke controversy as the two hundredth anniversary of its outbreak nears; discussion of the causes of the events of May has scarcely begun. Some Frenchmen subscribed to a variety of conspiracy theories. Was the CIA, everyone's favorite scapegoat, behind the events of May? Or were old-line Stalinists, the Chinese, the East German secret service? Not a shred of evidence has been brought forward against any of these alleged culprits, but conspiracy theories often need no other support than faith alone, and the willingness to see a plot in the events of May at least suggests that the French have not abandoned a cherished tradition. Some aging leftists saw the events as a spontaneous outburst against a society corrupted by American-style consumerism, and as such a revenge of the spirit against materialism. Many students were probably motivated by such feelings, but the workers were in the main after solid economic gains, which they presumably sought in order to enjoy more of the benefits of the consumer society. Perhaps revenges of the spirit are more likely to seize the privileged than groups wresting free of the pinch of want for the first time in their lives. Still another explanation has seen in the events of May the adumbration of a new form of class conflict. In place of the old conflict between the possessors of capital and labor, this new struggle internally divides the educated middle class, pitting the managers, who now possess most of the power of decision, against the technicians, who seek a share of that power. This is an intriguing theory, and perhaps it does afford a glimpse of conflict in an emerging society, but there is little evidence that would permit one to regard it as the driving force behind the events of May. A leading dissenter from the enthusiasm that overtook many of the observers of the crisis was the conservative sociologist Raymond Aron, who dismissed the events as a kind of "psychodrama," a release of pent-up energies and emotions for which French society, prosperous and at peace, afforded no other outlet.

If the causes of the events are likely to provoke controversy for a long time to come, the events themselves are still so near at hand that discussion of all but their most immediate consequences can hardly be other than speculatory. The crisis had severe short-term effects on the French economy and finances. The concessions that workers extracted from their employers gave another jolt to the inflationary spiral; speculation against the franc and the fear of unrest drained away the enormous gold reserves de Gaulle had piled up and eventually forced a devaluation of the currency. The events also left the authorities in an extremely jumpy mood, ready to call in vanloads of police at the first sign of trouble in the streets, behavior which merely maintained the yawning breach between themselves, a large segment of the press, and especially the young. The most positive immediate consequence of the events was the passage in September 1968 of the Faure Law, which promised, if carried into effect, to make sweeping changes in the structure of the French university system, where the trouble had all started.

De Gaulle's reassertion of his old powers of leadership was a fleeting triumph. It is doubtful whether he quite recovered from the events of May, either in his own eyes or the nation's. The French have had a weakness for saviors in military uniform. But they have also consistently shown a healthy lack of gratitude for being saved. As the man of June 18, 1940, de Gaulle had saved his country from dishonor; as the man of May 13, 1958, he may have saved his country from civil war. He had extricated France, as probably no one else could have done, from a futile colonial war. But the heroic mood that sustained de Gaulle for a lifetime could sustain a whole people only in the most exceptional moments. The presidential campaign of 1965 had already betrayed the French people's disenchantment with their distant hero. Indeed, perhaps the distance from mundane concerns that he had long ago identified as one of the precepts of leadership was in the end too distant, too detached.

In April 1969 de Gaulle chose to stake his presidency on a referendum on a relatively unimportant set of reforms. A majority voted against the reforms; de Gaulle immediately resigned. He returned to his country home and set to work on his unfinished memoirs. Perhaps he consoled himself with the thought that his own low opinion of the French people had once again been confirmed. His real love affair had always been with France. On November 9, 1970, de Gaulle died, two days before the anniversary of the armistice ending the First World War, when his own career had begun, and two weeks before his eightieth birthday.

Georges Pompidou, who for a time appeared to be the great victim of the events of May, turned out to be the great victor instead. Pompidou had spent his entire public career in the shadow of de Gaulle, but it was he, and not the General, who rallied a shaken government in the crisis of 1968. As an editorialist for *Le Monde* wrote at the time: "One has the impression that the government, and at moments even the state, no longer exist, just a solitary man who is courageously striving against the storm." Despite his dismissal as prime minister, Pompidou maintained his identification with Gaullism; this, along with the reputation he had established during the events of May, made him the leading candidate for the succession to de Gaulle. In June 1969 he was elected president of the Republic.

The new president is not simply the executor of the Gaullist political testament. Indeed, it may be doubted whether such a testament would be capable of fulfillment. The Gaullist style of leadership is not something that can be imitated or institutionalized. De Gaulle regarded himself as the unifier of the French nation, above the strife of parties; he was no one's man but his own. He held himself as aloof from the conservative bourgeoisie from whom he derived much of his electoral support as he did from the Communist party. He never showed much interest in the Gaullist parliamentary organization unless he needed its aid.

It is unlikely that parliament will remain as supine under his successors as it did under de Gaulle. The ten years of his lonely mastery of French public life may eventually seem to be a kind of parenthesis in the continuity of French political history. Pompidou, on the other hand, can be placed within a long political tradition. He is a representative of the outlook known as Orleanism, the down-to-earth but not unenlightened conservatism of the haute bourgeoisie, attached to parliamentary government, favorable to business interests, willing to concede social reform if not to agitate for it. He can count among his spiritual ancestors another professor, François Guizot, minister of the constitutional monarchy of Louis Philippe, and another self-made man, Adolphe Thiers, who characteristically served both monarchy and republic. Under Pompidou, defense and foreign policy no longer have that primacy over domestic affairs that characterized the rule of de Gaulle; social and economic issues occupy a considerable share of his attention. Or, as someone recently put it, Pompidou has substituted *bonheur* for *grandeur* at the top of the priorities of the government.

As Keith Botsford remarks, "Pompidou is ambiguous; the system is ambiguous; France is ambiguous." The French have a long tradition of confounding observers both foreign and domestic; anyone tempted to make predictions about even the immediate future has the experience of 1968 to remind him how risky such undertakings can be. Just as France seemed to have escaped the turmoil that has characterized much of the last forty years, it fell once again into a severe domestic crisis, and some people thought the French were up to their old game. Still, France has changed enormously since 1930. Do these changes amount to a revolution?

The recent French past is as ambiguous as the present of which Botsford writes. The France of the 1970's operates under essentially the same administrative and legal system as the France of the 1930's. The similarities between the political systems of the Third and Fifth Republics are as striking as the differences. The elites which dominate the economy, the society, and the political system in the France of today are drawn from the same social strata as they were in 1930. But a vigorous economy has supplanted the stagnant economy of the thirties. Despite the experience of 1968, the political instability of the Third and Fourth Republics has given way to stability and a consequent strengthening of the executive power. In the 1930's France remained the second-ranking imperial power in the world. The loss of Empire was an agonizing experience, but only a small minority of Frenchmen now regret the retreat of *La Grande Nation* to its European hexagon. Decolonization has not had the dire economic consequences some observers predicted; the abandonment of the imperial role has redounded to the benefit of French prestige abroad and has allowed economic and foreign-policy-makers to give their main attention to the potentialities of an economically and perhaps one day even politically united Europe. But perhaps the most significant changes which France has undergone in the last forty years have been those which have taken place at the grassroots level, whose subtleties elude the thick-fingered vocabulary of historians and social scientists. Perhaps it is well to remember that for the people experiencing them, the processes characterized by such flat and unemotional words as urbanization and modernization can mean bewilderment, anxiety, and loss as well as an improvement in material well-being and an expansion of cultural horizons.

But the last word can be left to Aléxis de Tocqueville, a great historian of his own times and a man who wrote of his compatriots about as well as anyone ever has:

"When I examine that nation in itself, I can not help thinking it is more extraordinary than any of the events of its history. Did there ever appear on the earth another nation so fertile in contrasts, so extreme in its acts—more under the domination of feeling, less ruled by principle; always better or worse than was anticipated—now below the level of humanity, now far above; a people so unchangeable in its leading features that it may be recognized by portraits drawn two or three thousand years ago, and yet so fickle in its daily opinions and tastes that it becomes at last a mystery to itself, and is as much astonished as strangers at the sight of what it has done; naturally fond of home and routine, yet, once driven forth and forced to adopt new customs, ready to carry principles to any lengths and to dare any thing; indocile by disposition, but better pleased with the arbitrary and even violent rule of a sovereign than with a free and regular government under its chief citizens; now fixed in hostility to subjection of any kind, now so passionately wedded to servitude that nations made to serve cannot vie with it; led by a thread so long as no word of resistance is spoken, wholly ungovernable when the standard of revolt has been raised—thus always deceiving its masters, who fear it too much or too little; never so free that it cannot be subjugated, or so kept down that it cannot break the yoke; qualified for every pursuit, but excelling in nothing but war; more prone to worship chance, force, success, éclat, noise than real glory; endowed with more heroism than virtue, more genius than common sense; better adapted for the conception of grand designs than the accomplishment of great enterprises; the most brilliant and the most dangerous nation of Europe, and the one that is surest to inspire admiration, hatred, terror or pity, but never indifference?"

Part 1

THE THIRD REPUBLIC

A Key to the Political Maze in France

by André Maurois

GREAT BRITAIN, the United States and France all live under a so-called "Parliamentary and democratic" régime. But in reality their institutions are so different that the citizens of any one of them have the greatest difficulty in understanding what is going on in the other two. Thus, during the recent French crisis, my American friends asked me innumerable questions: "How can a government that has a majority of sixty one day have ten the next, with the Deputies unchanged?" "How can the Senate upset the government, and what happens when the Senate and the Chamber cannot agree?" "In England, when one party is in power, it remains in power for the duration of the Legislature and, if the voting reveals an unexpected rift in the party, Parliament is dissolved by the Prime Minister. Is this impossible in France, and can you explain the constant changes which seem to us to be going on in a world of Alice in Wonderland?" It is difficult, but I will try.

I

It would be a mistake to blame France's Constitution of 1875 for her political fluctuations. This Constitution does not prohibit

From the *New York Times Magazine,* December 21, 1930, copyright © 1930, 1958 by The New York Times Company.

the formation of large parties which would come into power in turn, as in England the Whigs and Tories, the Conservatives and Liberals, and as in the United States the Democrats and the Republicans have done for so long. It recognizes and provides for dissolutions of Parliament.

President Doumergue, if he wished, could propose tomorrow in the Senate that the present Chamber of Deputies should be dissolved. In point of fact no President of the French Republic has availed himself of this right since 1877. Then Marshal MacMahon did dissolve the Chamber; but he did so maladroitly, at an inopportune moment, and the country replied with a slap in the face by sending him back the same majority.

Ever since this untoward incident the idea of dissolution, which should seem legal and natural, has been associated in the French mind with the idea of a coup d'état, a spectre which has haunted French Republicans ever since the 18 Brumaire and the 2 Décembre. This unfortunate memory of MacMahon has been a prime historical source of instability for the last forty years; it stopped a wheel in the Parliamentary machine that ought to be far from useless.

Let us consider the feelings of the average French Deputy and of the average British M. P. toward the Ministry in power, supposing them to be equally endowed with ambition and patriotism. What hopes are there for the British Parliamentarian who votes against his party and helps to upset the Cabinet? None to speak of. He places himself outside his party, and this renders his re-election difficult, if not impossible. He will have no chance of taking the place of one of the Ministers, because the Cabinet almost certainly will have recourse to a dissolution. Finally, this dissolution will entail on him the expenses of an election sooner than would otherwise have been the case. Even if he should become a Minister, without a dissolution, he will be required in accordance with the excellent British practice to offer himself again for election. Therefore the personal interests of the British parliamentarian lie on the side of stability. In England no premium is put upon the upsetting of Ministries.

In France there is such a premium, and the personal interests of the Deputy lie on the side of instability. What has he to fear if he helps to upset the Ministry? Will he be obliged to incur again the risks of an election? Certainly not, because, as we have seen, the tradition opposed to dissolution has become fixed. Will he be excluded from his party? Possibly, but there are so many parties in the French Chamber that he will easily find another.

Will he, on the other hand, take the place of some member of the Ministry that has been upset? It must be admitted that he has a chance of doing so. The head of the government, when forming his Ministry, frequently takes note of help given him by such or such a Deputy through an adroit manoeuvre against the preceding Cabinet. He prefers to have with him rather than against him a man known to be dangerous. Whence arises a temptation to even the most upright French Parliamentarian. Our practice has put a premium upon the upsetting of Ministries.

II

The temptation would be less strong if there were great organized parties contending for power. Such parties would maintain discipline within their ranks. Even in opposition they would be led by groups of men ready to form a Cabinet after a successful election. At the time of the last election in England there was no question at all as to who would be called by the King if the Labor party came to power; it was known that it would be J. Ramsay MacDonald, just as it was known that it would be Mr. Baldwin in the event of a Conservative victory. There may be conflicts within one of the parties in respect to the leadership (and such conflicts are frequent), but in Parliament a certain loyalty is traditional.

In France it is very difficult for great parties to come into existence. In the Chamber there are Communists, United Socialists, Socialist Republicans, Socialist Radicals, a Radical Left, a Social and Radical Left, Republicans of the Left, National Republicans, a Democratic Republican Union, Independents of the Left, Independents, and some Deputies so independent that they do not wish even to form a section of the group of Independents. Why this multiplicity of parties?

Every race has its qualities and its defects, and must be governed with due regard for both. In governing the French it must not be forgotten that they are individualists and have always been so. Caesar remarked that the Gauls submitted with difficulty to the authority of a single chief. France showed herself capable of discipline in the World War, and again under Poincaré, at the moment of the great effort to save the franc. She would always be so in situations of danger. But in tranquil times she likes to criticize her leaders. Since the last two Napoleonic experiences, especially, a large number of Frenchmen have felt an almost instinctive dread of every man who rises too swiftly and too high above the level of the rest. A popularity of a transcendent kind in the country would be, I believe, a handicap in Parliament for any French statesman.

This profound equalitarianism, as we call it in France, and this out and out individualism, stand in the way of anything like blind loyalty toward the leaders of a great party. In a Parliamentary group, apart from a few dumb, simple-minded and submissive individuals, every Deputy of any talent thinks that he ought to become at least an Under-Secretary of State, and that he will obtain such a post. If he is in disagreement with the senior members of his group, or even if, apart from any disagreement in regard to political dogmas, he is conscious that he has ahead of him in the group too many brilliant and self-assertive personages, he is tempted to form a new group of his own.

In this way from time to time we see various smaller groups formed and, hanging on to them, seceders from groups of similar bent.

Our Parliamentary game favors such secessions. Because no great party is numerous enough to take office by itself, every Ministry has to depend on a coalition of groups. In order to obtain the support of these groups it must welcome their representative leaders. Thus a man who has been an obscure member of the Radical party and who has never been a Minister, may become a Minister if he is head of a little group—a "social, anti-clerical Left," shall we say—founded by himself with a score of friends and very important to a government if it is to have a majority.

Let it not be said that such ambitions are to be condemned. They exist in every country. Spinoza has shown in his "Tractatus Politicus" that men's passions are always more or less the same and that the good institutions are those which turn to account human defects in such a way as to lead a nation wisely, just as a trainer of animals turns to account their appetites and their fears when putting them through their paces. The British Parliamentarian is as human as the French Parliamentarian. Like the latter he is at once mean and generous, ambitious and jealous, admirable and detestable. But the rules of the game are different.

III

This is not the only reason why the existence of great parties that alternate in office has not been possible hitherto in France. Great parties correspond to definite divisions in a nation. In the United States the two great parties had their origin in a conflict of interest between North and South. In England the cleavage between Whigs and Tories separated the rebellious nobles and often the Nonconformists from the partisans of the King and of the Established Church. When that dividing line disappeared it was replaced by the one between Conservatives and Liberals. Today the division between Conservatives and Laborites is very clearly defined. In France the lines of separation are much more numerous.

Before the Revolution the French were cut into two divisions more definitely than other nations. The privileged landowners who paid no taxes and who were absent from their estates, were separated more profoundly from the peasantry than was the English squire, who was himself often half a peasant and who, moreover, was subject to taxes like his tenant-farmers. The Church was a source of vexation to the French populace—although the populace were orthodox believers—because of its privileges and its alliance with the nobility; the Church and the Château were coupled together and the peasants had no love for either. Then came the Revolution, enlarging still further this abyss between France's "two nations."

The hatred, long felt on the one hand, was opposed, on the other, by a natural feeling of resentment. We must not forget that there exists in Paris a small cemetery—the most aristocratic of any in the city, because the oldest French families have themselves buried in it alongside their ancestors who were guillotined and thrown into the common ditch. The dividing line, between Revolution and Counter-Revolution, is tending gradually to become less accentuated, but it has been and still remains an important feature of the French political landscape. Only a few months ago the leader of the Radical party, speaking in the Chamber of Deputies, used the words: "Blancs contre Bleus." Such historic memories have their danger.

Now it must be noted that the dividing line between Revolution and Counter-Revolution, does not accord precisely with the dividing line between wealth and poverty. A rich peasant will not be in the same political party as his lord of the manor.

Some "petit bourgeois," economical, quiet, and a hundred times more conservative than many English Conservatives, will vote for the Radical candidate because he has an invincible distrust of the curé—a sentiment which seems astonishing when we think of the poverty and harmlessness and goodness of most of the French curés, but which is based on ancestral traditions. It is these traditions that lend a grave political aspect to all debates upon laws bearing upon French schools and French education, debates which in other countries would have nothing to do with questions of party.

In addition to these great dividing lines, there are countless others of a less pronounced nature. There are divisions between the North and the South, between the industrial regions and the agricultural regions, between agriculturists and wine-growers. Even among the Socialists there are Internationalists and Nationalists, and among the Radicals there are out-and-out Radicals and Opportunist Radicals. In addition, we must take into account the little groups and coteries that gather around an individual leader because he serves their purposes. All this makes clear why it is almost impossible to form two great political blocs in France, with an alternation in power that would assure stability in politics.

IV

"Good!" the American or Englishman will say to me. "But when out of this multiplicity of groups a political bloc has been formed numerous enough to accept office and to support a Ministry, why does this bloc not remain homogeneous, at least for the duration of a Parliament? How is it that a Chamber elected on a certain program will vote the Opposition into power? For that is what we have twice seen in the course of the last few years. The Chamber elected in 1924, the Chamber of the Cartel, the Chamber of the Left, finishes its fourth year under a man whom it began by getting rid of—Poincaré. The Chamber of 1928, the Chamber of the National Republicans, the Chamber of the Centre, runs its course in such a fashion as to render possible a Radical Ministry, if only for a day. Why and by what mechanism?"

It is not difficult to understand. In France, because the parties are not very well defined, there is not always strict discipline in the groups. The discipline is always much better in opposition than in power. It has been somewhat better preserved in the course of the present Parliament. Certain groups have expelled Deputies who have not respected decisions taken collectively. But a Deputy who has been expelled from one group can always join an allied one. Toward the centre of the Chamber there are certain groups which we call "charnières" (hinges) half of whose members vote for the Ministry and half against. At need, a Deputy who leaves a group will find refuge among the Independents. Therefore a party in opposition, like a party in power, can always try to wear out the bloc confronting it.

There are numerous methods for achieving this. The government is able to dispose of posts, decorations, favors. The Opposition can make use of promises and turn to account disappointed hopes. Above all, the Opposition has on its side, first, the fatigue inspired by every reign that is too long (the old story of Aristides), and, second, the natural difficulties that attend all action. A man in power is continually making mistakes. Give him enough rope, said Disraeli, and he will hang himself. That is what always happens. And when the Opposition sees the government tottering it is able, by raising a question which will disquiet the electors, to place the Deputies on the government side in the dilemma of having to choose between their re-election and their loyalty. It is not always their loyalty that wins the day.

The equilibrium of a Chamber of Deputies is a thing so unstable that the turn taken in a single sitting may change the whole political situation. A distinguished parliamentarian has declared that a speech has often affected his opinion, but never his vote. That was witty, but it is misleading. An adroit or maladroit speech may affect fifty votes. A French Chamber is extremely responsive to eloquence. It is not made of cast-iron parties upon which no orator can hope to make an impression. It is made up of individuals who are honest, but who are susceptible, and who are carried away by eloquent speeches.

I have seen Briand win over a hostile Chamber. I have seen Briand and Franklin-Bouillon win the applause of the entire Chamber within an interval of ten minutes for absolutely contradictory propositions. It was a subtle speech by Chautemps which, for a brief moment last year, gave the present Chamber the illusion that after all it was perhaps on the Radical side. It was a tactful silence on the part of Tardieu which afterward proved to it that it was not. For a clever tactician no struggle upon such a field of battle is ever quite hopeless.

In conclusion, it should be pointed out that this instability is less dangerous than it would seem. Its disadvantages are, of course, manifest. A head of the government is so occupied defending himself against relentless enemies in ambush that he cannot free his mind for serious matters. In particular it is regrettable that truces cannot be concluded at times of important international negotiations. But as a matter of fact, continuity of policy exists in France to a greater degree than foreigners imagine.

There are countries in which the surface seems to be united and in which division is really profound. In France the surface is broken up but the depths are homogeneous to a remarkable degree.

Just because the dividing lines are innumerable, there is little real difference among the programs of the different governments. Certain men are classed as being of the Left, others as being of the Right. If one did not know their political record, it would be difficult to understand why. The foreign policy of the country has for some years past been so consistent that M. Briand has been able to conduct it in all the Ministries, whether of the Right or of the Left.

Moreover, the task of the President of the French Republic is to secure a relative continuity by the choice of the men whom he calls to office. In appearance the President of France has no power. In fact, he has more power than the King of England, and he is always able quietly to correct the instability of our parliamentary institutions. For the votes of the French Chamber are like the oracles of the Sibyl: they can always be interpreted in more than one way.

The French View
of the World

by P. J. Philip

PARIS

WHOEVER ASPIRES to be considered a good militant of the French Radical and Radical Socialist party must wear a soft black felt hat. It is not a party uniform, for if one is a Radical Socialist one is very much of an individualist and will have nothing to do with uniformity in shirts or even in hats.

But in a soft black felt hat there is a great capacity for nice distinction. Its form is democratic, which is essential. Its sobriety of tone marks it as moderate and dignified. Being of soft felt, it can easily have individuality imparted to it, and, when it is worn for a considerable length of time, its individuality may become very marked. Finally, a soft black felt hat conveys just the right note of superior intellectuality. It can even be made to indicate a wide, generous culture which condescends to mix with less fortunate people.

Probably its choice as the party emblem just happened as natural things do. It was so essentially the right head-wear for a party whose leaders affect individual liberty, social equality and are slightly professional in their habit.

From the *New York Times Magazine,* December 11, 1932, copyright © 1932, 1960 by The New York Times Company.

There are, of course, no regulations as to its shape or the width of the brim. (Only Socialists, like Léon Blum, wear wide, stiff brims. They are more doctrinaire than our individualist Radicals.) Premier Herriot, after several choices, has seemed to select as his particular fancy something in the round pork-pie order. M. Chautemps's hat is heavier in form and substance, and, it may be his pale face that does it, rather funereal in aspect. M. Daladier gives his somehow an artistic touch. François Albert defiantly wears a large size—being a very small man. In a group one may easily pick him out by his hat without seeing him. Léon Meyor, Mayor of Havre, likes a high crown. Albert Milhaud, the General Secretary of the party, and several others affect little round hats which are as individual to Radicalism as tight black trousers to a Spanish dancer.

As soon as any young man obtains any administrative post in the party his first action is to select his particular type of hat—so long as it is black and soft. There are a few exceptions. M. Jammy Schmidt is one. He persists in wearing a black derby perched high above his long aquiline nose, but even his derby manages to have a Radical look and resembles in no way those that London city men wear for business. And there is Caillaux. But Caillaux never did conform. He alone in the party wears an eyeglass and he has been known to wear white spats. He persists even now in his seventieth year in sporting gray hats and brown hats and even green hats.

It isn't that Caillaux is not a good Radical Socialist. Many times, and to his cost, he has proved himself far more courageous in his radicalism than any of his followers or his successors. Perhaps that he does not wear a soft black felt hat is his final admission that he just cannot belong. He is not, except doctrinally, "one of us." There has remained through all his political adventures and misadventures a great deal of the aristocratic bourgeois in the gentleman who was baptized with the gentle-sounding names Marie Joseph Augustus Napoleon Caillaux.

This idiosyncrasy of the soft black felt hat apart, there is much in the Radical Socialist party in France which is comparable to the Democratic party in the United States. Perhaps it may prove fortunate for the world that there should be coincidence in their terms of office. For whatever successive governments France may have in the next four years—and a change may happen any day

—the Radical party, as the strongest single party in the Chamber and in the Senate, must remain the pivot of all governmental combinations.

It may be without real significance, but at least it is interesting as a point of similarity with the Democratic party, that the stronghold of the Radicals in France is the South. Toulouse is their Atlanta. There they have their most influential newspaper and there they recently held their Twenty-ninth Annual National Congress.

One would not wish to push the comparison too far, but it may be noted in passing that the South of France is less industrialized, more agrarian, than the North. The sun is hotter in the Summer time. The Winters are not hard. There is more leisure and ease of life. There is also an aptness for oratory among the people which finds natural outlet in political discussion in the corner café. When one has spoken eloquently, one seems to have done something if the sun is warm. And one is somebody when one belongs to a great organization of the eloquent who believe in liberty of debate and enjoy the discussion of great principles.

Also, it must in truth and justice be added, the "Midi" offers few chances to a young man who knows himself to have great ideas and a fine talent for expressing himself. He must go to Paris, at least occasionally, if he is to find scope. And what better road is there than the political road, along which so many Southern young men have traveled to comfortable jobs, including on more than one occasion the Presidency of the republic?

Politics in France's democratic party is always a shrewd mixture of high principle and mutual help. There are no Frenchmen so clannish in many ways as the Radicals; among them is a strong tradition of Freemasonry. Without reflecting on any—for all of us are human—there is a good strong touch of Tammany in France's Radical Socialist party.

There is another characteristic of the South which cannot be overlooked. Life being easier than in the bleak North, there is naturally a greater warmth of heart, a greater liberalism among its people. They believe very sincerely, very eloquently, in the principles which they profess and, if in action they sometimes do not quite live up to those principles—well, life is like that with all of us.

Though, as in all political parties in all countries, there are sections from all classes of society, it may be said of the French Radicals that, while their numerical strength lies in the South, they are essentially a middle-class party representing the middle classes from all over France. For nearly thirty years—with the exception of a few disastrous periods—they have been the predominant party in the country. In the words of one of their founders, Ledru-Rollin, they were formed "to bring into reality in the lives of men and of peoples the triple symbol of liberty, equality and fraternity."

It was a fine, high-sounding phrase, typical of both party and national rhetoric. In reality it amounted to saying that the middle class, which had never had a real chance at government, wanted that chance and was determined to get it. Though the origins of the party date back to the "bourgeois" revolution of 1848 and the "patriot" government of 1871 and Gambetta (these were radicalism's frock-coat days), the modern Radical and Radical Socialist party really began in 1904. Even then it was a party of combat, almost of civil war.

Until the end of last century, despite her many revolutions, control of the government in France had somehow always managed to slip back into the hands of the aristocracy and the very wealthy. It was the Dreyfus case, above all, which contributed to the organization of this middle-class party which adopted the name of Radical and Radical Socialist to mark its tendency rather than its creed. For, in trying to frame an opinion of just what the Radical and Radical Socialist party of Edouard Herriot is, the reader should disassociate from his mind the ideas which are conveyed in American speech by such a title.

It is one of the foibles of the Frenchman that he likes to think he is advanced and to label himself that way. Poincaré was always pleading that he was a man of the Left. There are only two groups in the Chamber which do not lay claim in their titles to Democracy or radicalism and there are three which profess some form of socialism. That does not in the least prevent any of them from being just as conservative as any Connecticut Republican who votes as his grandfather did.

Just how middle class the party is can be shown by its composition. Of its leaders, Herriot, Daladier, Milhaud, Nogaro and François Albert are or have been professors; Chautemps, Caillaux, Margaine and Julian Durand all began their careers in the upper branches of the civil service. Albert Sarraut is a newspaper owner. Many, like those two young intellectuals, Pierre Cot and Gaston Bergery, are lawyers. The party members are the shopkeepers, the State employes, the farmers, the doctors, the schoolmasters and all the lesser bourgeoisie of France, with, of course, recruits from the upper middle class and the workers. Many of them are Mayors in country towns.

By its very composition, therefore, it is conservative in the strict sense of the word. The heritage of liberalism to which it always pays tribute comes from the tradition of 1793 and 1848, from the revolt of the middle classes against the throne and the aristocracy which abused their power. These dates are still invoked—they were invoked the other day by Herriot.

But, though the modern Radical Socialist likes to think that he is of the race of the Revolutionaries, it would be more accurate to say he is the conserver of what the Revolutionaries won for his class, and he intends to hold on to his inheritance against all new challengers. For the rest his liberalism—more marked in some leaders than in others—might very easily be construed as a stout determination not to permit church interference with liberty of conscience, a warm desire to increase education and opportunity for the deserving, and a great anxiety to prevent the State, in the shape of the tax collector, from prying too deeply into his private affairs.

With the church he fought his battle twenty years ago and won. But since then, having established the laic principle, he has shown himself very lenient toward the activities of Rome. There is not any longer the old hatred of the clergy among the Radicals that there was when Gambetta declared: "Le clericalisme, voilà l'ennemi" and when Papa Combes separated the church from the State and the monasteries were closed.

For education the Radicals have undoubtedly done more than any other political party in France, though there is still a very great deal to be done in widening and improving general education. While opportunity is given to the clever boy, the State education in the primary schools is not carried to a sufficient age. There still lurks in many minds a suspicion that too much education is not good for the proletariat.

The great strength in doctrine and weakness in execution of the Radical party is its attitude toward public finance. It believes in a balanced budget, in economy, in the reduction of military expenditure, in the increase of education and social service and in the just distribution of the burden of taxation. But somehow it never seems to get the answers right in actual practice.

Therein, no doubt, it does not differ from any other democratic government in any other country. Every Parliament nowadays has its deficit, its tendency toward economy in the wrong place, its unfair taxation, its overinflated departments and its demagogic tendencies. Only somehow it seems that in France for many reasons these difficulties are more inherent and less exceptional than in other places.

Unfriendly people allege that it is because the French do not pay their taxes. That allegation is founded on an entirely wrong conception of what happens. The case should be put this way. If a Frenchman did pay all the taxes that the State demands of him he would have nothing left to live on and leave to pay his death duties. Therefore he dodges. Ways of dodging are indeed in many cases provided for him by the law. For the law-makers' argument is that the law can never take account of every circumstance and a little compensatory dodging is therefore only wise if the machine is to work smoothly.

Caillaux discovered years ago how ingrained is this habit of the French mind. There was enormous clamor against his "fiscal inquisition" in 1906 and the Finance Minister had to abandon his dream of a tidy taxation system. That fact does not prevent the party from solemnly demanding on every possible occasion the repression of fraud. Indeed, no resolution is ever more heartily applauded in a party congress than that calling for fiscal equality and the strict enforcement of the law. Where the catch is, is that most of those who applaud believe that they are the victims of an unfair system and that the strict enforcement of the law would in their case be a terrible injustice.

There is another aspect of the French Parliament's method of dealing with finance which, though it does not concern the Radicals only, is worth attention as typical. There is always much bother about balancing the budget and much discussion about appropriations and revenue, but there is no real control of expenditure. The figures are mostly hypothetical, and in a country which has two or three budgets of hypothetical figures it is only natural that the income-tax payer who never can know how his money is really spent should return a somewhat hypothetical figure.

In international affairs the Radical's doctrine is for cooperation. But representing as he does the commercial classes, his attitude is best summed up in his own phrase, "Donnant donnant," which may be interpreted, "Nothing for nothing."

Added to that the Radical has the French passion for juridic right, and so when one comes to a concrete case like that of the interallied debts he is always to be expected to show himself a firm creditor and at least a very argumentative debtor.

In all the departments of political life the Radical program is always more or less a compromise between doctrine and expediency. The Radical believes in fairly free trade except where the vital interests of "the nation," which includes his party, are concerned. Thus he can be counted on to protect the farmer up to the point where the price of bread does not cause active loss of support among the bread consumers. He can be expected to be active one day in attacking the problem of the cost of living and to be passive the next day when there is a recovery of basic prices on the Bourse.

With regard to disarmament and peace his reactions follow much the same rule. There is always an underlying contradiction between his doctrine and its application. Then, too, his doctrine is often complicated by logic and by his love of formulae. The "Liberty, Equality, Fraternity" of the Revolution has become: "Arbitration, Security, Disarmament" in this generation. The invention of these trilogies and their constant use by orators and in the press has many serious disadvantages. They express and so satisfy the aspirations and take little account of the possibility of practical fulfillment.

But there is no doubt whatever that in his heart every French Radical and nearly every Frenchman is sincerely attached to peace. He wants it for himself and for his children. He believes almost that he invented the idea and has a monopoly in this desire. He will claim passionately that France is not only a pacific country but the pacific country above all others. He always talks about Germany as if Germany had always been and would always be the great perturber of world peace. He never admits, if he ever remembers, that France has given the world far more scares than Germany ever did, and that Napoleon still looms bigger in the memory of the rest of humanity than Kaiser William II of Germany.

This forgetfulness is perhaps more on the surface than real. For the intelligent Radical of France's Third Republic seems somehow just at present to be devoting a good deal of his attention to tying up not only other people's war-like tendencies but his own also. That logic which dogs him all his life and is so difficult of comprehension to pragmatic Anglo-Saxons has led his professorial mind to the invention of a complete pyramid of pacts, covenants and conventions, whereby not only all others but he himself will be restricted and confined.

Perhaps it is because he recognizes that underneath his doctrine and his idealism, behind his democracy and his internationalism, there still is in him and his kind a strong instinct to battle. But he is a declining race. He is realist enough to take that into account. The day is past in history when France was the most numerously populated country in the world and the most inventive. War has cost her dearly under the Bourbons, under the Napoleons, and even under President Poincaré of the Third Republic. Her whole effort should be and must be toward preservation.

But the middle-class Radical is not sure that the other parties in France will accept that conception of France's rôle. He is not quite sure that in certain events, under certain provocation, he himself would accept it. When he talks of "security" he has in mind not only security from attack but also at times security from temptation to war.

Meanwhile, as it seeks to show the world the road to security and disarmament, which, with its national clearness and courage of mind, it knows to be the true road, France's Radical government with the whole Radical party behind it can be counted on to be prudent about abandoning the old system. There is not a single

Radical who will not continue to vote every penny necessary and possible for the upkeep of the army and navy and the air force at its full strength so long as the other peoples of Europe have not agreed to come into his mutual protection system.

As a party they stretch up to very high ideals. There are very few among them who will not individually admit that the case of Germany has been mishandled in and ever since the Treaty of Versailles. They will tell you that the Polish Corridor is a crime against reason. They will admit that the reparations claims of past days were folly. They will argue for good-will toward Germany more eloquently than any American. But they are a middle-class party, still rather unsure of themselves in the art of government, still rather terrified by the memory of war, and always hampered by the fact that, as in all democracies, their pace must be regulated by that of their slowest members.

And so, while as liberal humanitarians they reach toward their ideals—"Liberty, Equality, Fraternity"; "Arbitration, Security, Disarmament"—as Frenchmen they like keeping their feet firmly planted on solid ground.

France Feels the
Sweep of New Tides

by Harold Callender

PARIS

FOR A long time to come the politics of France will be governed by memories of the recent Paris revolt, when normally law-abiding young men longed for nothing so much as for an opportunity to unhorse the Gardes Mobiles and throw them into the Seine; when many threw marbles under the feet of the troops' mounts so that they might slip and throw their riders; when men proceeded deliberately and methodically to smash with hammers the glass enclosing traffic lights in the rue de Rivoli; when mobs tried to force their way into the Chamber of Deputies and the Elysée Palace (where the President lives) and were driven back by volleys of bullets and drawn sabers; when many thousands of Parisians of the most respectable classes—"the decent people" of the capital, as they have often since been called—engaged in a revolutionary demonstration against the French Parliament which turned into the most violent uprising that Paris had witnessed since the Commune of 1871.

If this spectacle haunts the minds of French politicians for years, there will be good reason for it. For when due allowance has been made for the prankish destructiveness of youth and the careful organization which preceded the demonstration, the fact remains that it represented an odd mixture of aggressive reaction, of real indignation at the scandals in public life, of economic discontent, of disillusionment with democracy as practiced: a combination of forces such as in other countries—though not yet in an experienced democracy like France—has threatened or overthrown parliamentary régimes.

While in France, particularly in the provinces, there are deeply rooted republican traditions and a profound distrust of "strong men" with dictatorial ambitions, the counter-revolution (if it may be called that) has considerable support in the upper middle class, especially in Paris. And it is prepared to make strong appeal to other classes, and to youth of all classes, by utilizing the worldwide unrest and confusion which economic disorganization has accentuated in all countries and under all types of government.

The republic in France has always drawn its principal strength from an inherited fear of reaction. To the peasant, the worker and the small business man the republic was a defense against the rich, the church, the aristocracy and all who might dream of reclaiming the privileges which the Revolution abolished. Years before the present crisis one was surprised by the challenging vehemence with which the Frenchman said, "I am a republican!" For were not nearly all Frenchmen republicans and was not the republic safe enough?

Not at all. Its supporters regarded the republic as being constantly in danger from some new Napoleon or Boulanger. The preservation of French liberties, they thought, demanded unremitting vigilance. The Third Republic, even after sixty years, still kept a watchful eye upon the enemies within.

The republic now has a new enemy. It has long managed to hold its own, even during four years of war and its tragic aftermath, against the remnants of the feudal aristocracy, the royalists, the reactionaries and the militarists. But now a new doctrine has appeared which, oddly allied to some extent with the old anti-republicanism, has cast a strange spell upon many of the younger generation of both "Right" and "Left" antecedents.

One refers, of course, to the doctrine of "authoritarian" government, of economic planning by capable technicians; the alluring conception of a society organized on economic rather than on political lines; the dream of a community where the traditional dogmas will have lost all meaning and where statesmen will be preoccupied not in restricting the clergy's privileges or safeguarding laical schools or upholding vague ideologies derived from eighteenth-century philosophers but in constructing a new type of State in harmony with the unprecedented requirements of a mechanized and troublesomely productive age.

These are the ideas and aspirations which have captivated many of the youth in France, at least many of the university youth, from whom future leaders will largely come. These young men look with something like contempt upon the pre-war politicians who have led France in the accustomed paths. They have no more use for the traditional terminology of politics, or the multifarious divisions and subdivisions of political groups in Parliament, or the pleasant abstractions which so long have been the stock in trade of party leaders than they have for the refined dialectics of medieval scholastics.

They are not yet at all clear as to what they want. They are not united under a leader or agreed upon a program. They may be moved by impulse more than by knowledge. But they represent perhaps the most remarkable and novel element, if as yet a somewhat fluid one, in the field of French political thought.

Without them it would be much the same old contest between "Right" and "Left," Conservative and Radical, Republican and clerical, capitalist and Socialist. But if these younger men are driven by economic events to push their way, perhaps prematurely, into the places that normally would be filled by the men who lie under white crosses in Northern France—men who would now be 35 to 55 years of age—the course of French politics may be radically changed. The middle generation is short of talent, many of its best having fallen in battle; there remain the old men with (as the youth would say) mostly old ideas, and the very young with startlingly new ideas.

Not that these ideas and longings were consciously championed by many of the mob which fought the police and howled at the Deputies. That mob was inspired by reactionaries of the old school, by Royalists, by Fascists and by people who genuinely believed that to give the deputies a fright would be a salutary measure. The mob represented, among other things, a revival of the rebellious, "frondeur," Boulangist spirit of Paris; and in consequence of its success Paris, which made the nineteenth-century revolutions, but since Boulanger's adventure in 1889 has had little influence upon French politics, may again take the lead, or at least play a more active role.

But the Parisian uprising was nothing if not anti-parliamentarian, and in this, at any rate, it coincided with the inclination of those, chiefly among the youth, who despair of the present political methods and machinery and seek something less cumbersome and better disciplined. Some rose against the present Chamber because it was dominated by the Left, others because they wanted a king or a dictator; but these diverse groups were at one in disliking the present Parliament, if not parliamentary government as such. Both their unity in opposition and their complete lack of unity as to program were revealed in the recent revolt.

In a recent procession in honor of one of those killed by Gardes Mobiles in the Place de la Concorde marched several thousand persons representing the following groups: The Action Française, the militant Royalist organization, which seeks to place the Duke of Guise upon the throne of France: the Jeunesses Patriotes (Patriotic Youth) in dark blue uniforms, an equally militant league of youth of the Extreme Right, which proclaims the need of a "national revolution" and maintains its "shock troops" on Fascist lines; the Solidarité Française, looking even more Fascist with their light blue shirts and their salutes; a group of Municipal Councilors of Paris, fifteen of whom had issued a vehement proclamation which helped to incite the city against the late Radical government, and the war veterans of the Croix de Feu and some members of the Union Nationale des Anciens Combattants.

Here, in formal array, was the organized advance guard of anti-parliamentarism as manifested in the recent demonstrations. The first three groups have decidedly Fascist characteristics, though the first places primary emphasis upon restoration of the monarchy. The youthful members of all three remind one of the militant and mystical young Nazis in German universities. The Municipal Councilors typify Parisian resistance to provincial radicalism and to what the "Right" generally regarded as an attempt by a radical government to increase its power and crush its enemies.

The veterans' organizations are more difficult to classify. They represent no avowed doctrine and profess to be republican, non-partisan and interested solely in good government, order and national defense; but the Croix de Feu, a recent organization of frontline soldiers, conducted an active campaign against the government and joined with Royalist and Fascist groups in an anti-parliamentary demonstration. A government which had the confidence of the Chamber was overthrown by a crowd in the streets of Paris, thanks largely to the Croix de Feu.

The commander of the Croix de Feu, Colonel de la Rocque, objects to comparisons between his organization and the Nazis, saying, "We are not romanticists," and pointing to the fact that his men wear no uniforms. But the comradery of the trenches, which the Croix de Feu represents, is not unlike that developed by the Nazis, though it perhaps resembles more closely that of the German Stahlhelm, composed, like the Croix de Feu, of war veterans. The Stahlhelm, too, stood for order, discipline and national defense; it, too, was made up of men of many classes; but it was frankly monarchist and military and closely allied to the Nationalist party.

The Croix de Feu are regarded by the "Left" as virtual Fascists, as tools of a conservative reaction. It will hardly be possible for them to remain aloof from the party and class conflict, in which they have, indeed, already taken sides, whether they intend to do so or not. In Germany the veterans' organizations were frankly political, one group being Socialist, one group Nationalist and some such split may come sooner or later in France. There is a marked tendency for many of the intellectual youth to ally themselves with the Croix de Feu; but others look upon the Croix members, whose ages range from 35 to 50 or more, as middle-aged and therefore hopeless.

In the Jeunesses Patriotes, in the Action Française, and perhaps in the Croix de Feu, are Fascist possibilities; but these groups are not united, are not led by a single dominant leader, and have not gained anything like the support among the youth which the Nazis had in, say, 1931. They would be resisted by the Radicals, the Socialists and the Communists and would be stronger in Paris than in the more sternly republican provinces.

While there are certain striking resemblances between the anti-parliamentarian movements in France and those that brought down the German republic, there are equally noteworthy differences. Both gained many followers among the youth, who were unemployed and without hope, and among the ex-soldiers. Both were supported by conservative middle-class interests and were regarded as enemies of labor and socialism. Both proclaimed, in almost identical terms, a "national awakening" and a cleansing of public life.

But while the German Nazi movement was directed against a republic that was new and weak, the French anti-parliamentarians and Fascists attack a republic that is sixty-three years old and has become firmly established. While the Nazis, though backed by industrialists, appealed chiefly to the lower middle-class masses who had hardly any property and hence cheered denunciations of bankers and promises of "national socialism," the French movement represents primarily the upper middle or propertied class and so makes no pretensions to economic radicalism, such as the Nazis made (before they came into power). The French movement shows no signs of anti-Semitism—though it may be expected to enjoy the support of the same classes that condemned Dreyfus—and it lacks the military spirit and form of the Nazi movement.

Most important of all perhaps, the French movement, far from having the marked anti-intellectual bias of the Nazis, is one in which intellectuals are leading. French fascism, if it becomes more than an aspiration, is not likely to be a revolt against intelligence.

The division among its enemies and critics will help the republic to resist the new attacks, though they are no longer the familiar onslaughts of a purely reactionary or clerical "Right." Moreover, the attacks come primarily from Paris, whose republicanism has long been tinged with Boulangist leanings and cosmopolitan skepticism. The real strength of the republic has been in the provinces, which are predominantly moderate and radical, even when they vote Socialist, while Paris tends to the Extreme "Right" and the Extreme "Left." It was the largest party in France, the Radicals, whose government was overthrown by the mob in Paris.

The provinces are habitually suspicious of Paris, which, as Professor Seignobos observes, is out of touch with the French masses. Most of the French political leaders come from the provinces. The Deputy from the provinces attending parliamentary sessions in Paris usually is a visitor living in a hotel. He must take care, says André Siegfried, not to become a Parisian, lest he be regarded by his constituents as a backslider from the republican faith. It should be noted that the recently developed anti-parliamentary movement is first and foremost a Parisian phenomenon.

But if the republic is to survive in substantially its present form, it may have to become far more efficient and more capable of meeting economic difficulties. It will have to meet the challenge of the "decent people" who have lost confidence in its officials and in its judiciary and resent the power of the trade unions of State employes, who even enjoy the right to strike. It will have to meet the attacks of the foes of liberal capitalism who want a planned economy and a strong central power. It will have to learn to act more decisively and to attain a higher standard of honesty among its representatives. It will have to become more attractive to the youth.

On the side of the existing régime is the stubborn republicanism of the provinces, a heritage of the past. Working against it are the trend of economic events and the contagious example of "authoritarian" political doctrines in the other major Continental countries —and also, strange as it may seem, the influence of the New Deal in the United States, whose President is widely regarded in Europe as a kind of benevolent but courageous dictator. Many times has the writer heard Frenchmen condemn their own Parliament while pointing with admiration to Mr. Roosevelt and wishing that France had a similar leader.

In Germany fascism, breaking from the reactionaries and monarchists who sought simply a return to the semi-feudal past, aligned itself with the more modern reactionaries who sought to crush the trade unions and federalism so as to establish a powerful State which they could control. In France the anti-parliamentary movement, and what incipient Fascists there are, have not decided how reactionary, in the old or the new style, they are going to be. The "authoritarian" movement has not yet crystallized and can hardly hope to do so until it finds a commanding leader. France has had her Bonapartes and her Boulangers and, on the whole, is not keen on repeating the experiment.

France is one of only three great free nations left in the world. If she should eventually adopt a dictatorship or go Fascist, she would be the first country with long experience of democracy to do so.

Puzzled France:
Which Way?

by André Maurois

PARIS

TO UNDERSTAND what has happened in France one must recall the traditional political alignment and how it had been transformed before the recent national election.

During the years following the war three great political groups were clearly discernible in France—leaving aside the finer shades of division. On the Right was a moderate group embracing many middle-class electors, a large number of peasants, especially in the West and East, and Catholic wage-earners. In the center were the Radicals, the most numerous group, representing the smaller business and professional people (the petits bourgeois), government employes and a part of the peasants of the central and southern provinces. On the Left were the Socialists supported by most of the workers, certain State employes (particularly school teachers) and intellectuals.

The Radical party held the balance of power. It was allied by sympathy with the Socialists, though in practice it often found itself at odds with them. André Siegfried defined the Radical party by saying that its heart was on the Left but its pocket impelled it

From the *New York Times Magazine*, May 31, 1936, copyright © 1936, 1964 by The New York Times Company.

to the Right. That party, composed of people with small savings, feared some of the financial measures the Socialists might adopt. But above all, being a patriotic party—the heir, as it often proclaimed, of the Jacobins of Valmy—it could not govern with the sole support of the Socialists, who refused to vote credits for national defense.

Consequently from 1919 to 1932 the Radical party was torn between its sympathies with the Left and the necessities of government. Sometimes it leaned toward the Right and France had a Poincaré or a Laval Ministry; sometimes it joined the Left in trying a Cartel (Left coalition) Cabinet in conjunction with the Socialists. This swing of the pendulum did not represent in France, as it does in England, a movement of the mass of voters in one direction or the other; it was merely the shifting of a parliamentary group in alternative coalitions.

As for the Communists, although they won a large number of votes in elections in those years, they obtained few seats in the Chamber. The reason was that in France an election consists of two ballotings, a week apart, and the outcome depends upon the alliances made between the first and second ballots. The Communists were on bad terms with the other Left parties. They were regarded by the Socialists as dangerous rivals and by the bourgeois and patriotic Radicals as international revolutionaries. In 1932 proportional representation would have given forty-five seats to the Communists, but they won only twelve.

If the Communists had remained enemies of the Socialists, if the moderates had remained on good terms with the Radicals, if the French voters had been fairly well satisfied with the government of the country, we probably should have witnessed this year the traditional comedy. That is, the voters would have given a small majority to the coalition of Radicals and Socialists, a Left government would have faced financial difficulties, and about 1938 the Left coalition would have foundered and been succeeded by a moderate government.

But new circumstances, combined with the errors of the moderates in their relations with the Radicals, altered the entire situation. The most important novelty was the transformation of the Communist party into a governing party. This was due to foreign causes. Soviet Russia, feeling itself menaced by Nazi Germany, had decided that the best defense lay in an alliance with the French Republic.

Two necessities were imposed by that alliance: *First,* that France should be strong, and therefore that the French Communists should support military expenditures: *second,* that France should have a government sincerely favoring the Russian alliance, and hence that the French Communists in the 1936 elections should seek the aid of the other Left parties and in turn should support the Radicals and Socialists.

This explains why the Communists, for the first time, were moved to ally themselves with the Radicals. But why should the Radicals have accepted such an alliance? Here is where the mistakes of the moderates played their part.

On the occasion of the Stavisky financial scandal the moderates made, or permitted, a campaign of extreme violence against the Radical leaders. That campaign had three results. It drove the Radicals toward the extreme Left; it convinced a part of the middle-class youth of the need to oppose the existing régime and, after the disturbances of Feb. 6, 1934, encouraged the formation of leagues like the Croix de Feu; and it provoked, as a reaction against the leagues and from fear of fascism, the formation of the electoral coalition of Communists, Socialists and Radicals called the People's Front. It was this People's Front which united behind a single candidate in each constituency at the second ballot in the recent election.

Any one acquainted with the political map of France could have predicted the victory of such a coalition and foreseen that it would give the Communists a much greater number of seats. But the victory of the People's Front exceeded the expectations of the experts. The coalition desired by the party leaders likewise coincided with the will of the mass of voters, who favored the extreme Left of this Left coalition—that is, the Communists and Socialists —at the expense of the Radicals.

Why did middle-class citizens, peasants and State employes vote for a change of leadership? Electoral strategy does not suffice to explain the sudden swing to the Left of so many voters. Let us then seek the reasons for it.

The most important reason was the extreme discontent among almost all classes caused by the policy of deflation. One need not discuss whether that policy was wise or not. It was necessary if the franc was to be defended. But it had painful consequences for everybody.

A series of decrees reduced the salaries of State employes, which naturally irritated that powerful class. The small shopkeepers suffered from the depression and from the absence of foreign tourists. Privately paid wages and salaries followed government payrolls in their descent to lower levels. Unemployment, though less acute than in the United States or in England, nevertheless caused much suffering.

The public had long waited patiently for the government to "do something." First the people were told that all the trouble came from politics and that a reform of the Constitution would remove the evils from which France suffered. During the administration of M. Doumergue, who assumed power after the 1934 riots, such a reform had been planned, but it was never carried through. Later the country was assured that deflation would bring back prosperity. Deflation was applied at the cost of great suffering, but the crisis continued. The least revolutionary of the middle class then began to wonder whether a change of government was not necessary.

These small, middle-class people had long been alienated from the Left parties by the question of national defense and by the religious question. But the Communists, 1936 model, spoke of the army with enthusiasm and of religion with sympathy. The influence of the Vatican, moreover, inclined the church toward social reforms.

To the small landowners who would have been frightened away by a too Socialistic or Communistic program, the candidates of the People's Front said: "It's not your wealth which is in question. Nobody thinks of touching your property, your land or your capital. Small and moderate fortunes will not be disturbed. It is only the great ones that are in danger. It is the 200 families who among them own nearly all the great business enterprises in France. They are the ones—the only ones—we are after."

Every effective propaganda campaign is founded upon a myth. "The 200 families" served as the myth of the 1936 French elections. It had among the masses a success not difficult to understand, for it offered a simple and naive explanation of all the country's troubles. It suggested easy remedies, and since it held a threat for only an infinitesimal minority, it provoked little opposition. It explains to a great extent why so many small property owners, middle-class Radicals, were willing on the second ballot to vote Communist or Socialist.

In domestic affairs the program of the Socialist and even of the Communist leaders is, at least for the moment, not at all revolutionary. It could hardly be revolutionary, for many of the new supporters of the Left parties do not wish a Left program. The Russian Communists, who seek the aid of France, have no desire to see France weakened by dissension. Above all, the most ardent wish of the masses is for economic recovery, which cannot take place in an atmosphere of apprehension and conflict. It must be added that the Right opposition has no more intention than the Left of carrying the struggle outside the parliamentary sphere.

"To assure the recovery of economic life"—that is the phrase now reiterated in newspaper articles and interviews by Léon Blum, the Socialist leader who is to become Premier. He desires, it appears, to undertake an experiment resembling that which President Roosevelt made in the United States and M. van Zeeland in Belgium.

But in those countries the point of departure, the fillip given to the national economy, was monetary devaluation. That would be difficult for the parties which have placed the defense of the franc at the head of their program. Some suggest that M. Blum would prefer to try a method somewhat analogous to that of Dr. Schacht; that is, of controlled exchanges and a semi-closed economy. Yet the export of gold, which since the elections has attained large proportions, might force him to devalue the currency.

In their election platforms the victorious parties promised to impose a levy on capital and to use the proceeds for public works designed to reduce unemployment. The specialists have no great confidence in the yield of such a tax. It would be difficult to collect because many forms of capital are such that they cannot be reached; it would reduce the yield of the income tax in subsequent years; it would hamper rather than help the restoration of normal economic activity. The Communists, nevertheless, have announced that they will propose such a measure as soon as the new Chamber meets.

The new government, on the other hand, will certainly attempt to nationalize the munitions industry. In so doing it will antagonize only certain private interests, for the bulk of the country is not hostile but rather favorable to this plan. Other monopolies will also be tackled.

There has been a suggestion to nationalize all insurance, but that apparently is not intended. Rather is it nationalization of the petroleum trade which is discussed. As importation is concentrated in a few hands, it would be relatively simple to take over the industry, and the intervention of the State could be justified to a certain extent by the importance of oil for national defense. Finally, the Bank of France certainly will be transformed and subjected to more drastic control by the State.

This immediate program is no more revolutionary than was that of the British Labor party, and it is quite possible that the Socialist and Radical parties in France will tend toward a kind of reform socialism after the fashion of the Laborites. That is, just now, the desire of several of their leaders. But one must take account of the inevitable resistance which always exasperates those who are resisted.

When the battle begins, will the majority behind the government remain faithful? Will the opposition have the wisdom to adhere to parliamentary methods, without having recourse to its great influence over owners of small savings accounts or bonds? Above all, will the Senate vote for State monopolies and new taxes?

If the Senate resists, we can expect a struggle like that against the House of Lords in England at the time of Lloyd George's budget in 1910. But the French Senate is elective while the Lords are hereditary, and until now it has not been unpopular. The Senate would defend itself, perhaps with the tacit support of the Radicals in the Chamber. The question is: Where, in the last analysis, is the real power in France? The Socialist victory, which is indisputable and undisputed, does not insure an easy path for the government, especially if the Communists refuse to share the responsibilities of power.

In foreign affairs the victory of the Left signifies first of all fidelity to the League of Nations and to the principle of collective security—precisely what Great Britain would have welcomed so eagerly a few months ago. But France and Britain seem fated to play at cross purposes, to wish different things at a given time or the same things at different times.

At this moment, when public opinion in France has by its vote sought to give a new lease of life to the League, the British Government contemplates a reform of the covenant so drastic that the League would not survive it. The French Socialist government will certainly ask the British to regard last year's difficulties as a misunderstanding and to give the League a few months more. But will they agree?

Regarding Germany, M. Blum says he desires to reopen negotiations for European disarmament, if that is still possible. He would call the Disarmament Conference into session again and ask Germany to participate. If she refused, a disarmament convention would be drawn up without her, and it would then be presented by the European States jointly to the German Government. That government has always said it favored such a project, and in these circumstances, M. Blum believes, the issue would have to be faced by Germany.

In foreign as in domestic affairs the new government's path will be strewn with difficulties. The three parties which compose its majority in the Chamber are not entirely in accord. The Communists wish above all a close agreement with Moscow; the Socialists favor a frankly pro-League policy; and it is no secret that M. Daladier, the Radical leader, used to urge a direct understanding with Germany and to support the Four-Power pact. There is no reason to assume that he has altered his opinions.

Will new leaders solve the old problems? In politics problems are never solved; or, rather, hardly are they solved before new obstacles appear. In France the great evil since the war has been the weakening of the power of the State. Governments of both the Right and the Left have complained of it and suffered from it.

If the Cabinet now assuming power re-establishes the authority of the State and governs with a realistic appreciation of the national interest, many Frenchmen who are neither Socialists nor Radicals will rejoice. If it falls into demagogy and takes orders from irresponsible party congresses, it will fail and quickly lose all prestige. Leaders and doctrines may change; they have just changed in France; but the principles of government are immutable. Votes do not transform men.

In What Direction?
A Puzzled France Wonders

by P. J. Philip

PARIS

WHATEVER THE outcome of the present political struggle in France may be, it is accepted here as almost certain that this country will not "go Fascist" or "go Communist," as these terms are understood and practiced in Italy, Germany and Russia. France will remain French. If a name must be given to the system which is most likely to evolve that name is "collectivist."

Everybody agrees that changes are coming. Events have been developing swiftly in France. Differences of opinion resulting from the Munich agreement and of the decree laws which led to the attempt to stage the recent general strike are growing. The signing on Tuesday of the "good-neighbor" pact between Germany and France is not likely to lessen the conflict over the social and economic policies of the nation and over the duties of the State and the rights of its citizens.

On top of the factional quarrels which are going on in France there has come the acute perception that economically this country is fast slipping from the rank it used to hold. The national income has shrunk to a greatly diminished number of billions of very greatly diminished francs. There has been little or no construction, little or no development in recent years. Housing has been neglected; even existing properties have been allowed to fall into decay from lack of the will or the money to keep them painted and repaired. Industries have fallen back because of the lack of the will or money to install new modern machinery. In shipping France has dropped back from third place to seventh. The commercial balance of the country continues to be unfavorable by hundreds of millions of francs a month.

Meanwhile, expenditure not only for armaments but for social service of all kinds has continued to pile up unendingly. M. Daladier recently gave the figures: National income, 250 billion francs; government expenditure, 137 billions; normal government revenue, 85 billions.

How to change these conditions and to achieve stability is the problem the country is facing amid great confusion of counsel. What is fundamentally at stake is the conception of the relations of the State and the citizenry which has established itself firmly in the French mind throughout a good many generations and especially in the last twenty years.

To understand the situation, or rather the conception the French have of the State and its duties, one must go back to the 19th of Fructidor, 1798, when Genenral Jourdan got the Council of Five Hundred to pass a little law making all men between 20 and 25 years old "defenseurs conscrits"—compelling them to take arms for the defense of their country. It is that little law—perpetuated throughout every regime ever since—which has made France different from other "democracies," however much the French may seek to conceal or to justify the difference.

That was the law which began the gradual conversion of France into a collectivist State. In return for military service the citizenry began to demand more and more from the government until even those governments and parties which were the declared opponents of socialism were compelled to join the procession, so that now the State seems to control and direct everything from the election of an academician and a schoolmaster to the railroads, the highways, the telegraphs and telephones, the manufacture of Sèvres pottery, the opera and some theatres, museums and art galleries. Add to this list huge forests, the manufacture of matches and tobacco, the refinement of oil, the Bank of France, potash mines in Alsace, coal mines in Flanders, steamship companies and mineral springs like those of Vichy.

There is scarcely anything in which the State does not take a hand and that, in the opinion of those opposed to such laws as the forty-hour week, is the source of the present difficulty. State intervention, it is argued, has killed private initiative; it has killed the desire of the capitalist to risk his capital in enterprise.

State intervention, too, runs the argument, has killed the desire of the workman to work and save. He has derived from his experience as a soldier—and of course the demands of the war veterans are cited in this connection—the feeling that the State owes him his livelihood. He obtained from the Blum government the forty-hour week and paid vacations. In themselves these improvements in the workers' lot in many industries are conceded to have been legitimate and beneficial. But it is contended that they spread the conception that the individual could "take things easy" and the State would provide.

If France were a sufficiently populated country with peaceful neighbors the task would be easier. But the awkward fact is that out of the profits and earnings of a Malthusian citizenry must be drawn, in addition to all that is needed for the upkeep and smooth running of the State, twenty-five billion francs a year for armaments, and that excluding the normal cost of the army, the fleet and the air force. If capital will not work and labor will not work, the necessary wealth cannot be produced and quite humanly they will not consent to work so long as the State would provide.

Neither capital nor labor is willing yet, it would seem, to admit that the State cannot go on providing. Capital wants labor to pull the country up by working longer hours. Labor, led by M. Blum, gives the old answer, "Tax the rich." It is rarely argued by the French capitalist that his indolence in attending to his business set an example to the workers or by the workers that there are very few "rich" left in France who can be so extensively and repeatedly taxed as to bring any real solution.

Out of this triangular struggle among the State, labor and capital there has evolved a political as well as an economic situation which to many observers has every appearance of becoming extremely dangerous. For there is no issue except a change of temper and attitude, and it is regarded doubtful whether that change can be accomplished without a change of regime.

Even in the country one now finds people—people who a few years, even a few months, ago felt and said that the republic was solidly built and would never need to be changed—who begin to say that the republic is "used up," that some firmer form of government is becoming necessary. In part the change of opinion is attributed to the disillusion caused by the Munich settlement. The mass of people are saying for the first time that France, the country which twice invaded the Weimar Republic to compel respect for treaties, had not sufficient confidence in herself and in what she wanted to invade Hitler's Third Reich.

Although the traditional collectivist spirit engendered by conscription sent 1,800,000 men to the frontier without question, there were people who professed to see only the form and not the substance of unity in the ranks. It was said that too much talking, the vanity of party leaders, their demagogy, their lip-service to strange doctrines, had sapped that spirit of national purpose which in the old days followed a leader, whether he was right or wrong, for the honor of France and the republic.

The great demand in France today is for a leader and discipline. During the mobilization in September both the regular army officers and the reservists were amazed to find that the men who were so troublesome as workmen and employes were so tractable and willing as soldiers. Once the soldier had donned his képi he seemed to forget that he had been a Radical, a Socialist, a Communist, a Doriotist or a member of de la Rocque's French Social party. He became a real collectivist and not merely a dependent on the collectivity. He seemed to be happier than he had been as a civilian faced with the problem of having to make up his voter's mind as to the rival merits of Reynaud's doctrine of recovery by individual action and the doctrines by the scores of different parties which the egoism of the French has created.

As to what will happen no one can prophesy. But if some different system of government from that which has controlled France for the past three generations has to be set up, one thing appears certain at this juncture—it will confine itself to the direction of the economic and military life of the country and not, as other dictatorships have done, interfere in the spiritual and free intellectual life of the people.

Part **2**

THE SECOND WORLD WAR

The Titanic Struggle Inside France

by Pertinax [André Geraud]

PIERRE LAVAL has just taken up the reins of command at Vichy. In choosing his colleagues he has been somewhat groping; but in his program he shows neither hesitancy nor doubt. Laval's political exile lasted sixteen months. The better part of this time he spent in Paris, under German protection, in endless conversations with Otto Abetz, representative of the Reich in occupied France, and Abetz's masters. He knows what he wants. And it is only too likely that he is in perfect agreement with the occupying power as to the way, the place, the time, the rhythm of the French contribution which will bring German victory—and he longs for it. But how can he carry out his promise against the will of the French people?

Today, all witnesses agree on the intensity of popular feeling against the Germans which rages in France under seeming resignation or even apathy. In vast numbers Frenchmen understand that they can never again become free and independent except by a victory of England, the United States and Russia. The majority of them also believe that the entrance of the United States into the struggle spells German defeat. And let us not forget that lasting horror branded on men's hearts by the mass killing of hostages, that burning indignation which occasionally bursts through in some violent gesture—in Paul Colette's pistol-shot. Is that comparable in essence to the knife thrusts of Charlotte Corday?

Even before America's declaration of war Laval had many times privately admitted that his compatriots detest the Nazi conqueror. But those who have had access to him say that the fact neither gives him pause nor bothers him. All the longings and hopes of his countrymen, he says, will not alter the inevitable reality. They will have to bow to Germany's triumph.

Laval has always scorned public opinion. No Minister is worth his salt, he thinks, who does not know how to mold that opinion as he thinks the interests of the country require. And in the present instance his task is all the easier, he boasts, because it is hitched to Hitler's star. Is his optimism justified? We are indeed forced to grant Laval a certain number of trump cards.

First, in a country without representative bodies, without a free press, without right of assembly or joint action, but honeycombed with police—in such a country public opinion takes shape only in private conversations, private letters, etc. Men are separated one from another. Each broods in his own little corner. A public opinion thus shaped must remain flighty, uncertain, vague. The politician who is in charge of the Ministry of Information (be it noted that Laval regards this post as equal in importance to that of Foreign Affairs or the Interior) easily persuades himself that he can do with opinion as he wills.

Second, particularly in unoccupied France, Marshal Pétain's personal prestige has kept up well among the "conservative classes," long living in fear of "popular fronts." In doubtful matters they will follow him without understanding what he is doing. They will allow him a generous drawing account. They will accept the assertions of the old soldier as against the English and American radio and even against their own judgment. Here is a great help to Laval in an hour of need.

But, third, there is something more. One result of collaboration with Germany has been the creation of vested interests. For at least eighteen months many industrialists, against personal preference, have had to work for the Germans in order not to be dispossessed of their machinery, of their family property, in order to live and give their employes a means of livelihood. They have become used to this collaboration, which is remote, scarcely felt, minor, tenuous. If its scope were little by little to widen, they would offer no resistance.

Alongside these collaborationists—timid, holding back, even a little shamefaced—there are the rich and the greedy who have staked their all on the Nazi cause and now feel too deeply involved to withdraw. For instance, a famous French family has had brilliant business dealings with the Germans—dealings which have restored that family's fortunes. Several million "occupation marks" were received in exchange for bottles of champagne. From that moment the wine itself became an unanswerable argument for collaboration. And, of course, there is Renault, the classic pro-Nazi industrialist, and his Cabinet Minister son-in-law, Lehideux. Such people will be collaborationists to the bitter end.

In the fourth place, we must always remember the million or so civil servants who depend upon the government for their salaries or their pensions and who are therefore at its mercy. And the reprisals, the persecutions, large and small, which are possible by reason of the 1,500,000 war prisoners held in German hands, by reason of France's being split up into separate administrative compartments, by reason of the fact that most daily necessities are obtainable only through favor.

Such are Laval's major weapons. But what about the basic question—his method of procedure?

The French counter-revolutionaries (by whom I mean that party which ever since 1815 has untiringly sought to destroy the 1789 "Rights of Man" and their social and political consequences) have always maintained that the greatest upheavals in a state are the work of resolute and violent minorities, and that the broad mass of people can be won over by them. Hence these men have held that the essential thing is to have within reach at the crucial moments and in the crucial positions men of daring who are brutal and unscrupulous.

At the beginning of this century in his "Enquête sur la Monarchie" (Inquiry into Monarchy) Charles Maurras said that sooner or later the Republic would lead France to military defeat. In order that France might not perish it would then be needful, he said, to overthrow the Republic. Force the will of the nation by means of small groups skillfully led: that is the system.

Laval and Maurras came together in that counter-revolutionary movement which sprang from bourgeois fear and terror of socialism and communism, and for which military defeat opened the road to power. All alone, through adroit manipulation of a few men, Laval succeeded in effecting the abdication of Parliament on July 10, 1940—in accomplishing the "National Revolution." He is confident that in external affairs he can now repeat what he succeeded in doing internally. It is merely a matter of horse-trading and flair, and boldness. The whole thing is to know when to grasp the fleeting opportunity.

Hence while major groups of Frenchmen—I should say the majority—can easily be prevented from following their feelings, impulses and desires, relatively small factions, both civil and military, will be able to achieve results entirely out of proportion to their number, affecting the destiny of their own country and also of the rest of the world—provided always that a well-chosen leader guides their efforts and that they themselves are carefully selected beforehand.

This idea requires some elaboration, for it is the crux of the whole business. What can a man like Laval expect from the armed forces toward the fulfillment of his schemes? It is clear enough that since June, 1940, in those instances that we are able to judge, the acts of a few men, or even of one man, have most often determined the attitude of the whole.

Thus what took place at Mers-el-Kebir resulted from a decision taken by the commander in chief of the French squadron, Admiral Gensoul. He could easily have concluded that there was no need for him to consult his superiors at Vichy—since all telegraphic and telephone messages were under German surveillance—before answering Admiral Sir James Somerville's ultimatum. But Gensoul did ask Vichy's advice and had to fight. Three days later, however, Vice Admiral Godefroy at Alexandria acted in very different fashion. Against Vichy's orders he came to an agreement with the English by which his squadron was neutralized. In both cases officers and men obeyed the admirals, in spite of the fact that their decisions were totally opposite.

These episodes, however, took place almost two years ago. Since then Vichy has gone over its civil and military servants with a fine-tooth comb, and in all posts of major importance we now find out-and-out collaborationists.

Such are the evidences of the past. From Laval's point of view they are encouraging. All the general officers judged capable of independent action are at present tucked away in second-rate berths. And what steps some of the officers took to make their conversion to nazism showy! A few of them went so far as to have their official files falsified, even to have documents manufactured, in order to prove their sympathies for the Axis. Note also that generals now holding important posts were released from German prison camps, that the thousands of French sailors captured at Dunkerque and Cherbourg were sent back to their ports—officers and seamen.

But the reverse of the coin shows a number of things that should offer Laval food for thought. In all naval establishments, among the mechanics, the stokers, the "black gangs," Communist propaganda has always thrived. Today it works to the same end as French patriotism.

Would Laval find as great a stumbling block in the army if, carrying Pétain with him, he tried to hurl French regiments against English or American Commandos in Brittany or Normandy? I have no recent information, but everything seems to indicate that the spirit of the troops is not different from that of the surrounding populations.

One must distinguish strictly between French units stationed in Syria, for instance, well within control of their military superiors, and units in garrison at home, immediately dwelling in an atmosphere not friendly to the officer class. The Vichy régime does not yet seem to have succeeded in building up a professional army cut off from the rest of the nation, and everything indicates that it will not succeed in doing so.

And if it is hard to imagine French soldiers going out to fight the English, the idea of a battle between French and Americans under Laval's orders is nothing less than fantastic. For the first time in history would Frenchmen fire upon Americans in order to prevent them from loosing the bonds of France? The only men who would hurl themselves into such a combat would be the "legionnaires" of the inner set, that is, the imperial guard of the régime, men recruited among the most fanatical elements of the counter-revolution, the men who, on the day when Anglo-American victory looms, would have the task of protecting Pétain, Laval & Co. from French vengeance.

Now we come to the puzzling side of the new Cabinet set-up. What is the true relation betwen Darlan, commander of the military forces, and Laval? In comparison to Laval, Darlan is a mere amateur in politics. His personality must be explained in terms of vanity and opportunism. His hatred of everything English is only a case in point. Darlan's position, to the extent that he opposes Laval and that Laval has the support of the Nazis, is equivocal. To keep his fleet whole and afloat, to avoid its dismantlement, which the Germans can require under the terms of the armistice, Darlan had to enlist the personal good-will of the conqueror. How could he afford any resistance to Laval—the protégé of Hitler— without laying his ships open to reprisal?

But from a broader point of view, and looking more deeply into things, the French people's reaction to Laval's criminal undertakings will not be determined by this or that part of the army or navy, by any general or admiral. Whatever Laval and his henchmen in the Ministry of Information may think, there is always a powerful and uncrushable popular feeling, even in the suffering and oppressed nations, among which the phrase "public opinion" no longer has much meaning. And for Laval, such a feeling is perhaps more to be feared, for it has the spontaneity and persistence of nature itself.

The killing of German soldiers, the execution of hostages, the sickening prostration of the multitude—from such things emerge political impossibilities which Laval himself, however much he has been won to the German cause, can never fathom. No matter what his heart's desire, Laval would not dare, on the day the news goes out that the Germans have massacred a thousand Frenchmen, to order French soldiers to kill English. And if—something not at all beyond the range of possibility—Frenchmen, determined to strike at "collaboration," started to raise their arms not against German soldiers wandering the streets by night but against the men of

Vichy, the "head of the government" would lose much of his boldness.

Laval, as ridden with superstitions as any Calabrian or Sicilian, believes that because Colette missed his aim he has paid his debt to the evil destiny threatening dictators, that now he is quits and that he will be spared a sudden death. But his opinion in this matter can easily suffer a sudden change.

Again Liberty, Equality, Fraternity

by D. W. Brogan

LONDON

ALL DISCUSSION of the future of France should begin by reaffirmation of the basic fact that even before all France was formally occupied, France as a territory, as a tradition, as a national group, was occupied—completely occupied in Paris and Dijon, imperfectly occupied in Lyons and Marseille. France was the greatest, the most famous, the richest prize of the Herrenvolk. For their own reasons the Germans permitted some liberty of action to the government of Vichy. But the brutal fact remained, incapable of denial, hard even to camouflage: when the Germans wanted to take over Vichy they could do it in a day. And when their hands were free, when the victory they counted on was at last secured, all French assets would be at the disposal of the victor who could have no more to fear than at worst a desperate and hopeless "point of honor" resistance in the French Empire.

Under the open or disguised yoke France has changed. But the direction of the change can only be inferred, can only be estimated, in most general terms. The years 1940, 1941 and 1942 probably have been the most important in the history of France since the

From the *New York Times Magazine*, February 14, 1943, copyright © 1943, 1971 by The New York Times Company.

Revolution. The "revolutions" that followed the Revolution were minor adjustments of political forms. They were not unimportant, but they did nothing to alter the social, cultural, religious and political settlement of the Revolution and the first Napoleon. No fundamental changes cutting down into the quick of the national life were made; they were hardly even attempted.

France in 1939 as in 1919 was a country deeply divided, but tolerating divisions. In 1939, it is true, the violence of the divisions was more openly expressed than in 1919. No government in the previous twenty years had been powerful enough to suppress for more than brief periods the extreme parties on the Left and on the Right. Old-fashioned Republicans asserted that the Republic was strong enough to disregard the froth; to ignore Doriot and Daudet, Thorez and Taittinger. Below, the still waters of republican loyalty ran deep, especially in the provinces neglected by Paris correspondents and foreign critics.

The confidence of old-fashioned leaders in the electoral fidelity of the provinces was justified enough. Fascism and communism alike seemed much less formidable in the Corrèze or the Cantal than they did in Billancourt or Passy. But the political immobility of the provinces was proof of a deeper immobility. In a world in flux the necessity of adaptation was stoutly denied by the normal leaders of the French countryside. And they were the political rulers of France.

It was not a peculiarly French fault to refuse to see that the old order was going to be changed if it did not change itself. But the error had immediate and disastrous fruits in France—defeat, surrender, loss of national independence.

After the disasters of 1870 Daumier drew a picture of a peasant, who had voted in the plebiscite of that year for Napoleon III, contemplating the ruins of his house, burned by the Germans, and saying, "I did not vote for that." The French peasant, the French townsman in 1940 had the same natural revulsion. He had not voted for the third and even more terrible invasion.

In the disaster of June, 1940, all but the strongest minds were torn from their anchorage. And the granting to Pétain of full powers by the Parliament of the Republic was certainly the expression of the public will or, at any rate, of the public despair. Had other leaders than the Marshal been in power, had other centers of public trust survived, a policy of resistance in the empire might have carried the day. France, like all the other occupied countries from Norway to Greece, might have pinned her hopes on a British victory which would ultimately deliver Europe from the monster. But the slow dissipation of the political authority of the French State was now complete and there was no national figure to set against the Marshal, no obvious alternative policy to set against that "honorable peace" between soldiers which the Marshal hoped would be possible.

The Vichy regime was faced with a task of immense difficulty; indeed, of insuperable difficulty. That it was difficult was admitted; more, it was stressed; that it was insuperable was naturally concealed. On the one hand, there was the material problem of restoring French life, profoundly disorganized by the invasion; on the other, there was the moral and political problem of creating a new State form. Indeed, only a more vigorous State organization could possibly cope with the problems presented by the collapse of 1940.

This was the primary justification of the "Vichy Revolution" for entrusting all powers to one man. France needed revolution—profound reorganization. For the moment the vested interests of the old political order were powerless. The French people had not voted for that.

The solution of the material problem was only impossible because of the German occupation and the continuance of the war. But that only illustrates the basic miscalculation of the founders of the Vichy regime. For the war could only end quickly by a German victory over England—after which the destiny of France would be decided by non-French hands; or the war would go on and Vichy would be more involved in the necessities of German strategy, political and economic as well as military. It was a total war and it was a naive mistake to think defeated France could make it a limited war—as far as she was concerned. Germany and England, the two main belligerents in 1940, learned that lesson which Russia and the United States learned later. And France was not even the sorcerer's apprentice but the prisoner of the sorcerer's apprentice.

The solution of the political problem was impossible for even deeper reasons. In the collapse of the parliamentary system the men of Vichy turned, as was natural, to the existing bureaucracy, to the existing hierarchies (the political alone excepted). The political personnel was discredited and, in any case, the victor could not permit the reconstruction of a democratic regime, discredited or not.

So Vichy had to be "reactionary." It had to turn (even if we abstract from the account) the natural prejudices of the marshal and his closest associates to the "notables," to the upper class economically, politically and socially. And that meant that it had to turn to the sections of French society which for a century past have lost every political battle they have waged as soon as they have antagonized the "people," the mass of Frenchmen and Frenchwomen in town and country, the workers, peasants, petits bourgeois or such proletarians as France possesses.

It was a wise British Ambassador who declared, after long experience of France, that he had only to listen to what his fellow-members in smart Paris clubs said and bet on the other side. They are never right. Ideas, doctrines, recipes for political cookery that have come from the Right, from Maistre to Maurras, have been mere obstructions. They have not been effective programs.

In default of the odious energy that the Paris-Nazified demagogues possessed, and possess, the men of Vichy, the more honest, patriotic and intelligent of them (and there were many in Vichy entitled to one of these epithets, if not many who deserved all of them) could, but for one handicap, have tapped that great reservoir of national feeling from which Hitler, Mussolini, Stalin and Churchill have drawn the strongest ingredients of their power. Vichy could have stressed that "All is not lost; the unconquerable will."

But the whole policy of the armistice, or the refusal to carry on resistance in Africa, in so far as it had other basis than the conviction that England must soon surrender too, was based on the conviction that France could not afford more heroism or heroics; the Gambettas, Dantons and Clemenceaus were outmoded. In any case it was evident that the Germans would not permit any defiant policy, any cultivation of "the study of revenge, immortal hate."

So Vichy was reduced to mere expedients or bogus gestures of energy. Its edicts were often well designed, often dealt with real weaknesses, real evils. But even when the proposed remedies were not (like the restoration of the old provinces) mere antiquarianism or window-dressing, the material and the moral means of carrying them out was lacking.

For Vichy had to be silent on the basic fact of French life. In the last war Clemenceau hammered on the theme "Les Allemands sont à Noyon." Pétain, Darlan and their collaborators had to keep silence on the fact that this time the Germans were at Strasbourg, Little Paris, Nantes, even though such outrages as the expulsion of loyal Alsatians or the murder of the Nantes hostages were events crying out at least for comment.

Because France was the greatest prize of the German war, the wealth of the country was not available for an economic restoration. Because France was all conquered and two-thirds occupied the moral power of a national insurrection could not be used—and Vichy had no other resources to draw on. The professional loyalty of army officers or of the navy, the discipline of civil servants, the claque provided by an enslaved press and radio were no substitute for a real movement of national resurgence that could only be directed against Germany.

In vain Darlan, Maurras, Cardinal Baudrillart and lesser scribes and pharisees tried to make the English and the Jews and the Russians serve as target for the hatred, self-criticism and bitter pride of the French people. Within a few months of the establishment of the new regime it was manifest that, with the facts so undeniable, you cannot deceive all the people all the time. Not that way lay the resurrection of France in a Europe that had seen the heroism of Greece and was soon to see in the blunting of the German sword on Russia's armor a light from the East.

As each month passed, as the prudential calculations of the armistice policy seemed more and more doubtful wisdom, the Germans accelerated the speed of French evolution. Inside France they were no longer "correct." Despite Vichy-inspired attacks on the British blockade, the French people knew why cold, hunger and disease gripped the pleasant land of France. As the Germans were forced to greater and greater efforts, they were forced to squeeze from France more and more ruthlessly the last resources, human and material.

French reaction provoked reprisals. There is now blood between the occupying army and the French people—and between the French people and the political allies, present and recent, of the Germans.

It is no wonder then that there is evidence of a revival of faith in the republic—not in the parliamentary machinery of the old regime but in the ideals of liberty, equality and fraternity which the old order so imperfectly embodied, but which, unlike the drab Etat Français, it did not deny. There is even a turn to the more dignified and respectable of the old political leaders, most of them now in prison. In so far as Pétain's system was accepted in 1940, it was not accepted for this enslavement of France to Germany.

And if Germany had a choice of winning or alienating France in 1940, she has none now. She must plunder and oppress. The consequence is not merely that resistance is stimulated but that the social revolution is carried on. Inflation is completing what the earlier inflation began, the ruin of the rentier—and how much of the stability and conservatism of France was due to the rentier! Bankruptcy seems inevitable.

Then, the Germany policy has accentuated the division between the industrial North and the rural South. It is the occupied North that has been most openly "Gaullist." In liberated France the old political predominance of the South will not have its old institutional basis. And France badly needs a reconstruction that will enable her to acquire that industrial power without which she cannot be a powerful nation again. So much will have to be done to rebuild from the foundations and even to alter some of the traditional ground plan that a new French revolution will be imposed by the nature of things. Another year of German exploitation and few in France will have much to lose but their chains.

It is a fact on which moralizing is unnecessary that the French directing classes and the officially recognized "élites" have been more deeply compromised by collaboration than any other groups. For it is the function of leaders to lead. Whatever the wisdom of their policies since 1940, the old élites have inevitably dissipated the only effective emotional asset they had to set against the dominant French revolutionary tradition, the asset of being par excellence the custodians of the national interests and the national honor. Ruling classes are pitilessly judged. And what can these rulers say to a passionate reviving French national spirit? What can they say to a Europe whose enslavement for two years they observed—at best—in silence?

Once liberated from the German bonds the purging of France from the taint of Vichy's compliance will seem to be, and will be, a necessary national act of purification. No free France in a free Europe will be possible on any other terms. For at times the only alternative to indicting a nation is to indict its rulers. The French people by their acts have indicted theirs.

In a Europe tainted with fascism, with racism, with inequality, France could be at best a feeble plagiarist, a servile imitator. France must be a trusted friend to her neighbors who have, like her, endured and resisted German tyranny. Those elements in French society that with varying degrees of guilt shared in policy of nonresistance to the enemy will be excluded from the construction of a new France which has been made more easy as well as absolutely necessary by the German tide.

That some of the men so excluded were guilty of no more than human weakness is true; that others may by later services redeem their past errors and even crimes also is true.

But historical necessity is under no obligation to be just. Inevitably, elements in France, mainly the working classes of the industrial and occupied North who have been the backbone of resistance to the Germans, and the men outside France who have made it true that some representatives of France have never been absent from the battle will provide the initial leaders in this remaking of France.

Whether they will remain leaders no man can say or even guess. But it is not a guess to say that Vichy cannot be salvaged and given new life in Africa—or in a liberated France. No man or group of men, no power or group of powers can force the marriage of a free France with a counter-revolution that is now in its last agony. They can but increase the chances of a civil war that can have only one possible issue.

Inside France:
The Conquered Stir

by André Philip

FOR MORE THAN two years France has been under the Nazi heel.
During that period the Germans have been in control of the press
and radio and maintained a strict censorship on all outgoing mail.
There is, as a result, an almost complete blackout of information
on developments inside France, particularly on the evolution of
public opinion in that country.

Having only recently escaped from France to England I am
able to provide something of an insider's view of what the people
are thinking in my country today, how their spirits have gradually
changed from deep despair to faith in ultimate Allied victory.

In the beginning morale was terrible. The Vichy people—and
this is their unforgivable sin—not only yielded to German military
force but also accepted defeat and capitulation. They gave to it
moral acknowledgment. Immediately after the armistice Marshal
Pétain spoke of the defeat as necessary punishment for our sins.
Newspapers, among them infamous Gringoire, declared openly that
France was guilty of having taken the initiative in a war against
poor, innocent Hitler. They declared that responsibility both for
the war and the defeat rested on the shoulders of the working class,

From the *New York Times Magazine*, November 1, 1942, copyright ©
1942, 1970 by The New York Times Company.

on the spirit of democracy of the great writers, the intellectuals and the spiritual leaders of our country.

All this produced a moral vacuum. France was knocked down and remained so for many months before beginning to recover. The military defeat, which, as we know today, was the result of the incompetence of our military leadership and the skillful work of a fifth column, came at the time as a complete shock to every one of us. The nation was scattered on the roads of the country. Administrative and industrial leaders had fled before the enemy and the people were left without guidance, without the élite to whom they used to look for leadership.

Add to this the personal prestige of Marshal Pétain, hero of Verdun, among many soldiers of the First World War, and the general feeling of chaos, and you will understand that the majority of the people simply thought in this fashion: "All this is too complicated. We don't understand anything any more. Let us have confidence in the great-grandfather who has taken charge of his children." (By the way, it is typical of France that the only type of dictator she would accept was the great-grandfather.)

"Let us believe that he is really for resistance, that he is lying to the Germans, double-crossing them in order to gain time to fight again if some day a miracle makes that possible."

Already at that time the first organization of resistance had been formed in Paris in the occupied zone and it gradually spread to what Parisians called with contempt "the Nono Zone." Its members came from different social groups, among which the most important were the working class (trade unions and Socialist groups), intellectuals and religious bodies.

The working class first: Here you find the greatest support of the resistance movement. With the treachery of René Belin, who became Pétain's Minister of Labor and dissolved the Federation of Labor, a hard blow was struck at the labor movement. The Trade Union Council, however, although strictly forbidden by a new law, remained strong and became the nucleus of our first group. Unity was realized between Socialists and Christian trade unions and it was they who began publication of our papers and organized massed demonstrations.

It is quite a symbol that just when the official Nationalists, who before were always inflamed against Germany, asking for her partition into small States, suddenly turned collaborationists the so-called Internationalist workers became on the other hand a bulwark of resistance; but it is quite logical. Men who believe only in force abuse it when they get it, become slaves when they are weak. Those who believe in justice give it to others when they are strong and fight stubbornly to get it when they are defeated.

Beside the working class you find the French intellectuals: On the whole they have behaved well. I do not speak, of course, of members of the French Academy living in the corrupted circles of high society without contact with the people, but of the really great French writers and also of the whole university body. French professors have carried on their lectures with independence and courage, refusing to obey the orders of Vichy and, I may state from personal experience, that until recently it was quite possible for a professor to mention in his lecture anything he desired without any one's reporting it to the Vichy administration.

As to religious groups: If official leaders of the church have been very cautious and noncommital, the rank and file, particularly laymen and humble clergymen, have been quite outspoken against Nazi rule and the autocratic methods of Vichy. I have heard from many pulpits striking condemnation of anti-Semitism and totalitarianism.

This merging in resistance groups of Socialists and trade unionists with liberals and Christian intellectuals who formerly were so opposed to one another is of utmost importance for the future reconstruction of our country, and it is in the presence of the religious element which has given our group one of its most important characteristics.

When we began work most of us did not believe in the possibility of victory. We admired General de Gaulle as a great spiritual leader but thought of him as a Bayard who fought to the end without hope rather than accept surrender. We did resist because nothing else was possible if we wanted to be faithful to the eternal values of our civilization. We believed that freedom and liberty are the supreme reality, that nothing is greater than respect for human dignity and individual responsibility—that it was better to die than to deny this.

We believed that ten tons of material reality do not make an ounce of verity; that possession of 5,000 tanks is not enough to change a lie into the truth, and this had to be told publicly, no matter what the result.

This attitude represented for us a great force. It meant that resistance does not depend upon success, that having spiritual roots it remains the same through the ups and downs of battle, independent of the results of our activity.

And the fact is, we did succeed. Our papers were read by more people; around each paper (Combat, Libération, Franc-Tireur, Coq Enchaîné, Le Père Duchesne and Le Populaire in the unoccupied zone; Libération, 1793, La Voix du Nord, La Quatrième République in the occupied zone) strong movements were built, the groups acting independently at first, then getting together through coordinating committees. They published in addition to their regular papers thousands of leaflets and began to organize public demonstrations like those of the First of May and the Fourteenth of July, when tens of thousands of people went out into the streets shouting, "Down with Laval" and "Vive de Gaulle."

Today our movements are growing strong. Two of the most important groups, Libération and Combat, have many thousands of members strongly organized and their papers are published every week with a circulation of 25,000 to 30,000 copies, which is quite important when one considers that every number is read by eighteen to twenty people.

Since the beginning of 1942 the prestige of Marshal Pétain has been gradually but steadily declining, for various reasons. First, with the return of the hope of victory more and more people began to think for themselves. What did they see? An incompetent administration unable to handle the food question or distribute properly the little that was left after the Germans' plunder; a foreign policy yielding more and more to the enemy, submitting French industrial life to Nazi rule and making French people suffer, work and die for Germany; the big trial at Riom, the only result of which was to enhance the prestige of the accused and demonstrate the real, big, personal responsibility of Pétain himself as well as the unpreparedness of our armies.

Finally, they saw the return of Laval, most hated and despised man in France, coming back to sell our manpower to Germany and introduce in "the Nono Zone" barbaric Nazi methods of dealing with the people.

Today Pétain's prestige is dead. Ninety per cent in the unoccupied zone follow General de Gaulle. They recognize him as their military and political leader and, for the time being, as the only legitimate representative of France.

This attitude is quite new; our resistance movements at the beginning hailed General de Gaulle as spiritual and military leader, but wanted to remain politically independent of what we called "the London people." Our opinions changed gradually, mainly for four reasons:

First, "the London people" have shown that they are just plain, free Frenchmen with free minds and free speech who defend on every occasion the permanent interests of our country even at the price of some discussion with our best friends; this independence has been the greatest cause of General de Gaulle's increasing prestige.

Second, in France there have been between the different groups some competition and conflict; there also have been attempts by military and political adventurers to put their hands on the movements in order to use them for their own purpose, sometimes by agreement with Vichy; the only way to avoid that appeared to be direct allegiance to General de Gaulle.

Third, psychologically also our attitude has changed. At the beginning we were full of sympathy for England and the United States, hoping that they would win the war and return to us on a platter our lost liberties. We soon realized, however, that if we wanted to rebuild something in France tomorrow and recover our lost honor, our country must re-enter the war in order to win back her liberty through her own efforts.

At the same time we realized that we had been becoming strong enough in our underground work to do something more than merely publish papers and organize mass demonstrations. We can become an army of the interior, ready to strike on the day a second front is opened; but for that we must be organized on a military basis, must receive from General de Gaulle's headquarters the necessary directives relative to the Allied Nations' strategic planning. It means that Free France and Captive France are unified in General de Gaulle's Fighting France movement.

Finally, we realized that when Germany collapses the situation in France will be tragic. The men of Vichy have been responsible for so many abuses, have been accumulating so much hate that, the day when Germany no longer is there to protect them, they will be murdered all over the country. The only way to avoid that is to have immediately a government strong enough to keep the people in order and give them assurance that the traitors will be prosecuted with due process of law.

Such a government cannot emerge from the former Parliament, which has lost face by surrender to Pétain; it cannot emerge from any former political leaders whose names have been associated with defeat and who have lost all political influence in a country which wants a new republic. It cannot emerge out of the resistance movements alone, which, if they were to form a government would immediately become divided into different factions and lose all their fighting power.

Here again there is no other possibility than a government with General de Gaulle at the head choosing its collaborators among the great economic and social powers of the country and representatives of the resistance movements. This can only be a temporary power lasting until the election of a National Assembly which with complete independence will choose the Constitution of the Fourth Republic.

In the meantime General de Gaulle remains for all of us the legitimate representative of France, the present incarnation of our lost liberties.

The New French Revolution

by Harold Callender

PARIS

A WAITER IN THE most conventional of tail coats gracefully poured wine into a glass. It was Château Latour 1938. One of the discoveries of the liberation period is that this was a fair wine year. Napery and silver were as choice as they had been under that roof in the time of the Third Republic or Second Empire. The waiter's movements were framed against the rich browns and blues of Aubusson tapestry hanging on the wall behind. By a slight displacement, one's eye fell upon a smooth green lawn and symmetrically placed trees seen through a huge plate-glass window of an eighteenth-century mansion. One might have imagined that nothing much changed in France, or that "plus ça change plus c'est la même chose." (The more it changes, the more it is the same thing.)

But a girl opposite was telling, while the level of the Mèdoc rose in glass after glass, how her father had been captured and tortured to death by Germans because he was a Resistance leader. As the waiter discreetly offered excellent Armagnac, a young man on my right described how he escaped madness when in solitary

From the *New York Times Magazine,* October 29, 1944, copyright © 1944 by The New York Times Company.

confinement by pacing diagonally from corner to corner of his cell while he composed a series of sonnets without pencil or paper. He was one of the many intellectuals who joined up with the workers to form the Resistance movement, and came out of it a changed man.

The setting in which we conversed seemed to carry one's mind back to the eighteenth century. But the stories my French friends told harked back to the worst periods of the Middle Ages, or even of barbarism. Yet these youths who had fought and suffered had faces turned to the future in a more hopeful mood than that of French intellectuals since the year 1870, at least.

The mentality of France today cannot be understood unless one begins to examine it by studying the Resistance movement—all of it—including university men who forsook their studies to slink up on Germans in the darkness or plant dynamite beneath trains, factory workers who skillfully bootlegged machine-guns, youths who fled to the Maquis and lived a gangster existence. Like the great French Revolution, this one had its encyclopaedists and its tough guys. It could have dispensed with neither.

In the intimacy of darkness and common peril the two groups became acquainted and got on together. The intellectuals grew tough, while the toughs were at least somewhat affected by what may be called the ideology of Resistance. Especially in France must men have an idea to justify fighting and dying. Out of privation, struggle, destruction and death there has arisen something greater than liberation or victory—something which in the minds of these tried and tested youths lends additional significance to those words.

The French often say that those who have not been under the heel of the Germans cannot conceive of what it was like. Many fail, at any rate, fully to understand that what the French were fighting was not only German power. It was the Vichy regime, which to them stood for something even worse—French acquiescence and participation in the German oppression of Frenchmen. The people of the Resistance were fighting against this national shame, as they call it. Also they were fighting against the humiliation of defeat in 1940. Thus they fought to regain for France her self-respect and pride as a nation. They have washed out the stain of defeat with their blood, and every Frenchman holds his head higher in consequence.

But behind the defeat which let the Germans into France, and behind Vichy which played their game, was something else—the defective political and social system which the Encyclopaedists of Resistance hold to have been ultimately responsible for France's downfall and for the suffering which it entailed.

It was inevitable, therefore, that in the cells and torture chambers where the Gestapo and its French agents put captured patriots, in the secret cellars where the faithful met and plotted as Christians met in the catacombs, in caves and camps of the Maquis, there germinated and grew what I have called an ideology of Resistance—a social philosophy which sought to take account of the causes of France's ordeal and to insure against their recurrence. Consequently, for these men liberation is not merely the negative achievement of getting rid of the Germans. It has more positive, and indeed revolutionary, implications. Liberation is to be a new chapter in French history, introducing, perhaps, a new French social structure, or at least one greatly changed and economically democratized.

Since coming to Paris a few days after the departure of the Germans, this correspondent has met many Resistance veterans from the President of the National Resistance Council to the boys who have matured in the underground struggle. Some of these are Catholics, others are without religion. Some are conservatives, others are Communists. But on this point all agree—that democratic capitalism as France knew it in the years before her downfall must never be restored.

Emerson wrote that in the New England of his time nearly everybody carried a design for Utopia in his vest pocket. One is reminded of this remark by what one sees in France today. Nearly every Resistance organization has a program for restoring to the French people control over their economic life and consequently over the physical sources of their national strength.

These programs have been neatly embraced, necessarily in generalized terms, in a plan adopted by the National Council of Resistance on March 15 last. A direct reflection of them is seen in the Government's action in taking over control of the coal mines and in Gen. Charles de Gaulle's speech at Lille, urging a planned economy under the supervision of the State.

The direction in which France is moving seems clearly marked. But her precise path remains to be determined. Between various groups there are differences of what the French call nuance. But often a French nuance assumes the proportions of the Grand Canyon.

Far more noteworthy than an agreement upon the need of social changes is the new sense of virility and confidence that animates the French, or, at least, these youths emerging from darkness and the Battle of Resistance. The feeling of weakness and frustration so conspicuous among intellectuals and university youths in the Nineteen Thirties, and the paralyzing pessimism over the future of France and democracy which caused so many bright youngsters to turn Fascist, seem to have been washed out, as the humiliation of defeat was washed out, by the ordeal and struggle from which the French have emerged.

The French, as represented by this élite that has gone through the fires of struggle, have acquired a new sense of their country, a new devotion to it, a new confidence in its destiny. It is as if the trace of degeneracy which had stained the French society of the Third Republic had been removed by a surgical operation.

Many now contend, as François Mauriac puts it, that "the former ruling classes now accept willy-nilly the Socialist experiment," which France seems destined to undertake as a new test of democracy.

It is probably difficult for Americans to appreciate the French aversion to their pre-war capitalism. Let it be noted that this French capitalism was very different from its American counterpart in that it did not bring to the working class anything like our standard of well-being, nor did it provide the State with anything like our industrial equipment for peace and war. Above all, it failed to unite France socially or to see her through a war; some say that it led her to defeat.

In this new French mood, suggestive in many ways of the utopian spirit of the seventeenth and eighteenth centuries, when human perfectibility seemed a natural assumption, one finds an older France. A passion for legality and order exists side by side with potent revolutionary impulses. The individualism of the past seems to have accommodated itself more or less to the hope or acceptance of socialism in the future. A proud nationalism to which the wartime traces of a new and also of an old struggle has contributed does not exclude a sense of the limitation of even France's renewed national strength or recognition of the need of powerful allies in building a less illusory peace.

Giving full weight to whatever qualifications may be imposed by judicious cynicism, there is a new spirit abroad in France. There is a new élite coming to the fore which is far younger than the elderly statesmen dominant in the Third Republic, and if less experienced, this élite is also less resigned to the evils and inequalities of the past. It is fired by faith in the future of the country which they have saved from defeat and humiliation.

To many Americans, as to this writer, France will seem little changed. Décor is still here, as in that room with the Aubussons and the Château Latour and the sedate lawn. But as familiar wine trickles into familiar glasses in a familiar Old World setting, I shall never quite forget those who sat there with me or the new France which is their vision and their aim.

In What Direction Will France Go?

by D. W. Brogan

"THE LAST TIME I saw Paris" before the catastrophe was a lovely late spring evening of 1939. I went with an old French friend of mine up to the terrace in front of the Sacré Coeur and we looked down on the great spectacle, guessing with melancholy resignation how much of it would survive the coming war. All of it, or almost all of it, has survived, and this is the first thing that strikes a visitor who has spent most of the war in London.

But apart from the old, tempting and dangerous error of confusing Paris with France, even first appearances are very soon seen to be deceptive. Those first appearances are of course very striking.

Paris, the Paris of the Grands Boulevards, of the Rue Royale, is more like New York than London is. London, which normally looks all right to me, suddenly seemed to my memory shabby in the Paris of 1945, as it had seemed shabby in the New York of 1944. I came quickly to understand the odd impression that Paris must make on the visiting British or American soldier—an impression of ease, beauty, extravagance, almost immunity.

No more than New York does Paris give to the casual visitor the

From the *New York Times Magazine*, August 26, 1945, copyright ©️ 1945 by The New York Times Company.

impression of being the chief city of a state that has been deeply involved in war. Still less does it give the impression of being the capital of a state whose political and economic future is the subject of bitter disputes and of conflicts of faith and skepticism.

Yet the moment you begin to move among French people the first impression peels off. There you find the nerves, the hopes and fears, the fatigue, the results of privations and still more the results of fears.

"We forget all the time," said a very competent French observer and actor. "We forget that the war and the liberation solved no old problems. It solved the new ones—we escaped being enslaved by the Germans. But all the old problems remained, made worse and more difficult by the occupation, by Vichy and by the material cost of liberation."

There is a deep truth in this and there is another truth to be noted. Liberation acquired during the German occupation a magical quality. It was like a party in the prophetic imagination of a child, like marriage and living happily ever afterward in an old-fashioned novel.

Just as no party or no marriage quite lives up to the publicity, liberation was bound to be a disappointment. People still recall with a touching nostalgia the magical days of August, 1944, the miracle of the rising of Paris, of the arrival of Leclerc's division, of the sudden transformation scene that made the captives captors. I have talked with several of the leading actors in this drama—romantic beyond the dreams of Hollywood—and in their voices and in the voices of many others there has been something of the inflection: "Bliss was it in that dawn to be alive."

I can remember in London at that moment how a friend of mine, active in the Resistance, got a message from a friend in Paris who had the chance to take part in the crowning of all their efforts, a message couched perhaps unconsciously in the spirit of Henri IV's message to Biron: "How I pity you for not having been in it."

There was, and is, bound to be a reaction to a hangover. The liberation was a triumph, a memory that will fortify millions of French hearts, but it was not, as some naively thought, a solution for more than the expulsion of the Germans from Paris. And the evil that the Germans did lives after them, even though there is no good to be interred with their bones.

At the very center of the French problem there is this disillusionment of the Resistance movement with what it has been able to achieve and with France herself. That disillusionment is creditable. noble, natural—dangerous. We should never forget that it was the Germans who decided to run France through Vichy; all that Pétain and Laval had freedom to choose was to play ball with the Germans; the rules of the game were decided by the Germans. That policy may have been from the German point of view a mistake in the long run; we won't know the answer to that for a long time.

It was the decision of some hundreds of thousands of individuals which first of all upset the German dream of profiting by a generally accepted government and then forced the Germans to abandon their tactics of "correctness" and show the French the real nature of the Third Reich.

The men and women who made that decision made it under conditions of terror of which nobody in America or England has any real conception, conditions in which so many fates were much worse than death, conditions in which entry into the underground called for rare and difficult combinations of virtue and character.

A man or a woman, a married couple, for instance, who made such a decision, burned their boats in a fashion that gave and gives them the force of conviction and something of the rigorous intolerance of men and women "converted" in the evangelical sense.

And these men and women are at the moment claimants to be a new governing class. Still more are they the apostles of a program for a France "dure et pure." The remedies they want their country to swallow are drastic and unpleasant and the patient shows some reluctance to take the dose. Humanly speaking, the impatience of the Resistance and the hesitation of the country are easily and not discreditably explicable, but they certainly add to the sense of unease.

There is nothing new in the organizing of a revolutionary government by a minority of eager, arrogant, bold, righteous and even self-righteous people. Some of the Resistance complaints about the apathy of many millions of French people are easily paralleled in the recorded opinions of Sam and John Adams. But the problems facing the leaders of the American Revolution were simple compared with those facing the present and any future rulers of France.

At the basis of the French disquiet, at the basis of the anxiety of the Resistance, is the realization that the future of France as a great power, as a modern society, is at stake. Victory in 1918 was bought so dearly that even before 1939 disillusionment with mere victory was widespread.

But whatever illusions were still held in 1939 about the slow but adequate adaptation of France to the needs of the modern world, they cannot be held now. France, still further impoverished by this new ordeal, can only recover by doing much more than recover, by breaking down in one way or another that paralysis of production that was so serious a symptom between the two wars.

The degree to which France was living on her assets, on the national patrimony, has been dramatically revealed now that so much of the patrimony has been stolen by the Germans. Twenty years ago André Siegfried told us that the modern world had to choose between Gandhi and Henry Ford; what most of many French friends tell me is that the choice must be Ford, that the religion of production must be engrafted on the French religion of thrift and individual skill and artistry.

But—and here is the dilemma—is it to be production in the manner of Henry Ford—that is, in the American fashion—or is it to be production in the Russian fashion? For, although it is in fact American production that is the visible miracle dazzling French eyes (and to some extent German production as seen by the prisoners), it is Russian production that provides the myth.

With all the will, the skill and the unity in the world, French recovery can only be slow without a shot in the arm, a blood transfusion from a richer society. And there is only one such society now, the United States, with possibly in a few years' time the auxiliary help of Britain.

But the vocal sections of French opinion which are most convinced of the necessity of a general transformation of French life on the economic plane are in general suspicious of, or openly hostile, to American "capitalism." It is not only the fear of economic exploitation that animates all debtors today, but something more doctrinaire and ideological. There is available a recipe for organization—"planning." The word is magical in France today. And Russia is the home of planning.

Of course, the campaign for Russian methods is not totally spontaneous. It is fostered by the French Communist party, totally devoted to Russian interests by passions—and its own interests. Moreover, the plugging of Russia frees French Communists from the necessity of defending their own role between 1939 and 1941. They cannot applaud General de Gaulle when he recalls the French declaration of war in 1939; they cannot celebrate the official birthday of the Resistance—the appeal from London on June 18, 1940.

It is wiser to insist on Stalingrad and on their own sufferings and achievements in the Resistance, after the invasion of Russia had made their ambiguous attitude toward the "imperialist war" obsolete. Their martyrs cover a good deal and the memory of Gabriel Péri's death stills speculation as to the activities of surviving leaders. But Russia is the trump card.

This is worth noting, since the Communists are now the most numerous, the best disciplined and the most active party in France. To look at the delegates at their congress of 1945 (the first since 1937; party democracy is intermittent in the "people's party") was to get an impression of a true mass party with deep roots—something very different from the English or American Communist parties. Here are real, vigorous and not very scrupulous candidates for the job of governing France.

But despite their widespread system of locals, despite the traditional provincial costumes of some female delegates, despite the exploitation of the grievances of fishermen and farm laborers, the French Communist party is the party of the cities and of the industrial workers in the great mass-production plants, in the mines and on the railroads.

However, if it were only that, it could not become by any normal democratic process a government, for the classes on which it draws for the bulk of its membership are still decidedly the minority classes in France. France was and is the European country in which the small business man—so small that he is hardly a business man at all—is a dominant factor in the economic life of the country.

It is not only a question of the peasant proprietor; there is also the small craftsman, the small shopkeeper, the small trader. According to Colin Clark's calculations, 33 per cent of French persons engaged in production were in family businesses or were "working proprietors." (Comparative figures for the United States were 25 per cent; Belgium, 20 per cent; Germany, 29 per cent, and Britain, 10 per cent.) France, that is to say, is largely inhabited and run by what, before they were liquidated, were called in Russia "Nepmen" and "Kulaks."

The country where Marxian concentration has reached its maximum is Britain, so the revolution ought to be imminent there. But despite the Labor victory, it isn't. Is it in France? Only if there is an economic *and* political breakdown at the same time. It must be remembered that in the Communist party itself are lots of Nepmen and Kulaks—either persons of the most unusual disinterestedness or, as is more probable, not very clearsighted people who "mean the other fellow." But a party doesn't need to have a clear-sighted rank and file to win.

The clear-sightedness is provided outside by the numerous allies or near allies of the Communists who face this dilemma. On the one hand, how can France be governed, be restored, without the collaboration of the leaders of the industrial workers, so important a body at any time, so decisively important a body today, with the needs of a reconstruction of industry paramount?

On the other hand, how can France be governed with the participation of a party with no political scruples, with a savage discipline that makes of its members in any government chartered spies for the party, and above all a party which in foreign affairs cannot have any policy that runs counter to the real or presumed wishes of the Russian Government?

The Communist members of a Cabinet cannot be really bound by any loyalty to their colleagues, the Communist leaders in the trade unions are no more bound, and had the Socialists accepted the Communist offer of union on the political front, they would have been swallowed—or if they resisted, would have become "social fascists" overnight as they have been before.

"France," said a very intelligent Socialist friend of mine, "is ungovernable"; and, were logic dominant in French life or in life generally, one would be inclined to agree. For it is easy to show that you cannot govern without the Communists and that you cannot govern with them. But as Mr. Dooley said of the divorce question: "In the Archey Road when a man and woman can't go on living together—they go on living together." And France may well be in this case the Archey Road rather than the home of logical consistency.

The constitutional controversy that now adds to French perplexities is in a sense the development of this fundamental question: Does France need and is she likely to get a revolution? She needs in a sense a revolution, but does she need a Revolution with a capital R? That question lies behind apparently academic disputes about the virtues of a single-chamber government, about a return to the old Constitution, about the rights and duties of a single Constituent Assembly.

The Communists, the Socialists and the Resistance groups, including the Catholic Democrats, are for a single Constituent Assembly to frame a new Constitution, but they are not agreed on what kind of Constitution is to be framed. The Communists have been playing their Jacobin card, complete with a parody of Citizenness Guillotine. It is possible they are overplaying the Jacobin card; that procession on July 14 recalling the good old days of 1793 is not going to be to the taste of millions of tired, worried, bewildered people in the small towns and in the countryside. A new "grande peur" might work against the Communists and against all the Left parties and destroy the hopes of a peaceful revolution or what General de Gaulle called a "renovation."

Some conservatives (many of them calling themselves, in the baffling French way, "radicals") already think so. Others more far-sighted think that since it is only by American help that the necessary lift upward and onward can be got, the delights of raising France by her own bootstraps will soon pall. And from a point of view in which economic prudence is all that matters, this last view is correct. But it is inadequate.

For, to go back to the beginning, the moral scars of the defeat and the occupation are as serious as the terrible destruction of Le Havre or Marseille. The shock given to the system of values by the invasion, by collaboration, by the failure of so much of the French élite to live up to its pretensions, remains.

The material resilience of the French people is one of the world's wonders. There are advantages, as well as disadvantages, in having a highly decentralized economic life that no one can really plan. A lot of people in France are probably minding their own business to their own profit at this moment—not necessarily to the nation's gain, but very often so.

But there is a danger that the French and their outside well-wishers (in Britain we have good selfish reasons for wishing the French well) may take too much comfort from that thought. For a great deal of French economic life cannot, in fact, be restarted in that automatic way. What was already in 1939 the very serious lack of adequate investment—as apart from savings—remains a problem reflected in the meager capital equipment of French industry and indeed of French agriculture. Complacency, routine—these will be very expensive intellectual faults.

So, too, will be taking the political question too complacently. A return to the old order would be a shattering blow to the hopes of the younger and more energetic Frenchmen and Frenchwomen, hopes that the old routine would not be allowed to reassert itself.

One of the great troubles of France at the present moment comes from the lack of an adequate basis for the authority of the state. For different reasons it was one of the great troubles of the Third Republic. The "Republic" is a general and generous idea that inspires hundreds of thousands of a true élite. The Third Republic has none of that magic in its recent record.

The memory of the great days of construction of the First Republic will be more appealing if the Communists do not revive the superstition that the First Republic was the Terror, and nothing else. But no government in France has ever survived or, if it has survived, done much without strong support from the people, without a dose of that passionate faith that fights in the French mind with ironical resignation. Only a new birth of freedom, ordered freedom, but not a mere revival of old forms, can give the future Government of France that sense of mission and of a people's mandate without which no shot in the arm from the outside, however well meant, can do permanent good.

I think it very unlikely that a genuinely democratic government in France could go in for total planning. But a genuinely democratic government would have sources of energy and faith at its disposal that mere technical proficiency cannot command. "Le peuple souverain s'avance" is the effective political text of the moment. And in what direction do they advance?

That, I—like all the world—can only guess at. But I do not think it will be a simple, dutiful pilgrimage to Moscow or a repentant return to Detroit. France cannot again know the greatness of size which was hers a hundred years ago. But she can use the good produced by that evil thing, the German occupation, to attack not only the gross evils bred by the occupation but older pre-German habits of postponement of decisions which must be taken if France is to survive as a great nation in any contemporary sense.

Part **3**

THE FOURTH
REPUBLIC

Tragic "Circus"— France's Parliament

by Jacques Fauvet

PARIS

ON THE BANKS of the Seine stands a vast building in the Greek style, a kind of Parthenon, blackened by the smoke of Paris. Passing in front of this monument, nine Frenchmen out of ten exclaim: "That's the circus."

The "circus" is the Palais Bourbon. Built in 1728, since 1815 it has sheltered the Chamber of Deputies, renamed in 1945 the National Assembly. It faces the Pont de la Concorde, a magnificent site, but a famous paradox. In spite of its name, this bridge has already witnessed three revolutions and numerous riots, the latest of which dates from only 1934.

In little more than two and a quarter centuries, the palace has seen the march past of four Republics, five kings, two Empires and —from 1940 to 1945—a French State. France's political history is a museum of defunct regimes, and there is every reason to believe that there are more to come.

Yet French Deputies do not deserve to be compared to clowns. In general, they are serious and, sometimes, courageous. One of them has remained famous. "Now," he cried, "you are about to see how a Deputy can die for 25 francs a day." That was in 1851, on the barricades, on a day of insurrection.

Today the Deputies are better paid. But their chamber still resembles a theatre. It is a semicircle with the stage—i. e., the rostrum—in the center, and, at the bottom of the tiers of seats, the Government, whose fate it is to be devoured. For if the Assembly recalls a circus, it is one in the Roman manner, in the days when wild animals were slaughtered there. Today it has become a place where Governments are put to death.

The French Parliament is composed of two chambers. The first is the National Assembly, numbering 595 Deputies. It is elected every five years by universal suffrage through proportional representation.

The number of Deputies from each of the six or seven existing parties is, in theory, in proportion to the number of votes the party obtains. But there has existed for the last six years the possibility of arranging *apparentements,* or local "marriages" of parties, which give several allied parties *all* the seats of a constituency if they have a majority of the votes. It was this system which made possible the reduction of Communist representation by one-third in the 1951 election.

The second chamber is the Council of the Republic, whose 320 members are called Senators. It is elected by delegates of the municipal councils of France and the overseas Territorial Assemblies. The electoral system is by majority, except in the seven most densely populated departments where it is proportional. The Senators can modify a law with the agreement of the Deputies, they can delay its passage, but they cannot veto it. Actually the Senators are important only once in every seven years—when they go into joint session with the Deputies to elect the President of the Republic.

It is, therefore, essentially the Deputies who make the laws, and they make a lot of them—more than 500 each year. A law is needed for everything in France. To create a marshal, as well as to increase the number of stallions in the national stud; to organize education, as well as to regulate the pressure in draft-beer apparatus. But before being passed in session, a bill must be examined in committee. There are fourteen of these, and they constitute fourteen little assemblies within the main one. When a bill emerges from this legislative mill, it bears little resemblance to its original form. It is mutilated, sometimes even destroyed. A law is no longer a law. It is 300 amendments, ten decrees, three administrative regulations. Even then, it is not necessarily put into operation. There was recently a case of a Deputy bringing in a bill to enforce a law already passed.

The Deputies also set up and overthrow Governments, and they overthrow them frequently. There have been more than 120 Governments since the Third Republic came into being in 1875. Their average length was six months. But the Deputies have no sense of guilt. In the first place, they know that the fall of a Government and a change of ministers are of little consequence. In actual fact, France is administered by high functionaries who, for their part, are permanent.

Secondly, the Deputies reckon that it is they in whom the power is really invested and who govern the country. Theirs is the Assembly system, inherited from the Convention, the Revolutionary Assembly of 1792, and completely different from the Cabinet systems of England or Germany. The Government does not rule; it gives effect to the decisions of Parliament; thus it can be dismissed like an unsatisfactory servant. In Léon Blum's opinion: "The Chamber governs just as much as the so-called Government." Maybe this conception is false, yet it has stood up against every political reverse, every defeat in war.

When a Government wants to escape from the tyranny of the Deputies, it often asks for "special powers" or "full powers." Sometimes it gets them for a definite period or a limited objective, though it does not always make use of them. It soon falls back under the almost daily supervision, suspicion and finicking, of the Deputies.

The Deputies, in fact, have the right to interpellate the Government at all times; it is enough that fifty of them demand a debate for it to be held, and for it to end in a vote of either confidence or censure of the Government.

The French Deputies do not like to recess; they prefer being able to keep an eye on the Government. So throughout the year, they remain in session for months on end, for many days each month and for long hours every day and night. This timetable—tiring enough for Deputies and ministers—is exhausting for the Premier.

Edgar Faure presided over his first Cabinet in 1952. "What makes Assembly rule intolerable to the head of a Government," he confided to someone shortly afterward, "is that the never-ending bout of catch-as-catch-can between him and almost 600 deputies is one-sided. The deputy organizes his life to suit himself; he can vote by proxy, dine and sleep when he likes. The President of the Cabinet is denied this relief." Governments often perish through physical exhaustion.

A minister is obliged to attend the Assembly's sessions whenever a question affecting his department is under discussion. The Premier, on the other hand, is obliged to be present at every debate of importance because, besides being the head of the Government, he is also the chief of the majority. This means he must always keep a lookout that the three, four or five parties on whom his majority depends are in agreement; he must conciliate the points of view—often at variance, sometimes even contradictory—of these parties, and must struggle, not so much against the opposition as against the individual or collective dissensions of his majority.

On their side, the Deputies are not obliged to be present even to vote. Their leaders can cast their ballots for them, except when the birth or death of a Government is at issue. Then they can be seen flocking in from every corner of France—of the world even, since there are fifty-two representatives from overseas, forty-one of them colored. When a Government is in difficulty, it may send a plane to Africa to fetch them, and they then vote for bills the greater part of which have nothing to do with their territory, but which can decide the fate of the Government. It is the African representatives who in this way arbitrate the quarrels of the parliamentarians of the mother country.

There are thirteen groups in the Assembly elected in 1956, but only two of them exercise discipline over their members: the Socialists and the Communists. The former number about 100 and the latter 150. These are two task forces which weigh heavily in Assembly battles. The other groups are less important and more divided. It is an unequal combat.

The Communist party has been excluded from Cabinets since 1947. It would, therefore, count for little, did not its members continually hold the fate of the Government in their hands. To be sure, there remain some 450 non-Communist Deputies who could, if they would, agree among themselves to form a majority and support the Government; but a sizable number of them are always ready to vote with the Communists against the men in office.

In fact, there are not one but two permanent oppositions. One is on the extreme Left, the other on the extreme Right. The first is made up of the Communists (since 1947) and, from time to time, the Socialists (from 1951 to 1955). The second consists of the Gaullists (from 1951 to 1953) or of the Poujadists (since 1956) and sometimes of the conservatives. When one opposition joins its votes to those of another the Government is in a minority, but as the two oppositions disagree on everything they can combine their efforts only to overthrow a Government, not to name a successor. So in comes a new team comparable to the previous one. Governments change; ministers linger on. There is only one man who has refused to play this game, where politicians turn each other out and then succeed themselves, and he is Pierre Mendès-France. He has been very popular in the country, but is very unpopular in Parliament.

These divisions in the Assembly are an exact image of the divisions in the country. Because there are so many and none of them predominates, a majority in the Assembly is impossible. It is true that there was none before the war either, when Deputies were elected by majority votes rather than by proportional representation. Governments were just as ephemeral. Those which lasted the longest were not the best, exactly as is the case today; for a Government that acts is turned out forthwith. That is why ministries do their utmost to carry out their programs in the early days of their existence: They know that Parliament soon becomes the master and ministers its slaves—then, before long, its victims.

Actually, French instability has a deeper and extremely paradoxical cause. Politics in France suffers, not because there is no majority, but because there are too many. There is a different majority for each important question.

For example, there is the educational problem: state aid to Roman Catholic schools. The Socialists are against such aid. They say: "Public funds for public schools; private funds for private schools." On the other hand, the Popular Republicans (M. R. P.) are in favor of it. They argue: "Educational liberty is an illusion if it does not have the material means for self-expression." It is an old quarrel and always bitter. So, although the Socialists and Popular Republicans are in agreement on other issues, they cannot govern together for any length of time.

A certain department in the Midi had two Deputies; more often than not they voted the same way, and they always traveled together when they left Paris. But when their train arrived in the south, each left his carriage by a different door. It would not do for their electors to see them together; they would not have understood. The two men were friends in the capital, but were obliged to appear to be enemies in their constituency.

The M. R. P., which has an understanding with the conservatives to defend the Roman Catholic schools (schools majority), is, on the contrary, in agreement with the Socialists against the conservative Right in defense of the workers (social majority). And the M. R. P., conservatives and Socialists are united in defending the parliamentary regime against the Communists and the Poujadists today, or the Gaullists yesterday (political majority). In short, there are as many possible ministerial combinations as there are parliamentary majorities—or problems. When the problem changes, the Government must change.

It is a very ancient evil, as old as the Republic, perhaps even as old as France. After the war, the Constitution and the electoral law were modified, but the situation only grew worse. Instability persists and the executive power was weakened.

There is only one way of assuring the stability of the executive power: a provision that the Assembly be automatically dissolved whenever it overthrew a Government. As things stand, in order that the Government may dissolve the Assembly, two Governments within a period of eighteen months must be defeated by an absolute majority of the Deputies. That has happened only once— in 1955. Edgar Faure then dissolved the Assembly. The one subsequently elected, the present one, has proved even more ungovernable.

Dissolution has as bad a reputation as Bonapartism. Republicans have never forgiven Marshal MacMahon for dissolving the *Chambre* in 1877, nor Marshal Pétain for dismissing Parliament in 1940, nor General de Gaulle for having demanded a dissolution in 1947. There is no likelihood of the Left Wing or Center parties agreeing to an automatic dissolution in the case of a defeat of the Government. At the most, they will agree that the right to dissolve the Assembly should be again entrusted to the President of the Republic, as it was under the Constitution of 1875. This is what Felix Gaillard proposes. But the French pass a part of their time making constitutions, another in modifying them and another in not applying them.

The evil goes deeper; it arises from divisions of a religious, historic and social order. It can be cured only by a radical change in the mentality of the élite and in the structure of the French economic system.

Like all peoples of a civilization essentially Mediterranean, the French are individualists and intellectuals; they have a passion for discussion and theorizing. They multiply their divisions *ad infinitum* and dislike discipline. More attentive to ideas than to facts, they are always quite ignorant of economic realities, and refractory to technical progress.

They are beginning to change. Science is replacing letters more and more in the universities; industry and even agriculture are being modernized with increasing rapidity. But today the incongruities between certain regions and a modern one in others are still adding new divisions and consequently new weaknesses.

In this respect, the National Assembly is truly a reflection of France. It is made up of idealists, even when they sit on the right, and conservatives, even when they sit on the left. This is not a matter of parties, but of temperaments.

General de Gaulle likes to quote a saying of Goethe: "At the beginning was the Word? No, at the beginning was the Deed." In France, things are just the reverse. The word takes precedence over action, the heart over reason; ideas come before facts.

Nearly half of the French Deputies practice some intellectual profession; 150 are lawyers or teachers. They love to talk; they talk well. A French audience likes to listen, even to conflicting opinions, provided that they are well expressed. A politician may be efficient, honest, industrious, but if he is not primarily an orator he will not succeed. Furthermore, his first subjects of discussion must be morality, history or philosophy, rather than politics.

It has been said of the Frenchman that he carries his heart on the left and his wallet on the right. He is as jealous of his revolutionary ideals as of his economic conservatism. As elsewhere, then, people are capable of defending their interests, but there is a great difference between methods on the two sides of the Atlantic.

In America lobbying is official and done in public. In France it is forbidden and therefore clandestine. It is camouflaged in the form of information offices and research organizations. They nourish the electoral funds of the Center and Right Wing parties. But the French employers and big businesses are not overly generous. Even the richest parties still remain very poor compared with those of other countries.

Any question that may arise about money, in fact, has something dubious about it. In ten years there have been only two such matters brought to the attention of the Assembly. A Deputy of a moderate party admitted to receiving money for his election campaign; he was not allowed to run again. Shortly afterward, a minister was accused of having distributed funds of an employers' organization before becoming a member of the Assembly; he was obliged to resign from the Government. In both these cases the Communists brought the charges. But now their adversaries maintain that the Communist party receives financial assistance from the U. S. S. R. Yet what is not permitted to an individual is forgiven in the case of a political party.

The average Frenchman is wholeheartedly for his Deputy and against Parliament, just as he is for his curé and against the Church. The French are always suspicious of power; they are afraid the Government is harming their interests and encroaching on their liberties. They count on their Deputies to defend both. The elector constantly keeps an eye on his Deputy, while the Deputy supervises the ministers. The Assembly is a vast observation ward.

Yet had not the French experienced so many different regimes, lived through so much history, suffered such frequent civil or foreign wars, they would not feel so detached from Parliament, they would not smilingly throw in one's teeth the word "Deputy" when they run short of jokes or insults. Nor would they brand the Palais Bourbon as "the circus."

Picture of an Average French Family

by Tania Long

PARIS

DÉSIRÉ LEFEBVRE, a postman, is typical of the civil servants of France who, with white-collar workers in general, have been hardest hit by the inflationary spiral which the Government is trying desperately to control. On the Government's success in this huge task may well depend its future.

Before the war M. Lefebvre could count on at least a little leisure and entertainment, but now even with tips and employment after regular working hours there is hardly enough income to provide the barest necessities of life. He and his family subsist —it cannot be called living—on "le minimum vital," which is officialdom's phrase for the lowest wage sufficient to maintain life at the lowest level.

It is the wives of men like him that one overhears in queues and on buses and in the Metro complaining that they "don't know how they're going to manage" until the end of the month. It is a comment which once uttered is invariably picked up by other women. Heads nod in agreement and the conversation goes on until it ends in a sigh.

"Ah, oui, c'est bien la misère."

For Mme. Lefebvre, as for millions of Frenchwomen similarly situated, the end of the month when resources are depleted and there is no reserve is a time of struggle and despair. Budgets they have prepared so carefully are unbalanced by rising prices, unexpected expenses and illnesses. This is apt to be a period when, if a family is to be kept alive until the next payday, it will have to be on potatoes, carrots and thin vegetable soup.

That is what "le minimum vital" means—enough to keep one alive from one payday to the next but not enough to replenish a dwindling wardrobe, to provide a glass of wine, an evening at the movies or toys for the children. A year ago it was estimated that 7,000 francs monthly would provide that minimum. Now it is 10,500 francs and French labor says the sum must be raised again.

Lefebvre earns just that minimum. He says it isn't quite enough to keep body and soul together for himself, his wife and three children. How then does he manage? The answer is by going without everything that isn't absolutely necessary and counting on tips to bridge the gap between income and expenses. Others in his wage group solve the problem by putting the wife to work, finding a job for the oldest child, working themselves in spare time and even dabbling in the black market.

Lefebvre is as average a Parisian of the working class as can be found and his recent history is typical of that of millions of other Frenchmen of his class.

Short, swarthy, agile and quick-witted, he was by profession a chimneysweep. He made a good living in this manner until 1939 saw him called to the colors. Taken prisoner in the Vosges early in 1940 by the Germans, he spent the next five years in a series of prison camps, slave-labor camps and concentration camps from which he managed to escape fourteen times, only to be recaptured on each occasion. Together with thousands of others he was liberated by Allied armies in May, 1945.

When he returned to Paris he began to work at his old profession. But he had been so weakened physically by his years as a prisoner and slave laborer that he found himself unable for long to carry with him on his job the heavy equipment required to sweep the huge chimneys of factories and large business establishments in which he had specialized. In June, 1946, therefore, he joined the postal service and he has been delivering letters and packages by pushcart ever since.

M. Lefebvre works eight hours a day, six days a week. He pays 1.5 per cent of his wage of 10,500 francs a month for social security and 6 per cent toward a pension fund, so that he receives 9,713 francs net. Because he has three children he receives a Government grant of 4,250 francs additional and since his wife is unable to go to work and he is the only breadwinner in the family, he receives another 4,250 francs. When he is paid at the end of the month he therefore can count on an income of 18,213 francs.

The Lefebvre family lives in a shoddy old tenement house in the Menilmontant district of Paris. The building has no central heat, no hot water and the plumbing facilities are of the most primitive. The kitchen sink serves equally as washstand and laundry. There is, of course, no bathroom. The only toilet in the house is a communal affair in the basement and this is shared by seven other families who live in the tenement. With some money the Lefebvres had accumulated—part of it saved by his wife during the war when she worked in a factory and the rest received as a Government grant when M. Lefebvre returned from Germany— they were able to install electricity and gas but many of their neighbors in the building are still doing without.

Lefebvre had just come in from work when I arrived and he and his buxom wife Louisette were sitting at the table in the living room, one of the two small rooms which make up their apartment. In the back room the 6-month-old baby Jocelyne slept peacefully in a cot while the younger of two sons, Maurice, aged 2, played with his blocks on the bare floor. The older boy, Georges, 10, was still at school.

When I asked about the basic monthly expenses, Mme. Lefebvre quickly got pencil and paper, gathered some old bills and sat down to figure. In a few seconds she showed me the minimum expenses for a month. The total came to 19,355 francs—1,142 francs over the regular income.

Mme. Lefebvre then explained that her husband received tips for delivering packages and registered mail.

"Without these tips," she said, "I don't know what we'd do. On some days they're better than on others, of course, but if he can average 60 francs a day, that gives us another 1,800 francs a month added to his salary and grants. And that's the margin which carries us over—just."

She demonstrated by quick addition and subtraction that there were some 658 francs left from her husband's earnings and tips after minimum expenses were paid.

"And what can you do with 600 francs?" she asked, shrugging her shoulders. "A smock for little Maurice, a simple cotton smock cost us 475 francs the other day. You can see how if we've any unexpected expenses, however small, we just cannot manage to get by."

Maurice, she went on to explain, had never owned a coat, for the simple reason that to buy him one would take over 2,000 francs. As a result the child rarely goes outdoors in cold weather and when he has to go, his mother wraps him in an old wool shawl, a relic of pre-war days.

The day-to-day existence of the Lefebvre family like that of others in the same category is one of unrelieved drabness. With no money to spare for even modest pleasures what happiness they get out of life comes from within their family circle.

Even so, when speaking of their life the postman and his wife seem surprisingly cheerful. Their conversation is full of Gallic humor and wit, they still laugh easily and with gusto and even when Mme. Lefebvre refers to "la misère," it's more by way of stating a fact than in complaint. The Lefebvres grumble, of course, shrugging their shoulders and pointing up their remarks with their hands.

"We always were great ones for grumbling, we French," says M. Lefebvre.

It is when they speak of the future that one realizes that the cheerfulness of the postman and his wife is merely a surface manifestation of French character and good manners. The daily grind of existence could be borne easily enough, as the Lefebvres told me, if there were some promise of easier days ahead, if they could look forward to a date, even in the distant future, when they could say to themselves: "Now we can relax, bad times are over, so let's enjoy life."

As the postman put it, "There we are, my wife and I, going on toward middle age, with three children to bring up and worse off today than when we started together twelve years ago. It's not so much for Louisette and myself that I care—we had a few years of normal, carefree living—it's the children I am worrying about. What will their world be like? Will there in fact be a world for them to live in?"

Uncertainty about the future and fear of another war color his thinking and poison his sleep. Although he doesn't speak of it often, he believes that if there is another war France, the first victim, will be annihilated.

What about the Marshall Plan, one asks. Does he think that will help France's recovery and assist in maintaining peace?

"It will help France, of course," Lefebvre replies, "but whether it will assure the peace, who knows? God knows my country needs assistance and we are grateful to the Americans for it. And if it helps bring Europe closer together it will be a wonderful thing.

"The question I'd like to know the answer to is whether the Marshall Plan will help in bringing the whole world closer or whether it will accentuate a quarrel already existing between East and West."

It would be giving a false picture, however, to say that worries in the realm of international politics are uppermost in the Lefebvres' minds. Such worries are there but they are generally buried beneath worries about the business of keeping alive.

A recent survey of the purchasing power of French money today as compared with 1938 illustrated remarkably well the difficulties of families such as the Lefebvres. In the year before the war the worker earning 48 francs for an eight-hour day could buy with that sum the following goods: a pound of bread, a half pound of meat, a litre of wine, a pound of beans, five eggs, a box of cheese, four pounds of potatoes, a pack of cigarettes, a quarter pound of chocolate, a half pound of butter, a quarter pound of coffee, a litre of milk, a half pound of rice and a box of sardines.

Today the worker earning the minimum wage of 420 francs for an eight-hour day can buy less than half of these items: a half pound of bread, a half pound of meat, a litre of wine, a pound of beans, five eggs, a box of cheese and four pounds of potatoes. In order to buy the remaining items—actually most of them are not available except on the black market—the French wage earner would have to have 700 francs at his disposal instead of 420.

Most of what Lefebvre earns goes to feed the family for, as his wife said, "The chief thing is to keep healthy." Because of the high price of food, she has to spend an average of 500 francs a day, which is nearly fifteen times more than the same food would have cost before the war.

The Lefebvres rise to a breakfast consisting of bread, usually dry, sometimes but rarely spread with butter, and two cups of ersatz coffee known as "café national." The children have milk.

Mother and children have their main meal in the middle of the day and this usually consists of meat stew or of a steak of horse meat accompanied by vegetables and followed by a little fruit. The postman has his dinner when he returns from work; he goes on his eight hours of rounds with nothing to eat between his breakfast and his dinner. Toward 7 in the evening the family gathers again for a light supper of bread and vegetable soup and perhaps a little cheese if the budget will allow it. Frequently there is no meat or fish during the last week of the month. Then Georges, who is growing, suffers most, Mme. Lefebvre says, for she and her husband have learned to tighten their belts and the two younger children have their milk. There isn't enough milk to go around so the Government sees to it that most of it goes to young children.

One of the greatest hardships for the postman is that he can no longer afford to buy wine for his table. The French are brought up to drink wine at both meals and in the old days before inflation even the poorest beggar could buy himself a glass to go with a crust of bread. But for people like the Lefebvres wine has become a luxury they no longer can afford, for even the cheapest brand costs around 50 francs a bottle.

While he was talking to me his wife finished drawing up a quick list of her daily expenditures for food.

"This is the very least I spend, you see," she said. "One hundred francs for milk, 48 francs for bread, 150 for a small piece of meat or fish, 150 for vegetables and about 50 for miscellaneous items such as noodles, ersatz coffee and so on. At that, we never have enough bread and when my ration tickets have run out I have to buy bread at black market prices, which nearly doubles the cost."

At the rate of 500 francs a day the Lefebvres' monthly expenditures for food average 15,000 francs—a huge slice out of a postman's wages. Their other regular monthly purchases are coal and wood for heating which average 3,500 francs, electricity 320 francs, gas 300 francs. Their rent of 235 francs monthly is still extremely low because it's a pre-war rate.

With only a few hundred francs left over, once the immediate necessities are paid for, at the end of the month the Lefebvres naturally are unable to give any thought to buying clothes or replacing household articles which wear out or get broken through the years. The mailman and his wife have bought themselves no clothes since before the war with the exception of one pair of heavy shoes which M. Lefebvre got for himself when he returned from Germany.

His wardrobe consists of one pair of thoroughly mended gray flannel trousers, two shirts, one sweater and a leather, fleece-lined jacket which his maternal aunt sent him for Christmas from her home in the provinces. Apart from that he owns nothing. The postman's képi which the Government has provided him with as a sort of token for the full dark-blue uniform he is supposed to have some day is, of course, national property.

Mme. Lefebvre's wardrobe is just about as depleted and she says that if things don't get any better in a year or two she'll have to cut down her curtains to make dresses. At present she has one eight-year-old black dress, a pale blue smock or house dress, a coat dating back ten years, one pair of black shoes—at home she usually wears felt slippers—and an old black hat which, on the day I visited her family, had just been lent to a neighbor who had gone into mourning and did not possess the black headgear required of her. A few articles of underclothes and a carefully preserved silk scarf complete the list of her personal possessions.

Mme. Lefebvre smiled wryly when I asked what the family did for entertainment. "I leave the house only to do my daily shopping," she said. "In the evening we stay home. My husband is too tired after his work to visit friends and we can't afford to have our friends here, so it's just as well. On Sundays we stay home all day with the children."

"We avoid temptation that way," broke in the postman. "Ah, those Sundays before the war. . . . When we'd go out and have our little apéritif at the corner bistro, then maybe take in a movie in the afternoon or walk in the Bois de Boulogne if it was a fine day. We lived well then, always had wine on the table and plenty of good rich food and, when we needed something, well, we'd just save up for it. . . . But what makes it so hard now is that we cannot do more for our children."

Lefebvre is a man of more than average intelligence. He has not, like so many of his colleagues and others who live on the margin of subsistence, turned to communism as the cure-all of France's ills. However, he is just as disillusioned about the present state of French politics as most Frenchmen.

"The French who vote Communist do so because they don't understand what it's all about," he says. "What we need in France is a real labor party, a party that will really work for labor, a party in which labor can have some faith. Right now nobody but the extremist has faith in any party, for the obvious reason that no party truly tries to represent its following but instead engages in a game of politics while the nation goes from bad to worse."

He shrugged his shoulders when I asked what hope there was of the right kind of party arising. "It's probably the fault of the people," he replied. "We can't seem to get together on anything and as a result we have these hundreds of small political parties, none of which accomplishes anything."

There are millions of Desiré Lefebvres in France. Their problem is common to all but the wealthiest classes. For the gap between wages and prices is one that afflicts nearly everyone in France in different degrees. The workman who is getting higher pay than he ever got before the war still cannot buy half of what he could on a pre-war salary nor can he live nearly so well. But for the Lefebvres it is no longer a question of giving up luxuries or even of improvising for necessities. They have struck rock bottom.

De Gaulle Waits, the World Watches

by C. L. Sulzberger

PARIS

ONE OF THE biggest questions on the continent of Europe is whether Charles de Gaulle will again come to power in France. If he does it will mean the end of the Fourth Republic.

Out of office nearly three years, the tall, serious-faced, religious General is today as much a man of mystery and as much a topic of discussion as when, in the early war years, he rallied the French people from London and North Africa and then, from 1944 to 1946, headed the Provisional Government of France. The reason is that de Gaulle has recently stepped up his political activities. After refraining from extensive speaking tours for a considerable period this year, he has renewed his call for a general election, has made it plain he is ready to assume power, and has taken his cause to the people.

Last month he journeyed through southern and southeastern France explaining his ideas to a region which contains a large de Gaullist faction. It was evident that his is an immense popularity, based on spontaneous enthusiasm, carefully fostered and organized by a trained political apparatus. There were a number of clashes

From the *New York Times Magazine*, November 7, 1948, copyright © 1948 by The New York Times Company.

with the Communists, who tried to break up the meetings. But the chief effect was a series of de Gaullist anti-government demonstrations.

Upon the General's evident bid for control depends this country's course, perhaps for years to come. The future of Europe, the Marshall Plan and the Brussels Pact are directly affected. And Europe's entire political development might well follow the trend of events in France.

What of the man who possesses such a tremendous power potential? What is de Gaulle like today? What does he stand for and who are his advisers?

The General, who will be 58 on Nov. 22, is an austere puritan, a devout Catholic and a retiring family man. In this he reflects the background from which he comes—conservative, perhaps somewhat royalist, and very religious. He is scrupulously honest and no breath of personal scandal has ever been whispered about him—in contrast with so many other French politicians.

Sincere and studious, he has a psychological make-up which appears to prevent him from being close to many people. For the most part he does not call those who work intimately with him by their Christian names. He is a man who lives in reflective solitude for considerable periods of time. There are those who have visited his family circle in his country home at Colombey-les-Deux-Eglises who say that, sometimes for hours, the General sits wrapped in his own thoughts and silence reigns. He is certainly distant and haughty; that was the impression both Roosevelt and Churchill formed.

At Colombey he follows a simple, country-gentleman's routine. According to some of his friends, he reads several newspapers each morning. Generally, he spends much time reading, even when he is actively engaged in public affairs.

As for his convictions, he seems utterly sure in his own mind of the rectitude of his thoughts, his analyses and his conclusions. There is undoubtedly a streak of the mystic in him. He appears to have an unusual feeling of "oneness" with France and his own destiny.

Cool and distant as he may be in private conversations, he has a curiously magnetic personality. Persons who have visited him or attended small meetings where he was present have been struck by this, whether they agreed with his ideas or not. His mind is precise and, aided by a gift of particularly fine phraseology he expresses his thoughts with special clarity.

As a speaker de Gaulle has a Gallic gift for moving crowds. His style would almost certainly not electrify American or other foreign audiences, but it appears to grip the French mind. His gestures are not overdramatized and they even give an impression of awkwardness when they are examined, for example, in the cinema. But they appear to be instinctively timed to the mood of a French audience.

His method of address is a combination of logic, sincerity and wit tinged with occasional sarcasm—something of especial appeal to *l'esprit Gallois.* Whether it manages to sway opponents or those neutral toward him is a difficult question to answer. But it excites the admiration of his sympathizers and the fury of his enemies.

His strength right now lies in the close-knit ranks of the "Rassemblement du Peuple Français." Despite the continuance of the Central Coalition Ministry, which may yet survive, the two most powerful political forces in France today are the RPF and the Communists. Together, grinding the center between their millstones, these two fundamentally revolutionary parties are managing to pursue a "politique du pire" (a "politics of making things worse") which forces the Government into a succession of pitfalls and toward a situation from which both the RPF and the Communists hope to profit.

The present organizational structure of the General's RPF is based on a select group of advisers, who are tantamount to a "shadow cabinet," and a "National Council," which has a structural resemblance to the "National Committee" formed early in the war. His "cabinet" is composed of eleven men, three of whom, comprising the Executive Committee, form the most important group around de Gaulle in terms of present influence. These are:

Jacques Soustelle, who is general secretary of the RPF and serves as political and administrative officer of that body.

André Malraux, the writer, who is in charge of coordinating the press, information and propaganda, and who also has a large influence on the general's sociological program.

Gaston Palewski, who is responsible for liaison and foreign-affairs reports.

Working with the eleven-man committee is a subsidiary body called the "Intergroup for True Democracy" and made up of former supporters of the Troisième Force. This is headed by Paul Giaccobi, a deputy from Corsica.

The RPF now claims a membership of approximately two million. It has one official journal—Le Rassemblement—which appears weekly in Paris, with special regional editions containing local reports. The organization is financed by annual membership dues of 200 francs and by voluntary contributions. It claims that it does not have its own police or parliamentary force, but it is safe to assert that, despite these denials, some protective body does exist.

What actually is the political theory and application which de Gaulle wants to put into effect in place of the Fourth Republic?

De Gaulle's supporters and the General himself explain it briefly in this way. They wish to establish a constitutional system similar to that of the United States, in which the three governmental functions—executive, legislative and judicial—are balanced, instead of a system of legislative control under which Parliament can continually bring about the overthrow of ministries.

The RPF insists on its respect for democratic theories and stresses that men and women of all the French religions, races and colors may be members. De Gaullists say that sociologically they wish to establish sounder relationships between the citizen and the government and more just nonpolitical relationships between labor and capital.

De Gaulle himself told this writer last year:

"The aim of the RPF is to group the French people in such a way as to permit a system in which policies can be decided and responsibilities assumed in the interests of France, independent of the aspirations of any single political party.

"The aim of the RPF is the reconstruction of France to its full productive capacity and power. It is necessary to restore productive capacity, and in order to do so we must provide for full free enterprise. . . . It is necessary to increase the volume of French production. Simultaneously it is necessary to find a solution to the problems relating to the working of capital and labor."

De Gaulle's critics and those who fear him can be roughly grouped in two large blocs. First of all there are the Communists. Curiously enough, much as they hate him, their obdurate refusal to cooperate in any way in alleviating the task of the Center Government is rendering de Gaulle's chances continually better. The Communists fear de Gaulle because there is not the slightest doubt that he will try to reduce and eventually eliminate their influence.

The other group comprises leftists and moderates who fear that de Gaulle—a second time in power—might head France along autocratic paths. They say he evinces too much faith in himself and too little in parliamentary democracy.

They fear the vagueness of his announced policy, his economic inexperience, some of his social ideas and the personality of many of his advisers.

De Gaulle himself has spoken on the subject both of dictatorship and democracy. At Bayeux on June 16, 1946, he analyzed dictatorship as "a great adventure" whose dynamism at first contrasts favorably with the anarchy it succeeds, but which then, in order to satisfy the public, leads it toward the path of disaster.

Nevertheless, those who fear his return are alarmed by several symptoms. First of all, they fear that despite public pledges a de Gaullist Government would not only terminate the Fourth Republic as now constituted, but might end the system of political parties and formal opposition. This, they maintain, would negate democracy no matter how well ordered.

There are many who, despite their own anti-Communist convictions, believe that a move by de Gaulle to outlaw the Communist party might pave the way to civil war and would certainly strengthen communism as it has been strengthened in other countries such as Italy and Greece where it was outlawed for years.

Finally, his opponents are frequently skeptical about flat assertions by de Gaullists that they have no paramilitary secret organizations supporting them. Old revolutionaries and resistance leaders like Malraux or Remy are certainly practiced at creating such bodies.

De Gaulle's enemies assert that Colonel "Passy," at one time the General's intelligence chief in London and often alleged to be a former Cagoulard [pre-war Fascist group], is playing a vital clandestine role in the RPF. The implication is that he has a lot to do with a secret "defense force." (RPF denies vigorously that "Passy" has anything to do with it.)

Some labor leaders frankly voice fears that the trade-union movement would be so drastically altered as to be vitiated if a de Gaulle government were able to install its "associations" of workers and capitalists. They assert that this idea—one of the planks in the RPF movement—has remarkable similarity to the corporativism of Mussolini.

Whether these suspicions and fears are well grounded or not is impossible to know. The French political atmosphere is replete with charges and countercharges.

But this is the kind of argument which involves all France these days and frequently ends up with harsh and bitter words. It enables the most vehement supporters of de Gaulle to engage in fisticuffs and even more vigorous battles with his enemies and it makes it easier for organized groups from both the RPF and communism to promote occasional scraps such as those which occurred toward the end of the General's recent speaking tour in southern France.

How would de Gaulle come to power? And what are his chances?

First of all, he clearly counts on a final collapse of what he has denounced as the unstable party system as it has existed in the Third and Fourth Republics.

He counts on the advent of a situation where a fed-up public will demand stability as represented by himself and his movement. Whether he could secure power through an election or a plebiscite —if that moment on which he bases his hopes arrives—cannot be said. It is illogical to expect a parliament which contains many members who would not be re-elected to dissolve itself.

If legal means were not available it is not impossible that the General might agree to unconstitutional methods to accomplish what he considers his mission of saving France. De Gaulle certainly has the authoritarian type of mind which is often associated with a military education and career. However, his term as head of the French state showed not the slightest sign that he sought to install an autocratic regime.

Can one count on this still? An absolute prediction cannot be risked. Should de Gaulle take over the reins again he might lean toward a dictatorial form of administration..

It is obvious that de Gaulle's chances are far better today than they were six months ago. But this does not mean either that the Fourth Republic has had its last fling or that the General's RPF will of a surety take control here.

It is no secret that neither Britain nor the United States would enthusiastically welcome such a development despite continual Communist charges that de Gaulle is an American stooge.

The General's strong Gallic pride, his diplomatic obduracy and his mystical faith in his ideas made him a difficult man for Anglo-American diplomatists to deal with during the war and just afterward. They are worried about possible autocratic tendencies should he again step to the helm.

But the decision will be made by France and Frenchmen regardless of foreign desires. And the situation this autumn contains many of those basic symptoms which are frequently preliminary to a political revolution.

Economic misery and inflation have not been eliminated. Workers and pensioners are not receiving enough real purchasing power. The regime of successive weak Governments has not been able to master basic issues yet. And de Gaulle's RPF is, in terms of political philosophy, a revolutionary organization clearly prepared to seek advantage from this situation and assume responsibility.

The only true test of the ability of the de Gaullists to govern democratically and successfully without infringing upon the civil rights of Frenchmen would be the actuality of a de Gaulle government. France will very likely have to decide whether it wishes to apply this test during the course of the next six months.

French Premier
with a Deadline

by Harold Callender

PARIS

LONG AGO George Bernard Shaw said his oculist had discovered with much amazement that Shaw had absolutely normal vision, which hardly anybody had. Shaw remarked that it was then clear to him why he saw the world about him so much more accurately than most other people saw it.

Pierre Mendès-France, the new Premier of France, has not the intellectual vanity that Mr. Shaw professed to have. But he has a remarkable confidence in his analyses and judgments and sometimes has not hesitated to express it.

Four years ago, M. Mendès-France said to the National Assembly:

"To win the war in Indochina, we shall need half a million men; you will never get them because you will never draw upon conscript troops."

Two years later he said France's position for negotiating a peace there was worse than it had been the previous year and probably would be worse still when another year had passed. These forecasts proved correct.

A year ago, after outlining a program for expanding French production, he told the Assembly he had placed before it facts that would be accepted sooner or later, the only question being whether that acceptance would be delayed until France suffered further from a stagnant economy. Ten days ago, he urged upon the Assembly the same facts and the same program he had proposed a year earlier, as confident as ever that he knew what France should do.

M. Mendès-France's intellectual vision has been proved by the test of time and events—and not alone in the field of economics and finance. Probably this clarity owes much to his self-criticism, his distrust of his own ideas until he has examined and analyzed them and subjected them to the comments of others. He is a man of studious and methodical habits, and his cautiously critical approach to the problems of his time causes him to make up his mind about them only very slowly.

A practiced lawyer, he can if he must make a speech extemporaneously, and some of his best speeches have been made in this way. But he writes laboriously and slowly since what he puts down is subject to reflection and self-criticism as he goes along. One of his friends said he sometimes spent hours over a paragraph. He spent more than three days drafting his thirteen-page speech asking the Assembly to make him Premier, but he spent about ninety minutes preparing an equally long speech answering his critics.

M. Mendès-France is an intellectual and as such is painfully aware of the inevitable disparity between thought and action, especially in politics. He seems to believe it is easier to serve his country as Mayor of the small town of Louviers than as a member of the National Assembly. He once remarked that as Mayor he could see real results of his labors—better roads, schools, gas and electric installations—but that as a Deputy about all he could take credit for was a law about rabbits, which, when passed, had quite ceased to resemble what he had proposed.

The French National Assembly is not the best place to acquire faith in the translation of ideas into facts. France has perhaps an over-supply of intellectuals, but in France, as in the United States, politics tends to be guided largely by the need to win the votes of the more numerous non-intellectuals.

Yet M. Mendès-France has not despaired of influencing policy through careful analysis of national needs, through the force of accumulated facts, through appeal to the intelligence of Frenchmen rather than to their sectional or professional interests or to their traditional doctrines.

He retains a hope that the disparity between the vision of the enlightened intellectual and the acts of political leaders may be diminished. Now he is going to put this hope to the test by trying a political experiment of bold proportions—that of revising France's policies toward her overseas territories and of freeing her national economy from the shackles that restrict production and trade.

M. Mendès-France has been called "a new man" in France partly because, although he has held Cabinet posts, he has not held the top ones and has never before been Premier, but mainly because his unexpected choice as Premier seemed to presage a change in the sluggish politics of the country and a Goverment that would at least try harder than its immediate predecessors to solve some major national problems.

Some observers have imagined him to be pessimistic because it has been his role to draw attention to unpleasant facts that others preferred to ignore, to sound the alarm for disasters that might impend. But he fought for his country when victory seemed hopeless, and he has fought for policies that seemed to have little chance of acceptance. He clings to the hope that France may improve her system of government and modernize her economy so as to play a greater role in world affairs.

His friends point out that no pessimist would try to learn to ski at the age of 43, as M. Mendès-France did. His sons, aged 18 and 19, consider his skiing a joke and he admits it is not brilliant. But he professes to understand perfectly the theory of skiing and persists in trying to apply it. Every winter he tries again, although he has repeatedly broken a leg or an ankle in the process.

In his adopted town of Louviers, west of Paris, where he practices law and meets constituents, M. Mendès-France seldom sits in cafes to gossip with the people.

He gives few dinner parties. But in the Department of Eure, which he represents in the Assembly, he apparently has won the confidence of farm workers, merchants and others, who continue to elect him.

M. Mendès-France is short and stocky, with almost black hair and a face that animates as he talks. He reads much, notably in history and economics, and sometimes plays the piano. In Paris he and his wife, who spent four years in the United States during World War II and speaks excellent English, live in a very modest apartment on the fourth floor of a fairly new building not far from the Bois de Boulogne.

Beginning his career as a lawyer and Deputy at Louviers, M. Mendès-France specialized in economics and finance. At the age of 19 he wrote a thesis on the stabilization of the franc by Poincaré. When World War II began he was in the French Air Force serving in Syria and later, from Britain, he was on bombing missions over France.

His first important venture in post-war politics was his proposal to General de Gaulle's Provisional Government to put an end to inflation by blocking bank accounts and issuing a new currency, as was done in Belgium. This plan was rejected and M. Mendès-France resigned as Minister for National Economy. The inflation continued and became a major post-war problem.

M. Mendès-France represented France at the Bretton Woods conference which established the International Monetary Fund and the International Bank for Reconstruction and Development. He became executive director and later a member of the board of governors of the fund. At Bretton Woods, he became acquainted with the British economist Lord Keynes, many of whose ideas he then shared.

Within the last year, he has been chairman of the Finance Committee of the National Assembly and he directed the huge work of a committee of specialists analyzing and severely criticizing the French economy. The evils of a protected system with little competition were depicted with complete frankness in an elaborate report often cited by the studious but little read by the public.

M. Mendès-France's speech as candidate for Premier a year ago was essentially a lecture on economics. He insisted that "to govern is to choose," and that France must decide how to use her resources and how to adapt her aspirations to her means. He questioned whether France could pursue the war in Indochina and at the same time build up her strength in Europe, and he contended she must choose which she would do.

He thus approached international problems from the point of view of France's military and economic capacity.

He urged increasing her economic power by expanding production. To this end he proposed a better use of resources, greater competition in place of cartels and the elimination of unproductive or high-cost industries. He wanted to expand, above all, exports and building, the latter chiefly to produce the houses that France has been slow to build.

At the same time, he urged greater progress toward self-government in Tunisia and Morocco, as he did again in his speech ten days ago outlining his program as Premier.

M. Mendès-France has been cited by conservatives as a bogy man who might come into power with Communist support and withdraw from Indochina. By others he has been considered the only man who might organize a Left bloc without the Communists. By his friends and many of the younger generation he is regarded as a man who might rejuvenate the Fourth Republic by breaking down the rigid party lines that divide and paralyze it.

Sometimes he has been accused of "neutralism," but in his speech of June 3, 1953, he said the neutralists were wrong in imagining that, if another world war came France could stay out of it.

But he argued that France must limit her objectives and not indulge in the "illusion of grandeur." The first article of foreign policy should be the build-up of the internal economy, he contended.

In his speech June 9, last, he insisted that France's vulnerability to Communist propaganda should be taken as a basic problem of

Western strategy. This vulnerability he attributed mainly to France's backward economy. Here again is the economic approach to foreign policy which dominates M. Mendès-France's thinking as he surveys France's position in the world in relation to her internal weaknesses, both economic and political.

The French Empire: "Time Runs Out"

by D. W. Brogan

IT IS unnecessary to underline the importance for a great imperial power of a military and political defeat such as that which France suffered in Indochina. The defeat, it is true, is not only a defeat for France; it is a defeat for France's allies, for all the nations threatened by the Communist powers. But it is for France a time for an agonizing reappraisal of the role and the future of the French Empire, or, as it is now called, the French Union. That the reappraisal is taking place is indicated by recent moves in Paris. One is Premier Mendès-France's plan to establish an all-Tunisian Government and to grant that strife-torn protectorate full internal autonomy under conditions that would protect the rights of French settlers. And the continuing tension in Morocco calls for fresh decisions.

It may and it will be said in America that this decline of the French Empire is a good thing. But in the American attitude on the question of imperialism there is often to be noted a belief that imperialism, *all* imperialism, is intrinsically evil. Yet the world is a bigger and more complicated place than an old-fashioned Fourth of July oration would suggest. In any case, the French Empire is

From the *New York Times Magazine,* August 15, 1954, copyright © 1954 by The New York Times Company.

still there and there is no guarantee nor, in my opinion, any probability that its disappearance would either promote the strength of the West or even the material well-being of the liberated inhabitants. It is, that is to say, to the interest of the United States and of Great Britain that the problems, the grave and very present problems of the French Empire, be solved in a manner that does not involve the dissolution of one of the main bastions of order in a world so badly in need of them.

An epigrammatic Cambridge professor said more than two generations ago that the "British Empire was created in a fit of absence of mind." He was at best half-right. It could more truly be said that the French Empire was created in a permanent fit of absence of mind by the majority of French voters and French ministers. It was created by a comparatively small body of soldiers, sailors, administrators, missionaries and business men, supported rather than led by a handful of politicians who saw in the empire the means of redressing the balance of power in Europe or (so their enemies alleged) of distracting the hopes of the French people from the dream of the recovery of Alsace and Lorraine to the more practical dream of finding compensation on the Niger and on the Red River.

The French Empire, like so many great French achievements, was not the direct, planned achievement of the French state. So that, today, when more and more attention is being paid in France to imperial problems, it is being paid in a country that, in the mass, is not accustomed to thinking about them.

This is not a peculiarly French phenomenon. Few Americans, today, can even vaguely remember the imperial oratory of Senators like Albert J. Beveridge. In British politics the living and difficult problems of imperial policy are discussed, too often, in terms that recall the bitter fights between the imperialists and their opponents who were scornfully called "little Englanders."

But the French situation is more complicated and probably more dangerous. It is not only that the country of the "Declaration of the Rights of Man and the Citizen" has never found it easy to invent a formula that could fit in the imperial fact to the republican theory. It is that the French Empire was largely created by people whose adherence to the principles of 1789 was tepid, at best. For example, one reason and a politically important reason for the French intervention in and then conquest of Indochina was that Annam was one of the greatest fields of French missionary endeavor.

We all know the psychological importance of the missionary connection between the United States and China. But France (proportionately to its population and resources the greatest missionary country in the world) had an equal interest in Indochina. The same interest was, in part, behind the occupation of Madagascar and of a great part of Africa. Trade, prestige, military power were all elements in the creation of the French Empire. But missionary zeal was at least as important, and one of the disasters of the present "settlement" in Indochina is the abandonment to the Communists of so many flourishing Catholic communities in Tonkin.

It is not accidental that, even today, some of the most lively discussions of the problems of the empire take place in Catholic circles, that Indochina, for example, has been regarded as a fief of the Catholic Democrats, the M. R. P., that the first and, possibly, fatal decisions when French authority was restored there, were made by the sailor-monk, Admiral Thierry d'Argenlieu of the Carmelite order.

It was not only a question of missionaries. Some of the most brilliant makers of the Empire were men like Lyautey, men of royalist families who found in a career in Indochina or Morocco a field of action denied to them in republican France. It was not merely a gesture when the Socialist party expelled Alexandre Varenne for accepting the post of Governor-General of Indochina. The empire was a "Right-Wing affair"; in the eyes of many, a Right-Wing racket. But apart from denunciations of imperialism in general and of abuses like the Congo concessions in particular, the amount of knowledge or thought that the Left-Wing parties were prepared to devote to the empire was small. And one of the tragedies of the defeat of the Government of Léon Blum after 1936 was that the necessary adjustments in Syria and in North Africa that were planned for were lost in the confusion of the years before the Second World War.

The Second World War suddenly gave to the empire a new

importance. For with the whole of France occupied, the empire *was* France. From equatorial Brazzaville and then from Algiers came the rallying cries that reinforced the voice of de Gaulle from London. The greater part of de Lattre de Tassigny's army of "the Rhine and Danube" came from the empire. The successes of the war that restored French faith in French arms, the feats of Leclerc, Koenig, Juin had their roots in the empire. For the first time, the empire became not a thing of specialists and special interests. It became an emotional reality to the mass of the French people.

Unfortunately, this emotional appeal was not backed up by a realistic assessment of the position of the empire. The new imperial institutions, loosely compared to the dominion status of the British Empire (itself busily becoming a Commonwealth), were, in part at least, based on a view of a France "one and indivisible," as they said in the Year One of the French Revolution.

Not many people were willing to notice the implications of the British withdrawal from India. Once that was done, the French position in Indochina was undermined. If the British, whose rule was so much older, whose prestige was so much greater, decided to go, it was impossible that the French should stay on anything like the old terms. Many French resent the British withdrawal in India and Egypt as a betrayal. Be that as it may, it is a fact.

But however odd it may seem to Americans, the problem of Indochina, the ulcer that has drained France for seven years, was, in French eyes, not the real imperial problem. Far more serious were the problems of Africa. For Africa is not very remote from France. Algiers and Marseille are a day's steaming apart.

Since 1830, immense amounts of men and money have been poured into Algiers, then Tunisia, then Morocco. During the late war and after, Morocco attracted even more people and more investment. There was created, across the Mediterranean from France, a new France. There were created the new European cities of Algiers and Tunis beside the old Arab pirate ports. There was created the great city of Casablanca where there had been, in 1906, a fishing village. There was imposed on the torpid or fanatical world of western Islam, the "Maghreb," a Western economy.

Some of the problems of Casablanca are those which New Yorkers are or ought to be familiar with in the Puerto Rican slums of Harlem. But, of course, they are magnified by the fact that the French are intruders, that North Africa did not ask for this sudden projection into the modern world. Its dogmatic slumbers might have continued, but for French energy and French capital.

Then the Maghreb could not hope to escape the stirrings of the Islamic world, especially of the Arab world. French authority has disappeared from Syria. British authority has disappeared from Egypt and from the Sudan. After centuries of torpor, the Islamic world is awakening. The results of that awakening, from the point of view of order, military security and modern techniques, may not be, are not, impressive in Java or in Egypt. But the movement is there. And that has presented the French with a special problem, for they alone among the Western powers have a great personal investment in the Islamic world.

It was one thing to find ways of evacuating the British troops from the Suez Canal. It is another thing to find ways for peaceful co-existence between the Arab-speaking Moroccans or the Tunisians on one side and the French "colons" on the other. It is difficult to make the fiction that Algiers is "just three French departments" fit in with the reality that its problems cannot be separated from those of Morocco or Tunisia. Indeed, it is painfully obvious how close are the connections, for some of the Deputies and Senators for Algeria in the National Assembly in Paris act as the spokesmen for their spiritual (and often their blood) kin, the "colons" of Morocco and Tunisia. More than once the chances of a settlement in Tunisia or Morocco have been sacrificed to the need for the votes of these spokesmen for the "colons."

Outrageous as it may seem, there is a case for the "colons." When the "colons" say that they *made* modern North Africa, they are telling the truth. When they express skepticism that the "Arabs" would have done much with the country, they are at least plausible. When they point out that the unity of Morocco (like the unity of Indochina or, for that matter, of India) was the work of the foreign imperialists, they are more than plausible. Nevertheless, the "colons" must adjust themselves to a world in which their old, exclusive, superior position must be abandoned. And that is the opinion of a great part of the French people which thinks about imperial problems.

The problems of North Africa are difficult, but not yet desperate. The complete disappearance of French authority would probably produce a breakdown of order and communications in Tunisia and Algeria. It might well produce a bloody civil war in Morocco. But —and the text should be studied in Paris as well as in Rabat and Tunis—Burke was right, "Great empires and little minds go ill together." There have been no great minds in North Africa for quite a long time.

South of the Sahara, the situation is different. Here the French are dealing with a fluid and plastic society, just entering the modern world. Here their role as teachers is still accepted. But the rapid approach of the Gold Coast to dominion status in the Commonwealth is being noticed. Which will prove more appealing, the career of M. Senghor, who plays an important role in Paris, or that of Dr. Nkrumah, who is Prime Minister of the Gold Coast? Will the élite which the French wish to produce and do produce, be content to seek their ambitions in the politics of metropolitan France or would they rather be bosses in their own backyard? No one knows.

Both Britain and France, in different ways, have undertaken to stimulate and push forward the mechanics of modern democracy in West Africa. In the Congo the Belgians, with no visibly bad results, have not. The French solution has been, roughly, to promote the subjects of the French Empire to the rank of French citizens, making them, as far as may be, French in spirit as well as in legal form. The English, perhaps because they think that attaining the rank of Englishman is something that only Providence can provide for, have chosen to allow their subjects to develop in their own ways.

Time is running out. It is running out fastest in North Africa. Only a strong government in Paris can impose on the "colons" a due regard for the Moslem majority and, at the same time, guarantee that the great work of construction is not undone. Yet the élite whom the French have created will have to be given the place in their own country that their education entitles them to.

South of the Sahara, the problem is less urgent. But the "promotion" of the Africans must be speeded up. And as France is poor in capital, the jealous mercantilist spirit of French business must be taught that its interest lies in encouraging foreign investment, not only in Africa but in Madagascar and other French possessions.

Frankly, few people in Paris expect the settlement in Indochina to last long. There it is five past twelve. In North Africa, it is five to twelve. In the rest of the French Union, it is eleven o'clock. There is still everywhere an appreciation of French culture and French ideas that can be used. There is a pro-French party everywhere. There is, in France, an increasing undoctrinaire interest in the Empire and a genuine concern about it.

If the two forces—the generous desire to make the French Union a spiritual reality that animates so many Frenchmen, Catholic and *laic,* and the reluctance that animates so many citizens of "France Overseas" to lose their status as members of the Union— can be brought together, the Union can emerge from the crisis strengthened. If that is not done, the winners will be not the Nationalists of Rabat or Tunis or Dakar, but the Kremlin. And the losers will be all of us in the West. The next two or three years at most will decide one way or the other.

Part 4

THE FIFTH REPUBLIC

"We Are All Victims in Algeria"

by Joseph Kraft

ALGERIA CAN be summed up in a mot: *"Ce n'est que le provisoire qui dure"*—"The temporary is what lasts."

Forty-three months, five Premiers and three U. N. debates have passed since hostilities began. Repression has been mixed with reform, and alarm has crowded upon excursion. In season and out, generals and proconsuls have signaled what one of them once called "the last quarter of an hour." Still, the war goes on, and nothing—not even the revolts of the generals—changes the basic features of that unshakable reality.

Horror—the horror of a war visited upon civil populations and with heavy overtones of social and racial conflict—is the most striking of those features. No day passes in Algeria without reports of violence, a bloody engagement in the Aurès Mountains, a grenade exploded in an Oran cafe, a throat cut in Constantine, an Arab tortured to death in Algiers. Gutted schools and leveled villages stand everywhere in mute testimony to the rival terror tactics of French and nationalist soldiers. A European, missing an arm or a leg, or with an ear sliced off, is no longer an object of curiosity in the cafes. Along the back-country roads broken men,

From the *New York Times Magazine*, May 25, 1958, copyright © 1958 by The New York Times Company.

and near blind, stumble their way home—Arabs released from the torture chambers, each with a white note fixed to his clothing to indicate he is harmless. "This," one Arab doctor says, "is our daily bread."

One way or another, it is everybody's bread. "We are all victims in Algeria," Père Scotto, a Dominican priest in a working class section of Algiers, once said. But the victims are no more members of a single community than fifty men are a centipede. At least four major groups—the French Army, the nationalist rebels, the European settlers, and the mass of Moslem natives—can be counted.

Within each group the majority is passive, while firebrands force the pace. Relations between the groups, in consequence, are badly distorted. Poorly connected with each other, where they are not wholly cut off, they go their separate ways at cross-purposes, only dimly aware of the vast aggregate of a country four times the size of France. Here are some quick sketches of the four main elements in the Algerian picture:

The Army

French military forces, probably 450,000 in number and certainly the largest army ever sent overseas by France, are spread across Algeria in a *quadrillage* operation aimed at dotting the whole country with strong points. Draftees and recalled veterans, by profession farmers from Normandy or upholsterers from Arras, the overwhelming bulk of the soldiers have no love for the settlers and little stomach for fighting the nationalists. Day after day they go through the weary rounds of garrison duty in provincial towns so deeply steeped in ennui as to make Madame Bovary's Rouen seem a Babylon. On dusty parade grounds and in the muddy courts of newly built posts, they may be seen endlessly rolling little wooden balls, one after another, in a game something like the Italian *boccia*. "It's the national sport," a press officer once said.

A not dissimilar mood prevails in the very highest circles of military authority and in some of the sector commands. In the afternoon of lackluster careers, wary of harming innocent civilians, and conscious of being dependent upon the politicians for promotion, the top French generals go through their paces with one eye cocked on Paris, and in an air bordering on futility. One sector commander, not long ago, took his leave in Paris with the idea of selling a series of articles on Algeria to the newspaper Le Monde. His plan was that French forces, instead of manning fixed posts, should course back and forth across the countryside on permanent patrol. But asked why he didn't use that system in his own sector, he said: "Too hot."

The dust of battle, in these circumstances, has been borne by a relatively small group of professionals—notably the paratroopers. Superbly trained, in almost constant action since World War II, equipped with the most modern American arms, the paras are among the best troops in the world. To them belongs the credit for the only indubitable French victory in Algeria—the cleaning out of the Casbah of Algiers, a rabbit warren of interconnecting homes.

Assumption of security duties in the cities, though, has brought the paras into close touch with the ultra elements among the settlers and the local administrators. It has confronted them too with the ugly dilemma—the dilemma of "talk or else"—facing most police forces. Repeatedly they will capture a nationalist who can give intelligence that might lead to the saving of French lives. Making no headway by routine questions and egged on by the die-hards, they not infrequently resort to torture, sometimes of wholly innocent people. Whenever the facts get out, cries of protest go up in Paris.

Moreover, despite their valor, the paras have not been a winning force. They did not win World War II, nor in Indochina, nor in Tunisia, nor in Morocco, nor at Suez in November, 1956. Algeria they see as a last stand. "Here," one colonel, a fiercely blue-eyed man who spoke grandly in the Shavian manner of war, God and destiny, once put it, "the politicians can't cheat us."

In these conditions—brutalized by security duties, conscious of their strength but bitterly frustrated by their failures, idolized by the settlers but chastened by Paris—the paras became a hotbed of political dissension. "What France needs," one of them once said, "is a regime *pur et dur* [hard and clean]. What we have is a regime *pourri* [rotten]. Minister X took a hundred million francs from the Sultan for giving him Morocco. Deputy Y is pro-Arab because his wife has a department store in Cairo. They are all *bradeurs* [a rare French word, now much in vogue, meaning a peddler who, after crying up his wares, sells cheap]."

The Rebels

Like the war itself, the Algerian nationalists, or National Liberation Army, are everywhere and nowhere.

Everywhere, because in any city a foreigner can meet Arabs, many of them working for the French administration, who can put him in touch with the nationalist forces. Probably no village in Algeria is without a nationalist political officer, dunning the locals for funds, setting women and children to spy on the French, storing up food for nationalist soldiers who may happen by, yet, withal, unknown to the French. Many of the political officers have dug in as local nabobs, running the towns and billeting their wives and children and, in one known case, an elderly mother.

Nowhere, because the rebel troops—not more than 30,000 in all —move by night in the back country and in tiny units.

A thirty-man section is the usual fighting force, though sometimes companies of a hundred take the field and once a battalion was mustered. Troop leaders maintain only tenuous liaison with the five regional nationalist headquarters in Algeria, and these in turn have but the loosest ties with the topmost political leaders— scattered through the world, in Tunis, Cairo, Damascus and even New York.

In consequence, there is a large degree of local autonomy. "If I think I can take a French post," one sergeant once told me, "well then, I'll try it." But inevitably, the temptation is to pick easier marks—defenseless settlers' farms, for instance, or Arab villagers suspected of helping the French.

The rebel troops are largely fresh-faced boys, many still in their teens, but well-trained in camps in Morocco and Tunisia. They wear uniforms not unlike American fatigues, and are equipped with small arms—including machine guns and a few mortars—taken from the French, or transported across the Moroccan and Tunisian borders from sources as distant as Cairo, Belgrade and London. Like almost everyone else in Algeria, the nationalist soldiers have settled to a routine. "We get food and we're out-doors," one medical orderly once said to me. "What more do you want?"

Of ultimate victory, the rebels seem to have no doubt. "We may not beat the French," one captain said, "but they can't beat us. Not in a hundred years. Sooner or later something's bound to happen in France. When it does, they'll give way."

Istiqlal—independence—is, of course, the word on every na-tionalist lip, and sometimes it seems the only one in their patriotic songs. "Independence for what?" though, is a question that on more than one occasion has reduced the soldiers to embarrassed silence. And they accorded to one sergeant who answered, "To get the French off our backs," the kind of respect Aristotle might have received had he popped up in the twelfth century to settle a nice point for a pack of schoolmen.

In the rebel camp, too, in the very midst of determination, there exists an incongruity and aimlessness, of a piece with the rolling of wooden balls. A lieutenant once borrowed my typewriter—to write an order, he said. At the top of the sheet, he wrote, in capital letters neatly centered, "National Liberation Army." Evi-dently there then occurred to him a French phrase used in typing schools to employ every letter key in a single sentence. What he wrote on the order was, in translation: "I imagine a Zouave, play-ing the xylophone while drinking whiskey."

The Europeans

Few people can have been so much maligned as the million so-called "French *colons*" in Algeria. *Colons* they are not, for that term implies rich landowner, whereas nine-tenths of the settlers live in cities and work as clerks, artisans and shopkeepers at wages averaging 20 per cent below the prevailing French standard. A typical European apartment in downtown Algiers includes two small, ill-lit rooms—one serving as kitchen and eating quarters; the other, with a triple-decker for the children and a double bed for the parents, as sleeping quarters.

Neither are the settlers exactly French. Half, at most, are of French descent, the rest coming from all over the Mediterranean with a specially heavy sprinkling of Spaniards and Italians. Living with much less formal manners in a softer climate, and in day-to-day touch with the Moslems at home, in schools, at work and almost all public places, the settlers have taken on non-European mores. There is truth as well as pride in the claim, "We are Algerians."

What they have not taken on is a politics of their own. A heavily outnumbered minority, the settlers always have looked at times of duress to whatever powers may be. During World War II, they embraced in rapid succession the Third Republic, Vichy, the Germans, the Americans, the Free French, the Fourth Republic. More recently, in the absence of a strong lead from Paris, opinion has slipped its moorings. "They change ideas," Mayor Jacques Chevallier of Algiers says of his fellow settlers, "like the smile on the Cheshire cat."

To be sure, there are men and institutions working among the settlers to calm tempers and maintain good relations with the Moslems. Mayor Chevallier, a builder on the scale of Robert Moses and the Levitts combined, is one. Another is the Roman Catholic Church. "It is the duty of every man to avoid violence, not only in acts but in words," Monsignor Duval, the Archbishop of Algiers, said in a recent pastoral letter. Working with young men and women of the purest religious feeling, Père Scotto has established social service missions in the worst of the Moslem slums. "I deeply wanted," one of his workers said, "to fill the gap [between Christians and Moslems] by the performance of common tasks." But he said that from the dock of a military tribunal where he was convicted on charges of aiding the enemy. And a European spectator at the trial, questioned about the name of the Archbishop, replied: "Mohammed."

The truth is that die-hard extremists have increasingly come to dominate European opinion in Algeria. A handful of rich wine-growers, dependent upon French subsidies for their income and likely to go to the wall if independence came, take the lead. The dirty work is done by clubs, professional and veterans' organizations and other private groups. A university students' association, located on the second floor of a bank building in Algiers, is perhaps typical.

The stairs leading up to the office were plastered with posters showing Europeans mutilated by the rebels and bearing captions saying: "Frenchmen, meditate on this." On a table by the door was a pile of medical pamphlets, thick with pictures of bloody corpses, and purporting to show that ritualistic murder was an innate racial trait of the Arabs. Inside, a group of teen-agers—the boys in shorts, the girls in cotton dresses—lounged at their ease. Several days before, in reprisal for the nationalists' bombing of a casino, the boys had led a raid against some Arab merchants, actually pitching two of them off a cliff into the sea. "I don't regret it," one of them said. "My sister might have been killed in that casino, or worse, maybe lost an arm. Anyhow, the Arabs insulted us."

Minutes later a company of paratroopers paraded past in the street below. All the students crowded to the window, cheering and waving. What did their visitor think of the paras, they wanted to know. They were good troops, he believed, but not very different from the Wehrmacht. "That's what we like about them," one of the girls said.

The Moslem Mass

The Moslems—a thickly mixed blend of Arabs and Berbers making up 85 per cent of the total population of nearly nine million—were victims long before the fighting began. A backward people sent reeling into the modern world by the impact of France, they have been keyed up to demands their poor country cannot possibly support. Their population, thanks to medical science, doubles every twenty-five years, only to find not enough houses, not enough schools, not enough jobs. They remain largely rural, but in desperate straits hundreds of thousands have crowded into the *bidonvilles* (tin-can cities) around the major Algerian towns, or moved to France as industrial workers.

On the Moslems, too, has fallen the great burden of the war. Total deaths number roughly 100,000, of which less than a thousand are French civilians, with perhaps 6,000 in French military ranks. The rebel forces have lost perhaps 20,000. All the rest, nearly three-quarters, are Moslem civilians.

Even so, it is no easy task to determine Moslem public opinion in the struggle. Go into the countryside with the rebels, and the villagers will turn out in enthusiastic welcome. Go in with the French, and the same thing will happen. Traveling with the French once, I came upon an Arab playing checkers with a French officer at a command post, high atop a mountain. Spontaneously, it seemed, he began talking about what would happen if the French were forced out. "Half my people would be wiped out in a year. Like that," he said, sweeping the counters from the board.

Amidst much uncertainty, however, there are two clear points. One is that the best educated and most successful Moslems lean decidedly toward the rebels. Not half a dozen eminent Arabs in Algeria, if that many, support the French cause. Among the rebels' supporters, literally thousands speak Parisian French. France's civilizing mission, in short, has done its work. Having risen from the dead mass of their people, the educated Moslems want to lead them. As the Moslem hero of an Algerian novel modestly puts the complaint: "I am a one-eyed man in the kingdom of the blind; but I am not king."

The other point is that the French reforms, big or small, seem to make almost no dent. One big one which would have given the Moslems a considerable voice in local government was laughed off. "We want meat, and they give us milk," one educated Moslem said. As to the small reforms, they convince nobody. In Batna, for instance, the French have changed the name of the native quarter from Black Town to New France. But no European can enter New France without an armed guard.

What emerges in sum is the spectacle of thousands of men— life-sized but no bigger—caught up in the sweep of a gigantic event. Preoccupied with their own problems and prejudices, almost void of practical political programs, the actors on the Algerian stage play out their roles by rote, mindless of the consequences in the total drama. Purposeless drifting, punctuated by bursts of furious violence—that, in essence, is the Algerian tragedy.

Tormented Officer
in a "Dirty War"

by Henry Tanner

THE FRENCH ARMY in Algeria is one of the most tormented, most self-searching and self-doubting bodies of men that ever fought a war. Now in its sixth year of combat, it numbers about 400,000 men. Of its 30,000 officers, an estimated two-thirds are professional soldiers. Paris editorialists who write about "the Army"— what it does and thinks, and whether it is loyal or likely to stage another *putsch*—are writing about this corps of highly trained, highly intelligent, articulate and troubled regular officers.

What is the French officer in Algeria like? Captain Claude-André de V. is a valid example. He is 41 years old. The men in his family have been soldiers since Napoleon.

Captain de V. is a member of the last class to graduate from Saint-Cyr, the French military academy, before the Germans overran the country in 1940. After his graduation he joined the Resistance as a civilian. He was captured a few months later and spent the rest of the war in the concentration camp of Buchenwald.

In 1945, almost immediately after his liberation, he volunteered for Indochina. When asked why he was so eager, after years in the

From the *New York Times Magazine,* June 26, 1960, copyright © 1960 by The New York Times Company.

concentration camp, to go from one hell to another, he answers evenly: "My country had trained me as a soldier. It was time I started to be one."

Captain de V. served a total of seven years in Indochina. Between tours he was trained as a paratrooper in France. After Indochina came Morocco, then Tunisia and finally Algeria. He was a young company commander in the first paratroop regiment that was sent into the Aurès Mountains of eastern Algeria shortly after the outbreak of the nationalist rebellion on Nov. 1, 1954. Recently he was sent back into the Aurès after having served in Kabylia, another crucial mountain region, and on the general staff in Algiers.

The central experience in Captain de V.'s life was Indochina. It formed him, he says, and adds wryly: " 'Sensitized' perhaps would be a better word."

To begin with, he remembers his last day in Indochina. On that day he had to face the 150 Vietnamese soldiers fighting in his company. He had personally selected and trained them. They were his men. Now he had to tell them that France was leaving Indochina, that he, their commander, was going home and that they would have to stay, probably to be tortured and killed.

"I betrayed them. I betrayed their faith in me," he cries, and in a startling, abrupt movement, as if bent under the enormous burden of that guilt, he leans forward and sobs, his face covered with both hands. After a moment, attempting a smile, he says: "You must think we are a sentimental army."

Today, too, the captain commands about 100 local soldiers. Nearly 130,000 Moslems have been enlisted into the French Army as auxiliaries and are carrying French arms. Thousands of others have been organized in "self-defense" units and are guarding their villages with antiquated rifles. Thousands are cooperating with the French police and the Army's intelligence officers. And thousands have committed themselves by running for political office or accepting administrative jobs.

The captain tells of one of his friends, a much-decorated career officer, who resigned his Army commission last year and emigrated to Canada—partly, the captain suspects, because he feared that if he stayed he would one day have to tell his Moslem soldiers, as he had told his Vietnamese, that he was letting them down. This feeling of guilt and shame is one of the reasons for the vehemence with which some of the French officers here have turned against successive Paris Governments whenever they feared, as they did before May 13, 1958, and again last January, that the Army would be drawn into another "ignominious" withdrawal.

This fear has been revived to a considerable degree by General de Gaulle's latest offer to the rebels to go to Paris to discuss a cease-fire in Algeria—an offer that was quickly accepted.

"We are no *ultras,* no reactionaries," cried a major who had demonstrated his sympathy with the extremist insurgents last January. "On the contrary, we are the true liberals, the true Christians. We love these people [the Algerian Moslems]. We have nothing in common with the *colons.* We will never be rich, here in Algeria or elsewhere. But we are afraid of what the intentions of Paris might be. Let Paris dispel our fears, and all will be well."

Many of these officers have been agitating for "integration," the slogan of the civilian *ultras,* because they feel that the door will be finally closed to "abandonment" only if Algeria becomes permanently a part of France. But many of them, in fact, care little about the future status of Algeria and would go along with any solution, including independence, if it were attained in such a way that the Army would emerge from this "dirty war" with "its honor intact." Army control of the referendum, in which Algerians will choose their future, is thus the Army's frequently heard minimum demand.

The presence of General de Gaulle at the helm of the French state has not changed the basic outlook of these officers. Fifteen out of seventeen commanding generals, including the Commander-in-chief in Algeria, were replaced in an unprecedented command shakeup following the January insurrection by European extremists. Confirmed Gaullists or apolitical officers now hold all the most important commands. General de Gaulle's hold on the Army thus is stronger than it ever was, but nobody is in a position to know whether it will prove strong enough for all contingencies.

Except for a steadily decreasing number of aging colonels and generals, the great majority of today's career officers has no special loyalty to de Gaulle. These younger officers will tell you that *"le grand Charles"* is a fine figure of an old soldier but that he belongs to another world and another generation and that he has never really grasped the methods of revolutionary warfare which the Army has been waging in Indochina and Algeria.

These officers respect de Gaulle for what he was twenty years ago. But they have deep misgivings about his present role. They do not give him any blank checks. Their attitudes toward him and his Government will be determined in each new situation that arises by the actions he takes and the results he produces.

Captain de V.'s command post is an isolated village in the mountains. Once a week a heavily armed convoy moves slowly up the winding Army-built road with food, mail and soldiers returning from leave. On rare occasions a helicopter lands to evacuate a wounded soldier or bring in a superior officer for a quick inspection.

In the village and the ten square miles of empty country around it the captain is king—or, as he puts it, "almost God Almighty." Since this is one of the worst fighting zones in Algeria, there have been no local elections in the village. The captain is Mayor, judge, head schoolmaster and many other dignitaries all in one. Two of his soldiers are the community's only teachers. His company doctor is the only doctor.

The captain, far from enjoying his power, is overwhelmed by it. "How can a man have such a hold on people and keep from misusing it?" he asks. "And how can an Army which plays this kind of role keep from getting mixed up in the country's politics?"

A few years ago the population of the captain's village was eight thousand. Now it is nearly 20,000, all of them Moslems. The Army has emptied the mountains around it, liquidated the isolated *mechtas* (hamlets) and forced the peasants to bring their families to the village. A new community of squat, windowless structures of pressed earth, odd wooden planks and sheets of corrugated iron, sackcloth and straw mats has risen on the edge of the old village with its old but solid stone houses. This new community is what the Army calls a *regroupement*.

The Army has "regrouped" about two million Moslems or about a fifth of the Moslem population of Algeria. "Regrouping" is an essential part of the methods of "revolutionary warfare" which the Army has devised to meet the nationalist rebels on their own ground.

The theory of "revolutionary warfare" stems from the writings of Mao Tse-tung. It was practiced by the Communists in Indochina, where the French adopted and adapted it for their own use as the only possible answer to rebel strategy. The theory holds that the rebels need the support of the civilian population "as a fish needs water." Without it, they would be without food, shelter, clothes and information about the Army's moves. By the same token, the theory holds, the civilians start to live only if they are protected against the rebels' political commissars, tax collectors, recruiting agents and plain terrorists.

Finally, the theory continues, it takes all-pervading "psychological action" by the Army to restore the health of the civilian population once the process of subversion by the rebels has begun.

Thus the Army has adopted three commandments: The civilian population must be "protected," "engaged" and "controlled." To this end, it has developed a complex machinery for getting a total hold on the civilians through *regroupements,* self-defense units, re-education camps for brain-washing, networks of informers, sports teams, needlework groups for women, hospitals, schools and a vast general propaganda program.

Captain de V. believes in the necessity of "revolutionary warfare" and "psychological action." Like almost all officers in Algeria, he is convinced that the French Army here is the last bastion of Western civilization.

French officers here are in turn angry and deeply hurt that France's allies do not see them as they see themselves, as the last crusaders against communism. Mindful of the failure of the United States to support France fully in the U. N. debate on Algeria, Captain de V. says, *"Eh, non,* we didn't bear you in our hearts when you let us down."

One of his junior officers put it differently. "Well, how are things in Little Rock this morning?" he likes to ask the American visitor. For the only thing these officers resent more than the allied "betrayal" is the charge, or implied charge, of racism.

Frequently they will say, with mock admiration: "You were smart, of course. You solved your problem when you killed off your Indians. We pampered our Moslems and now we have ten million of them on our hands."

The worshipers emerging from the early mass at Algiers Cathedral the other Sunday included a famous general, a bevy of colonels and captains wearing the red or green berets of the paratroopers and scores of less conspicuous officers and men. They filed past the Tommy-gun-carrying police sentries who guard the church and, like the rest of the congregation, lingered in the sun-lit Moorish square to shake hands with neighbors and bow to the priest.

The spectacle is the same every Sunday morning at almost every church. The French Army in Algeria is a praying army.

Gen. Jacques Massu, whose removal from command touched off the abortive extremist uprising last January, is a devout and ardent church-goer. Most of the regimental commanders of the Tenth Paratroop Division, Massu's old outfit, which has fought some of the most merciless campaigns of the war and which fraternized with the extremists during the uprising, are equally strict in the observance of their religious obligations.

The Army's interest in religion is one of the many things that have combined to turn this total and "dirty" war into a bitter conflict of conscience.

Officers like Captain de V. are well aware of this. The captain speaks with relative serenity of summary military justice, arbitrary arrest and even torture, because, he says, his "conscience is clear— as clear at least as that of any police captain in Chicago or Birmingham."

He is trying as faithfully as he can to keep the war "clean" in his sector. And he relates how some time ago he had to detach an officer to keep an eye on a unit of the D. O. P. *(Détachement Operationnel de Protection),* a kind of military police and intelligence agency, which entered his sector. Moslem civilians had complained to him that people were unaccountably missing and that others had been brutally mistreated.

"Those are the boys who pull the rough stuff," he says of the D. O. P. And he adds: "It's always the guy from outside, from another neck of the woods, who commits the crimes, never the one who stays in an area. It's true of the rebel side, too."

In spite of his efforts the captain has no illusions about some things happening under his command that he isn't proud of. This kind of war is a tremendous emotional strain for every man and officer, he says.

"You are combing the mountains day and night—for nothing.

It takes a company to hunt down one man, and maybe miss him. Then you see some shepherds and you ask them questions. They haven't seen or heard a thing, and they grin. And so there is that wall again. And how do you expect a man to keep his temper all the time? One night he is going to lash out at the wrong people."

The captain knows that since General de Gaulle's return to power both civilian and military authorities have been looking for means to end all practice of torture by the Army. He thinks they have made some headway, but not very much.

There has been a suggestion, rejected in the end, to relieve the Army of the "dirty work" and create a special agency for it. He scoffs at the hypocrisy of the idea. And he says he is afraid that certain types of reprisals—immediate execution of a terrorist caught throwing a bomb into a Sunday crowd, for instance, and exhibition of his body in the public square—are indispensable weapons at times in this war.

The captain knows about the letter sent some while ago to the French College of Bishops by a number of Catholic priests who were serving their terms as reserve officers in Algeria.

The priests wrote that the war was fought with "means which our conscience reproves" and that interrogations too often were made with what "we must classify as 'tortures.' " They warned that these practices might haunt young officers and men in their later lives either as moral corruption or as unbearable conflicts of conscience.

The captain is aware of such dangers. He has heard that at Maillot, the military hospital of Algiers, and in various hospitals of the mainland, an increasing number of young officers, veterans of Algeria, are being treated for nervous disorders.

Captain de V. and his like are able to talk dispassionately about this side of the war only if they do not feel they are being attacked. Let a Paris newspaper or an American politician or an African delegate to the United Nations talk about "French tortures" and they will explode.

"We are no angels, and things will happen in a war," they will say. "But if one of our guys is quick on the trigger or touches a woman or kills a man, he is abominated. He becomes an outcast even to his friends and buddies. Not so on the other side. They kill. They cut the throats of a family, their own Moslem families, down to the children and the baby in the crib and the family dog. And then they proclaim the killer a national hero and make speeches about him and issue communiqués about his achievements.

"That's the difference. And you invite them into your palaces in New York and Washington. That's what we don't understand."

No one is able to predict what "the Army" will do if Algeria ceases to be French. Some of the officers were close to the European extremists in the abortive January uprising. Yet, at the same time, some powerful commanders quietly gathered the men and the means to intervene in Algiers and to save the Republic not only from the civilian extremists but, if necessary, also from the extremists in their own ranks. Some officers would not hesitate to march on Paris if they thought they could take it; others, fearing chaos and civil war, would hesitate and, in the end, obey the Government.

Immediately after the insurrection, a representative officer said: "The Army has obeyed this time, after pondering its moral obligations for a day or two. It is glad it did. But if there are more broken promises and if the threat of a sell-out is raised again— well, I wouldn't take the Army for granted then."

As Chanzeaux Sees the French Crisis

by Laurence Wylie

THE TOWN clerk and the constable were trying to explain the implications of the local vote in the last elections, and inevitably this led to a discussion of personalities. For all villagers the discussion of personalities is a major sport, but it is in bad taste for public officials to sit in the Town Hall and analyze the citizens' political behavior, so we dropped the subject. I tried a less personal opening.

"How will Chanzeaux vote in the referendum?"

The clerk did not have to ponder this question: "You know Chanzeaux. You know what we say about de Gaulle. You can answer that one yourself."

Given Chanzeaux and given de Gaulle, the answer did seem obvious, and if Chanzeaux felt the way it did, then many other rural communities of France would feel the same way. I had chosen to make a study of Chanzeaux precisely because it is a representative community in its region. Now that I had lived there with my family for ten months I knew that beneath traditional labels and slogans it had much in common with the village where we had lived in the opposite corner of France.

Chanzeaux is in the Maine-et-Loire Department, about a six-hour drive from Paris, in western France. Of its 1,200 inhabitants about 300 live in the *bourg,* the village in the center of the commune. The 900 others live in isolated farmhouses or in the ten hamlets scattered through the countryside. There is a little basket factory owned by Monsieur Nicolas, the Mayor, but most of the people make their living by farming.

In the northern end of the commune, where the land slopes down to the Layon River, there are rich vineyards that produce some of the sweet white wine sold in Paris bars to men who order *"un coup de blanc d'Anjou."* On the plateau, at the other end of the commune, the farmers raise cattle for both meat and milk, and their crops are all for fodder—hay, oats, fodder cabbage, fodder beets. On the rest of the land a wide variety of crops is grown—wheat, camomile, potatoes, tobacco, seed pansies. By the variety of its economy Chanzeaux mirrors the economy of rural France.

Chanzeaux's distinction is in its history. It was one of the counter-revolutionary centers from which the Vendée War spread in 1793. The Catholic, conservative tradition is still strong, but in the last fifty years there has been a silent revolution. Inflation, a growing taste for city life, the fragmentation of the land through inheritance have weakened the domination of the nobles and left the land and the power in the hands of the farmers themselves. They no longer bow low to *M'sieu' notr' maîtr'.* Instead, they pity the poor noble who slaves at his business in the city in order to make money to keep the old château from falling apart.

When one settles in a rural community one is tempted to judge the whole community by the people living in the *bourg.* This is inevitable because contact with the villagers is easy and natural, but it is difficult to meet the farmers. Only after months does one make friends with enough country people to know really what life on the farms is like. It is essential, however, not to judge the farmers by what one knows of the villagers. The two groups share many ideals and attitudes, but the economic problems they face today are quite different.

As an administrative and spiritual center the *bourg* has a real function, but economically it is becoming obsolete. Farmers have cars and motorbikes, and the little city of Chemillé is only seven miles away. Angers is not much farther. Instead of shopping in the village of Chanzeaux the farmers do their errands in the city when they go to sell their cattle or eggs or butter at the weekly market. Country women also buy from the grocery trucks that drive out of the cities and crisscross the countryside, stopping at every farmhouse. There is little business left for the merchants of Chanzeaux.

Most of the artisans work at crafts that are dying out. M. Cesbron, the wooden shoemaker, retired several years ago, but he cannot even sell the stock he has left. Rubber boots and factory-made plastic sabots have taken the place of wooden shoes. M. Martin, the tinsmith, does not have enough work because people use so many plastic buckets and pans. M. Ragneau, the cabinet-maker, used to make the furniture for the young ménages in the commune. Now the young people prefer to buy ready-made furniture in Angers.

Our landlord, M. Boussion, was the harness maker, and he still has as much business as he can handle. Most of the farm work is done by horses, although since the Marshall Plan brought the first tractor to the commune the number has increased to twenty-three. When I asked M. Boussion what he intended to do with our house when we left, he said he would like to live in it himself if only he could retire.

"What keeps you from retiring?"

"I've looked everywhere for someone to take over my work," he said. "There aren't any apprentices any more. What boy wants to become a harness maker today?"

"So what's the answer?"

"I'll keep going as long as I can and then shut up the shop. There's nothing else to do."

The only artisans with a future are those who have been able to roll with the technological blow. M. Mosset started his career as a blacksmith but gradually gave that up to repair bicycles—and now motorbikes. His older son has become the electrician for the commune, and the next son is learning electronics in the army.

The other people living in the village are mostly public officials —the clerk, the constable, the postmen, the teachers, the priest— and retired people. Needless to say, this part of the population has been hit extremely hard by inflation. M. Durand, for instance, once owned the village cafe and hotel. His business was prosperous, but in the late Nineteen Thirties his health began to fail. He was told that he had to drink less.

"I didn't mind cutting down on wine," says M. Durand, "but I knew this meant the end of my business. You can't run an inn if you aren't ready to drink with your customers when they ask you."

So he sold out. Today the value of the money he received is less than a twentieth of what it was in 1938, and he can scarcely make ends meet. Fortunately, he did not sell his little vineyard and fortunately he is still able to work it himself.

"But it's hard at my age," he says. "My vines are a kilometer away from the village, uphill, downhill. I had to trade in my bicycle and get a woman's bike so I wouldn't have to swing my leg over. I have to rest a lot, but I get the work done. I've got to."

"Don't you have a pension?"

"My retired worker's pension, but that's not enough. Too bad I wasn't wounded in the first war. I'd been called up for maneuvers a month before it started and went through the whole thing down to Armistice Day without a scratch. I thought I was lucky then, but if I'd gotten a little wound I'd be getting a pension for that."

As a whole, then, the villagers are economically a rather depressed group. On meeting them you would not realize this because they are cordial, almost gay people. M. Cesbron cannot sell his wooden shoes, and he is going blind from cataracts, but his conversation is sprightly. Mme. Cimon's grocery is losing money, but as she gossips with her occasional customers their conversation is not gloomy.

It is when the Government is mentioned that the bitterness emerges, because it is the Government the villagers blame for the taxes and inflation to which they attribute their ruin. When Pierre Poujade started his anti-tax revolt many of the Chanzeaux villagers thought he might bring a solution to their problems. Now they have lost faith in him, but they are still ready for a change.

Traditionally the farmers as a group complain more than the villagers, but today they have far less reason to complain, for they are relatively well-off. M. Robineau can serve as a good example of the average Chanzeaux farmer. I met him when he brought us a load of wood for our fireplace, but I did not know him well until we took a walk one night. He had invited me to go with him to the cattle market, and one day in early June he sent word that we would go the following Thursday.

I arrived at his house at 1:30 in the morning. We had breakfast, drove four steers out of the barn and started down the road. His two sons went with us, and a neighbor, who was driving a cow to market, joined us a mile down the road. With the five of us the task was simple. The neighbor walked ahead to make sure the road was clear. The boys walked on either side to keep the steers from going into the fields. Robineau and I walked behind to see that they did not turn back. It was a beautiful night. Chemillé was seven miles away. All Robineau and I had to do was follow the cattle and talk.

"I should have sold them last week," he said. "With this Algerian business they've never brought a better price."

"Well, for once you farmers can't complain."

Robineau said nothing for a few steps. Then he answered: "There's no denying it. We've never been so well off. We run the land and our business as we like. My land still belongs to a noble, but I haven't seen her for years, and her agent comes around only to collect the rent. She doesn't modernize the property, but then I pay less rent because of it."

"But all of you complain that taxes take away your profits."

"Of course, taxes are too high. It's the Algerian business. But still the Government gives us lots of breaks."

He went on to point out that farmers pay less in taxes than any other economic class. The Government banking agency supplies ample credit at reasonable rates. Tariffs have protected key products. Farmers receive coupons so that they may buy gas more cheaply for their tractors. All sorts of advisory services are available, so that farmers may increase their production. Cooperatives are not taxed like ordinary businesses, and the farmers of Chanzeaux buy most of their equipment at the best possible prices. Its cost has gone up, but they pay for it with the inflated money they receive for their products.

"But what do you farmers do with all this money you make?"

This is not a question you can usually ask a farmer—or anyone. But when two men are walking together in the middle of the night they talk more freely. Still, Robineau answered at such length, in such detail, so indirectly and technically that I had only a vague idea of what he was saying—which was perhaps what he wished. He reads the government bulletins and the financial pages of the newspapers carefully, and he has definite ideas about the relative advantages of investing in gold or gold louis or stocks or bonds or land. Gold and government bonds guaranteed against inflation seemed to interest him most. M. Robineau is certainly making money and putting it aside.

So is M. Caillau. He is a wine grower, and normally the wine growers are even more prosperous than the other farmers. Along with all the other vintners of France, however, Caillau is experiencing a temporary squeeze. For the last two years a spring freeze has decimated the harvest, and his financial reserves are low. Of course, there was some compensation in the fact that the price of wine rose steeply, but now to force the price down the Government has imported quantities of wine from Spain and Greece. What M. Caillau says about this measure is not fit to print. However, his 1958 wine will be plentiful and of good quality, it appears, so that he feels his worries are temporary.

The fact that the farmers of Chanzeaux are prosperous does not mean that they have no problems. They have serious problems. Their equipment is not sufficiently modernized. Living conditions on the farm are often inconvenient and unsanitary. There is a shortage of labor, and at the same time farmers complain that their children are forced to work in the city because there is no land for them to farm. Roads need improvement. Hedges should be torn out and fields enlarged. One of the most desperate problems is the fragmentation of property, which prevents efficient use of the land.

However, the farmers have lived with the problems a long time and do not feel their urgency. The prosperity of the farmers today makes them economically as satisfied a group of people as the villagers are dissatisfied.

Still, there is a preoccupation shared by all the people in the commune so acute that it dominates every other consideration. It increases the bitterness of the villagers, and it outweighs the contentment of the farmers. The people of Chanzeaux are utterly exasperated with sending their sons to Algeria to die or to risk dying for a cause which seemed hopeless until de Gaulle took over last spring.

On Candlemas some boys asked me to take a group picture of them. After mass the class of 1958—that is, the boys who were going to be drafted in 1958—passed the *baton* to the class of 1959. After the traditional ceremony the younger men went off to the wine cellar belonging to one of their fathers. The class of 1958 ordered two bottles of wine in the cafe, filled the ten glasses put before them and sat glumly around the big table. Gérard Audiau had already passed his physical and would leave as their twentieth birthdays arrived.

"Algeria . . . Hmmmm!" Jean Oger made a motion of a knife being twisted into his ribs.

"Stop it, Oger," Audiau said.

"What's the matter? Are you afraid?"

"Sure, aren't you?"

"Just as your ancestors must have been afraid when they climbed the church tower and fired on the Blues," I suggested.

"At least they had something to fight for," said Lelu. "They had religion. And what have we got? Oil! Money in the pocket of someone in Paris."

"Don't think I wouldn't die for religion," Oger said, "but I don't see what religion has to do with this business."

At this moment Louis Mosset came by the table, overheard the conversation and stopped. He is 23 and has already put in his two years in Algeria.

"You've got France to fight for, and if that's not enough you'll find a good reason when you get down there. Wait until your best friend is killed beside you. Then you'll catch on. You'll want to kill every damned Algerian you see." Mosset walked off to join his own group.

"Now there's a noble reason to fight—personal revenge," said Lelu sarcastically. "No, the only reason I can see is that if we give up we'll feel ashamed, the way we did after Indochina. . . . No, there must be a change anyway!"

There must be a change! That is what everyone said. They might disagree on what the change should be, but they knew there had to be a change. The atmosphere was like that of the summer of 1939 when everyone was saying, "There must be an end to it." And, of course, things have changed. When the blow-up came and de Gaulle intervened, the people of Chanzeaux welcomed him with a tremendous feeling of relief. The vagueness of his intentions permitted wide interpretation, so the enthusiasm was unanimous. Or almost, since there are a dozen or so Communists in the commune. Everyone else felt that de Gaulle offered the only hope in a situation that had seemed hopeless.

For the *Fête-Dieu* (Corpus Christi) the community prepares a half-mile carpet of flower petals and colored sawdust arranged in a series of religious emblems and designs over which the priest carries *le bon Dieu* in the procession. M. Horeau, the blacksmith, was going to make de Gaulle's profile and the Lorraine Cross in flower petals in front of his house. After much discussion the neighbors persuaded him not to. The mixture of politics and religion seemed inappropriate. They consoled him, however, by making it clear that they shared his enthusiasm.

How will Chanzeaux vote in the September referendum? Obviously for de Gaulle. But the constitution itself? Are the people for it or against it? "A good farmer can make a living with a horse and a plow," says Robineau, "and a poor farmer can go broke with a tractor."

The people of Chanzeaux hope the new constitution will be a tractor run by a good farmer, but the man is more important than the machine. When men fail their mechanisms fail. The failure of the Fourth Republic is blamed more on the men who formed the Government than on the constitution of the Fourth Republic. If the Fifth Republic succeeds, it will be because of the men running it. No one knows who they will be, but the people of Chanzeaux believe they have nothing to lose in a change. For the present, at least, there is de Gaulle. Their vote in the referendum will be a vote of confidence for him.

In its attitude toward de Gaulle and the referendum, Chanzeaux is no exception among the thousands of rural communes in France. Normally these communities are turned against each other politically by the traditional conflicts that have arisen in the course of history, that are complicated by each new national crisis and that are perpetuated partly by the political parties themselves. Today, as at other points in French history, the people of the villages of France are united by an anguish so acute that the divisive influence of the old labels and slogans is no longer effective. The people of all rural France, except for those of the extreme Right and extreme Left, will vote for the same reason and in the same sense as the people of Chanzeaux.

Whether the new constitution will foster this sense of unity is another question. The tragedy of French politics—as with politics anywhere—is that the traditional labels and slogans keep old fears so stirred up that the deeper causes for unity are overlooked. We went to live in Chanzeaux so that we might be able to compare it with the village of Peyrane in the Vaucluse Department, about fifty miles north of Marseilles.

Peyrane has always been a community of the Left, as Chanzeaux is traditionally to the Right. The elected representatives of the districts in which these villages are situated are consistently at each other's throats in the Chamber of Deputies. One might assume that the people of the two villages are basically antagonistic to each other. This is not true. The people of Chanzeaux and those of Peyrane are not really very different. If their representatives could leave off fighting old battles, which have little real meaning for the people today, they might discover that the basic interests of the communities are very close.

In Chanzeaux M. Aligon votes Independent, and M. Robineau probably votes M. R. P. In Peyrane M. Pelloux votes Socialist and M. Tamisier, Socialist-Radical. Their deputies in Paris have, to cite an example, perpetuated the battle over the relationships of church schools to the state, so that this problem is no nearer settlement than when it arose 125 years ago. M. Robineau, Aligon, Pelloux and Tamisier could reach an agreement on this divisive issue in a morning's conference and then they could go to the cafe and enjoy a bottle of wine together.

Once the old slogans are put aside, these men have no quarrel with each other, they agree on what is right and what is wrong, what is fair and unfair in human behavior. They share a common dream about the sort of life they would like to lead. They have much the same attitude toward their families and their communities. They face the same economic problems and could easily agree on means to solve them. Above all, they are far more tolerant and reasonable in religious and political matters than their elected representatives.

De Gaulle believes that by reducing the influence of the political parties he may weaken the traditional distrust which they perpetuate. This will certainly help, but a mere political solution is not enough in itself to liberate the essential unity of the people so that it may become a constructive force. There are many other forces, especially in the opinion-forming institutions of the country that perpetuate traditional quarrels. If de Gaulle is to succeed, he must seek reconciliation at all levels.

The danger is, of course, that in his drive for unity de Gaulle may destroy the freedom of expression of these institutions and the individual citizens. The people of Chanzeaux and Peyrane are aware of this danger. M. Durand says, "If he becomes dictator, we're finished. Louis XIV, two Napoleons, Pétain! Dictators mean disaster." But again, the distress of the Algerian situation overrides every other fear. M. Durand will still vote for the new constitution —that is, for de Gaulle—and hope for the best.

French Dilemma:
How Strong a Man?

by Robert C. Doty

PARIS

FRENCHMEN ARE engaged today in a new phase of their 300-year-old struggle to strike political equilibrium between authority and weak but representative government. From the absolute control of the 17th-century monarchy down to the incoherence and impotence of the closing days of the Fourth Republic in 1958, the pendulum has swung at least half a dozen times without ever coming to rest on a durable solution.

At one extreme, it produced a series of strong men—Louis XIV, Napoleon I, Napoleon III, Clemenceau, Pétain, Charles de Gaulle —to whom, for a time, France turned over her destinies. There were others who aspired to the strong man role but never quite made it—Preisident Patrice MacMahon in the eighteen-seventies and the tragicomic Gen. Georges Boulanger, a decade later.

These men brought France both moments of intoxicating glory and of black despair. In the cases of all but Clemenceau—because he worked within the republican framework—and de Gaulle— because his story is not finished—the periods of strong rule ended

From the *New York Times Magazine,* October 28, 1962, copyright ©
1962 by The New York Times Company.

only with the death of the strong man or a great national disaster that brought him down.

At the other end of the swing, the pendulum has brought periods of government—the Great Revolution and the Terror, restoration kings and Second, Third and Fourth Republics—marked, at best, by instability and, at worst, by anarchy.

It is against this background of three centuries of unsuccessful experimentation that the current struggle between President de Gaulle and the traditional political forces of the country is now being played out. The issue on the surface is comparatively simple. The President wants to amend the Constitution so that his eventual successor will be elected by popular suffrage instead of by a limited college of some 80,000 "notables" who represent and are controlled by the party organization as specified in the Constitution.

De Gaulle seeks to do this by appealing directly to the voters in a referendum being held today, instead of risking having his project blocked in the Senate if he were to choose the method defined by the Constitution for amendment—submission to Parliament. The pros and cons of this proposal are being endlessly debated across all of France. The debate recalls the historical sources of France's alternate fear of and fascination with the strong man, and suggests an assessment of the extent to which de Gaulle conforms to the classic figure of the strong man and an estimate as to whether fear or fascination is uppermost in French minds today.

The strong man has always been more popular with the masses, from whom he draws his strength, than with the normal political cadres of the country—whether nobles, party leaders, economic interests or social and professional organizations—which he largely displaces. The strong man's opportunity comes always with the decline of the efficacy and prestige of these traditional forces of leadership.

But if strong men find their opportunity in failure, they themselves are condemned to perpetual success. So long as they are winning, they are almost invulnerable. But let them once slip—at Waterloo, at Sedan—and the personal prestige on which their power is exclusively built is destroyed irrevocably. The contract they made with the apolitical masses to conduct their public affairs in such a way as to relieve the masses of direct concern with them is dramatically broken. And the masses turn on them unmercifully.

This is a fragility that the cabinet governments of the party system do not share. Socialist Premier Guy Mollet survived the disaster of his Suez Canal expedition in 1956 by more than six months because responsibility for the unsuccessful policy was diffused in the Cabinet-Assembly system of government. And when he fell it was on a matter completely divorced from the Suez affair.

In the bright light that beats upon a strong man there is no place to hide. The major decisions, the rewards of success, the responsibility for failure—and the punishment for it—all are his and his alone.

De Gaulle, in his imperious contempt for lesser men and notably politicians, in his impatience with opposition, in his reliance on "direct democracy"—referendum and plebiscite—to the virtual exclusion of traditional intermediaries, conforms in many respects to the characteristics of previous French strong men. Debate today centers on the question of whether he can escape the historical forces that pushed his predecessors along the fatal course to full dictatorship.

The debate is complicated by the tendency of Frenchmen—at least those of the political cadres—to draw excessively on precedent. All the history France has lived through has strewn the ground with political clichés and personal stereotypes. When a Frenchman of the political élite is discussing current events he reaches almost instinctively for a historical parallel and is not really happy unless he finds one.

The tacit threat of military intervention that brought de Gaulle back to power in 1958 is automatically likened to a new 18 Brumaire, the date of Napoleon's first coup against the Parliament of the Directory a century and a half before. And, of course, in the current political struggle, the traditional parties are campaigning at least as much against Louis XIV, the two Emperors Napoleon and even General Boulanger as they are against President de Gaulle.

However convenient this type of political shorthand may be, it also has its disadvantages. The application of historical references to current events tends to evoke, often with specious logic, not only the old event itself but a whole set of automatic emotional reactions to its context.

Thus, the conditions—of public education, of communications, of economic and social structure—that made it possible for Napoleon III to impose himself no longer exist. The people to whom de Gaulle turns for support in periodic referendums are in every way better informed and more politically sophisticated than was the electorate a century ago.

And yet, when Senate President Gaston Monnerville brands de Gaulle's policy as "enlightened Bonapartism" he stirs Pavlovian reactions of hostility in French republican breasts.

Former Premier Pierre Mendès-France presses on the same nerve when he writes in his current survey of French affairs.

"If Louis Napoleon, a century ago, and de Gaulle in our day, crushed the Assembly, it is not by chance. It is because their system [of personal power] leads directly to it."

But shortly after Mendès-France wrote those words the "crushed" French Assembly rose up and defeated the Gaullist Government of Premier Georges Pompidou. The President responded, as is his constitutional right, by dissolving the Assembly and turning the issues over to the voters to arbitrate in new legislative elections. This would appear to be reasonably democratic procedure.

But here, too, historical precedents come into play to cloud the issues. In 1877 the monarchist President Patrice MacMahon dissolved the Chamber of Deputies to rid himself of what was deemed a too republican majority and seek election of a more royalist chamber. Because of the obviously partisan nature of this precedent, dissolution of Parliament fell into permanent disrepute although it remained among the rights of governments of both the Third and Fourth Republics. Successive Presidents and Premiers preferred to struggle with chambers in which no stable governing majority existed rather than to incur the odium of imitating MacMahon.

When, in 1955, Radical Premier Edgar Faure at last revived the dissolution procedure after his defeat in the National Assembly, he won disapproval for not "playing the game"; it still haunts him and his political career. Similarly, de Gaulle's use of the threat of dissolution and appeal to the voters to get his way with Parliament for the past four years is one of the principal sources of his unpopularity with the parties and their leaders.

But, as yet, it appears that the fear that de Gaulle is leading France toward outright dictatorship, under either himself or his eventual successor, is limited to the political circles of the country —the so-called *pays légal*—the "legal country." In the *pays réel*— the "real country"—soundings intimate that his popularity remains high. The researchers of so anti-Gaullist a journal as the weekly L'Express returned from studies in five representative sections of the country concluding, with resignation, that de Gaulle would again carry the day with the masses.

With these ordinary voters subtle evocations of the Napoleons, of the violation of the constitutional amendment procedure by de Gaulle, weighed little. The reporters for L'Express found that the most oft-repeated sentiments were that de Gaulle, after all, was *propre*—meaning, approximately clean and correct in his dealings —whereas the parties—*eh bien,* the parties were that old tangle of feuding ambitions that had landed France in the soup before.

This is really the heart of the matter. To the average voter there just is no satisfactory substitute for de Gaulle on the scene. Regardless of their personal merits—which in many cases are notable —the political leaders of the opposition still symbolize a return to the weaknesses and humiliations of the Fourth Republic. As most observers read public opinion, the voters are far more afraid of that possibility than of the risk that de Gaulle or a successor in the Presidency might turn France into a dictatorship.

So strong is this revulsion against the old regime that not a single responsible voice is raised to defend it. Even the men who used to operate its shaky controls now deny with indignation Gaullist charges that they wish to taste again "the delights and poisons" of the sovereign-Assembly system.

The party leaders, despite their temporary and fragile unanimity and the support of most of the intelligentsia and provincial political personnel, have an uphill fight in opposing de Gaulle.

In the first place, they have been able to unite effectively only against something, as they used to do in overthrowing governments of the Fourth Republic. But, thus far, they have been unable to get together on a positive program to oppose de Gaulle's.

Secondly, their arguments against the strong man and his current initiative are sophisticated and juridical. The President's arguments are simple and direct.

The parties would be in a far easier position if they dared openly oppose the very idea of a strong executive. But, embarassed by the record of the Assembly regime and aware of a current of opinion favorable to strength at the top, they must concentrate their fire on what, to the average voter, are relatively abstruse considerations.

They must say, for example: "We are for a strong government but against personal power"; "We approve the principle of popular suffrage and sovereignty but the way de Gaulle proposes to bring it into play is dangerous, unsound and unconstitutional."

There is every reason to believe that the professions of reform by the old-line leaders are sincere. They *do* believe in the necessity for a strong executive and they *do* believe the one de Gaulle outlines would be dangerously overbalanced in the direction of strong man rule. But it is hard to make the voters believe it.

It is child's play for Gaullist propaganda to convince the voters that what the parties really mean by their position is: "We want to get back to the good old days of revolving-door governments where every man could at least hope to be a minister"; and: "You, the voters, are just intelligent enough to elect the Deputies but cannot be trusted to choose wisely a President of the Republic."

At the same time, the President is shamelessly blackmailing the country by threatening to resign if he does not get the massive support of the voters in today's referendum. In contrast to the subtleties of the party position, he is able to say to the voters, with simple flattery, looking each in the eye from the television screen: "I ask you, very simply, to decide that, from now on, you will elect your President by universal suffrage."

What could be more appealing than to vote "yes" and thereby affirm one's own status as citizen-arbiter and, at the same time, keep the President from resigning and casting the future into uncertainty? For it is true—unfortunately, from the viewpoint of the parties—that de Gaulle's withdrawal from the scene would leave a void that might be filled by chaos. Technically, Gaston Monnerville, President of the Senate and a leader of the opposition to the President's plan, would become interim President of the Republic until new elections could be held not later than 40 days after the vacancy. Depending on the referendum results, these would be held either by universal suffrage or with the limited college of "notables."

In either case, a vacancy of power would provide a tempting opportunity for some of the really sinister forces lurking just off-stage—the Fascist-minded elements in the army, the remnants of the Secret Army Organization of uprooted Europeans from Algeria and the classic extreme right that has always existed in France. It would require fast, effective coalition action by the traditional "republican" forces—faster and more effective action than they have demonstrated in the past—to close the door to a coup d'état.

Against the simple, deadly appeal of such argument, the political leaders struggle in anger and frustration. Furthermore, as individuals they are badly overmatched.

Paul Reynaud is a lucid, intelligent man who, at 84, has the vigor of one 20 years younger. His arguments against the Gaullist regime are cogent and well documented. But he is also the victim of his own stereotype. He is the Premier who presided over the downfall of France in 1940, a downfall prepared largely by those who preceded him in power, but with which his public image is irrevocably tarnished. A battle for public confidence between de Gaulle and Reynaud is clearly no contest.

Guy Mollet is a high-minded Socialist, devoted democrat, intensely "European" and "Atlantic" in his outlook. He, too, inveighs brilliantly against the perils of personal power. But for the average citizen Mollet is still the Premier who was in office when the Algerian rebellion took several turns for the worse, whose Government sponsored the Suez disaster and left the state considerably worse off financially than it found it. Again, a mismatch with de Gaulle.

So it is, too, with most of the other leaders of anti-Gaullism—a Félix Gaillard, whose brilliance as a financial expert was incapable of checking the Fourth Republic's slide toward bankruptcy; the coldly intellectual Mendès-France, whose career has been spent in denouncing the weaknesses of the old regime as vigorously as have the Gaullists but who, fairly or unfairly, must remain identified with it in the popular mind; a Maurice Faure, relatively untarred, personally, with the failures of the Fourth Republic, but president of a party—the Radical Socialists—that was the very epitome of all that was compromising and uninspiring about it.

In the simple—the oversimple—judgments of the average Frenchman, these men, collectively, represent failure, while de Gaulle represents success; they stand for the divisions of a multiplicity of doctrinaire parties, de Gaulle for unity and a regrouping of political forces into big formations capable of operating a Presidential system.

Not even the ghosts of the two Napoleons are likely to reverse that assessment now.

A New Revolution Transforms France

by Stephen R. Graubard

FRANCE IS IN the midst of a major revolution. The absence of violence conceals the extent of the change, but those who know the country best understand that this is not the France they knew immediately after Hitler's defeat or even the one which they recognized as recently as 1955. In political life, as in everything else, the pre-1939 world seems strangely remote. The historian, looking back at the French 1962 Parliamentary elections in which Charles de Gaulle's party won an absolute majority in the past fortnight, will be impressed by the calm which characterized the nation in what was supposed to be a critical time. He will be struck by the number of men and women who refused to become excited, who absented themselves from the polls and who did not believe they were living at a historic moment, privileged to choose between the forces of order and disorder, between freedom and autocracy. The specter of another Napoleon III obviously did not haunt very many.

Perhaps the election experience will be viewed as one more evidence of the fact that old-fashioned French party politics is dead, having no more relevance to today's political situation than is offered by 19th-century armaments in the military sphere or traditional diplomatic methods in the relations that exist between France and her neighbors. France has a new opinion of itself, as it does of Europe and the rest of the world. In its relations with Germany there is revealed a spirit which no Frenchman, now alive, recognizes as issuing from the past. A new generation is coming to the fore, and there is little to suggest that it is prepared to accept the values of those who were middle-aged in 1939. Economically and socially, France is experiencing a change as great as any she has ever known. The change is affecting all classes—in the way they think as much as in the way they live. This is a revolution in everything but name. All the traditional caricatures about France seem suddenly dated.

In the sphere of foreign policy the revolution is at once apparent. The French are no longer frightened of Germany. It is not that they trust Adenauer; they did not flock to see him as the Germans did to see de Gaulle on his triumphal tour last summer. Their feeling about Germany and Europe is indeed very complex. In the present world, France is simply not large enough to mean anything by herself; she can realize herself only in and through Europe.

In one way or another, this idea is expressed by almost all who talk in anything but the old clichés. France is excited by Europe; she is curious to know it; she is even prepared to help invent the myths which will make it real for those who cannot yet feel its presence.

The French businessman who tells you that he is prepared to accept France as a province of Europe does not imagine that he is making an extraordinary concession to some abstract metaphysical or historical entity. Europe is real for him—and not in the old pre-World War I sense, in which Europe existed as a group of independent and rival nations, and the Government urged him, for patriotic reasons, to buy Russians bonds as a way of checking the German menace.

Those who search for the symbol of today's revolution a century hence may choose to find it in the automobile. Before the Second World War, the French bourgeois lived in Paris or in the country, and ventured forth each summer to "rest" in the country with a parent, a sister or some other close relation. The worker spent his brief holiday in the village from which he had come, or at the shore. The peasant remained on the land; there was no one available to take over for him. Travel abroad, except for the rich or the well-educated, was uncommon.

The nation was quite satisfied to know itself; nothing more seemed to be necessary. With this provincialism went other habits which cut across class lines. The French did not think it necessary to learn modern foreign languages; anyone who chose to visit France was expected to know French and to use it. Foreign books were sometimes translated; there was no great sale for those which were not. The United States was a world away; one neither went there nor thought overly much about it. The supremacy of French civilization was taken for granted. Events at home commanded the interest of the country; for most Frenchmen, there were no others.

Trade with overseas French territories was extensive, and in many foreign markets the products of particular French craft industries knew no rivals. The French Empire gave the country an interest in Africa and Asia, and this circumstance made France, or at least Paris, a major world center. The object, however, was always to export the French language, and with it the distinctive culture based on its use.

While it would be a serious mistake to suggest that all this is now changed, there can be no question but that these qualities no longer define even approximately the French nation. A lawyer's son, aged 20, tells you that he has visited Italy and Spain many times; he spent July and August with a family in Sussex to perfect his English; last Christmas he skied in Austria; this coming Easter he plans to go to Greece. Next summer, if all works out well, he will be going to America on a charter flight. What does he hope to see? New York and Mexico.

Conversations like this are standard in Paris today. More surprising, perhaps, is the talk of a mason, a master of his craft, and not a young man, who lives outside Chartres. The summer is too busy a time for him or for any of his employes to be absent. However, by law, his workers are entitled to three weeks of paid vacation, and he now regularly gives them four. "After all, monsieur," he says, "the workers in the large factories are given a month during the summer. Why, then, should my own have less, particularly when they take their vacations in the autumn or winter? Those with young children are inconvenienced because of school but the others like to be away when the hotels are un-crowded and when prices are less high. In any case, all seasons are made for travel."

Why so much talk about travel and vacations? Are they of such consequence to the ordinary people of France? The answer, very simply, is yes. Europe is no longer an abstraction for a great part of the French people. They have seen it—Milan, with its sky-scrapers; Vienna, with its baroque monuments; Amsterdam, with its quiet canals. The automobile—four years ago, a simple 2-horsepower model for those of modest means; today, a rather more elaborate affair—has given a freedom inconceivable before the war to any but the rich. It carries ordinary people to distant and hitherto unknown places. "Europe is remarkable, monsieur; not a dying continent at all, but alive and healthy." These are the words of a worker whose father never traveled 300 miles from the place where he was born.

It would be a mistake, however, to imagine that French interest is wholly consumed by the discovery of the outside world. There is too much happening within France for such a topic to dominate.

France, for the first time since 1914, has a normal complement of young people. When it is realized that one of every two French-men between the ages of 20 and 32 in 1914 lost his life in the Great War, it is possible to understand why the mood of the nation was so cautious and grim in the twenties and thirties. One generation was lost and another was not born as a consequence of the fighting that raged along the Western Front from 1914 to 1918. This kind of slaughter did not happen again in 1939-45. The old fears about a declining population are gone.

France now has to concern itself about its youth. Schools in vastly increased number must be built. The technological advances of the last 10 years make it essential that a greater number of students be admitted to the *lycées* and universities. The old élites are no longer sufficient for the tasks which now require to be done.

Likewise, the situation of women is entirely altered. Marriage and life within the family are no longer an acceptable solution for tens of thousands of middle-class girls who crave a different sort of existence. Their wish is not to live as their mothers did. The "great days" were not in the past, not in the nineteen-twenties, and probably not even in *la belle époque* before 1914. There is very little romancing about the past among those who are young.

For the first time in this century France is giving serious attention to its housing shortage. The end of the Algerian war, and the return of hundreds of thousands of Europeans, has only exacerbated a situation which existed before; there is insufficient housing for all classes in almost all urban areas.

To meet the need, whole new suburbs are being built. In and around Paris, quarters which remained untouched for decades now begin to have a new appearance. The creation of these new dwellings makes possible a life for tens of thousands of low-income and middle-income families which would have seemed inconceivable a decade ago. If the unimaginative architecture leaves a good deal to be desired, there is still a sense of space and modern convenience which the old tenements never afforded. The unfilled demand remains enormous, and is a source of constant complaint, but at last something is showing above ground.

In these situations, what can old political party labels mean? What are the Socialists, for example, to fight for? Expanded social-security measures? France boasts a system which will stand comparison with any in the world. More economic planning? The French planning effort is as extensive and as intelligently executed as any undertaken in a democratic society. Higher wages? This is always a welcome proposal, but elections are rarely won on this plank alone. The fact of the matter is that the French worker is not today economically underprivileged. While many continue to earn insufficient wages, particularly in the public sector of the economy, the pressure even among state employes, while serious, is not overwhelming.

As for the middle class, it has rarely known a more prosperous time. Superb financial management has made the franc one of the most stable currencies in Europe and has contributed to increasing the gold reserves of the country. Profits are high and there is no evidence that traditional French "thrift" is leading people with money to defer spending until prices become more reasonable.

Everywhere, in Paris as well as in the provinces, there are evidences of renovation, building, spending and consuming. The middle class does not appear to be saving for a stormy tomorrow.

The class which has not yet shared in this prosperity is the one which shows greatest evidence of discontent. The peasant disturbances that began quite suddenly several years ago reflect the fact that this group does not feel that it has profited in the way that others have. Peasants own tractors, motorcycles, automobiles and other major industrial appliances, at least in the more prosperous regions; even there, however, they do not appear to be satisfied. In the poorer regions, the extent of agrarian poverty is immediately apparent.

Peasant manifestations constitute a new problem for France; all this came upon the country like a sudden storm. No one was prepared for it. While the Government boasts about its plans for reform, the farmers are impatient and show their feelings in various acts of overt resistance—blocking traffic on the roads, dumping quantities of agricultural produce which would otherwise sell at low prices, and raiding the properties of absentee landlords.

To date, none of the traditional political parties has known how to take advantage of this discontent, or how to channel it in such a way as to improve its own electoral position. In a country where there is no single workers' party, it is not likely that we will soon see a peasants' party.

Under these new circumstances, conventional party labels now mean little. The old political distinctions between Left and Right are becoming increasingly irrelevant, at least to the young. They no longer describe what exists, and a generation unfamiliar with the old slogans is no longer led to think in those terms.

The Communist party retains its hold on those who have voted for its candidates since the liberation, but one has no sense that new cadres are developing. The man who sells L'Humanité each Sunday at the street corner is growing old. What will lead a new generation to embrace Communism? A high regard for the Soviet Union? That is unlikely; too many Frenchmen have been there, or have read about it, and they are not impressed. Internal social discontent? There is not enough for a party to nourish itself at this source.

Around the Sorbonne, the leaflets that are distributed by students are generally religious in character. Roman Catholic groups are strong and active. Even the trade unions seem to reflect the growth of Catholic influence. The major strikes in public utilities last spring were led not by Communist-dominated unions, but by the Catholic labor movement. Among intellectuals, Catholic opinions thrive as they have not done in many a year. Being a good Republican no longer seems to mean that one must also be anti-clerical.

The empirical social sciences have a new importance in the country. The young are interested in the problems of industrial growth, economic planning, urban reform, education. These are very real issues for them; they have little use for those who treat these questions too abstractly. Decisions are waiting to be made in all these areas; this is not a time for idle speculation or endless talk. The work of American economists and sociologists is much admired in certain intellectual quarters in Paris.

Many who visit France today remark on its resemblance to the United States. Their impressions are hasty and mistaken. Automobiles, neon and self-service restaurants do not define a nation's character. While France's rapid industrial expansion is unquestionably leading her to adopt practices and forms which resemble those that exist here, a close scrutiny even of these will suggest important differences.

France is, and remains, a province of Europe. Its experience, on the deepest level, in both the First and Second World Wars is one which it shares with Germany and not with us. Its imperial adventure, again, was of a European sort, and not at all like what we did in Puerto Rico or in the Philippines. Peasants are not farmers; they do not resemble those who live on the land in Vermont or Iowa. Workers have not yet begun to confuse themselves with the middle class. All this may yet come, but it is not the situation of today.

France is changing but it is not at all clear that she is becoming like us. She seeks her new destiny in a new unity, which is European. We would do well to reflect on what this may mean in the next several years, for if it creates problems for us, as it will, it also opens up vast opportunities.

France knows that it is not an island unto itself. Events abroad may still prevent the realization of important plans already made. Also, the continuing political problem may at any time take a serious turn and cause difficulties which will not be easily resolved. Europe is far from being an accomplished fact.

The French remain sufficiently skeptical to estimate with some detachment their present achievement. They are neither overwhelmed by it, nor are they dissatisfied. One thing they know— the France of today is alive and changing. Few regret the past; few look back to it.

France Transformed:
Seven Years of de Gaulle

by Henri Peyre

WITH NEXT month's election, France will begin the eighth year of
a presidency which is, for all practical purposes a constitutional
monarchy. No other ruler in Western Europe or North America
has wielded powers equal to Charles de Gaulle's in the past decade.
The President's critics are numerous and vocal in his own country
but when all is said, he has used his powers skillfully and mod-
erately. At 75, de Gaulle leads a nation that has changed the
agonizing crises of seven years ago for some complacency in
prosperity.

De Gaulle apparently commands the allegiance of two-thirds of
his countrymen. The opposition is hopelessly divided, powerless
to offer a constructive program or suggest new ideas. The general
is not loved and he has not tried to make himself loved. But for
the present, millions of French men and women see no other
choice. De Gaulle's announcement that he will seek re-election on
Dec. 5 to another seven-year term was greeted with significant

From the *New York Times Magazine,* November 14, 1965, copyright ©
1965 by The New York Times Company.

calm; the French are only vaguely worried about the inevitable problem of succession. They realize that France has changed more profoundly under his regime than since Bonaparte consolidated the results of the French Revolution and established a national framework which was to last a century. Except among a few politicians who find it hard to renounce their old views and who cling to the shadows and labels of old parties, there is little nostalgia for the pre-de Gaulle era.

When the general was called from retirement in 1958 by the frightened politicians, the regime was moribund, the treasury empty, the army officers threatening civil war over Algeria. France's prestige abroad was shaken. As a wit put it, the Fourth Republic had died almost as soon as it was installed in the late nineteen-forties—to make way for the Third. Between 1948 and 1958, France lived in the past, split by party squabbles, mouthing meaningless slogans. But while Cabinet ministers played musical chairs, the country worked to achieve record levels of productivity and regain its health after the scars of war and occupation.

France yearned for a better Government and deserved one. But only a violent trauma could bring about the overdue revolution.

Though de Gaulle's achievements have been enormous, they are not all admirable. He has sown seeds of discord and eventual turmoil. It is disturbing for a country to have no alternative to the Government in power, and almost no alternative policy.

Many people wish the haughty President would occasionally pay a warmer tribute to the economic, administrative and cultural achievements of the Fourth Republic. A majority of de Gaulle's countrymen also would consider it fair and fitting of him to recall, in his public utterances, the debt of liberated, prostrate France to the "Anglo-Saxon" armies and American generosity. Instead, de Gaulle advertises his contempt for the materialistic "Americanization" of the Western European masses.

Then, too, de Gaulle has been needlessly imperious in rebuffing his partners in the Common Market, members of the French Parliament and trade union leaders. Of him, as of wrathful Coriolanus in Shakespeare's drama, it could be said:

> *You speak o' the people,*
> *As if you were a god to punish, not*
> *A Man of their infirmity.*

But whatever the manner and the Machiavellian opportunism of a leader who antagonized a number of his early supporters (generals and admirals, statesmen like Georges Bidault and Jacques Soustelle), the first seven years of de Gaulle's rule have completely altered the foundations of France as well as its facade.

In the financial realm, confidence in a strong and stable regime quickly reversed a previous trend that had emptied the coffers of state. Saving deposits climbed, gold and dollars flowed back into the country, the total national income grew. When de Gaulle advocated converting France's large holdings of dollars into gold, the move was misrepresented in the United States as a hostile act by an ungrateful country. In fact, other European countries—West Germany, in particular—bought gold from the American treasury before France did and bought more than France. West Germany, Holland, Belgium, Spain and Switzerland all have a larger percentage of their dollars converted into gold than France does.

France is again a rich country and the franc is among the stable currencies of the world. Such prosperity has not been experienced since Poincaré's monetary measures of 1926.

This year, against the protests of many industrialists and bankers, the Government stubbornly adopted a policy of mild deflation in order to stop a rise in prices and combat inflationary tendencies. As a result, prices rose less in France during 1965 than in any other Continental country. At the same time, total production increased by 5 per cent and reserves climbed to $5 billion, an increase of $500 million.

De Gaulle himself never claimed to be an expert in finance or economics. But he won the willing cooperation of brilliant civil servants and able men like Finance Minister Giscard D'Estaing. Today the French have finally shaken off the inferiority complex which made them believe they could not compete with the Germans or the British in industrial equipment and the export trade.

They have, contrary to what French industrialists long feared, done so well among the six nations of the Common Market that they have profited from the alliance more than any other power.

Neither the prolonged Algerian war nor the expenses entailed in building a French atomic bomb and the projected missiles and nuclear submarines have proved to be a drain on the economy. France has fewer superhighways and higher gasoline prices than any other industrial nation. But she still ranks third (after the U.S. and Canada) in the ratio of cars to population.

Frenchmen are eager for more enjoyment of comfort; *"le mieux être"* has replaced mere "well-being" as the goal outlined by the Government. And though it resembles American slogans ("You never had it so good") and those which lately assured Ludwig Erhard's re-election in Germany, de Gaulle does not seem to think the phrase contradicts *"grandeur."*

The changes resulting from seven years of stability and prosperity have, in turn, caused far-reaching social and psychological consequences.

Families are not afraid of the future; the baby boom continues in France while it has slackened in other countries, including the U.S., in the last two years. The population is likely to reach 50 million before the end of the decade, a rise of more than 25 per cent over 1938.

Even more significant than such an act of faith in the years to come is the change in working-class attitudes. Though French workers have traditionally felt alienated from the rest of society and ready to turn against it, they appear reconciled to the existing order and converted to the benefits of an affluent society. The Communist vote is still large in national and municipal elections, but party membership has shrunk to one-fourth or less of what it was in the immediate postwar years, when it reached almost 1,000,000.

A sizable number of Communist workers (and especially their wives) are expected to vote for de Gaulle in the coming presidential election. Behind the Communist decision to accept Socialist François Mitterand as the candidate of a "united" left against de Gaulle, there clearly lies the reluctance of the Communists to stand up and be counted—to find perhaps that half their usual voters prefer the aristocratic President whose foreign policy (and distrust of America) is more appealing than the program of the left.

The truth is, the French masses are fast becoming "depolitized," as the phrase goes. Utopian socialism of the 19th century, the mystique of Communism, the once-fond belief that only leftist Governments could prevent war are dead and gone. A mere fraction of factory workers belong to labor unions, especially in the new industries of electronics, chemicals and oils. Strikes are relatively scarce and of short duration.

De Gaulle may not be an admirer of democracy, but he has increased the benefits enjoyed by the masses. He has adopted the goals of the now-weakened Socialists and fulfilled them with deeds. On Sept. 16, 1964, de Gaulle's Premier, Georges Pompidou, bluntly declared: "France has a Socialist economy and it has come to stay."

That indifference to politics, or to what used to constitute the typically Latin aspect of political life (heated debate, vituperation, reluctance to agree to disagree, differences of philosophy becoming passionate affairs of the heart) carries perils, too.

The French have become tranquilized, eager for social peace and for tangible benefits—social security, paid vacations, yearly raises, more consumer goods for more families. They enjoy these rewards under a paternalist ruler who talks to them benevolently on television and radio and during his tours of the provinces. Parliament counts for little in the new regime and voters seem unconcerned by the demotion, and at times, the snubbing, of their elected representatives.

Political life at the municipal level is, in compensation, more active. The people feel closer to the mayor of their city or town and expect from him, whether he is a Communist, Radical, Catholic or Gaullist, an efficient administration. They also feel close to the President, austere and inhuman as he sometimes seems, and are flattered by the system of referendums and plebiscites which bypass the Assembly and the Senate.

De Gaulle pours scorn on the old parties as powerless fossils and few would contradict him. The multiparty system is discredited. The two-party system apparently is unworkable in any country except Britain, the U.S., Canada and Scandinavia. The French left should have triumphed after 1945, when much of the right had been discredited by its failure to resist the German occupation. But, as in the past, though the left's emotional appeal to the French people is great, it proved unable to govern. The masses are resigned to their new presidential regime.

The wide powers granted to the President by the new constitution were tailor-cut to suit de Gaulle's wishes in 1958. Unlike the President of the United States, he even has the right to dissolve Parliament. He selects his own Cabinet outside the National Assembly, as in the U.S., and public opinion has apparently accepted such an innovation—startling in France—without demur.

No Supreme Court exists to help offset presidential prerogatives. Since France is not a federal republic and states' rights have no equivalent, the strong presidential regime has no counterweight in a deeply rooted local government. In the hands of a less popular ruler, or a reckless one, such immense powers could be dangerous.

A number of intellectuals have voiced their fears. But the people as a whole, during the last legislative election in 1962, gave de Gaulle the majority that he wanted—the largest in France for 130 years. They clearly approved, for the time being, an efficient Government led by almost anonymous technocrats.

Criticism is rife, to be sure. The press has been left free. Caricaturists, *chansonniers,* satirists mock de Gaulle freely. Opponents such as Bidault and Soustelle publish violent books against him. Television and radio, both Government-controlled, grant only limited time to the opposition, but relatively few people are indignant.

The bitterest opponents of the President include those who accuse him of having betrayed compatriots who dreamed of keeping Algeria French. Others say he has demoralized the army, spent too much on atomic weapons and not enough on education, jeopardized French agriculture and trade by threatening to break up the Common Market.

Yet on these scores, too, de Gaulle's achievements are imposing.

He alone could have freed Algeria, left the Sahara oil wells to the new Government and given nearly 20 African colonies their independence. Of course, some form of economic and financial neocolonialism has replaced the French Empire, but nowhere is de Gaulle more popular than in those African territories and no country, not even Britain, has managed to remain on such good terms with its former colonies.

The army is disgruntled, but it is being rebuilt along new concepts. It is clear de Gaulle's pursuit of an independent nuclear force and his brutal attitude toward NATO and U.S. domination of its European allies has been inspired, in part, by the need to restore the French Army's confidence. At the same time, he sought to encourage French science through autonomous nuclear research.

The lack of adequate educational facilities, due to the lack of foresight of the Fourth Republic, is acute. So is the shortage of adequate housing. Just the same, the budget for education, including funds for cultural relations and teachers' retirement pensions, in 1964 amounted to 20 per cent of the total French budget, double the 1958 figure and considerably higher than the defense budget.

On de Gaulle's foreign policy, there is no evidence the French as a whole strongly disapprove of his refusal to promote a European federation in which supernationality would overshadow the all-important "national fact." A number of idealists and intellectuals regret the President's nationalism. But I am convinced that de Gaulle's foreign policy, including the temporary exclusion of Britain from the Common Market and the assertion of French independence from NATO, would be approved by 80 per cent of Frenchmen—even by those who try to soothe their American friends by appearing to deplore the Gaullist style and ingratitude.

It would be a mistake for U.S. planners to expect a reversal of basic Gaullist foreign policy (at best, they could expect a gentler and less arrogant tone) if and when that strange Catholic general relinquishes power. Indeed, there is much to confirm the view that de Gaulle wants to make Europeans ("from the Atlantic to the Urals") think and act like Europeans, to become convinced that their fate cannot be decided without them. He may well be viewed by history as a European, rather than as a French, nationalist.

Gratitude has never swayed the people's votes very long, either in the Athens of Themistocles, the France of Clemenceau or the Britain of Churchill. The French are as fickle as any other nation, if not more so. They will probably give de Gaulle at least two-thirds of their votes on Dec. 5. But the question in their minds, and often on their lips, is: What next?

Gaullists have often cited 1970 as the crucial date for consolidating the changes in the social, economic and political structure of France initiated or confirmed by their chief. By 1970 France's independent foreign policy will have reached the point of no return. In another five years France intends to have her own H bomb, missiles and modest means of delivery. By then, the Common Market will either have been broken up or expanded to include Britain, opening new outlets for surplus French agricultural products.

By 1970, de Gaulle will be 80, two years short of completing his second presidential term. Will he live until then? "Be reassured, I shall die some day," he told journalists at the Elysée Palace a few months ago. But can he have ordered his eventual succession smoothly?

History would not justify optimism. One thinks at once of Alexander's feuding generals, of Charlemagne's empire disintegrating after him, of the sequel to Cromwell's rule. Some, like Pierre Mendès-France, conclude that no authoritarian personality like de Gaulle—who thinks of himself as a Promethean savior— has ever died without leaving behind the seeds of revolution.

France, however, seems very remote from a revolutionary mood. Neither Parliament nor political parties, nor labor unions, are likely to recapture much power. The state will remain strong and some sort of a presidential system is likely to remain the rule. Dissenting intellectuals have lost much of their influence in today's France. Literature and the arts do not flourish brilliantly in a regime where the chief of state writes the best prose of any French ruler in five centuries. Then, too, the general is surrounded by former professors: Pompidou, Joxe, Peyrefitte, Jenneney, Paye and others.

A power vacuum seems inevitable after such a portentous figure steps down or disappears. Who will try to fill it? It seems clear at present that Premier Pompidou—as different from his chief as Eden was from Churchill—suave, flexible, superbly intelligent, is de Gaulle's first choice as his successor.

A long biography of Pompidou, the son of a modest family who became an able *lycée* teacher, then a banker, then de Gaulle's confidant and Premier, was published last July, probably with de Gaulle's blessing. The President's, and perhaps the nation's, alternate choices would be Louis Joxe, another teacher-turned-diplomat and administrator or, more probably, Giscard d'Estaing, the brilliant and more aristocratic Finance Minister.

Those of us who live into the next decade may be surprised to see how little the economy and politics of post-Gaullist France will differ from the present. France *will* be different in manner and style. That may be the reason why the French strike us as much less anxious about the transition after de Gaulle than the friends of France abroad.

The hopes of some Americans to see a new French foreign policy are likely to be frustrated. Other European nations, less tartly to be sure, tend to agree with de Gaulle that the U.S. can no longer play the role of guardian for a healthy and arrogant European continent. They will clamor for a voice on the use of the U.S. nuclear arsenal, if they are to provide troops and bases in return. Also, they vaguely fear being relegated to a secondary role if the Russians and the Americans become reconciled to peaceful coexistence.

Gaullism, in that sense, is not limited to France and it will survive de Gaulle.

Raymond Aron once remarked, when France seemed hopelessly bogged down in the Algerian war, that a nation of skeptics (as France is supposed to be) has always proved the readiest to appeal to saviors or providential men. The French are in truth more Bonapartist than monarchist—or perhaps even republican.

Bonaparte swept away the litter of the past when he understood his role as the continuation of the Revolution. De Gaulle has also swept away much which deserved to die, and a few things which did not.

His successors are not likely to be endowed with similar charisma, to use the word which Max Weber, borrowing from St. Paul, made fashionable. But they may well, under another guise, pursue similar aims.

Two Who Bridge
the Generation Gap

by Sanche de Gramont

PARIS

IT WAS July 21, half of France was on vacation, maintenance crews with steam rollers were spreading tar over paved streets of the Latin Quarter, several hundred of the riot policemen who fought the students in May had been shifted to their usual summer duty as lifeguards, and in the National Assembly a generation of fathers was holding a debate on the future of higher education and the unruly behavior of their sons.

In tones ranging from petulance to anger, deputies of the Gaullist majority (the Union for the Defense of the Republic) conducted their post-mortem on the spring events. Then David Rousset, a sort of overweight Danton with a congested, blotchy moon face, a thick, bristly mane of white hair and a booming bass voice, rose and began a lively exchange by saying: "Let's not get too indignant about students on barricades when we say nothing when peasants draw them up."

VIVIEN (U.D.R.) "They were *voyous*." ["Young hooligans" or "louts."] *Laughter. Lively exclamations. Noises.*

ROUSSET: "They were serious young men, devoted to their

cause. This country will someday need these youths. We can and we must discuss with them." *Protests and clamor on the Gaullist benches.* "I am pleased, Monsieur Fanton, that we do not hold the same opinions."

FANTON (U.D.R.): "I, too, am pleased."

ROUSSET: "The decree on dissolution permits the Government to arrest young people for reconstituting dissolved movements, while what we should be doing is practicing a policy of appeasement. We cannot both initiate reforms and maintain repression. The vast majority of students, and not only revolutionary students, are bound to react." *Protests on U.D.R. benches.* "There is a deep solidarity among all students which one would be wrong to ignore."

This sort of exchange is common enough in French parliamentary practice and would hardly be worth mentioning were it not for two special circumstances. First, David Rousset is a Gaullist deputy. In the foregoing excerpt from the National Assembly record, he was arguing with members of his own party, which won an overwhelming majority in the June election but is split by the student revolt into rival Whig and Tory factions. Second, while David Rousset was speaking up for the students at the National Assembly, his 21-year-old son, Pierre, was awaiting trial in a cell at Santé Prison for his activities as a leader of the May riots.

Pierre is a founder of the Revolutionary Communist Youth, an anti-Stalinist party that broke with the French Communists in 1966 and was outlawed by them as heretical. It was one of the dozen or so "groupuscules" (tiny groups) in the Latin Quarter which gained some notoriety during May. Pierre Rousset spent so much time on the barricades that he feared at one point that the amount of tear gas he had absorbed had permanently damaged his eyesight.

The Ministry of the Interior, on the simplistic assumption that such groupuscules as the Revolutionary Communist Youth and Daniel Cohn-Bendit's Movement of the 22nd of March had planned and coordinated the spring uprising like some grand Napoleonic campaign, decided that by ordering the dissolution of the movements it would strike at the root of the evil. "Typical police thinking," says Pierre. "There has to be a guilty party. They think that by liquidating the organizations they will liquidate the problem."

Militants of these dissolved groups became active in other organizations, such as neighborhood action committees. And thus it was that on July 10, Pierre Rousset was present at a meeting of the 11th Arrondissement action committee in an auditorium on the Rue Charonne lent by a parish priest. About 40 persons attended this barricade alumni meeting. "I see some unfamiliar faces," a young lady said. "Since we don't all know one another, why doesn't each person identify himself before we begin the discussion?" Two of the unfamiliar faces promptly rose and identified themselves as those of police inspectors. Five of the 40, including Pierre Rousset, were held. An informer had given the inspectors his description: tall, husky, curly brown hair, tortoise-shell glasses.

It is one of the peculiarities of the Fifth Republic's judicial system that citizens can be detained for up to 10 days under suspicion of plotting against the safety of the state without going before a judge or having any charges brought against them. Pierre and the others were held for eight days in this manner, incommunicado, and were then charged with "attempting to reconstitute a dissolved movement." It is another peculiarity of the Fifth Republic's judicial system that bail is rarely granted, so Pierre and the others swelled the ranks of the Santé Prison inmates awaiting trial, who represent 70 per cent of the total prison population.

Pierre Rousset was puzzled by some of the Santé regulations. No singing or whistling (he had not been planning to sing or whistle); no lying down on your bed in the daytime; no hanging pictures or calendars on the walls, which must be kept bare. But soon he was moved to the section reserved for political prisoners. It had just been vacated by the last convicted members of the Secret Army Organization, including some of the terrorists who tried to assassinate General de Gaulle in 1962. They were amnestied by de Gaulle during the June election campaign as a gesture to win the support of the French right.

Political prisoners in French jails have reasonably comfortable regimes, which is only natural in a country where today's chief of state may become tomorrow's political prisoner, as Marshal Henri-

Philippe Pétain did. Pierre Rousset and his friends had their own courtyard, equipped with a badminton court. They had access to the prison canteen and to an unlimited supply of books and newspapers. They were allowed four one-hour visits a week. And there was always the hope that a change in the political climate would spring them.

It became clear to certain members of the de Gaulle Cabinet that keeping popular student leaders in jail on flimsy charges was not the best way to prepare for a quiet academic year. The new Minister of Education, Edgar Faure, came out strongly for the liberation of the students. Faure, a holdover from the Fourth Republic who has served in all the key Cabinet posts, including that of Premier, is emerging in his latest incarnation as a 1968 French version of Mr. Chips. He quotes Mao ("We must cure the illness without killing the patient"); he agrees with the students that their crisis is the crisis of modern man examining the foundations of his society, and he shocked the Gaullist right wing when he came out for political freedom in the university. He said he would never give in to "the pessimism of those who believe that if political freedom is allowed the most extreme viewpoint will prevail, whereas in fact extreme positions are the easiest to refute." Thanks partly to Faure's influence, Pierre Rousset and his friends were released "in provisional liberty" after six weeks in jail. There is a 50-50 chance that their case will never come to trial.

The 56-year-old Gaullist deputy and his 21-year-old revolutionary son: It would be tempting to make the French crisis fit into the neat category of generations. The sons rise up against their fathers, who have bequeathed them a botched civilization. The fathers see the image of their failure in the revolt of their sons. Subversion has not come from abroad but from within the family circle. The wisdom and institutions of one generation are held in contempt by its successor.

The story of Rousset *père* and Rousset *fils* does not, however, fit this comfortable stereotype. Instead of two generations in conflict, it shows the generation of sons taking over from the defeated generation of their fathers in a world where the problems have changed but the methods have not. Like his son, David Rousset was an extreme left-wing revolutionary student. Like his son, but for different reasons, he rejected orthodox Communism. As a philosophy student in the nineteen-thirties, he saw the hope of the Russian Revolution of 1917 grow into totalitarian Stalinist dictatorship. As an economics student in the sixties, Pierre Rousset broke with the French Communist party because he considered it counterrevolutionary, reformist and the stooge of the Soviet Union.

David Rousset grew up in a Europe in which the forces of the left were defeated in every major test. In Germany, with Hitler's rise to power. In Spain, where the Fascist powers ensured Franco's victory. In France in 1935 and 1936, when the parties of the left failed to exploit the revolutionary possibilities of popular discontent with governmental instability and the Depression, which led to a massive occupation of factories, settling instead for the reformist program of Léon Blum's short-lived Popular Front.

Like his son, David Rousset was a militant. He joined a Trotskyite group. Disgusted by the Popular Front's neutrality in the Spanish Civil War, he recruited volunteers and supplies for the International Brigades. He fought in a celebrated 1934 riot against right-wing groups trying to storm the Concorde Bridge and capture the National Assembly. The police opened fire; there were 17 dead and 2,329 wounded. David Rousset was beaten up more than once in clashes with right-wing groups. Thirty years later, in 1966, his son was distributing pamphlets in front of a *lycée* when he was attacked by a right-wing commando. He was cracked over the head with an iron bar and suffered a fractured skull. His assailant was identified but released after some of his political friends provided him with an alibi.

Thus, David Rousset's young manhood was marked by the failure of the left to provide a successful alternative to the rise of Fascism and by the failure of the Russian Revolution as an example for the non-Communist left. In this context, World War II seemed a penance being exacted from European liberals. After the disillusion of liberal hopes, the trauma of war. Rousset became a key member of a Resistance network which penetrated German Army groups stationed in the Breton port of Brest. He and his friends found anti-Nazi German soldiers who were willing to contribute to a German-language resistance newspaper secretly distributed to the occupation army. The network had created three cells of anti-Nazi soldiers by the time it was infiltrated by the Gestapo. Rousset was arrested and sent to Buchenwald in 1943.

When American troops liberated the camp in 1944, he recalls, "I had lost 80 pounds. I was concave instead of convex. I had also caught typhus, but I didn't tell anyone because I would have been quarantined, and I had to get out of there. I drove out in a truck with some Americans and I pointed out to them a fleeing Gestapo staff car. They let it go, saying, 'We won this war and we have to be good sports.' When I got back to Paris I saw a doctor. Fortunately I was not the cause of a typhus epidemic."

Rousset spent the next two years writing what has become the French classic on the camps, "The Concentrationary Universe." He had a disturbing insight: that the concentration camp, far from being a monstrous denial of civilization, was a possible model for a future civilization. The camps were such models of efficient bureaucracy that they formed a workable kind of society. They were not primitive but overrefined. Men did not die there as men but as part of an administrative system, according to a strictly defined bureaucratic mechanism. The concentration camps were the supreme example of planification.

This is what Rousset calls "the advent of a new barbarism." It was, he says, "the most profound kind of exploitation of man," far worse than the kind of exploitation Marx described as taking place in capitalist societies. Just as Stalinism had been the failure of a revolution, the new barbarism was the failure of an ideology. Nothing Marx wrote was relevant to this new and terrible form of human exploitation, the concentration camp. More than that, the camps also existed in the very country which claimed that it practiced Marxism-Leninism, the Soviet Union.

The other lesson David Rousset drew from his political experience of the thirties was that political parties were bankrupt. He had seen the liberal parties powerless before dictators. In France, the system led to the revolving-door governments of party hacks. So in 1948, with the existentialist philosopher Jean-Paul Sartre, he founded an antiparty movement called the Revolutionary Democratic Assembly, which proclaimed itself both anti-Communist and anticapitalist and stated its opposition to both the Soviet and the American blocs.

For a man destined to become a Gaullist deputy, Rousset had some harsh words for the general, who had just founded his own Assembly of the French People. He compared de Gaulle to Stalin, saying: "De Gaulle says to French society what Stalin says to the world proletariat: 'I am your savior and I mean to impose your salvation.' " With heavy sarcasm, he added: "De Gaulle is the man who possesses the revealed truth of the French bourgeoisie. He does not need to consult anyone, he does not need to examine himself, he knows ahead of time what is just and necessary."

But after a year and a half, Rousset broke with Sartre, who was moving closer to the French Communist party, and devoted himself to exposing the labor camps in the Soviet Union. He did not become a Gaullist until 1966, and says he was won over by the general's anticolonialism and by his foreign policy, which—like his own—refuses to choose between the Soviet and American blocs. Recruited by the Gaullists as a well-known left-wing intellectual and potential vote-getter, Rousset ran unsuccessfully for Parliament in the 1967 elections, but was elected in the Gaullist landslide this June in a northern industrial district.

Rousset sees the major failure of his generation in its inability to provide an ideology for the youths who are rebelling today. "Because of this," he says, "they still use the worn-out political vocabulary of Marxism-Leninism. They do not realize that the problems with which they must deal are not even broached in Marx or Lenin—the tremendous productive forces of the industrialized Western countries, for instance, which divided the world into underdeveloped and overdeveloped regions.

"Marx is no longer prophetic. He believed that one of the most important benefits of Communist society would be to give each man sufficient leisure time to fulfill and improve himself. Well, many of us have this leisure time today in our neocapitalist society, and we are discovering that it can be used to enslave man instead of emancipating him, thanks to sophisticated methods of persuasion.

"Today's young revolutionaries, those who are contesting the form of society they live in, have problems that the Russian revolutionaries of 1917 did not have. They are the first revolutionaries of the affluent society, in which goods and services are plentiful and want is no longer the principal problem. They are not revolting for bread, but from a surfeit of material goods. Everyone thought revolution in the second half of the 20th century would come from the Third World, from Africa and Latin America, but instead it is coming from the most industrialized states, from the youth and intellectuals in France and Czechoslovakia, and from the Negroes and the New Left in the United States.

"But since these new revolutionaries have not got their Lenin, they must formulate their ideology as they go along. They are still stumbling, they only partly understand their own action. Here in France they still believe in a tight party organization, but the May events proved the futility of that. No party can claim to have controlled or directed that great explosion. Events spread spontaneously, without any central directive. The May events marked the failure of the professional politicians who claim to speak for the people."

Student leaders agree with David Rousset that their organizations were taken by surprise. Jacques Sauvageot, secretary of the largest national student organization, says: "We were so poorly informed that it was not until I was jailed with Daniel Cohn-Bendit and we had a talk that I learned what had been going on at Nanterre."

Pierre Rousset adds: "We were astonished, although we recognized the spontaneity of the movement as proof of a latent crisis in French society. And we saw that some of the ideas we had been stressing all along had seeped to the masses.

"We believe that there is no possible alliance with the French Communist party, and the majority of the students sensed this. [Rousset says the French Communists gave the police membership lists of groups such as his that had broken away from them.] We believe that no revolution is possible without the collaboration of the working class, and the movement did spread to the workers. Finally, we stressed the international aspect of the struggle—it's the same struggle in Berlin, Rome or Berkeley."

If Pierre Rousset maintains his faith in Marxism-Leninism and in the party as the best possible political structure, it is perhaps because he has not suffered the same disappointments as his father. His is the first generation of French youths in this century which has not been involved in a war. Stalinism, Fascism, concentration camps—these are to him pages from history textbooks, while to his father they are spiritual and physical scars. His generation is undefeated because it has not yet really been tested.

It is also a generation which sees the world through a different set of problems. David Rousset grew up in a period of European conflict which led to World War II. Two conflicting ideologies, Fascism and Communism, fought within the framework of traditional 19th-century European nationalism.

Pierre Rousset grew up in a period of European peace in which the key problem was the emancipation of the colonial world. Too young to fight in Indochina or Algeria, he could analyze colonialism impersonally. He saw a French society in contradiction with itself, stressing the values of Western humanism, freedom, human rights, while denying those values to the colonial peoples it exploited.

He is unresponsive to the appeals of nationalism, for his generation has never had to feel that France was threatened. The deep strain of French chauvinism, which since 1870 has been essentially a compensatory mechanism for defeat, is absent from his mentality. He is incapable of feeling, as de Gaulle feels, that there is a certain idea of France and French grandeur to which everything else must be subjected.

On the contrary, he considers that the problems of his generation are not national, but applicable to Western civilization as a whole. To him, there are no national values to defend or national faults to condemn, but a certain number of diseases secreted by Western society. He feels he is part of an international more effective than the Comintern ever was, because the Comintern was imposed by a government which used it both to spread world revolution and to pursue the imperialist goals of Greater Russia, whereas the international he belongs to grew organically from small groups of students in different countries who found that they had identical goals. Just as Marx said that a French worker should feel more in common with a German worker than with a French bourgeois, Rousset feels greater kinship to Rudi Dutschke than to Edgar Faure.

Although he was surprised by the timing of the May events, he and other student militants had been preparing for such an occasion. "We were among the first to fight police in Vietnam demonstrations and we had some street combat experience," he says. "Then some of us, including myself, went to Berlin in February for a Vietnam demonstration. We had quite a fight with the Fascists there."

For a time, Rousset and his friends thought the movement in France would be able to topple the Gaullist regime. "We saw the signs of a vacuum of power," he says. "The ministers were incapable of making decisions. The policemen's union was grumbling. We knew that if de Gaulle called out the army the draftees would resist. But everything depended on the unions and the opposition parties, and the Communist party was the first to call for an election. Finally, the Communist party and the Communist-led unions saved the Gaullist regime; the call for a new election meant an end to the strikes and the demoralization of the revolutionary groups."

Pierre Rousset rules out another explosion of student rioting when the Sorbonne reopens. "We would be isolated," he said, "the workers would not go along. This will have to be a period of meditation and reorganization. We saw in May that outside the Latin Quarter we were powerless. We have to permeate the masses, create a national party. It's our duty to use the electoral system to advance our ideas, even if our ideas are anti-parliamentarian."

This is the dilemma of the student revolt. To pursue their action they are compelled to make use of the available instruments of the society they are condemning. In the same manner, the student author of a book on the May insurrection wrote in the preface: "The consumer society poisons everything it produces by turning it into merchandise. Everything is commercially exploited, even the barricades. My book does not escape that objection, but between the risk of doing nothing and the risk of doing something, I decided to publish." The writer also runs the risk of becoming a best-selling author and being completely swallowed up by the consumer society. Pierre Rousset, if he helps found a party and runs for office, runs the risk of being elected. Perhaps revolution is only for the young. Perhaps in a few years he will move closer to the Establishment, as his father did. Perhaps in some future regime he will be a Cabinet minister.

For the moment, he expresses his willingness to work within existing institutions in order eventually to scuttle them, and he remains loyal to his Marxist-Leninist ideology. "I see nothing else," he says. "The condition of the worker has not changed. He is still a merchandise on the labor market. Bourgeois thought is degenerate. French students have a Marxist formation and do not read Marcuse. Sartre has taught us nothing. Existentialism is dead. The sad thing is that there are no great new Marxist thinkers, because Stalin froze Marxist thought for a generation. We realize we are confronted with new problems to which we are applying dated categories of thought. Marxist thought must make a great leap forward."

Pierre Rousset believes the proven methods of political agitation and mass movements will change society. His father, although he is one of the Gaullists most sympathetic to the student movement, believes as a Gaullist deputy that revolution must come from the top, and that no one has a better chance of profoundly changing French society than the general himself.

David Rousset's faith is based partly on a private conversation he had with de Gaulle last April, 10 days before the start of the crisis. Rousset was summoned to the Elysée because he had long been writing about the need for social reform. After greeting him, de Gaulle sat down behind his desk and put on his glasses. Rousset felt relieved, for he had been warned that when de Gaulle wears his glasses it means he is interested in the conversation, but when he removes them it means that his mind has wandered to some private dimension.

At that time the student problem at Nanterre centered on whether the girl students should have the right to receive male students in their rooms. "First they wanted classes and teachers," grumbled the general, "now they want beds and mistresses.

"The French left," de Gaulle went on, "can't forgive me for carrying out the policies it was incapable of implementing itself.

They will only forgive me after my death when they will call me their precursor."

Then de Gaulle announced that he intended to devote his last years in office to the social transformation of France. In his most oracular tone, he said: "We must condemn capitalism, David Rousset, we must expressly condemn capitalist society. We must also condemn totalitarian Communism, for its solutions are unadapted and inadequate to our society. We must find a new way, a new solution."

De Gaulle went into an explanation of participation, in which workers, students and all citizens have a share in the highest responsibilities of the state. "If it's a matter of institutions," de Gaulle said, "I'm not worried, for when it comes to forming a concept or a policy, *la stratégie, c'est moi.* But the problem is that this society must be transformed at the same time it is being administered." De Gaulle indicated that some of his ministers would be reluctant to go along because a radical program of change makes day-to-day governing so difficult. "I need popular support for this," he confided. Since that April conversation, de Gaulle has received massive support in the June elections and most of the key ministers have been changed.

This leaves three principal possibilities for France: a revolution from the top masterminded by de Gaulle, a revolution from the bottom fomented by political agitators and student leaders like Pierre Rousset or no revolution at all, thanks to the inertia of the average citizen and to the resistance of those classes whose interest is to defend the social and economic status quo.

I have bets with David and Pierre Rousset that are really bets on the future of France. David Rousset has bet me that in two years de Gaulle will have succeeded in his "mutation from the summit."

Pierre Rousset has bet me that within the next calendar year he will be in jail again.

A "New European Man" Runs France

by Keith Botsford

PARIS

ONCE THE home of Mme. de Pompadour, now housing the President of the Republic, Georges Pompidou, the Elysée Palace in Paris is a building in refined 18th-century taste: elegant and symmetrical, chaste without and ornate within.

French politics has often seemed romantic, emotional and theatrical. France wept even as it executed its king; it manned revolutionary barricades which brought tyrants into power. While the Left has been sanctified in word and sporadically in deed, the Right has been more truly representative of the national craving for authority. Only the extremes have drawn the passionate attention of Frenchmen and in a country which makes much intellectual capital of Reason, only the rational Center seems to have had less than a fair chance.

All that is changing now. France has become richer, more European, less grandiose and more bourgeois, if you like. Its last king was Charles de Gaulle and he, as if realizing that after him the race of kings would die out, left two bequests to the nation: one was the new Constitution and strong presidency which he

From the *New York Times Magazine,* August 29, 1971, copyright © 1971 by The New York Times Company.

created with such effort, and the other was naming as his heir the man who had been closest to him, in and out of politics, for the last 26 years of his life, and the man who, in his opinion, understood the new France best, Georges Pompidou.

Pompidou was not the man closest to de Gaulle in any romantic, emotional sense, as were the general's companions in the war, but he was the most *central*, the most indispensable for his sober skills and that homely, elegant, brilliant mind and manner that so perfectly mirrors the palace in which I recently talked to him.

For an audience with the President one walks in off the Rue St. Honoré into the *Loge d'Honneur;* a policeman conducts one across the gravel courtyard to the vast double doors of the palace itself; a lackey in black swallowtails leads one up the ornate marble stairs where one is met by the presidential usher; he, chain of office discreetly settled on his waist, seats one in a large *salon* on a formal, uncomfortable chair and between two allegorical Gobelin tapestries representing October and March; then the President's aide-de-camp, a colonel resplendent in air-force blue, his breast invisible behind campaign ribbons, his shoulders under braid, accompanies one through the antechamber into the presidential office. It is solid gilt, walls and ceiling; the furniture is encrusted in gold leaf; the presidential desk, which could have been Mme. de Pompadour's, is covered with red leather and in perfect order.

So far, all is as it ever was. One was received in this manner by Napoleon I and Napoleon III. Intervening revolutions, periods of use as a printshop, then as a gaming house, have affected the building little. Even with Charles de Gaulle residing there, fingering the revolving globe and pondering on the world and France's place in it, there can have been little discontinuity with the past. But now?

Now de Gaulle's globe is gone. It went the first day Pompidou moved in. Now behind the President's chair, on a little stand of its own, stands a strikingly modern abstract expressionist drawing: the economical, minimal culture of our times, one thinks, the taste that money can afford. But then on a high chest of drawers of exquisite marquetry, there sit photographs of Mr. and Mrs. Pompidou, their son and grandchildren, all in the special bright tan and disparate blue of sky that Kodachrome gives, and one thinks, ah, he is one of us! The man, just turned 60, tall, bulky, striped in suit of sober blue, a blue tie randomly patterned and scrupulously knotted exactly bisecting his white shirt, steps forward to shake one's hand: this is the Pompidou whose discretion, modesty and financial cunning made him so acceptable to the politics and the money of the time that he could become both Premier of France and director-general of the Banque Rothschild and seem to alter his basic self not at all. Then when he sits down, lights up a filter cigarette and while talking leaves it dangling straight down from his lower lip, when one begins to listen to the deliberateness and pith of his conversation or watches him laugh, one recalls the stubborn, hard-working peasants of France from whom Pompidou descends.

So at one moment the *ancien régime* is still with us and Pompidou can say how he feels "completely at home" with "advanced" trends in the arts, with those painters whose works now hang in the palace, and then say, with a mixture of regret and lordliness, "No, I no longer visit painters now, I *receive* them." The next moment he will explain the presidency in terms of husbands and wives: "What is a quality in a private individual can be a defect in a man who has responsibilities. Lots of husbands are good husbands because they're a little weak. Well, there's nothing worse for a head of government or head of state than to be weak."

This blend of certainty and loftiness persists in many of Pompidou's declarations. When his party seeks to launch a "Year of Change," Pompidou can refuse the slogan, saying, "Social change is not yearly, but daily." Or, on quitting the premiership in 1968: "The business of a deputy is to meddle with things and talk, and what I want is to stay at a distance from things and shut up."

To spend any time in French intellectual milieus is to live in a world of loudspeakers and no receiving equipment: there is much talk and little listening and what counts is less what is said than the brilliance with which it is expressed. Pompidou's make-up is absolutely typical of these circles in which he and his wife—who is both very much an intellectual herself and a *mondaine,* a member of higher society—always have moved and still do; yet there is a difference. One feels that Pompidou could produce all that flash if he wanted to, but that he considers it both wasteful and foolish. He measures his words; he rations them. When they emerge, they are not brilliant words; they are simply clear, comprehensible and reasonable. And it is obvious that he has that rarest of gifts among Frenchmen: the ability to listen, to doubt, to question, to evaluate and hence to learn.

There are those in France who see in Pompidou Balzac's Rastignac or Stendhal's Julien Sorel, those heroes with the passionate desire to "make good," and to some extent this must at one time have been true of the man. But now Pompidou has *arrived* and in a real sense his is a "success story" of a kind that would not have been possible in prewar France. Not without some extraordinary deed: neither Rastignac nor Sorel could have risen as Pompidou has by sheer application, absolute self-confidence and so relatively minor an accident. And one might be tempted to think of Pompidou's "making it" as a freak, a sport of the times, were it not that we can clearly see other "New European Men," in the ascendancy: men as new as the united Europe of which Pompidou is such an ardent advocate, men as diverse and antithetical to their traditional national political and social patterns as England's Edward Heath and West Germany's Willy Brandt.

Pompidou's grandfather tilled the poor, hard soil of Auvergne with a hoe. His son, Léon, as a shoeless peasant boy, was, in the educational reforming zeal of the Third Republic, as sought-after for school as American blacks today are for business, faculties or government. In the ruthlessly competitive structure of French education, to be called is not enough; one must also succeed. Leon succeeded—becoming first an *instituteur,* then marrying one and ending his days as a professor of Spanish in a *lycée*—and his son succeeded even more brilliantly. "When I was 8 and I was asked what I wanted to be when I grew up, I answered without a moment's hesitation that I would be a *normalien,*" the President told me.

To understand what this meant—the flat declaration is still characteristic of Pompidou, who seems never to have doubted that he belongs by right among the elect—one has to understand that the Ecole Normale Supérieure, like Sciences Politiques, which Pompidou later attended, is one of the *Grandes Ecoles.* These are particularly French institutions and can continue to exist and flourish only because France remains, of all modern nations, the most absolutely centralized and hierarchical. It is as though Harvard and Yale, or Oxford and Cambridge, were recognizably and beyond dispute the *premier* educational establishments in their countries and that every young boy could aspire to go to them. To do so, he would take a national examination and be admitted— as well as, later, graduated—strictly on the basis of his rank in examination. Pompidou was admitted No. 1 written and No. 8 orally; he was graduated, naturally, at the head of his class. About which he said, again characteristically: "The result didn't surprise me. Of course, I was pleased."

Graduation gave Pompidou his *agrégation*—that is, his academic rank, but also much more. In France, this brings with it a position in society that is recognized and accepted not only by "top people," but also by the whole society; also, the graduates of the *Grandes Ecoles* form, at the apex of national life, not merely a network of connections, but also a society within a society that shares a common language, a common approach to problem-solving and a common system for dealing with the real world. In the most literal sense, Pompidou was a man not only groomed for success but perfectly conscious of the fact.

The only indeterminate in Pompidou's life as a young man in the early thirties was: In what field would success come?

Would it be politics? No, at first it was Greek, then literature; later it was administration, then banking. "No, politics was completely an accident," Pompidou said. But, *Monsieur le Président,* you never thought of an active role in politics? "When I was a young man," he answered, "I was interested in politics. I was not as extremely politicized as some, but still committed. I was of the Left, of course. What young man isn't? Or of the extreme Right? No one took that seriously. One of my classmates could yell out, 'Kill all Jews!' . . . That was the way it was to be a *Normalien*. In 1933 I was a card-carrying member of the Socialist party. I made a trip to Germany. I saw one of those massive Nazi demonstrations in Munich. . . . Its power, its violence, its mass, its order, its discipline, left an indelible mark on me. I was horrified and impressed. When I got back to France I tore up my party card. What could a political party in the Third Republic do to withstand such a force? Nothing. It was better to turn away from politics altogether."

Still in that mood, having married the young law student (who was also the charming, intelligent and lively daughter of a successful provincial doctor) he had met one day on the Boulevard Saint-Michel, he lived, as he put it, a "private life." He fought the war, as long as it was still being fought by France, as a lieutenant in an Alpine regiment. Then, when it was lost, he lived through four long years of German occupation without, he admits, much more than superficial difficulty; a teacher of literature in a Parisian *lycée,* at the Liberation he was preparing a critical edition of Racine's "Brittanicus." As for the romanticism of the Resistance, the heroes both real and self-proclaimed . . . "I hate all that business," he said with a quick wave of his hand and sharp displeasure in his bright eyes, "I hate medals, I hate decorations of all kinds."

Until 1944, then, French politics seemed to him either futile or sick (and therefore responsible for the debacle of 1940) or simply romantic. Charming but silly. Wasted energy. The institutions for viable politics just did not exist at the time; they were not to come into existence until de Gaulle created them.

In 1944, de Gaulle, who throughout the war has been bereft of money, support, staff and power, returns to Paris to create a Government out of nothing. He needs men around him, he needs bright young men. A fellow *Normalien,* René Brouillet, who had been the head of Bidault's personal staff when Bidault headed the National Council for the Resistance, heard from Pompidou—then 33 and beginning to realize that teaching would not satisfy his ambitions—that he was "looking for something to do, some job where he might make himself useful." Pompidou meets the hero he, like every Frenchman in his heart, has been looking for, his life is transformed.

To Pompidou at first fall such tasks as drafting letters, writing memoranda, analyzing and reducing to order immense, complex files, and the skills he learned were such as unobtrusiveness, brevity, accuracy, unbiased evaluation, clear summary, style, loyalty, discretion. After much work and long study, Pompidou learns to operate as de Gaulle operates; he can take some of the load off the general; and he cultivates his own special talents—especially those dealing with figures, economics being a subject that profoundly bores de Gaulle. Discretion and loyalty, which are for de Gaulle the greatest (they are the most Roman) virtues, come so naturally to Pompidou that in all the years of their association, there is no single exchange of words between the two men ever recorded by Pompidou or by any third party. He is twice as useful to de Gaulle precisely because he is self-effacing and easily overlooked: the bright stars in the political firmament think of Pompidou as a superior office boy. He is never irked by this, for the mistake is theirs: the secret of success is to get on with the job, whatever it is, and, as he has said, "to let life come to one."

But Pompidou is more than just "useful." He has a great capacity for friendship. The man who starts working for de Gaulle unburdened with a past, either glorious or awkward, who serves in a humble capacity out of conviction, goes on to become the *friend* who can be trusted with any task and who will always *understand*. In 1946, de Gaulle gives up power for the first time; nearly all his collaborators at the period thought the general was finished; they left him to look after their own political careers. Pompidou continued to serve his master. He is de Gaulle's political secretary during that first exile. By sorting out the raveled finances of the Foundation for Handicapped Children established in memory of their dead daughter, Anne, Pompidou earns the personal gratitude of the de Gaulles, and more important, the unswerving support of Mrs. de Gaulle. It is while working on behalf of the foundation (he is still its president), that Pompidou becomes friendly with René Fillon, who moves in the upper levels of high finance. Fillon covets a senatorial role, Pompidou is able to assist. . . . As one of Pompidou's closest associates put it to me: "Pompidou has always known how to make friends and how to keep friends. In all those years in which his chief profession has been government, I do not know a single friend or contact he has ever lost. Each step in his career has simply added new contacts and new friends."

Political skill of a high order. But after the 1951 elections, de Gaulle retires again to Colombey, and Pompidou, who has excelled at every stage of his career so far—the scholastic, the administrative, the personal—now makes a third decisive change. "I could not see an administrative career being a live, interesting career for me," Pompidou has said. "I like the law, but I don't find it gives sufficient scope for activity." This time the general's return to private life seems absolute and final. Pompidou's similar return would have been equally final for any other man: he enters the Rothschild Bank, thanks to René Fillon, and once again he begins to ascend with dizzying speed; in no time at all he is director-general.

In 1958, there is the attempted coup in Algiers; de Gaulle comes out of retirement and "borrows" Pompidou from his bank. After six months, as agreed, Pompidou returns to the Rothschilds: "Despite the interest of the work, I still felt a sort of doubt toward the servitude of public life. . . ." In April, 1962, he is Premier. It is another switch, but it is no longer so great a leap. It is like moving to another chair, but all the rest remains the same, the milieu, the friends—artists, intellectuals, politicians, financiers.

A new man of this sort is in some way bound to be both en-slaved by his superiority and deeply conscious of it, and when Pompidou talks about his political peers, this sense of being a more complete, more self-sufficient man than they, comes out sharply. Perhaps because he is a classicist, he tends to think of character as being inextricably mixed with history, and yet few men who have grasped as much power as he have been less concerned with "destiny" or with their role in history. If there is any abstract vision with which Pompidou is closely attuned, that vision is the *New* Europe.

He has just come back from a weekend of wine and Lorelei on the Rhine and . . . I get the impression that the President thinks of the Germans as being preoccupied with thoughts of power. "Of course, they do not always do so consciously. I do not think that with Hitler it was conscious; but with Bismarck, yes it *was* conscious." And with Brandt?

His "summit" meeting with Edward Heath has been a personal triumph for both men; it has cleared the way for Britain's entry into the E.E.C. And yet, Pompidou recognizes that although he admires Heath, he finds him puzzling: "He is a complex man, not at all simple." Perhaps a kind of British eccentricity, that peculiar insularity, remains the main obstacle to the Europeanization of England: "Ah, yes, Mr. Heath, he has his yacht." However, what strikes Pompidou most is a feeling that he and Heath must have shared: that whatever one's ideas, real responsibility toward those ideas comes only with power. "Heath," he says, "has been a European for 20 years, but it is only since he has headed his Government that he has really and truly been *convinced.*"

Mr. Nixon might be, were he European, much the same sort of man. Of course, Pompidou says jokingly, though some Americans are very much Europeans, the majority cannot be: "They take everything much too seriously." He does not know Nixon well, but two things commend him to Pompidou. First, "I said when he was elected that here at last was the President who would finally extricate America from that disastrous war in Vietnam, and I was heavily criticized for doing so, but more than ever I believe that to be true." And, second, Nixon's penchant for private correspondence between heads of state that bypasses protocol and routine; Pompidou says the correspondence is "regular" and "very useful." (This correspondence apparently didn't forewarn the French President of Nixon's new dollar policy, and when the surprise announcement of it came, Pompidou, obviously displeased, interrupted his vacation to huddle with his currency advisers.)

Pompidou's enjoyment of his job is apparent. That is why most observers seem to feel that, barring an unforeseen political crisis (which many feel could stem from the unrest of the young, from the lack of outlet for aspirations and ideals, or ultimately from an economic stagnation that at this moment in France is, unlike in the United States and Great Britain, no more than a shadow on the horizon), or ill-health, Pompidou is almost certain to run for re-election in 1975: in a straight fight against the Communists and a Left-coalition led by François Mitterrand. It is a subject on which Pompidou refuses to speculate. Asked on a recent television interview if he liked being President, he answered: " 'Like' is the wrong word. I am possessed. . . . I mean 'possesed' in the literal sense. In the Dostoevskian sense. Don't forget that in Russian, the title of the novel ["The Possessed"] is 'The Demons.' "

The presidency, then, is Pompidou's demon. But where is the anxiety, the fear, the real "possession" that drives the character Stravrogin to ever greater excesses?

Sometimes it is the very professionalism of Pompidou, limitless neutrality and common sense, that seems likely to cause him the gravest problems. After all, behind the Elysée facade, is France, is Europe, in such rosy shape? Perhaps not.

He has enemies. The deputies, shorn of their real power under de Gaulle's Constitution, are restive; there are those who hold Pompidou's success against him, who see a sinister connection between high finance and political power, and those for whom he is the archbetrayer of Gaullism, and his rivals for 1975, and those who whisper about land-acquisitions through straw men. What can the rising generation of young men in France—whose economic freedom is threatened by the new giant international combines, who feel their identity threatened by the abstraction of a "New Europe" they see as little more than a "market" which benefits the financial potentates and the poor hardly at all, for whom political life in the Fifth Republic has become a politics of absurdity—what can they feel toward a man who says their problems "[don't] weigh on my mind?" That he is "concerned, of course, but their protest was perfectly natural" and that "they wouldn't grow up to much if they didn't protest?" Who dismisses them, in short, as just nice kids?

The least the young are going to feel is that Pompidou does not speak their language. And that sometimes he speaks the same old language that French Governments have always spoken, the language of repression. "Order is respect for law, and law the expression of the general will," Pompidou has said. "But that belongs to a society of the past. We face a different situation. There are individuals and groups who deny not just the law but the expression of the law, who turn their backs on the elections by which the general will makes itself felt. And then, more and more, there is in the modern world a kind of need for violence. . . . The old outlets, colonial wars, explorations, are gone. . . . There could be general subversion, an attempt to overthrow the Government. . . . Well, I'd repress subversion with patience, firmness and, if needed, harshness. And then there is this generalized, scattered, sudden violence. . . . One cannot foresee everything. Ultimately order may be respect for law, but above all it's respect for human beings, respect for others and self-respect. Which is why order isn't in the streets; it's inside the citizenry and it depends on them."

True, these are the words of moderation, of a patient man. But to many they are also the language of an administrator, a technocrat, a man who, for all his *bonhomie,* for all the smiles and friendliness he dispenses in his ceremonial functions, remains faceless. Such people may conclude, as did one of his former associates, that Pompidou is not at all a natural neutral, a moderate, a representative of the new European Center, the rational consensus. "That face," they say, "is merely the mask." "Do not forget," this man told me, "that men who have risen to high position in society, very largely because their society is organized in such a way that men *can* rise to the highest offices, have every reason to congratulate themselves: not only on their native skill and talent, but also on the nature of the society which made their ascension possible. They are bound to feel that society is, in fact, the best possible society, and they have every reason to defend its interests." The answer that one might make to this charge is that, if true of Pompidou, it may also be true of the majority of Frenchmen. Pompidou then emerges as the natural leader of the French silent majority.

Being President hadn't changed Pompidou in any essential way. He still read at lot, he still had a private life, he had not ceased being an intellectual. He still saw his intimate friends; the same writers and painters and connoisseurs of the good life he had known as the director of the Rothschild Bank, people like the novelist Françoise Sagan and the painter Bernard Buffet. They could come and dine with him; they could still talk freely. Of course, it was more difficult as President. Mrs. Pompidou was less restricted. On the whole, he had ample contact with the public; it was something he insisted upon. A President need not feel isolated.

He didn't think he was out of touch with the young. He had his son, who was now a doctor, and he saw quite a few of his son's friends: because he liked to see young people and because he thought talking with them "kept him in shape."

And, no: "There are some things that are less interesting than others, but, no, I am never bored."

Some of the ambiguity which people see in Pompidou is undoubtedly due to the nature of the French presidency itself. The "strong" presidency is still an innovation but in many respects it seems like a repetition of the old: there's the cutting of ribbons and the bussing of Olympic heroes, for the presidency is part ceremonial and part symbolic. The President *is,* after all, the nation. Certainly, de Gaulle was the living incarnation of that truth. But Pompidou?

Like so many "solutions" to the perennial problem of politics in France, the Fifth Republic was created as a reaction to its predecessors; the creation of a "strong" presidency was based upon the scorn de Gaulle, Pompidou and most Frenchmen felt for the "parliamentary game" of the Third and Fourth Republics.

The innovation, not unsurprisingly, has worked well so far: the nation relishes leadership, and voters a direct vote as to who leads them; the professional politicians recognize and covet the greatest power. But that greater power has never been precisely defined. In appearance, there are two parallel powers: the President and the Premier, Pompidou and Jacques Chaban-Delmas, deputy from Bordeaux and also mayor of that city. As for many years there was General de Gaulle and Georges Pompidou. Pompidou is head of state, Chaban-Delmas head of the Government. Pompidou is the apex of the nation, Chaban-Delmas the pinnacle of a legislature of deputies, of ministers, of other political powers.

The two men see each other constantly, nearly every day. Pompidou is very precise about that. Punctilious even, as he was when *he* was Prime Minister and many mistakenly thought that because de Gaulle was President, Pompidou was just his lackey.

Pompidou explained his relations with his Prime Minister: "Chaban-Delmas," he said, "that's the daily business of the state. I don't have to do that; that's what I have a Premier for. Take the budget. That's an important matter. Well, once a year, it costs me two or three hours' work. But Chaban-Delmas, for him it's 50, 100 hours' work." The President, then, deals less with the formulation of policy than with decision. "Yes," Pompidou answered, "ultimately power rests in this office, but it is a question of how and when one exercises it."

Was there, I asked, a *réserve spéciale,* as there had been under de Gaulle? The President exclusively concerned with matters of major moment, almost exclusively international, and everything else left in the hands of the Premier?

As head of state, obviously the President was especially interested in foreign affairs; it was he who had negotiated with Heath, who had just come back from meetings with Brandt; but it was not correct, any more than it was true with de Gaulle, that "the rest" was left to the Premier to handle. In the first place, everything is discussed mutually; in the second, while the President, like the kings of France, has the right of *evocation*—that is, the right to say that such-and-such a thing shall not be discussed but is His and His alone to decide—the business of government would become impossible if the President interfered, either too little or too much. "And those," he added, "who think the President has too much power are always the first to demand that I exercise my power when it suits their own requirements." He was thinking, he said, of a deputy who had asked him to use his Presidential power to prevent the mayor of a provincial town from prohibiting the showing of a particular film.

Pompidou's argument was that if a President was to be President of all the nation he must use his power sparingly, and mainly in those areas where it sprang naturally from the nature of the office.

As for his relations with the legislature and with "his" ministers, he had known "from before the war that power had to have another source besides Parliament," but also that "Parliament was necessary." A constitution had to check the penchant of any executive toward authoritarianism, "which exists just as any parliament has a penchant toward anarchy. When the executive rules alone, the people tire of it . . . an elected legislature is there to prevent that happening." He insists that despite rumors to the contrary, there is no "inner cabinet" or "executive staff" *à la White House,* parallel to the ministries.

But it is a curious system and the French themselves do not yet see it very clearly defined. For one Gaullist deputy on the left wing of his party, the division of powers actually seems to be as follows: each man responding to his own inner nature, Chaban-Delmas had been assigned the liberal, progressive, socially minded sector, and Pompidou the traditional and conservative. Another said: "It is just as it was under de Gaulle: the Premier takes care of France, the President busies himself with the rest of the world." In his recent television interview, Pompidou seems to have cast himself in the role of the "heavy" vs. Chaban-Delmas as "the People's Friend." "By nature," he declared, "I am really a rather nice man. I like to please. And in the job I have . . . I seem to be forced to refuse all the time. . . . I find it harsh to quash demands that seem to me perfectly understandable and which seem, however, to be quite impossible to comply with. And yet I try, I try. . . . I remember a piece of advice General de Gaulle gave me: 'Be tough, Pompidou!' he said. I try, but I find it very hard."

Many I talked to seemed to find this explanation of Pompidou as President a piece of calculated disingenuousness. But then in Paris you can find men to theorize about anything: that the Republic will collapse because President and Premier are at war; that Chaban-Delmas is Pompidou's lackey; that he is his stalking horse for 1975; that Chaban-Delmas only tolerates Pompidou because he himself is running for the presidency; that. . . .

Pompidou is ambiguous; the system is ambiguous; France in 1971 is ambiguous. But the "New European Man" is the one subject on which Pompidou himself is totally unambiguous; it is the only shred of ideology to which he seems genuinely attached. Many see this "New European Man" as a creature of selfish interests; he is motivated only by profit and not by humane values; he operates as a great leveler, rubbing out national, regional, even individual distinctions; he wants to turn us all into one mold, to make us all into his own image. "No," Pompidou says passionately, "the New Europe cannot be all alike." He considers it his most important task, in France itself, to decentralize, to allow of variation.

No, he sees the New Europe in a different way. "I see it more as a restatement of the age-old quarrel between the Ancients and the Moderns," he says. "The Moderns claim pre-eminence over the Ancients. They have progressed further; they know more. But at what cost? What have they lost? Does the Modern really imply the tearing down of all tradition?"

The Europe Pompidou sees is, as he said on the Rhine, conservative, rural France wining with socialist, urban Germany, as if distinctions had vanished in a river mist. No, emphatically no, Pompidou does not want the Moderns to triumph by the destruction of the Ancients. "For me," he says, "European Man is the man who is constantly renewing himself, and when I think of the Europe we are building, what comes to my mind immediately is the Middle Ages. I think of the *cité,* that good place in which all men know each other, in which there is a real sense of community, of belonging. And I wonder," he adds with an ironic smile, cigarette—another, the third or fourth—still dangling straight down from his lower lip, "if I am not, after all, becoming a reactionary. . . ."

Then, as I am ushered out the great double doors of the palace by the chamberlain with his chain and start down the stairs, I see on either side of me the Republican Guard, brilliant in their cuirasses, bandoliers, helmets of shiny steel and horsehair plumes, curved swords held motionlessly upright by their chins, arranged in a hemicycle. . . . I am supposed to exit through that? I take two steps backward into the arms of the frock-coated chamberlain. *"Mais non, monsieur,"* he murmurs politely, "It is quite all right. . . ."

And it is all right. From the depths of a black Citröen emerges the Co-Prince of Andorra—cloaked, shriveled, his mouth full of gold teeth and a *bicorne* on the top of his narrow head—come (as he and his ancestors have done without fail since 1607) to pay his yearly feu duty of 960 francs to his suzerain, the Co-Prince of France. . . .

Suggested Reading

So many people have written good books on modern France that making choices among them is nearly as hard as finding a good cheap French restaurant in New York City. The following list is no *Guide Michelin;* it covers only a few main courses and skips over much tantalizing fare. Only books that have appeared in English are included.

The best study of France under the Republics is David Thomson, *Democracy in France Since 1870* (5th ed., New York and London, 1969). Gordon Wright, *France in Modern Times, 1760 to the Present* (Chicago, 1960), affords a longer and broader perspective on the French past. Stanley Hoffmann's contribution to Hoffmann, *et al., In Search of France* (Cambridge, Mass., 1963), is indispensable reading for anyone interested in France since 1930. Other contributors discuss aspects of the sweeping social and economic changes which have overtaken France in the twentieth century. These changes, along with certain intellectual trends, are also assessed in John Ardagh, *The New French Revolution* (New York, 1968). Ardagh concentrates on the period since the end of the Second World War.

One of the best studies of France in the 1930's remains Alexander Werth's eyewitness account, *The Twilight of France, 1933–1940* (New York, 1942). An unsurpassed essay on the debacle of 1940 is Marc Bloch, *Strange Defeat* (London, 1949). On

France during the war years see Robert Aron, *The Vichy Regime, 1940–1944* (New York, 1958), and the same author's *France Reborn: The History of the Liberation* (New York, 1964). The best source on the Gaullism of de Gaulle is, appropriately enough, Charles de Gaulle himself: *The Complete War Memoirs* (New York, 1964); *Memoirs of Hope: Renewal and Endeavor* (New York, 1971). As studies of the London-based Resistance and the Allied coalition, however, the *War Memoirs* need to be read with great care and compared with other accounts. An excellent short biography of de Gaulle—perhaps the best of any length—is Jean Lacouture, *De Gaulle* (New York, 1966).

The best analysis of the Fourth Republic in any language is Philip M. Williams, *Crisis and Compromise: Politics in the Fourth Republic* (3rd ed., London, 1964). On the French phase of the Indochinese war see Ellen Hammer, *The Struggle for Indochina* (Stanford, 1954). George A. Kelly, *Lost Soldiers: The French Army and Empire in Crisis, 1947–62* (Cambridge, Mass., 1965), examines the causes and consequences of the army's entry into politics. Philip Williams, in collaboration with Martin Harrison, has carried his investigation of postwar French politics into the Fifth Republic with *Politics and Society in de Gaulle's Republic* (London, 1971). Social change at the grass roots is best examined at the grass roots: Edgar Morin, *The Red and the Black: Report from a French Village* (New York, 1971), and Laurence Wylie, *Village in the Vaucluse* (rev. ed., New York, 1964), are local studies done with great sensitivity. A fairly straightforward account of the events of May is Patrick Seale and Maureen Mc-Conville, *Red Flag/Black Flag: French Revolution 1968* (New York, 1968). An excellent short analysis is David Goldey, "A Precarious Regime; The Events of May 1968," in Philip M. Williams, *French Politicians and Elections, 1951–1969* (Cambridge, England, 1970).

Two episodes whose significance transcends the frontiers of France have recently received excellent treatment at the hands of documentary film-makers: Marcel Ophuls, *The Sorrow and the Pity* (1971), on France under the German Occupation; Yves Courrière and Jacques Perrin, *The Algerian War* (1972).

Index

A Note on the Editor

John E. Talbott was born in Grinnell, Iowa, and studied at the University of Missouri and Stanford University. He is the author of *The Politics of Educational Reform in France, 1918–1940*, and is now at work on a study of France and the Algerian War. Mr. Talbott teaches history at the University of California, Santa Barbara.

THE WORLD TO COME

The World to Come

FROM CHRISTIAN PAST
TO GLOBAL FUTURE

Lloyd Geering

POLEBRIDGE PRESS

The World to Come: From Christian Past to Global Future

This edition first published in 1999 by Polebridge Press, P. O. Box 6144, Santa Rosa, California, 95406. Also published in 1999 in New Zealand by Bridget Williams Books Ltd, P O Box 5482, Wellington, New Zealand.

Cover painting: Detail from 'Ben Ohau', oil on linen, 1220 x 1220 mm, 1991, by Grahame Sydney, as published in Timeless Land, Longacre Press, 1995. Reproduced by kind permission of the artist.

Cover design by Mission Hall Design Group

Library of Congress Cataloging-in-Publication Data

Geering, Lloyd George.
    The world to come : from Christian past to global future / Lloyd
    Geering
      p. cm.
    Includes bibliographical references and index.
    ISBN 0-944344-76-3
      1. Christianity – Controversial literature. 2. Religion and culture –
      Forecasting. I. Title.

BL2776 .G44 1999
200'.1'12 – dc21
                                                              99-040098

*To the affectionate memory
of my parents*

GEORGE GEERING (1875–1976)
ALICE GEERING (1879–1957)

CONTENTS

FOREWORD

It gives me great pleasure to introduce Lloyd Geering to American readers for the first time. It is unfortunate that his pioneering spirit and theological genius have been confined largely to New Zealand, his home, to Australia, where he taught theology for a time, and to Great Britain, where he is known as a friend of the Sea of Faith movement initiated by Don Cupitt. With the publication of this book, we hope North Americans will discover why he enjoys the high reputation he does elsewhere in the world.

Professor Geering is a forerunner of the Jesus Seminar. Back in 1966, long before the Seminar was organized, he published an article on the resurrection of Jesus that anticipated many of the findings of the Seminar twenty years later. In 1967, he published a second article on the immortality of the soul that stirred many Presbyterians in New Zealand to take action. He was charged with doctrinal error and disturbing the peace of the church, of which he is an ordained minister. A two-day televised trial before the Assembly led to his exoneration and contributed to his fame. Yet the experience was perhaps what moved Lloyd Geering to enter on the next phase of his career, which was to become the theological pied piper of New Zealand.

In 1971, he resigned as Principal of Theological Hall, Knox College, Dunedin, to become Foundation Professor of Religious Studies, Victoria University in Wellington. As has so often been the case in the twentieth century, the church attempted to silence one of its truly prophetic voices only to find that it had depleted its own treasury of wisdom by so doing. Lloyd Geering served as Professor in Victoria University until 1984, when he retired. Meanwhile, he was much in demand as lecturer and commentator on religion on both radio and television. In 1988 he was made a Companion of the British Empire.

In 1998, I was privileged to tour New Zealand in the Jesus Seminar on-the-Road programs organized by James Veitch. On that occasion, I appeared with Professor Geering and found, much to my delight, a precursor of such wit and wisdom that we immediately became friends. Subsequently, I invited him to the United States to be a featured lecturer in our Once and Future Jesus series (October 1999) and we offered to publish his new book, *The World to Come. From Christian Past to Global Future*, which you now have before you.

In his previous book, *Tomorrow's God* (1994), Professor Geering argues that in the past we created our gods and religions by means of our stories, stories that no longer function they way they once did. We have passed through several revolutions – the cosmological, the biological, and the anthropological – that have created a radical shift in human consciousness. The old mythic certainties have died as a result. The loss of meaning has resulted in greater personal freedom, but it has brought with it new challenges. The future was once encompassed by the future of the tribe (in the ethnic age), then human beings looked to a personal future in heaven (or hell) (in the transethnic age), now (in the global age) they must begin to think of their future in terms of stewardship for the planet and care for each other. Jesus is not coming back to help us. In place of that hope, we must now think of creating a new global spirituality that will serve us in the centuries to come. In *The World to Come* Professor Geering announces the end of the millennium, of Christendom, of Christian orthodoxy, of old mythic certainties, while sketching his vision of a new global spirituality that incorporates the best of our legacy from the past and promotes care for all living creatures and the earth itself.

I am certain you will find Lloyd Geering's clear thinking and lucid writing as stimulating and enlightening as I have.

Robert W. Funk
Director, Westar Institute
Founder, Jesus Seminar

PREFACE

Some of the material in this book has, in earlier drafts, been delivered as lectures to a variety of public audiences. Chapter 6 has drawn extensively from some lectures published as *Relativity: the Key to Human Understanding*. Some lectures recently published as *Does Society Need Religion?* are reflected in chapter 12 and elsewhere.

Throughout most of the book the traditional notation for dates, BC and AD, has been replaced by the modern convention, BCE (Before the Common Era) and CE (Common Era). This change of convention is itself illustrative of the theme of the book; the traditional notation has been retained only where it is necessary to support the reasoning.

Reference is frequently made to the Axial Period (approx. 700–300 BCE). This term, coined by Karl Jaspers, is commonly used to refer to the period of creative and radical cultural change out of which came the great religious traditions sometimes known as the world religions. The current phenomenon of cultural change, now on a global scale, may be regarded as a Second Axial Period in the known history of humankind. I have discussed the Axial Period much more fully in my earlier books *Faith's New Age* and *Tomorrow's God*. To some extent this book may be regarded as a sequel to them both.

Lloyd Geering
WELLINGTON, 1999

Introduction

This book had its beginnings in the English summer of 1997, during a three-month spell in Oxford. Since the idea of the year 2000 CE was already creating some excitement, I began to ponder the questions posed by the century's end. And so, in the Bodleian Library, I read around the theme of the millennium.

What, after all, does it commemorate? If we really wished to celebrate the two-thousandth anniversary of the birth of Jesus Christ, the year 1996 would be nearer the mark (though this is only an intelligent guess). Even by traditional reckoning, the start of the new millennium should be 1 January 2001, as the Royal Greenwich Observatory has declared and the title of the popular film, *2001: A Space Odyssey*, suggests.

The Christian calendar, long believed to be commemorating a divine event, is not only the product of the creative human imagination but also reflects the errors so often made by fallible human beings. So the year 2000 is but a human convention which rests both on a miscalculation and on convictions which have now become outmoded. Yet Mikhail Gorbachev, himself instrumental in altering the course of events in the former Soviet Union, was probably right when he said that humankind stands today at a watershed in its history. Thus, for reasons quite different from those associated with the origin and meaning of the western calendar, the year 2000 appears to mark a significant turning point in human history.

Some look forward to the new millennium with keen anticipation; others approach it with foreboding. The optimists see it as a golden age of unprecedented prosperity sustained by expanding knowledge and technology. The pessimists fear that the third millennium, perhaps even the first century of it, may bring crises of colossal proportions for the human species.

This striking ambivalence is sufficient to make us pause and take stock of what lies ahead. It is not only the second millennium which is coming to an end, but also much of what we have taken for granted in the past.

We are living in a whole series of 'end-times'. People who have already distanced themselves from traditional Christian beliefs may well question the
need for a book about the end of conventional Christianity, when this
seems self-evident. However, the end of the Christian era is likely to have
far-reaching consequences, and we need to understand the reasons for its
demise. Many who have abandoned all commitment to the tradition over-
look the fact that many aspects of Christian civilisation are also under
threat in the post-Christian age. The end-times of the late twentieth century are on a global scale, and it is not only Christians who are at risk.

Most people who are still practising Christians, in one form or another,
will not want to contemplate the possibility of the Christian era ending.
Yet, in turning to the Bible to defend the traditional Christian teaching,
they will find that concern with the end-times is a dominant theme of the
Bible itself. The anticipation of the end of the age, along with the hope for
a new world to come, has had a long history in Judeo-Christian tradition.
The Israelite prophets used words like these:

> It shall come to pass in the last days that the mountain on which
> God dwells will be established as the highest of all mountains.
> All the nations will stream towards it to learn from God how to
> walk in the paths designed by him. He will establish justice
> among the nations, so that they beat their swords into
> ploughshares and their spears into pruning hooks and abandon
> war for ever. Thereafter they will sit by their vines and under their
> fig trees fearful of no one.[1]

Yet the prophets also warned that the God who had created the world
could end it by destruction. About 620 BCE the prophet Jeremiah, observing the signs that the Kingdom of David was about to be swallowed up by
invasion from the east, spoke of the end not just of the people of Israel
but of the whole earth in these alarming words:

> I have seen what the earth is coming to,
> and lo, it is as formless and empty as when it began.
> And I have seen the heavens;
> their light has gone, only darkness is left.
> I have seen the mountains and they are quaking,
> and the hills are shaking to and fro.
> I looked and there is not a human to be found,
> and all the birds of the sky have fled.
> I looked and the garden-land has become a desert
> and all its cities are in ruins.[2]

Christianity emerged during a resurgence of this Jewish concern about the likely end of the age. It was a period of widespread cultural change and turmoil not unlike that which we have now entered. The Graeco-Roman civilisation had just passed its zenith. The Jewish people, after a dramatic political recovery in the time of Herod the Great, were experiencing their second expulsion from their ancestral land. The first Christians were Jews who shared this expectation of an imminent end with many of their fellow Jews. But they also believed that the Messiah had already come – a Messiah who would usher in a new age, and thereby bring the Jewish tradition to its logical end or fulfilment. They went out proclaiming the advent of an entirely different world. Thus, for a variety of reasons, the first Christians saw themselves living in the *eschata* (end-times or last days) and this belief permeates the writings of the New Testament.

Today there is some doubt among scholars as to whether the idea of an end-time was actually taught and shared by Jesus, but it certainly became dominant in the rise of Christianity after his death. The imminent end-time is described in the New Testament in such striking passages as:

> In those days the sun will be darkened and the moon will not give its light and the stars will fall from heaven, and the powers of the heavens will be shaken . . . this generation will not pass away till all these things take place. Heaven and earth will pass away, but these words will not pass away. Of that day and hour no one knows . . . but the Father only. As were the days of Noah, so will be the coming of the Son of man.

> In the last days there will come times of stress. For men will be lovers of self, lovers of money, disobedient to their parents, inhuman, slanderers, haters of good.[3]

> I saw a new sky and a new earth, for the first sky and the first earth had passed away and the sea was no more.[4]

The earliest of the New Testament writings also refer to it; in his letters, Paul wrote with passion and complete confidence about the approaching time when

> the Lord himself will descend from heaven with a cry of command, with the archangel's call, and with the sound of the trumpet of God. And the dead will rise first; and then we who are alive, who are left, shall be caught up together with them in the clouds to meet the Lord in the air; and so we shall always be with the Lord.[5]

Paul clearly expected the end of the present age and the coming of the new world to occur in his own lifetime. His attention was so focused on the immediate future that he showed little interest in the words and deeds of Jesus, as remembered from the latter's earthly ministry. Paul saw the now glorified Jesus as the first of a new kind of human being, the new Adam.

The Jewish Christians came to see Jesus as a new Moses, who would lead not only the Jews but the whole of humankind out of enslavement to the Devil. The Gentile Christianity shaped by Paul went further in the second century, even debating whether to cut its links with its Jewish past. Thus Christians joyfully hailed the Christian Gospel as a new beginning, saying, 'The old has passed away, behold, the new has come.'[6] They looked expectantly to the forthcoming time when the world of the past would be completely replaced by a new world of peace, order and wholeness.

The early Christians' expectation of the world to come was not fulfilled, at least not in the way they imagined it. As someone has succinctly put it, the first Christians looked expectantly for the coming of the Kingdom of God, but what they got was the church! By the end of the first century, and certainly during the second century, a good deal of readjustment in Christian thinking had to be done. What eventually emerged from the chrysalis of early Christianity was Christendom, ruled by an ecclesiastical institution which inherited the structures of imperial Rome. The church affirmed an increasingly detailed body of authoritative Christian doctrine in which hope for the world to come had been subtly transferred to a distant future, to be reached only after death and resurrection. Right up until recent times the Christian west was being openly shaped and motivated by what Christianity had ultimately become.

But we have now come to the end of Christendom. We are nearing the end of the global supremacy of the Christian west. We are even seeing the collapse of conventional Christianity. We are suffering the loss of what we long took to be verities and certainties. We are already caught up in a process of cultural change more rapid, more deeply rooted and more widespread than ever before in human history. We are now entering a post-Christian and uncertain global future. The sandwich-board message of the proverbial Hyde Park preacher, 'The End is Nigh!', has unexpectedly become relevant to everybody, Christian or not.

Conventional Christianity is, somewhat ironically, declining in the context of great cultural change not unlike that in which Christianity emerged. There are some clear parallels between now and the time of Christian origins, as there are also between the disintegration of the Christian west and the decline of the Roman Empire. Much of what the west has long taken for granted is now disappearing: the security provided by Christendom; the Christian way of interpreting reality; the confidence that the Christian path leads to eternal salvation; and the belief that Christian doctrine embodies the essential and unchangeable truths by which to live. All these are passing away. We face a future without them, a post-Christian future which will be very different from the past.

There are, however, some significant differences between New Testament times and ours. Christian fundamentalists, who read the New Testament at face value, and who look at today's events through the lens of the New Testament, are inclined to treat the passing of the last 2,000 years as if nothing has substantially changed. They still look expectantly to the bodily return of Jesus descending from the heavens, the battle of Armageddon in the Middle East and the replacement of this present world with a 'new heaven and a new earth'. But the end-times of the first Christians, on which Bible-believing Christians of today fasten their attention, are very different from our current end-times, described in Part I of this book. For the latter reflect the history of the Christian era and all that has happened in the centuries since Christianity came into being.

Today's fundamentalists who proclaim that the end is nigh are apt to anticipate the destruction of the world with enthusiasm. Recently, for example, planeloads of American fundamentalists have been travelling to Israel to view the site, Megiddo, where they believe the great clash among the nations will break out, and the battle of Armageddon will bring to an end the world as we know it.[7] As this event is believed to herald the return of Jesus Christ, they have no fear for their own future, understanding from the words of Paul quoted above, that they will be 'raptured' (lifted up into the sky and preserved from destruction) and that only non-believers will perish in the death of the old world.

Most mainline churches have little sympathy with this talk about end-times, whether it comes from the fundamentalists or from those who warn of the end of conventional Christianity. Mainstream Christians tend to look to the past rather than to the future, and to search for ways to restore Christianity to its former glory, as manifested in the flowering of Christendom. Only a minority of Christians show any awareness of the crisis now facing Christianity.

There are a few who are looking more seriously into the future of Christianity, and writing about it. They include: Stanley Romaine Hopper, *The Crisis of Faith* (1947); W.H. van de Pol, *The End of Conventional*

Christianity (1968); David Edwards, *The Futures of Christianity* (1987); Ewert Cousins, *Christ of the 21st Century* (1992); Donald English, *Into the 21st Century* (1995); Douglas John Hall, *The End of Christendom and the Future of Christianity* (1997); John Shelby Spong, *Why Christianity Must Change or Die* (1998); and Don Cupitt, *After God* (1997). By and large, however, there has been great reluctance on the part of the churches to acknowledge that we are entering a post-Christian age.

An examination of today's end-times is, however, highly pertinent to Christian and non-Christian alike. And what better time to attempt it than as we pass into the third millennium? What does the end of the Christian era mean, not only for the post-Christian west, but for the world as a whole? What will follow this series of end-times? What sort of post-Christian future can we expect in the twenty-first century? What does the world face beyond 2000 CE?

In Part 2, this book attempts, tentatively, to take stock of just where we humans are in the evolution of human culture on this planet, to explore the significance of entering a new era that is both global and post-Christian, and to look into the future.

Humans have long been used to contemplating their own personal future. Unlike other animals which (as far as we can tell) live in a timeless present, we have a sense of the passing of time. We humans are aware of change in personal development, as described in Shakespeare's 'seven ages of man'; so we are used to planning for the next day, the next year or even for a lifetime as when, in early adulthood, we choose a career or a spouse. But in the past this contemplation of a personal future normally took place with the idea that the cultural and physical environment had some permanence. The physical world in particular seemed to be changeless. Its mountains, rocks and rivers had such apparent reliability that God's eternal presence was likened to a rock.

With the advent of the modern world view, humans have become increasingly aware of the phenomenon of change as something which permeates the whole of reality. From geology we have come to understand that, in geological time, the earth is continually changing its surface and the physical environment within which life is to be lived. Hard on the heels of the idea of a slowly changing earth came the notion of biological evolution. The planets' innumerable living species are not fixed but are subject to slow evolutionary change, leading sometimes to the emergence of new species and sometimes to their extinction.

The ideas of evolution and historical development in the distant past were barely accepted, before the current process of cultural and religious change gained momentum. The widespread consciousness of this in the latter half of the twentieth century caused Alvin Toffler's *Future Shock* to be a runaway best-seller. It struck a chord with what people were beginning to feel.

Thus it seems that nothing in the world stays the same. The Buddhist idea of universal impermanence has largely been confirmed. Moreover, the process of change is now accelerating, both in human culture and in our physical environment. So radical is human change that many national and minority cultures are threatened with extinction and are beginning to take desperate measures to try to preserve themselves. We can therefore no longer take the future of the world for granted as our forebears used to. But neither can we afford simply to ignore the future and stoically await what comes. If there are still different possible futures for planetary life in general, and for human existence in particular, those futures have come to depend increasingly on decisions made by the human species. We now have to plan not only for our personal future but also for the future of the earth itself.

Part 2, in assessing the trends now dominant in the global cultural change we are facing, will sketch the process of globalisation, humanity's threat to itself, the human threat to the planet that sustains its life, and the possible scenarios that may result from these threats. It will conclude by exploring the possible emergence of a new kind of society – a global society, whose cohesion and harmonious life rest upon the rise of a global culture.

Every culture in the past has had a religious dimension, which motivates the culture and supplies it with its values and goals. As the word 'religion' has, in popular usage, become associated with an outdated supernatural world, we need to return to the original meaning of the word if there is to be any profitable discussion about the religion of the future. The Latin word *religio* meant devotion or commitment, 'a conscientious concern for what really matters'; the English word 'religion', while often implying a sense of the sacred, originally referred to the human attitude of devotion. To be religious in any culture is to be devoted to whatever is believed to matter most in life. As we shall see, religion has been usefully defined as 'a total mode of the interpreting and living of life'.[8] That is the sense in which the word will be used here.[9]

The religious dimension of global culture, if it comes at all, will be naturalistic and humanistic in form. Yet it will evolve out of the many cultures which have preceded it – and in particular its Christian heritage, simply because the civilisation of the Christian west indirectly caused the modern world to come into being. But what could the Christian tradition (long wedded to a supernaturalist format) possibly contribute to the growth of a humanistic global culture? Curiously, the religious dimension of the new global society may draw on some of the long-neglected elements in the biblical tradition itself. The books known as the Wisdom Literature, also referred to as the documents of Hebrew humanism (Proverbs, Job, Ecclesiastes, Wisdom of Solomon, Ecclesiasticus), describe a religious way of thinking drawn from the lessons of daily experience. It was humanistic and universalistic, and it almost completely ignored the historical and theological themes which dominate the rest of the Old Testament. It drew freely from non-Israelite sources. And recent New Testament scholarship suggests that Jesus of Nazareth had much more affinity with this stream of thought than previously realised. 'Jesus may well have been a wisdom teacher – a sage,' concludes Robert Funk of the Jesus Seminar.[10]

There are other (often forgotten) voices from the Judeo-Christian past which are now being heard more clearly – people whose work or writing has contributed to the rise of the contemporary naturalist worldview. Modern ecologists (usually non-religious) are singing the praises of the mediaeval Francis of Assisi, a man who abandoned material riches and the life of sensual pleasure to adopt the simplest and most frugal of lifestyles. In particular, he turned back to the natural world, long neglected by earlier Christianity, and acknowledged his kinship with all living things. The order of friars that Francis founded was forbidden, at first, even to own property; they had to live by the work of their hands. The Franciscans also produced some remarkable thinkers – Roger Bacon, Bonaventure, Duns Scotus and William of Ockham (who indirectly influenced Luther and Feuerbach) – men who pioneered some of the ideas that led to the modern world several centuries later.

Exploring the idea of Christ in the twenty-first century in 1992, Ewert Cousins wrote: 'with a penetrating spiritual insight, Francis saw an organic relationship between nature, the human and God . . . For him nature was sacred, an expression of God himself; it was a divine gift which bore God's imprint'.[11] He suggested that Francis' integral humanism is even more relevant to the global context of the twentieth century than it was to the thirteenth.

The seventeenth-century Jewish philosopher Spinoza (1632–1677) also affirmed the relationship between divinity and nature. He began to speak of 'God or Nature', as if these were alternative concepts. Convinced of the unity of all reality, Spinoza effectively eliminated the great gulf previously thought to exist between the Creator and the Creation, between the spiritual and physical. He was far ahead of his time, however, and was completely rejected by both Jew and Christian. Yet his ideas later flourished in the writing of Hegel, Schelling, Schleiermacher and Feuerbach in the nineteenth century and in Buber, Teilhard de Chardin and Tillich in the twentieth.

Ludwig Feuerbach shocked the western Christian world in 1841 with what might be called in current terminology the 'deconstruction' of Christianity in his book *The Essence of Christianity*.[12] While he set out to expound Christianity positively, he did so on a completely natural basis and without any reference to supernatural forces. Feuerbach already sensed the radical cultural change beginning to take place. He spoke of the coming of a new era in human history and the need for a new religion. In his lectures to students in Heidelberg he concluded:

> We must replace the love of God by the love of man as the only true religion . . . the belief in God by the belief in man . . . My wish is to transform friends of God into friends of man, believers into thinkers . . . candidates for the hereafter into students of this world, Christians, who, by their own profession are half-animal, half-angel, into men, into whole men.[13]

Feuerbach further offended the people of his day by suggesting that the ancient nature religions remained superior to Christianity since they were sensuously in touch with the earth and with nature, whereas Christianity had become separated from nature, and had made of God a separate, sexless, spiritual being. Some of his words could have been written today.

The Christian tradition has contained many different elements in the past, some of which were in their day rejected and condemned. Ironically, it is some of those dissident elements of the old tradition that may well contain seeds of the religious dimension of the future global society. The global era will, in some respects, be very different from the Christian era which preceded it, but there will also be continuity. The transition from one to the other forms the subject of this book.

PART I

The End
of the Christian Era

CHAPTER I

The End
of the Millennium

The year we call 2000 is a human convention created by western culture, projected upon the planet as a convenient way of measuring historical time. In the natural world of celestial bodies, the year 2000 has no actual existence, let alone significance. Not one of the astronomical cycles within our solar system (giving us days, months and years) is a simple multiple of the others, nor are any of them naturally divisible by thousands.

The factors leading to the convention now called 'the millennium' are various. In the first place, our ancient ancestors created a 10-digit numbering system only because we happen to have 10 fingers. There are plenty of other possible systems, some of them now considered better than our decimal system. Even to speak of a millennium, or 1,000 years, is to impose one particular numbering system on the measurement of time – and a humanly invented one at that.

Secondly, the calendar which numbers the years from the supposed birth year of Jesus of Nazareth was established by Christians, and is peculiar to the Christian tradition. It has never been shared by other cultures. The Jews, for example, number their years from the first day of the creation of the world, as calculated from the Books of Moses. This they determined to be 3,760 years before the beginning of the Christian era. The year 2000 AD for Christians will be the year 5760–5761 for Jews. (The Jewish year does not begin on 1 January but on Rosh Hashanah, which varies slightly from year to year, according to the cycles of the moon.)

The Muslim calendar differs further from the Christian calendar. The Islamic year consists of 12 exact lunar months (or cycles of the moon around the earth) and hence is shorter, by about 11 days, than our solar year (the time of a cycle of the earth around the sun). The Islamic calendar starts neither from the birth of Jesus nor from the birth of Muhammad but from the *Hijrah* ('flight') of Muhammad from Mecca to Medina, which resulted in the establishment of the first Islamic state.

Thus the Christian calendar is far from being observed worldwide. Only about one fifth of humankind is even nominally Christian. It is chauvinistic of Christians to assume that the other four-fifths of the human race should have any special interest in the year 2000 and the transition it marks from the second to the third millennium.

The year 2000 has, moreover, become suspect even for Christians. Although the calendar starts from the supposed birth of Jesus Christ, no one really knows what year Jesus was born! The year 4 BC is now seen as more likely. (That is why a group of leading New Testament scholars, known as the Jesus Seminar, named their 1996 conference *Jesus at 2000*.)[1]

So when we refer to the end of the second millennium and the beginning of a third millennium we are talking only about a human construct. And if we pay too much attention to the year 2000 we are in danger of being deceived by our own cultural creation, like a spider entangled in its own web. People, who make plans to travel the world in order to view the dawning of the new millennium, are caught in a similar sort of web. For they are observing yet another convention – the now universal practice of imposing on the globe a meridian passing through Greenwich, a line arbitrarily chosen by the sea-faring people of Britain. Sunrise in the Chatham Islands off New Zealand's east coast on January 1, 2000, has no meaning in the natural world. By endowing such 'millennial' events with some kind of absolute significance, we humans merely dupe ourselves with our own creations.

Any meaning associated with the year 2000 rests solely on certain religious beliefs held exclusively by Christians. For Christians the year of the birth of Jesus Christ *was* a year of cosmic significance: one by which, as they believed, the divine Creator of the universe and Lord of history had inaugurated an entirely new era for the world. It marked the moment when God had chosen to cut human history in two. Everything which came before that event was to be measured backwards, occurring, as they later said, so many years *Before Christ* (or BC). Everything which came afterwards was in a particular year of the Lord, *Anno Domini* (or AD).

Even in this more secular age, people in the western world tacitly, even if unintentionally, acknowledge Christian faith when they refer to a particular year by number, since the words Anno Domini, strictly speaking, are always implied. Some secular protest in the west against the continuing use of the traditional calendar might perhaps have been expected. Indeed, when Auguste Comte (1798–1857) promoted his new Religion of Humanity in the mid nineteenth century, he introduced a calendar of 13 months, named after such people as Moses, Aristotle, Caesar, Shakespeare and Descartes. The year of the French Revolution was Year One of his Positivist Calendar.

The year we call 2000 CE is not only religiously based, and hence cultur- ally relative, but it is also based on doubtful calculations. It was a Scythian Christian monk called Dionysius Exiguus (Dennis the Short), living in Rome in the sixth century, who first suggested that our years should be dated from the birth of Jesus of Nazareth. In 525 AD, at the request of Pope St John I, Dionysius prepared a new schedule for the calculation of Easter; almost as an addendum, he suggested a reform which was little noticed at the time. He discarded the current Alexandrian practice of dating the years from the beginning of the rule of Diocletian (284 AD) on the grounds that it perpetuated the name of the Great Persecutor, and proposed that the years be numbered from the 'Incarnation of the Lord Jesus Christ'. (Coptic Christians retain the Alexandrian calendar to this day on the grounds that it honours the martyrs put to death by Diocletian.)

Dionysius argued that, just as the Romans had come to regard the foun- dation of Rome as the beginning of the civilisation of ancient Rome, so the coming of Jesus Christ into the world marked the beginning of a new era in the history of the world – the Christian era. He placed that event in the year 753 of the Roman calendar. By then Christians were already cele- brating 25 March (nine calendar months before Christmas Day) as the Feast Day of the Annunciation to the Virgin Mary. So Dionysius put the New Year's Day of the first year in his new calendar on that date, believing it to mark the time of Jesus' conception in the womb of his mother Mary. (Only in 1582 was New Year's Day restored by Pope Gregory XIII to 1 January, where Julius Caesar had earlier placed it.)

The acceptance of the 'Christian era' of Dionysius spread because of the use made of his new Easter tables. It was promoted by the influential 'Doctor of the Church', Isidore of Seville (*c.*560–636). In England the Christian era was adopted at the Synod of Whitby in 664, but it did not become general in Europe until the eleventh century, and in the Greek world not until the fifteenth.

The Christian era was perfectly consistent with the way Christians had come to understand the world. For them, the birth of Jesus Christ was a turning point in world history, a cosmic event just as basic to the universe as the creation of the earth, sun and moon, and the creation of humankind. Did not the biblical story of the birth of Jesus report that a new star appeared in the sky to mark the event, and that this enabled the magi of the east to find their way to Bethlehem? Was not Jesus Christ referred to in the New Testament as the new Adam? Such things made it clear to them that the coming of Jesus Christ was on a par with the cre- ation of humankind.

This conviction about the central place of Christ in human history seemed convincing at that time and came to be universally accepted throughout the Christian world until less than 200 years ago. As Christians approached the beginning of the second Christian millennium (which, according to some authorities, they more correctly calculated to be the first day of 1001 AD), a huge crowd gathered in Rome, expecting the end of the world, and others flocked to Palestine to witness the Advent of the Saviour as the Last Trump sounded. There was not even a hint in those days that the Christian picture of the universe would not stand up to careful scrutiny.

As we come to the end of the second millennium, however, we are aware of the subjective foundations of the Christian calendar, and of the legendary character of the data used by Dionysius Exiguus. The date of 25 December for celebrating the birthday of Jesus cannot be traced back with any certainty beyond 336 AD, and has no historical connection with Jesus. It probably resulted from the Christianisation of the Mithraic festival, held at the winter solstice, which celebrated the rebirth of the unconquerable sun, Invictus. (Mithraism was the chief religious rival to Christianity in the pre-Constantinian days of Rome.) The Christian festival of the Annunciation on 25 March was arrived at simply by going back nine months from the supposed birthday of Jesus.

In fact we know neither the day on which Jesus was born, nor the year. Just how Dionysius calculated the year of Jesus' birth we cannot be sure, but it is not consistent with what we find in the New Testament. According to the Gospel of Matthew, Jesus was born 'in the days of Herod the King'. Since we know that Herod the Great died in what would now be reckoned the year 4 BC, Jesus was perhaps born no later than that year. Luke also assigns the birth of Jesus to the days of Herod but goes on to associate it with an enrolment ordered by Caesar Augustus when Quirinius was governor of Syria. But the rule of Quirinius is now reckoned to be about 6–9 AD, more than a decade after the death of Herod. Thus Luke's dates, and other clues in the New Testament, are not at all reliable, partly because they were written nearly a century after the event and partly because they were determined by religious interests rather than by a concern for historical accuracy. Modern attempts to date the birth of Jesus by astronomical calculations concerning the brightness of a star are not reliable either, since the visit of Wise Men from the east is almost certainly legendary. Our traditional dating of the years thus rests upon quite late and unhistorical traditions, and in no sense does it mark a supposed significant event with historical accuracy.

Today, even the significance of the birth of Jesus is open to question. Jesus may still be regarded as a wise and innovative teacher who has exerted a great deal of influence during the course of the last 20 centuries, but he is now coming to be seen as one great teacher among others, rather than the incarnation of the one and only God, and the absolute Saviour of all humankind. The date of his birth, if we could know it, would still hold some significance for Christians, but it has lost its universal meaning as a turning point in history.

Within the Christian tradition, however, the millennium is also regarded as significant for reasons quite other than the supposed birth-date of Jesus Christ. Some of this has to do with a numbering system based on the numeral 10. We all use the figures 10, 100, 1,000, and 10,000 as handy approximations for particular periods of time and these all occur frequently in the Bible, as they do in other religious traditions. The millennium, or a period of 1,000 years, can thus be seen as a convenient way of delineating a substantial piece of time. But the millennium has come to mean much more than that, largely because the Judeo-Christian tradition believed that God not only created the world but was unfolding its history step by step according to a divine plan.

The twentieth-century philosopher of history, R.G. Collingwood, judged the early Christians to be the first to conceive of writing a universal history of the world going back to the origin of humankind, and instanced Eusebius of Caesarea (*c.*260–340). But, long before Eusebius, the ancient Israelite scholars had laid sketch plans for such a universal history in their Hebrew Scriptures (the Christian Old Testament), and this was carried further by the Jewish scholar Josephus (37–100 AD) in his book, *Antiquities of the Jews.*

These early Israelite traditions (compiled in their present form during the period of the Babylonian Exile) were set out in eras divided by strategic turning points, such as the Great Flood (which led to a new beginning for humankind), the Tower of Babel (which led to the dispersion of peoples), the Abrahamic migration (by which the offspring of Abraham became the 'chosen people'), the Exodus from Egypt (which led to the possession of the Promised Land) and, finally, the establishment of the Kingdom of David. It was in such ways that figures and events became milestones on the path of a universal history which revealed the supposed plan of divine salvation. History was viewed through theological spectacles, effectively imposing a supposed divine plan on the sequence of historical events.

Belief in such a plan motivated not only the calculations of Dionysius in

525 but also those of Bishop Ussher (1581–1656) a thousand years later. Ussher, noting the time of Herod's death, decided that Dionysius must have been in error and placed the birth of Jesus in the year 4 BC. Already, the Venerable Bede (c.673–735) had carefully calculated from the Hebrew Bible that the Creation occurred 3,952 years before the birth of Christ. Ussher, influenced by the fascination with millennia which had become an integral part of the Christian schema, had little difficulty in making a few minor corrections to Bede's calculations. He concluded that the Creation occurred exactly 4,000 years before the birth of Christ, in 4004 BC – at noon on 23 October. (His calculations were still being printed in the text of the King James Bible well into the twentieth century). Since, according to tbe Bible, the world had been created in six days, and 1,000 years are but as a day for God, Ussher believed that the world would last 6,000 years. (This conclusion had already been reached by the ancient Christian scholar Lactantius, c.240–320). The building of Solomon's temple was finished at the halfway mark, 3,000 years after Creation. Christ came 4,000 years after Creation; this left a further 2,000 years to run. By his calculation the world should have ended in 1996.

This brings us to an even more important reason for the current interest in the new millennium, one which has very ancient roots. The special significance attached to a period of 1,000 years eventually became so widespread that the term millennium now appears in the *Oxford English Dictionary* as 'a period of happiness and benign government'. Such a meaning can be traced back directly to a few verses in the biblical book of Revelation (Chapter 20:1–7). The writer, purporting to reveal the future of the world, speaks of a period of 1,000 years in which Satan will be held chained to a bottomless pit. During this period Christ, along with all those martyred for their faith in him, will reign, unhindered by the evil designs of Satan. But after the 1,000 years Satan will be released from his prison, and the nations from the four corners of the earth will engage in a gigantic conflict until fire comes down from heaven. Satan, Death, Hades and all people whose names are not found written in the Book of Life will be thrown into a lake of fire.

The writer of this strange apocalyptic book regarded the millennium as an interlude before the final cosmic battle – an interlude in which peace and joy reign supreme and all evil is completely, if temporarily, suppressed. In his 1957 book, *The Pursuit of the Millennium*, Norman Cohn examined the influence of this belief in European history. He found that, between the end of the eleventh century and the first half of the sixteenth century, there was a succession of highly emotional mass movements, motivated by the desire of various groups to see the material conditions of their lives greatly improved. These movements varied in tone from violent aggression to mild pacifism, but their motivation could all be traced back to Jewish and Christian prophecies in the ancient world, of which the few verses about the millennium in Revelation are the best example. They are therefore often called chiliastic movements (*chilias* being the Greek word for 'thousand').

Cohn was interested in the possible similarities between these chiliastic movements and the twentieth-century totalitarian movements of communism and German national socialism. These latter, in a far more secular age, lacked the supernatural elements of the earlier more apocalyptic movements (which reflected the mediaeval beliefs of the time), but they did have strong religious overtones. Each was led to ruthless and irrational behaviour because of the eschatological ideals. Communism looked to the imminent coming of the classless society and Nazism was committed to the achievement of the pure Aryan race. Hitler's Third Reich was intended to last for 1,000 years.

But where did the idea of a glorious future age come from? What led to the expectation that there would 'shortly be a marvellous consummation, when good will be finally victorious over evil and for ever reduce it to nullity; that the human agents of evil will be either physically annihilated or otherwise disposed of; that the elect will thereafter live as a collectivity, unanimous and without conflict, on a transformed and purified earth'?[2]

Some 20 years later, Cohn published his findings in *Cosmos, Chaos and the World to Come: The Ancient Roots of Apocalyptic Faith* (1993). Until some time around 1500–1000 BC, peoples as diverse as the Egyptians, Sumerians, Babylonians, Indo-Iranians, Canaanites and pre-exilic Israelites all had myths implying that, in the beginning, the world had been organised and set in order by immutable divine decrees, but that this order was continually under threat from evil and destructive forces. The conflict between the intended orderly cosmos and the ever-threatening chaos was given symbolic expression in a combat myth, in which a young hero god, or divine warrior, was charged by the gods with the task of keeping the forces of chaos at bay, and in return was awarded kingship over the world.[3]

Cohn contends that the Iranian prophet Zoroaster made a break with that static, yet anxious and unstable world view. (Cohn dates Zoroaster about 1200 BCE, while other scholars date him later, as far down as 588 BCE.) Zoroaster, according to Cohn, introduced a radical re-interpretation of the Iranian version of the combat myth. In Zoroaster's view the world was not static, but was already moving, through incessant conflict, towards a consummation which would result in a perfect and conflict-free state. This perfect time would come when, in a prodigious final battle, the supreme god and his supernatural allies would defeat the forces of chaos with their human allies, and eliminate them once and for all. From then on, the divinely appointed order would be established for all time. Physical distress and want would become unknown. No enemy would threaten. Within the community of the saved there would be absolute unanimity. In other words, the world would be for ever untroubled and secure.

The impact of Zoroastrianism on Judaism (and hence on Christianity and Islam) is now widely, though not unanimously, accepted. As D.S. Russell noted, 'The influence of Zoroastrianism, and indeed of the whole Perso-Babylonian culture, is amply illustrated in the writings of the Jewish apocalyptists'.[4] There are a number of elements which the Judeo-Christian tradition and Zoroastrianism have in common, which do not appear in Judaism until after it came into contact with Zoroastrianism from 540 BCE onwards. They include the naming of angels (Michael, Raphael and so on); a personal Devil (which Satan later became) with accompanying demons; a Book of Life which records the deeds of people during their lifetime; a coming cosmic conflict in which the forces of evil will be finally overthrown; the separation of the soul from the body at death; a general resurrection and a universal judgement; and an afterlife with rewards and punishments. Of particular interest is the division of time into successive significant periods (usually a millennium in length); in Zoroastrian teaching the world would last for a period of 12 millennia, consisting of four eras of 3,000 years each.

R.C. Zaehner claimed that 'from the moment that the Jews made contact with the Iranians they took over the typical Zoroastrian doctrine of an individual afterlife in which rewards are to be enjoyed and punishments endured . . . the idea of a bodily resurrection at the end of time was probably original to Zoroastrianism'.[5] Cohn also concluded that the similarities between Zoroastrianism and the ideas found in the Jewish Apocalypses were too remarkable to be explained by coincidence.[6]

Only some Jewish parties, such as the apocalyptic writers of Daniel, 1 Enoch and Jubilees, and the Qumran Sect and the Pharisees, embraced some or all of these Zoroastrian notions before the beginning of the Christian era. The Pharisees, practising a puritan and separatist form of spirituality, accepted the belief in a general resurrection (the more conservative Sadducees rejected it) and they left a huge deposit in subsequent rabbinical Judaism. There were other Jewish groups more marginal to the life of Judaism and these later included the Christians. As Cohn points out, Zoroaster's view that 'the time would come when, in a prodigious final battle, the supreme god and his supernatural allies would defeat the forces of chaos and their human allies and eliminate them once and for all' deeply influenced certain Jewish groups which, in turn, 'influenced the Jesus sect, with incalculable consequences'.[7]

Since the 1890s New Testament scholars have been rediscovering the importance of apocalyptic literature among Jews and Christians in the ancient world, represented in the books referred to as Apocalypses, which offer visions, revelations of the future, and other divine mysteries. The term 'apocalyptic' refers to a religious outlook which contrasts the present, temporary and perishable age with a new age which is to be imperishable and eternal; it contains the belief that this new age is of a transcendent order which, in the imminent future, will suddenly break in from beyond by divine intervention. It is now acknowledged that much of the New Testament was written within a context of apocalyptic or eschatological thought, in which the early Christian movement looked towards the imminent end (*eschaton*) of the present age and the breaking in of the new age (the Kingdom of God).

There is much evidence of these views in the Gospels, where they are placed by the Evangelists in the mouth of Jesus, in Mark 12, Matthew 24 and Luke 21. While these are the longest and most explicit examples of apocalyptic thinking, there are many shorter examples. Scholars still debate the extent to which Jesus shared these apocalyptic beliefs and intended his teaching about the coming Kingdom of God to be interpreted in their light. Certainly apocalyptic beliefs were dominant among the early Christians and pervade the New Testament. They are clearly present in 1 Thessalonians 4, 5, the earliest of Paul's letters.

The Apocalypse of John is not so out of keeping with the rest of the New Testament as much later readers were inclined to think. Indeed, by the second century it had become the most frequently quoted New Testament book. Although this was the only Christian apocalypse to gain inclusion in the New Testament canon, there were other early favourites such as the Apocalypse of Peter and the Shepherd of Hermas. Further, the Jewish Apocalypses remained popular among Christians for several centuries – and it was Christians and not Jews who were responsible for their survival.

Just as the Apocalypse of John made the specific reference to the miraculous character of the millennium, so Papias (60–130 CE), bishop of Hierapolis in Asia Minor, expressed apocalyptic and millenarian convictions. He held that, in the 1,000 years after the general resurrection soon to come, Christ would establish his Kingdom on earth in material form; he believed that Jesus had described the coming millennium thus: 'The days will come in which vines shall appear, having each 10,000 shoots and on every shoot 10,000 twigs, and on each twig 10,000 stems, and on every stem 10,000 bunches, and in every bunch 10,000 grapes, and every grape will give 25 metretes of wine'.[8]

By virtue of being canonised in Holy Scripture, the many pieces of apocalyptic writing in the New Testament, including the Apocalypse of John, have become permanently associated with the cardinal Christian doctrine of the expectation of the Second Coming of Christ, as expressed in the Creed: 'He shall come again with glory to judge both the living and the dead and his kingdom shall have no end.'

It has been mainly at times of cultural change and social crisis, however, that apocalyptic beliefs and millennialism have been revived in Christian thought and practice. At other times this kind of thinking has been marginalised and strongly discouraged. The reason is simple. The apocalyptic has a special appeal to the downtrodden, the persecuted, the dispossessed and the wretched, for whom the idea of a sudden period of bliss brings new hope. The Jewish Apocalypses were written to bring hope and comfort to the Jews suffering domination by the Greeks and Romans. The Christian Apocalypses flourished in a time of the Roman persecution of the Christians. But in more settled times, and particularly after the Constantinian adoption of Christianity as the state religion, the church looked with disfavour on any movement which threatened the status quo.

There was an outbreak of apocalyptic thought and activity in the late second century, led by the prophet Montanus and his women supporters Prisca and Maximilla. Even the great Tertullian (c.160–c.220), second only to Augustine among the early theologians of the western church, embraced Montanism. Over the course of history the years 500, 1000, 1260, 1420, 1533 (the supposed fifteenth centennial of Christ's death), 1843, 1844, 1845, 1847, 1851 and 1914 have in turn been awaited expectantly as the beginning of the millennium.

Amid the unsettled times of the Protestant Reformation millennial expectations were championed by the radical Protestant reformer Thomas Münzer (c.1490–1525), who became the leader of the Peasants' Revolt. There were further apocalyptic outbreaks in the nineteenth century and these gave rise to new sects, such as the Millerites, the Seventh Day Adventists and Jehovah's Witnesses. William Miller, the founder of the Millerites, had a following of more than 100,000 and announced that Christ would return and engulf the world in a conflagration in 1843. The millennialist sects have fallen into two groups, differing in their conviction as to whether Christ will return before the millennium (the pre-millennialists) or after the millennium (the post-millennialists).

It is only to be expected that the approach of the year 2000 would once again revitalise millenarian expectations. In the 1970s the evangelical preacher Hal Lindsey wrote *The Late Great Planet Earth*, which sold 25 million copies around the world. In this and later books he prophesied the imminence of the battle of Armageddon, which would start in a war between Israel and the Arab peoples and end with the destruction of all the major cities before the Advent of Christ and the coming of a new world. The same message was being preached by the American tele-evangelists and eagerly accepted by millions of viewers, including, it has been claimed, Ronald Reagan and some of his supporters.

In the expansion of Christianity around the world in the wake of European colonialism, new converts from the various indigenous peoples have not infrequently fastened on the apocalyptic component and blended it with their own cultural beliefs to create fresh millennial movements which offer their people hope of deliverance from imperialistic conquest and the arrival of a new age of bliss. Mainline Christian denominations have distanced themselves from millenarian and apocalyptic thought, finding its presence in the New Testament something of an embarrassment. But, as we shall see in later chapters, the mainline denominations have been declining. The conservative and more fundamentalist denominations are growing and these usually set much store on millennialism and the Second Coming of Christ. Ironically, although they commonly pride themselves on being the guardians of a pure and unadulterated Christianity, they unknowingly reflect the long-term influence of the Iranian prophet Zoroaster.

This serves to illustrate the first theme of this chapter: that cultural influences are often at work in ways that are both unexpected and undetected. This, we have seen, is true of the Christian calendar and the millennium: they are simply cultural conventions, dependent on the Christian civilisation that produced them.

But what is the future of Christian civilisation? There are many signs that all is not well. To this topic we now turn, for, just as the ancient Roman calendar disappeared with the decay of Roman civilisation, the decline of Christian civilisation may ultimately lead to the adoption of a new and non-Christian calendar for universal use around the globe. If this is so, then we could be living through the end of the millennium in more ways than one. The year 2000 AD could be marking the end of the last Christian millennium, and the end to all Christian millennia.

CHAPTER 2

The Decline
of Christian Civilisation

In 1940 Winston Churchill declared: 'The Battle of Britain is about to begin. Upon this battle depends the survival of Christian civilisation.' Scottish theologian John Baillie responded in the question posed by his Riddell Lectures of 1945: *What is Christian Civilization?* He claimed that the essential element of Christian civilisation is that the population as a whole believes what the church teaches.[1]

But how long is it since that could be said of the so-called Christian countries? In 1946 Christopher Dawson, a notable Roman Catholic historian of western culture, wrote:

> Today Christendom no longer exists and we are moving towards a world in which the Christian peoples or the peoples that have formerly been Christian will be a minority . . . We no longer have any solid grounds for believing that the post-Christian era is likely to realise any of the humanitarian utopias in which the idealists of the nineteenth century put their faith.[2]

A similar judgement made in 1922 by German philosopher and historian Oswald Spengler had shocked readers. In his book *The Decline of the West*, Spengler argued that all cultures pass through a life cycle, and that western civilisation was already in unavoidable decline. The time had passed when spiritual forces and values were determining the character of the western world; a new era had begun in which the scholar, the artist, the seer and the saint were being replaced by the soldier, the engineer and the politician, resulting in a technical civilisation which was no longer Christendom.

Churchill's solemn warning at a critical point in European history only drew widespread attention to what was already happening. The survival of Christian civilisation did not depend on who won the Battle of Britain; it had already ceased to exist. World War II was itself a sign that Christian civilisation was in an advanced form of disintegration. Dissolution has not come about as a direct result of enemy military action, Nazi or otherwise, but as a result of forces of quite a different order. And to borrow a phrase from the nursery rhyme, neither all the king's horses nor all the king's men can possibly put Christian civilisation back together again.

We need to examine what we mean by Christian civilisation, or 'Christendom', a word often used as a synonym. The term Christendom was coined to name the domain or realm where Christ was believed to rule. It may be defined as that society, with its own geographical area, which was subject to the rule of Christ, and whose culture and way of life had become so permeated and shaped by Christian beliefs and values as to form a cohesive whole. Christopher Dawson, in his book *The Formation of Christendom*, offers this description:

> A culture and its language together form an autonomous world of meaning and existence which is indeed the only world of which the individual is conscious. It is man-made in the sense that it is the product of man's creativity and his power of symbolic communication. But the individual is not aware of this, since both culture and language are unconscious processes in which men are immersed from their earliest infancy and on which this earliest social and intellectual activity is based.[3]

In the case of Christendom, the 'autonomous world of meaning and existence' was supplied by the complex of myths, goals and values of the religious tradition we now call Christianity. Both terms are relatively modern, first used (synonymously) in the seventeenth century. The reason why both these terms came into use comparatively recently is that when one lives within a culture like Christendom, there is no call to give it a name; as Dawson observed, it is 'the only world of which the individual is conscious'. The practice of giving names to religious traditions is likewise a modern phenomenon, as Wilfred Cantwell Smith has pointed out,[4] and it derives from the growing awareness of other cultures and civilisations. As soon as one feels the need to name one's own culture or religion, one is no longer living wholly within its horizon; rather, one has taken, at least in imagination, the first tentative step outside it. This process of looking at one's world and culture more objectively and analytically has made it necessary for us, first to create such terms as Christianity and Christendom, and, more recently, to distinguish between the two. Douglas Hall makes this distinction clearly in the title of his book, *The End of Christendom and the Future of Christianity*. It may be true that Christendom no longer exists but that Christianity, in a variety of forms, is still very much alive. In this chapter we shall examine the decline and fall of Christendom, leaving to later chapters the definition and destiny of Christianity.

The two terms Christianity and Christendom have been linked for so long that it was commonly assumed that the two must stand or fall together. Yet Christendom is at least some three to five centuries younger than Christianity and in some ways is a cultural product of Christianity. Christianity is a cultural tradition of religious belief and practice which, by its own reckoning, is 2,000 years old in the year 2000. Beginning as a Jewish sect, formed by the followers of Jesus of Nazareth after his death, the embryonic Christian church eventually broke away from its Jewish beginnings and became a new religion for Gentiles. It has long been independent from, and even antagonistic to, the Judaism which gave it birth and with which it still has so much in common. Within three to four centuries Christianity had outstripped all of its rivals, such as Mithraism and Manichaeism. But, as the modern study of Christian origins has made clear, the idea of establishing a Christian civilisation was entirely foreign both to Jesus of Nazareth and to the early Christian movement. It was not until the Roman emperor Constantine decided to adopt Christianity as the new state religion of the empire, shortly after the beginning of the fourth Christian century, that the vital step was taken towards the formation of Christendom.

Even the fall of Rome, although disastrous at first, nurtured the growth of western Christendom eventually. The barbarian invaders were in time converted to Christianity; the bishop of Rome adopted the Roman emperor's title of Pontifex Maximus; and the church, by stages, inherited the mantle of power which had previously been the Roman emperor's in the west. The eastern church, by contrast, always remained more subservient to the emperor at Constantinople and later to the czar in Russia. Only in the west did the church largely fill the power vacuum left by the fall of Rome.

But the formation of Christendom depended on more than imperial authority. In the first few centuries of the Christian era, a synthesis of thought took place between the declining Graeco-Roman culture and the still-evolving system of Christian thought which had burst out of Judaism. This amalgam of Israelite prophetic zeal and the more abstract concepts of Greek philosophy constituted the belief system that provided Christendom with its 'autonomous world of meaning and existence'. By the end of the first millennium, the newly emerged Christendom had extended its power and cultural influence even further than the boundaries of the former Roman Empire.

In this process Christendom had to defend itself from both external and internal threats. After vanquishing all its earlier rivals, it had to withstand both the intellectual and the military impact of Islam. Islam expanded much faster than Christianity and had established an impressive civilisation in only half the time it took Christianity to reach the High Middle Ages. Eastern Christendom bore the brunt of the military and cultural advance of Islam and suffered quite heavy losses. Western Christendom, under Charlemagne's leadership, just managed to stem the spread of Islam, and later counter-attacked in the Crusades.

Threats just as serious to the vitality of Christendom came from within, from a succession of schismatic and heretical movements. Its unity and catholicity were sorely tested, but Christendom was able to contain these threats, absorb new ideas and knowledge (such as Aristotelianism in the twelfth century) and cater for the whole range of human emotions and intellectual levels. By the High Middle Ages (the twelfth and thirteenth centuries) western Christendom manifested an impressive depth of intellectual culture, and an internal unity. Its confidence is reflected in the building of the great European cathedrals. It is easy to look back nostalgically and ascribe to the Middle Ages a perfection they did not possess. To be hypercritical is just as tempting, for by present moral standards life in the Middle Ages left a great deal to be desired. Nonetheless, it can be claimed that the Christian world of the High Middle Ages attained such a homogeneity of culture, one so permeated by Christian values and beliefs (as then understood), that it can be quite properly referred to as Christendom: that is, a domain or realm where Christ was believed to rule.

This Christendom was such a living, complex unity that it could be likened to an organism, in the way any healthy homogeneous society can be called a social organism. But just as all living organisms have a beginning and an end, going through a life cycle between conception and death, so it is with social organisms. This is why civilisations come and go, as Arnold Toynbee demonstrated in his study of world history. So it has been with Christendom.

Christendom rose out of the death of the Graeco-Roman civilisation and advanced to maturity during the Middle Ages. But that phase of maturity is now long past and Christendom (or Christian civilisation) is now facing its demise. And as the dying process of an organism can stretch over some time, so the demise of a social organism which has enjoyed a life span of some 1,500 years may be a lengthy process. At what point are we in that process? Is it premature or a gross exaggeration to assume the demise of Christendom?

In the wake of the colonising expansion of the European nations, Christianity travelled faster and wider during the nineteenth century than in any previous period. As it spread around the globe, particularly in the American and African continents, Christianity was intent on incorporating the newly colonised areas into Christendom. There still existed in the Christian west a mood of triumphant conquest. By the beginning of the twentieth century all the churches of Europe and North America were heavily involved in what they called Foreign Missions, by which they meant their God-given task of Christianising the rest of the world. An American Methodist called John R. Mott published a book in 1900 entitled *The Evangelisation of the World in this Generation*, and this became a widely used slogan. It was fully expected that during the course of the twentieth century the whole race of humankind would be incorporated into Christendom. This was to be *The Christian Century*, as indicated by the journal which took that name.

Yet the twentieth century has witnessed severe and quite unexpected setbacks to the viability of Christendom itself. Firstly, the two greatest wars ever waged by humankind were initiated within Christendom and were largely fought by the so-called Christian nations. Globally, Christianity's claims to be a harbinger of peace are far from justified. Secondly, the most horrifying act of mass murder or genocide ever perpetrated by humans occurred within a leading Christian nation; and this grew out of an anti-Semitism long present within Christendom. Thirdly, the Christian nations, made economically strong by both their political imperialism and their advanced state of technology, have not only constructed the weapons for nuclear war but also been most to blame for the selfish exploitation of the non-renewable resources of the earth, for the accumulating mass pollution, for the gross interference with the delicate ecology of the planet. All of these together endanger the future not only of humankind but of all earthly life.

The mood in the Christian west at the end of this century is entirely different from the confidence expressed at its beginning. It is hard to believe that, after two millennia, such drastic changes could have occurred in only one century. In relative terms, the collapse of Christendom is happening as fast as the collapse of the communist world following the fall of the Berlin Wall. Christian expansion is still occurring in such places as Africa and South America. But no longer is Christianity triumphantly conquering the world, as it still appeared to be doing at the beginning of this century. The so-called Old World, which set out to incorporate the New World into Christendom, has itself entered what is now called a post-Christian era.

Scottish theologian Ronald Gregor Smith said in 1966: 'The tide of secularism has swept over the whole of the western world, the world that was once called Christendom, and beyond that it has reached into every land . . . It has flooded over every island and the remotest parts of the world'.[5] No longer can it be said that Christian beliefs, values and aspirations are shaping our public life. The so-called Christian countries of the West have become increasingly secularised and no longer see themselves as subject to the rule of Christ. During the course of this century the observance of Sunday and the annual festivals of Whitsunday and Easter have almost disappeared as public Christian festivals. These once *holy* days have become merely *holi*days. They emphasise the fact that Christendom within the countries of the west is a mere shadow of its former self. Christendom has virtually ceased to exist.

How has this come about and why? The decline of Christendom in fact began just after the period of its greatest flowering. There is general agreement today that the Renaissance marks the starting point of modern times. (As we shall see in Chapter 4, this needs to be qualified by going back to the influence of the Franciscan philosopher William of Ockham, *c.*1285–1347). The Renaissance was much more than the rediscovery of the classical texts of ancient Greece and Rome. The study of these texts, written as they were by pagan, pre-Christian authors, led to such a new appreciation of the creative capabilities of humankind in its unredeemed state that it has been called a revolution of consciousness. The leading thinkers of the Renaissance began to look with new eyes on the human condition. Pico della Mirandola (1463–1494) wrote (when only 24) *Oration on the Dignity of Man*, in which he imagined the Creator saying to Adam something like this: 'I created you to be neither heavenly nor earthly that you might be free to shape and master yourself. You may descend to be lower than the beasts or you may rise to be as gods. Your growth and development depend on your own free will. You have in you the germs of a universal life.'[6]

Attention was no longer so focused on other-worldliness; as a result, the natural and material world came to be revalued. Humans came to be seen less as fallen creatures living in a fallen world and more as autonomous, rational beings, capable of choice, of doing good of their own free will, and of creativity. The men of the Renaissance began to turn away from the eternal and the absolute (as commonly conceived) and to concern themselves with the world of nature and of internal human experience. The Greek and Latin classics they studied became known as the humanities, for in Cicero's day *humanitas* meant the education of humankind. So the leading figures of the Renaissance commended the study of the classics as the means of nurturing our human potential. Because they placed such emphasis on the value and dignity of the human condition, their philosophy came to be known as humanism. The humanists eagerly sought the rebirth of the free and creative human spirit which they believed to have flowered in the ancient world and to have been lost in the Middle Ages. Thus the Renaissance brought to birth our modern awareness of historical change, our passion for freedom, our respect for human reason, and our eagerness to investigate the natural world and to extend our knowledge.

The Renaissance humanists were not atheistic or anti-Christian, as some modern humanists are. They were aware of the need for spiritual renewal within the church, but they sought to promote reform from within. They were critical of the papacy, which had been passing through its most dismal period, but they saw no reason to doubt Christian institutions as such. In 1381 an association was founded, open to both clerics and laymen, called the Brethren of the Common Life.[7] It set out to counter decadence in the church, to promote spirituality and to provide general education. One of their students was Nicholas of Cusa (c.1400–1464) who has often been regarded as the model of a 'Renaissance man'; he became a cardinal, yet he was also a mathematician, a diagnostic physician, and an experimental scientist. Erasmus (c.1466–1536) spent the first 30 years of his life in the schools of the Brethren of the Common Life before becoming the greatest of the humanist scholars. He wrote merciless satires against the church, and for this he lived a somewhat uneasy existence. Yet when the Protestant Reformation took place, he did not join it, partly because he was a man of moderate and tolerant temperament who abhorred violence, and partly because he was repelled by the anti-humanist element in so much of the Protestantism of his time.

Nevertheless, the Protestant Reformation was the logical outcome of the Renaissance, both because of the new sense of human freedom it created and because the resurgent interest in the study of biblical texts gave the Reformers the authority and courage to challenge the church hierarchy. It was said that Erasmus laid the egg which Martin Luther hatched. In seeing the Protestant Reformation as an assault on Christendom from within, the Catholics were partly right: the Protestant Reformation was destined to sound the death-knell to Christendom.

Protestants, of course, have long seen the Protestant Reformation as the resurrection of Christianity to new life, after its burial beneath the mass of superstition accumulated during the late Middle Ages. They too were partly right; even Catholic scholars now agree that the mediaeval church was in dire need of reformation. However, the Protestant Reformation was only partially successful, and there were heavy costs – the fragmentation of Christendom and, ultimately, its dissolution. From this time onwards, Christendom increasingly lost both its unity and its all-embracing catholicity.

The splintering of the western church into denominations was much more serious than the schism between the eastern and western church that had taken place in 1054. The east–west schism left Christendom intact but in two sections, geographically separate from each other. The Protestant–Catholic division, however, split communities into warring Christian factions, creating conflict akin to that which smoulders to this day in Northern Ireland. Christians came to spend much of their activity in countering one another.

The Protestant movement never achieved any organisational unity. The attempt to unite the Lutheran and Calvinist traditions at the Colloquy of Marburg in 1529 foundered on the doctrine of the Eucharist. Failure also met the attempt to unite the churches of the British Isles at the Westminster Assembly of 1643. Subsequently the Protestant denominations splintered even further, so that catholicity came to be replaced by sectarianism. The fragmentation of the church meant that western Christendom no longer had a unified organisational structure. What survived of the former Christendom was the fact that all (except the Jews) stoutly professed their commitment to the Christian tradition and their faith in Jesus Christ as Lord and Saviour, but they differed strongly about what this entailed. There was no longer consensus on the doctrines of the church, the priesthood, the sacraments and the mode of Christian salvation. And because they no longer had a common personal head, Christians came to depend more and more upon the civil authority of the emerging nation states. Although these states saw themselves quite clearly as Christian, this process of state formation was the first step towards the emergence of the modern secular (or religiously neutral) state.

The fragmentation of Christendom which took place from the Reformation onwards did not lead directly to any questioning of the basic Christian beliefs; on the contrary, sectarian strife fostered so much bitterness and even fanaticism that the humanistic philosophy of the Renaissance was temporarily submerged. Not until the Enlightenment of the eighteenth century did it surface again.

It was partly because of sectarian strife that the humanist concern with the importance of human reason reappeared. Catholics were content to submit themselves to the authority of the Pope. Protestants turned to the Bible as to a 'paper Pope' but could not always agree on what it required them to do and believe. Christendom now lacked one central authority to which appeal could be made. For an honest and inquiring person, this posed an enigma. Since Catholic and Protestant could not both be right, by what criterion was one to make a judgement about their competing claims? And further, since one of them was clearly wrong, how could one be sure they were not both wrong? The first to give expression to this enigma was the French humanist Montaigne (1533–92), though he himself chose to remain a practising Catholic.

Thus, on the margins between the surviving fragments of Christendom, more searching questions were being asked. As the Reformers had earlier appealed to the Bible in order to challenge the authority of the Pope, so human reason emerged as the only criterion by which one could challenge the different seats of authority acknowledged by Catholic and Protestant. The Age of Reason began to supersede the Ages of Faith. The leading thinkers of the Enlightenment (as the age came to be called) began to submit the basic tenets of Christianity to rational examination and produced what was called 'natural religion'. They did not see themselves as atheistic or anti-Christian, but were intent on taking the Protestant Reformation to what they believed was its logical conclusion by removing the supernatural additions. The titles of their books indicate their intent: *Reasonableness of Christianity as Delivered in the Scriptures* (John Locke, 1695), *Christianity Not Mysterious* (John Toland, 1696) and *Christianity as Old as the Creation* (Matthew Tindal, 1730).

In the course of this examination of Christianity, there emerged the first signs of modern unbelief, as exemplified in philosopher David Hume (1711–1776), the father of modern scepticism. As Roman Catholic scholar Johann-Baptist Metz observed in 1995, the processes of the eighteenth-century Enlightenment resulted in the secularisation of religion, the growing freedom of people to think and speak for themselves, the demythologising of the powerful religious images and the end of theology's cognitive innocence. This led to a profound crisis for Christian thought and teaching.[8] Christendom had been a cohesive whole in which Christian beliefs and values shaped both public and private life. In such a world, it did not matter much whether people talked about Christendom, Christian civilisation or simply Christianity. But when the cohesive whole began to disintegrate, it became necessary to distinguish Christendom from Christianity. From the Enlightenment onwards, public life became increasingly emancipated from the fairly rigid social structures that Christianity had shaped over the centuries. Christianity continued to shape people's private lives, however, and would do so for at least another 200 years. The decline of Christendom meant that public life was becoming increasingly secularised and Christianity was being privatised.

This has not been all bad. In so far as people had private lives within the former Christendom, they were largely contained by uniform and pre-scribed patterns; the opportunities to develop one's unique individuality were strictly limited. In Christendom there were standard ways not only of being a Christian but of being truly human. These differed somewhat for those in a monastic order, for the clergy, and for the lay people; Christian duties also differed for the aristocrat and the peasant. But the patterns were firmly set out, and peer pressure, as much as the authority of the church, ensured that this remained so. By contrast, post-Christian secular society provides much more freedom for individuals to be themselves. We now regard this as a value that we would be reluctant to surrender. In post-Christian society there are not only many ways of being Christian but also many more ways of being human. And the tolerance we have inherited from the Enlightenment enables us to accept this diversity and even to cel-ebrate it.

To appreciate how the Enlightenment marked the end for Christendom, we must look at the new kind of culture that then began to emerge. In the progression from the mediaeval world to the modern world, there have been three main steps – the Renaissance, the Protestant Reformation and the Enlightenment. If the modern world was conceived in the Renaissance, it came to birth at the Reformation and entered adolescence at the Enlightenment. As Dietrich Bonhoeffer said, we are now living through humankind's 'coming of age'.[9]

Many of the values and interests which we take for granted in the mod-ern world have been widespread only since the Enlightenment. Take, for example, our passion for freedom of speech and expression. In pre-Enlightenment Christendom, one was expected to think in ways that were consistent with what the church taught; it was heresy to think or express thoughts at variance with orthodoxy or 'right opinion'. This is why the word 'freethinker' (coined during the Enlightenment) gathered the sinister overtones which it has to this day, even though it meant at first what it lit-erally said. But with freedom to think came freedom to explore new ideas and new knowledge. Already at the Renaissance, scholars had begun to pore over the ancient writings which included the original Greek and Hebrew texts of the Bible. From the Enlightenment scholars began to ask questions about the history of those texts and to develop a greater historical awareness. A static view of reality began to give way to the acknowledgement of change, and then to an evolving view of reality. The whole mental picture of the world we live in began to alter.

Thus the 'Christian west' is today very different from the 'autonomous world of meaning and existence', which it was when known as Christendom. Christendom is no more, and the so-called 'Christian west' is only the shell of its former self. The shell remains clearly visible in many structures, both physical and social, but they are no longer parts of a living whole. With the demise of Christendom or Christian civilisation in the western world, what kind of civilisation is left? Is it only the ghostly remnant of Christian civilisation? Does it have any substance of its own which will enable it to survive, or is it living on past capital? Alvin Toffler, author of *Future Shock*, recently said: 'We are witnessing the sudden eruption of a new civilisation on the planet'.[10] This is certainly not the Christian civilisation which Christians expected and hoped for at the beginning of the twentieth century. Yet it manifests many of the values and ideals of western Christendom (partly because this new civilisation was fostered by the spread of European culture). Is Christianity thus continuing, rather like a leaven in the new global civilisation, as many Christians would like to believe? Or is Christianity destined for the same fate as Christendom? To this question we now turn.

CHAPTER 3

The Disintegration
of Orthodoxy

Since Christianity existed for at least three centuries before the formation of Christendom, there is no reason why it should end at the same time. Indeed, during the gradual demise of Christendom, Christianity has increased in vitality and spread its influence much further afield – rather like a living entity released from the protective shell which it had produced for itself. Thus, as the framework of Christendom began to crumble under its own weight from the sixteenth century onwards, Christian belief and allegiance experienced a surge of new life, first in Protestantism and then in Catholicism. As recently as the middle of the twentieth century, church historian K.S. Latourette described the period 1815–1914 as 'the greatest century which Christianity has thus far known' in its 2,000-year history.[1] Christendom might be dying but Christianity was very much alive. Some Christian leaders have even rejoiced in the dissolution of a Christendom that allowed, or perhaps encouraged, an excessive degree of nominal Christian allegiance: the impact of modern secular society has challenged people to make a conscious choice about whether they are either for or against Christianity. Such leaders prefer to speak of the present as the post-Constantinian age rather than a post-Christian one, and some claim that Christianity is stronger than ever today.

But what sort of Christianity are we talking about? The term Christianity is, as we have seen, relatively modern in its current usage. And it has come to mean different things to different people. From the Protestant Reformation onwards, Roman Catholics saw themselves as the guardians of the only genuine form of Christianity, and they judged Protestants to be heretics and apostates. The Protestants were equally adamant that they alone were faithful to the original and only true form of Christianity, and they condemned Catholics as idolaters. So were there now two (and perhaps even more) forms of Christianity?

For many centuries before the Reformation, there was substantially only one form of Christian teaching and it was clearly set out in a set of doctrines now often referred to as Christian orthodoxy (literally meaning 'right belief'). What became Christian orthodoxy was largely hammered out by debate in the ecumenical councils of the first few centuries, sometimes using concepts of Greek thought used by non-Christian philosophers. In the early centuries, Christian faith was sufficiently flexible to incorporate valid criticisms of its various verbal expressions. Only later did it assume the steadfast rigidity that it then displayed until modern times.

To deviate from established orthodoxy in one's beliefs was to be guilty of the heinous sin of heresy. The Inquisition was set up in the thirteenth century to search out, condemn and put to death all heretics. This assumed its most violent form in the Spanish Inquisition which lasted from 1479 to 1820. Defending orthodoxy by the severe punishment of deviants was not only a Catholic practice. The Protestant Reformer John Calvin (1509–1564) was instrumental in having Michael Servetus burnt at the stake in 1553 for denying the doctrine of the Holy Trinity and the divinity of Christ. At first, the critics of orthodoxy were often lone voices that could be quickly silenced. But from the time of the Protestant Reformation, and more particularly over the last 200 years, criticism of Christian orthodoxy has grown.

More latterly a succession of voices from within the Christian tradition itself has warned that Christian orthodoxy is coming to an end. In 1963 Bishop John Robinson's *Honest to God,* advertised with the slogan 'Our Image of God Must Go', became a runaway best-seller. Some months before, in 1962, a course of lectures began in the Catholic University of Nijmegen, Holland, entitled 'The End of Conventional Christianity'. The lecturer, W.H. van de Pol, later published a book with the same title in which he sought 'an answer to the question of why it is that conventional Christianity has become so undermined that we are experiencing its collapse'.[2]

By the term 'conventional Christianity' van de Pol did not mean the Christianity of the first three or four centuries, but rather Christianity as it was believed and has been practised since the Christianisation of Europe; that is, since the formation of Christendom. This Christianity is expressed in the creeds, confessions, hymns and liturgies, and is substantially what may be called Christian orthodoxy.

To understand the demise of Christian orthodoxy we must turn to four particular areas that are vulnerable to what have been called the corrosive acids of modernity – that is, the church, the Bible, the person of Jesus Christ and the reality of God.

The Church

The church had long seen itself as a divine institution, different from all natural institutions such as the family and all humanly created institutions such as the monarchy. The church was believed to have been founded by Jesus Christ, who remained its king and head, exercising his rule through his vicar the Pope. Thus the church mediated a unique and divine authority, wielding a power that could not be matched by kings and princes. The church claimed to be able to speak with finality on all matters of essential truth. The remnant of this is still to be found in the Roman Catholic Dogma of Papal Infallibility. Belief in the divine institution of the church became an article of faith, as in the words of the Creed, 'I believe in one, holy, catholic and apostolic church'.

Various aspects of this doctrine of the church were challenged at the Protestant Reformation. Yet the Reformers, critical though they were of the Pope and of the mediaeval church, were anxious not to throw the baby out with the bathwater. First they identified the church with the Christian people, rather than with the ecclesiastical institution which now ordered their lives. Secondly, they conceded that church councils were not infallible but were prone to error. Thus, although the church consisted of people who professed the Christian faith, its institutional form was human and fallible. Yet for a long time after the Reformation much of the traditional holiness was believed still to adhere to the church and its officers, the holy ministry.

The fact that the Reformers rejected the Pope entirely (even referring to him as the anti-Christ) meant that the Protestant churches lacked an authoritative personal voice. They were thrown back more and more on the words of the Bible, the very instrument they had used to bring criticism to bear upon the church. This proved something of a two-edged sword, leading to two extremes. Either the Bible was absolutely infallible, as it is for the fundamentalists; or it was subject to the same type of rational criticism that the Protestants had already brought to bear against the papacy. Thus Christian orthodoxy lost first a divine and infallible church and later, a divine and infallible Bible.

The Bible

Prior to the Enlightenment, Christian thought and practice appeared to be built on the firmest of foundations – the Bible. Both Catholic and Protestant accepted the Bible as the divine revelation of infallible truth. As the Westminster Divines of 1643 declared: 'The authority of the Holy Scripture depends not on the testimony of any man or church, but wholly on God, the author thereof; and it is to be received because it is the word of God.' The Bible was therefore believed to reveal without error the origin of the world, the meaning of history, the moral laws by which all should live, and the only path to salvation. People, whether educated or not, generally accepted at face value everything written in the Bible. Until the beginning of the nineteenth century there seemed little reason to doubt its stories of creation, the Great Flood, its history of humankind, and the story of Israel culminating in the birth, death and resurrection of Jesus Christ.

But in the nineteenth century this widespread confidence in the Bible was badly shaken, as biblical scholars began to study it with the modern tools of literary and historical criticism. These pioneers often found themselves rejected by their churches, and even dismissed from their university posts as a result of their publications. Only slowly did their work come to be known by the general public. The process by which people lost their faith in the Bible as an infallible source of knowledge is thus a complex one, stretching over some two centuries. From time to time fierce theological debates took place, such as that which followed the publication of Charles Darwin's (1809–82) theory of biological evolution in 1859. If Darwin was right, then the opening chapters of the Bible were false and misleading. If the Bible was found wanting in its account of Creation, how could one be sure of it anywhere? Although liberal Christians quickly found ways of accommodating the idea of evolution, more conservative Christians reject Darwinism to this day.

Fuel was added to the fire by the work of the seminal biblical scholar Julius Wellhausen (1844–1918) about 1880. This led scholars to reject the tradition which regarded Moses as the author of the first five books of the Bible. Behind these controversies lay a growing awareness of the human origin of the Bible. For scholars were discovering that the Bible – far from being the 'Word of God', dictated by God – was written by humans. Its various books reflected many aspects of the cultural environment in which they were composed, including even the prejudices and limited knowledge of their authors.

This new understanding of the Bible has by no means dampened the interest, indeed the enthusiasm, of scholars and the Bible has been more studied in the last 150 years than in the previous two millennia. This has enabled us to gain a more reliable picture of the ancient world reflected in the Bible. The Bible's value remains high, but it is value of a quite different order. The Bible remains our chief collection of extant records describing the origin and early development of the Judeo-Christian path of faith, but it no longer prescribes, as it was once thought to do, what devout people of all later ages should believe and do. The churches have found it difficult to come to terms with this fact, and often refuse to acknowledge that they have lost for ever what they took to be an authoritative source of religious truth. This revolution in our understanding of the Bible has had serious consequences for two other key concepts in Christianity: the person of Jesus Christ, and the reality of God.

Jesus Christ

What Christian orthodoxy meant by the term Jesus Christ is best understood by quoting from the Nicene Creed:

> (I believe) in one Lord Jesus Christ, the only begotten Son of God, Begotten of His father before all worlds, God of God, Light of Light, Very God of Very God, Begotten, not made, Being of one substance with the Father, By whom all things were made: Who for us men and for our salvation, came down from heaven, And was incarnate by the Holy Ghost of the Virgin Mary, And was made man, and was crucified for us under Pontius Pilate. He suffered and was buried, and the third day rose again according to the scriptures, and ascended into heaven, and sitteth on the right hand of the Father. And He shall come again with glory to judge both the quick and the dead: Whose kingdom shall have no end.

This Jesus Christ stands at the centre of Christian tradition and is the foundation of Christian orthodoxy. But what sort of person or being is the Creed referring to as the Lord Jesus Christ? Up until 200 years ago the term Jesus Christ implied all of the following things at one and the same time, for they were implicit, if not explicit, in the language common to all Christians in their devotions and their theology:

1. the *Divine Son of God,* who existed from the beginning of time, having been begotten before the Creation of the world, and who became the maker of all things;
2. the *second 'person' of the Holy Trinity,* who became incarnate in the man Jesus to become the Christ and Saviour of the world;
3. the *historical figure of Jesus,* who lived in Palestine some 2,000 years ago, who became a travelling teacher and healer before being crucified and who did and said all the things the four Gospels ascribed to him;
4. the *Christ who rose from the dead,* ascended into heaven and, while sitting at the right hand of God, is also now eternally present everywhere, sharing the timelessness of God;
5. the *church,* since it is called the 'body of Christ' and since Christ

resides spiritually in all Christians and all Christians are said to be 'in Christ';

6. the *Eternal Judge,* who now hears the prayers of his followers and who will come again in judgement at the end of the world.

These ways of thinking of Jesus Christ were all accepted as simply different facets of the one spiritual reality. As a result of the new understanding of the Bible, from the study of the last 200 years, the once seamless robe into which all these strands of thought were woven has been torn apart, just as surely as the curtain of the Jewish temple was said to have been rent in two on the first Good Friday after the death of Jesus. The Jesus Christ who is the foundation of Christian orthodoxy has disintegrated into a collage of history, myth and devout imagination. Based initially on personal memories of the historical figure of Jesus, the Jesus Christ worshipped in the Christian tradition has been shaped by the collective imagination and devotion of the Christian community.

The traditional mental picture of Jesus Christ was not dismantled intentionally by scholars hostile to Christianity. On the contrary, the long and complex process which has forced us to distinguish between the historical figure of Jesus (who is open to historical research) and the religious figure of the Christ (who can be affirmed only by Christians and who is subjectively 'known' in Christian devotion) has been undertaken by Christian scholars bringing the best of contemporary analysis to their study of the Bible.

First came the pioneering work of the Enlightenment scholar Hermann Reimarus (1694–1768), who made a critical study of the New Testament running to 4,000 pages of manuscript, entitled *The Defence of a Rational Worshipper of God.* He so surprised himself by his conclusions that he dared not publish this work during his lifetime but entrusted it to his friend G.E. Lessing, a dramatist and philosopher. Reimarus showed that it was impossible to reconcile the stories of Jesus as told by the four different Gospels (and particularly their accounts of Jesus' Resurrection), so the Gospels could not be accepted at face value as genuine records. He concluded that the disciples, distraught by the unexpected end to the ministry of Jesus, stole his crucified body, concocted the story of his Resurrection and turned the message *of* Jesus into the message *about* Jesus. After the death of Reimarus, Lessing published seven excerpts from the manuscript under the title *The Intention of Jesus and his Disciples.* It caused such an outcry that the King of Prussia forbade any more to be published.

The second step occurred when David Strauss (1808–74) published a two-volume work, *The Life of Jesus Critically Examined,* in 1835.[3] This is a most remarkable book to have been written by a young scholar of only 28 years. Strauss was the first to introduce into the study of the Gospels the categories of history, legend and myth. He defined legend as a story which has expanded and embellished the memory of an original historical event. A myth he defined as a story wholly created by devout imagination on the basis of an original idea. Strauss showed that the portraits of Jesus in the Gospels were already a mixture of history, legend and myth. In creating their stories, Strauss wrote, the early Christians drew largely upon Old Testament motifs and themes; they used them as models with which to describe how they saw the role of Jesus. In this way Strauss was able to see where Reimarus had gone wrong and why his hoax theory was false. The Gospel writers were not presenting eye-witness accounts, but simply collecting the stories already circulating about Jesus in the expanding oral tradition.

Strauss's book, translated into English by novelist George Eliot, was widely read. It aroused such opposition that various attempts were made to have the book suppressed and Strauss lost all chance of a career in either the church or university. Many recognised that if his interpretation of the Gospels were true, then Christian orthodoxy had no future. Strauss overstated his thesis, but he opened up such a problem for Christianity thereafter that Bishop Stephen Neill, a moderate scholar, wrote in 1964 that 'this book marked, as few others have done, a turning point in the history of the Christian faith'.[4]

Ever since Strauss's first book, and his later book *The Christ of Faith and Jesus of History* (1865), it has been necessary to distinguish between the historical figure, now known as Jesus of Nazareth, and the symbolic object of Christian worship, called Christ. The original Jesus became Christ by being clothed and partially hidden in the stories of early Christian devotion. The Gospels can no longer be read as an accurate account of the historical Jesus of Galilee. Jesus *became* Christ, not in human and cosmic history, but in the experience and thinking of the first generations of Christians.[5] This distinction between the historical Jesus and the Christ of faith meant that the traditional picture of Jesus Christ, as portrayed in the Creeds, was being torn apart. The only words in the Creed (as quoted earlier) that are historical are 'was crucified . . . under Pontius Pilate. He suffered and was buried'; the rest is the language of myth.

Attention was then fastened on the historical Jesus as the founder of Christianity, and this led, through the rest of the nineteenth century, to an intense historical search for the genuine and original Jesus. The search was brought to a climax with the third milestone, the publication by Albert Schweitzer (1875–1965) of his book *The Quest of the Historical Jesus* (1906). In this book Schweitzer surveyed the whole of the critical research into the life of Jesus that had been undertaken in Germany in the previous century. He showed that the attempt to penetrate the Gospel portraits and recover the original historical Jesus of Nazareth failed, because each of the written histories of Jesus unconsciously reflected the subjective hopes and ideals of the author. He put it this way:

> The Jesus of Nazareth who came forward publicly as the Messiah, who preached the ethic of the Kingdom of God, who founded the Kingdom of God upon earth, and died to give his work its final consecration, never had any existence. He is a figure designed by rationalism, endowed with life by liberalism, and clothed by modern theology in an historical garb.[6]

The failure to recover the historical Jesus did not unduly worry Schweitzer. He said: 'The truth is, it is not Jesus as historically known, but Jesus as spiritually arisen within men, who is significant for our time . . . Not the historical Jesus, but the spirit which goes forth from him . . . is that which overcomes the world.'[7] This was also the conclusion of a slightly earlier book which never received the publicity of Schweitzer's work. In *The So-called Historical Jesus and the Historic Biblical Christ* (1896), Martin Kähler described the search for the historical Jesus as a 'blind alley'. Not only, he said, does it fail to recover the historical Jesus but it actually 'conceals the living Christ'. Thus we do not have the necessary sources for writing 'a life of Jesus', for the Gospels are proclamations (or extended sermons), reflecting the testimonies of the first believers in Christ. As Kähler said, 'The risen Lord is not the historical Jesus *behind* the Gospels but the Christ of the apostolic preaching, of the *whole* New Testament.'[8] The real Christ, therefore, is the one who was proclaimed by the Apostles and who continues to be preached on the basis of the biblical proclamations.

For both Kähler and Schweitzer, Christ is the name of *the spiritual influence* which has flowed from the original Jesus, now lost in the mists of history. This is why Kähler referred to the biblical Christ as 'historic', in contrast to the 'historical' Jesus. 'The truly historic element in any great figure,' he said, 'is *the discernible personal influence* which he exercises upon later generations.'[9] This means of course that the living Christ is not open to historical enquiry and 'Christian language about Christ must always take the form of a confession'.[10] The only real Christ is the Christ who is preached, and the Christ who is preached is precisely the Christ of faith.

From Strauss onwards, when the distinction was first being made between Jesus and Christ, attention switched from the Christ of dogma to the Jesus of history. At the beginning of the twentieth century, from Kähler and Schweitzer onwards, attention switched from the Jesus of history to the Christ being preached. It was on this activity of preaching that both Karl Barth (1886–1968) and Rudolf Bultmann (1884–1976), fastened – not unlike St Paul, who not only showed little interest in the historical Jesus but also spoke in mystical terms of the in-dwelling Christ and of Christian believers being 'in Christ'. So long as the Christ who was preached continued to influence people spiritually, as was the case for some decades into the twentieth century, Christianity remained very much alive, even if some aspects of Christian orthodoxy were being quietly ignored. But by the middle of the century it was becoming apparent that the Gospel was falling on deaf ears. Rudolf Bultmann, arguably the greatest New Testament scholar of the twentieth century, and in many ways the logical successor of Kähler, blamed this failure on the outmoded mythological language of the New Testament. In a celebrated essay published during World War II, he acknowledged that the classical form of Christian proclamation (kerygma) in which the living Christ was communicated was couched in terminology drawn from the now obsolete cosmology of the ancient world.[11] Since this had become quite unbelievable to modern humankind, he called for a radical programme of re-interpretation which he called 'demythologising the Gospel message'.

After World War II Bultmann's plea for demythologising the Gospel led to widespread theological debate. Conservatives rejected his approach entirely. Many others agreed that he made a valid point but they could not accept his existentialist re-interpretation. Some of Bultmann's own pupils began what has been called 'A New Quest for the Historical Jesus'.[12] These scholars, recognising the pitfalls of the first quest, were more modest in their aims. They were primarily concerned to investigate the overlap between the genuine memories of Jesus embedded in tradition and the church's proclamation of him as Christ. More recently a group of New Testament scholars from USA and Germany, calling themselves the Jesus Seminar,[13] have initiated a third quest for the historical Jesus. The results of their work are to be found especially in Robert Funk's *The Five Gospels, What Did Jesus Really Say?* and *The Acts of Jesus, What Did Jesus Really Do?*[14]

We now know that the most we can really say about Jesus of Nazareth as an historical figure is that he was a first-century Jew who developed a reputation as a teacher and healer. He antagonised the authorities of his day, both Jewish and Roman, and he was executed by the Romans. What he actually taught has become so integrated with what his followers taught about him that it is difficult to recover his own words. The Jesus Seminar has concluded that only about 20 per cent of the words attributed to Jesus originated with him. He almost certainly reflected the beliefs of his day. He may have been a teacher of wisdom rather than a prophet. He did not claim to be the expected Messiah, the Saviour of the world or the divine Son of God. The stories of his birth, transfiguration, resurrection and ascension are not historical but belong to the categories of myth or legend.

Whether these radical findings of New Testament scholars mean the end of Christianity we have yet to discuss. They certainly entail the demise of Christian orthodoxy, which is wedded to the divinity of Jesus Christ. And this brings us to the fourth and ultimate foundation of Christian orthodoxy – the being of God.

God

The understanding of God as the supreme personal being has been basic to Christian orthodoxy from the beginning. Christians inherited this from the Jewish religion, out of which they emerged and of which they were originally a sect. The concept of one supreme being was readily adopted, as it seemed greatly superior to the plethora of gods that were worshipped in the ancient world. Christians drew upon this understanding of God in order to interpret the significance and role of Jesus, whom they recognised as the one anointed by God to be Messiah.

The first rift in Christianity occurred when the first Christians, being Jewish, continued to affirm the full humanity of Jesus, while the Gentile Christians led by Paul increasingly affirmed the divinity of Jesus. As the Christians moved away from Judaism into Hellenistic culture, their understanding of God and of Jesus Christ was influenced by the Greek concept of God (*theos*), particularly as it was defined by both Plato and the Stoics. This influence can be documented clearly during the first five centuries when the orthodox Christian doctrine of God was debated and expressed in the creeds of the ecumenical councils.

The reality of God as the spiritual Creator of the physical universe seemed to be self-evident. In the ancient world, it was not atheism against which Christianity had to defend itself but polytheism, the belief in too many gods. Christians even found themselves being called atheists because they dismissed the gods that people had traditionally worshipped. The various attempts of Christian philosophers through the centuries to prove the existence of God were never much more than academic exercises, for the reality of a heavenly designer and sustainer fitted the pre-modern view of the universe so convincingly. John Calvin was able to declare in 1555 without fear of contradiction: 'There is no nation so barbarous, no race so brutish as not to be imbued with the conviction that there is a God.'15

That was soon to change, but those who dared to question openly the reality of God faced the punishment of death. Giordano Bruno (1548–1600), an admirer of Copernicus, was burnt at the stake for contending, among other things, that God was not to be understood as a personal being distinct from the world but was to be encountered as immanent in nature. The divine life, he said, permeates everything including ourselves.

This kind of pantheism, shared by the Jewish philosopher Baruch Spinoza (1632–77), and to some extent by the earlier mystics, was the first alternative to traditional theism to be expressed. It was not until the eighteenth century that real doubt began to be raised about whether the concept of God referred to any kind of objective reality. The universal acceptance of the God reality was then beginning to weaken. Friedrich Nietzsche (1844–1900) gave dramatic expression to this in his parable of the madman who declared that 'God is dead'. He was describing the fact that the traditional understanding of God (theism) was becoming dead for the modern human mind, because the modern view of the universe was vastly changed from that in which monotheism had arisen. Nietzsche's announcement surfaced more widely in the 1960s, when even Christian theologians began to accept the significance of what he had said.

At the beginning of the twentieth century there were still only a few who dared to call themselves atheists. In the western world they remain a minority, but they are still growing in number. Traditional theism is declining even more rapidly, and is being replaced by agnosticism or by a use of the word 'God' that is both vague and variable from person to person. The God concept no longer has any agreed or universal meaning. There have, however, been some valiant attempts to defend the continuing use of the term God. Paul Tillich has spoken of God as 'being itself' or as the symbol which points to whatever is of ultimate concern for us.[16] He spoke of the 'God above God.'[17] Don Cupitt has expounded what he chooses to call a non-realist view of God, saying, 'God is the mythical embodiment of all that one is concerned with in the spiritual life.'[18] In this non-objective view, God is a symbolic term referring to our highest values and aspirations. Similarly, Gordon Kaufman has written: 'The symbol "God" presents a focus for orientation which claims to bring true fulfilment and meaning to human life. It sums up, unifies, and represents in a personification what are taken to be the highest and most indispensable human ideals and values.'[19]

No matter how the concept of God is to be understood, the fact remains that this central religious symbol on which Christian orthodoxy has always depended is today severely eroded. As Catholic theologian Johann-Baptist

Metz and Lutheran theologian Jürgen Moltmann have said in their book *Faith and the Future*, there is 'a permanent constitutional crisis for theology' because of 'a withering of the imagination and a radical renunciation of symbolism and mythology'.[20]

When we turn to the concept of relativity in Chapter 6 we shall find further reasons why such concepts as Jesus Christ and God have, during the twentieth century, lost their significance as absolutes. The Bible, the church, Jesus Christ and God have all lost their absoluteness in modern times, and the attempt of the guardians of Christian orthodoxy to restore any of them to the pillars from which they have fallen becomes only a new form of idolatry.

Of course there is much more to Christian orthodoxy than these four pillars, but they do support a system of thought which, within the cultural context of its time, was both impressive and convincing. Today, these pillars no longer offer a firm and absolute foundation, and, as a consequence, the system of thought built upon them comes tumbling down like a house of cards. Traditional Christians refuse to accept that orthodoxy is in any kind of crisis. In vindication they point to the large numbers of professing Christians who remain. Is this because Christianity is broader and more flexible than orthodoxy?

CHAPTER 4

The Failure of Christian Modernism

Why is Christian orthodoxy disintegrating? Why does it no longer have the power to bring conviction and win allegiance in the way it used to? We have already seen that orthodoxy first faltered in its encounters with the inquiring spirit of the Enlightenment. Today, those who valiantly try to defend Christian orthodoxy often blame modernism for its failure. But what is this 'modernism'?

The term modern is often used simply as a synonym for 'contemporary', but there is more to it than that. Coming into English usage about 1500 from the late Latin word *modernus*, the word 'modern' was used to describe obviously new things (as Shakespeare did frequently). Later, the period from 1500 CE onwards became known as the Modern World, following the Mediaeval World or Middle Ages (500–1500 CE), and the Ancient World (500 BCE to 500 CE). This division of history into three ages can be properly applied, of course, only to the Christian west, which also, for better or worse, produced modernity.

The dividing lines between the ancient, mediaeval and modern ages cannot be located with any precision because cultural history is always evolving and does not fall neatly into periods. So the mediaeval age grew out of the ancient world by a complex succession of steps or minor events, just as the modern age, in turn, emerged from the mediaeval age. It is somewhat easier to pinpoint the central or high point of each of these ages. The Graeco-Roman culture of ancient times, for example, had already reached its highest point by the beginning of the Christian era. Similarly, the thirteenth century is somewhere near the apex of the mediaeval age.

What makes the modern age significantly different? Some trace its beginning to the influence of William of Ockham (1285–1349), whose nominalist teaching at Oxford was called the *via moderna* to contrast it with the traditional teaching, the *via antiqua*. Nominalism drew inspiration from the rediscovered teaching of Aristotle that all reality consisted of individual things; it opposed the mediaeval scholastic philosophy which followed Plato's view that reality consisted ultimately of universal archetypal ideas.

These universals, said Ockham, were only names (*nomina*) which humans have created. This simple but radical insight was to have far-reaching philosophical, cultural and scientific consequences. From this seed-thought grew the modern recognition that language, culture, religion and even such basic terms as 'God' originated in the creative human imagination. Along with the *via moderna* came the *devotio moderna*, a form of spirituality promoted by the Brethren of the Common Life, described in Chapter 2. Its most well-known text was *The Imitation of Christ* of Thomas À. Kempis (*c*.1380–1471).

Modernity became a little more evident, however, in the Renaissance (whose leading thinkers were even then called humanists); this in turn gave rise to the Protestant Reformation, led by Martin Luther, a nominalist (1483–1546). But since the Renaissance humanists and the Protestant Reformers were each still trying to revive the past, many see the real beginnings of modernity with people like Francis Bacon (1561–1626). By separating the study of nature from theology and by laying the foundations of empirical science as he did in *The Advancement of Learning* (1605), Bacon encouraged his fellow humans to increase their knowledge of the natural world in order to gain mastery over it. It was this that led to the modern idea of human progress, and so later to industrialisation and the use of technology, both drawing heavily on empirical science. This early modern age, however, retained much of the supernatural superstructure of the mediaeval age, whereas the later modern age has become increasingly secular (or this-worldly) and non-theistic by comparison. In pre-modern times people saw themselves as living in a fixed and eternal cosmic order, which the structures of society were expected to reflect (for example, 'Thy will be done on earth, as it is in heaven'). Truth consisted of eternal and absolute verities waiting to be revealed or discovered. The modern age, by comparison, slowly began to question the permanence of the cosmic order. Whereas all cultural change was once contemplated with trepidation, as a further removal from the golden age in the past, people from the Renaissance onwards began to view cultural change positively, seeing it as the harbinger of welcome improvement in both social well-being and, later, standards of living.

Out of this reversal of mood came the belief in progress that has been such a hallmark of the later modern age. R.G. Collingwood pointed out in 1946 that by the late nineteenth century the idea of progress was becoming an article of faith. He quoted the words of historian Robert Mackenzie, writing in 1880: 'Human history is a record of progress – a record of accumulating knowledge and increasing wisdom, of continual advancement from a lower to a higher platform of intelligence and well-being . . . The nineteenth-century has witnessed progress rapid beyond all precedent, for it has witnessed the overthrow of the barriers which prevented progress.'[1]

Progress was possible and seemed to be assured because modernity took a much more positive view of the human condition. In the pre-modern ages human consciousness was dominated by a feeling of helplessness in the face of all natural and supernatural forces, causing people to acknowledge their absolute dependence on divine help, whereas the modern age has been marked by a high degree of human self-confidence and the belief that humans can at last master the forces of nature, justifying an optimistic hope for the human earthly future.

Belief in human progress was continually generated by the success of the emerging sciences, along with the new technology which scientific discoveries made possible. As the twentieth century progressed, modernity almost came to be identified with science itself. Science was commonly thought to hold the key to the human future, so that there was no problem or obstacle which it could not eventually overcome. Also associated with modernity, and perhaps even essential to it, has been the rise of democracy as the fairest, though not necessarily the most efficient, form of government and social order. Allied to democracy has been a new awareness of the value of personal freedom, individual human rights, and gender and sexual equality.

In 1900, therefore, the beginning of the new century was being welcomed with enthusiasm and expectation. The majority of people, at least in the western world, rejoiced in modernity and were reasonably happy with where the world was heading. Everything new and modern was praised and assumed to be superior to the old. Most were firmly confident that conditions could only get better. Just as implicit faith in science has been called scientism, so this trust and confidence which people put in modernity may be called modernism, a term found as early as the eighteenth century.

Modernity came into being in the west and is a product of Christian culture, however much conservative Christians today want to disown it. As the Christian west saw modernity at first, it seemed that a new and better social order was emerging, thus enabling the Kingdom of God at last to be built on earth. The early pioneers of modernity, such as William of Ockham, John Wycliffe, Erasmus, Martin Luther, Francis Bacon, Galileo and John Locke, were all Christian by conviction. All through the nineteenth-century leading Christian thinkers, while not condoning everything new, enthusiastically welcomed and embraced modernity. Among them was Friedrich Schleiermacher (1768–1834), often referred to as the first modern theologian. He was the father of what became known as Protestant Liberalism, which can be seen as the expression of Christian thought in a form more appropriate to the modern world. Thus, as the coming of modernity gathered speed, there were Christian thinkers and biblical scholars who were not only keeping pace with it but, in some areas, promoting it.

It is often forgotten today that, at the time of the furore over Darwin's epoch-making book *The Origin of Species* in 1859, there were theologians who quickly accepted his theory of biological evolution. In 1860 the famous Cambridge New Testament scholar, F.J.A. Hort (1828–1892) wrote to a friend: 'Have you read Darwin . . . In spite of difficulties, I am inclined to think it unanswerable.' The more liberal Christian thinkers were still confident they would be able to reconcile the Word of God in the book of nature with the Word of God in the Bible (as some of them put it). They believed that, even when the Bible was studied like any other book, it would still be found that there was no other book like it.

A group of Anglican scholars from Oxford gave their support to modernity in their *Essays and Reviews* in 1861, a book that caused an even greater storm than Darwin's. Professor Baden-Powell (father of the founder of the Boy Scout movement) wrote: 'Mr Darwin's masterly volume . . . must soon bring about an entire revolution of opinion in favour of the self-evolving powers of nature.'[2] By 1890 J.R. Illingworth, an influential Anglican theologian, was able to write: 'The last few years have witnessed the gradual acceptance by Christian thinkers of the great scientific generalisation of our time, the Theory of Evolution.'[3] Many books were written by theologians on the problem of how to reconcile Christian thought with evolution. The notion of evolution was itself applied to the origin of culture and of religion, as by the Scottish theologian Edward Caird in *The Evolution of Religion* (1890).

The rise of Protestant Liberalism may be said to have reached its climax in the thought of Adolf Harnack (1851–1930). A leading historian of the Christian church in the late nineteenth and early twentieth centuries, he was also deeply involved in the advancement of science, as a member of the Academy of Sciences in Berlin and president of what later came to be known as the Max Planck Society for the Advancement of Science. Harnack set out to show from his penetrating studies of early Christianity that the relevance of Christianity to the modern world lay not in theological dogmatism but in the understanding of Christianity as an historical, changing, evolving process. He argued that, within this process, there existed an unchangeable essence of Christianity which, in the course of history, had gone through one metamorphosis after another. He sought to separate this essence from the subsequent accretions of dogma.

The original Gospel of Jesus, in Harnack's view, had little in common with the ecclesiastical statutes and doctrines of orthodoxy. He was convinced that if the Gospel were to retain power in the modern world, it must be freed from its connection with the dogmas of God and Christ with which it had been clothed in order to survive in the ancient Hellenistic world. In 1900 he delivered his findings in a series of public lectures, later published as *What is Christianity?* There he reduced the essence of Christianity to the Fatherhood of God, the Brotherhood of Man, the infinite value of the human soul and the coming of the Kingdom of God – themes that were already becoming dominant in late nineteenth-century hymns.

The development of Protestant Liberalism contrasted strongly, at first, with the response of Catholicism to modernity, partly because the Roman Catholic Church has been a much more authoritarian structure, and partly because the Roman Catholic Church remained more firmly committed to the mediaeval age after the Protestant Reformation. It saw no reason to depart from the teaching of the great mediaeval theologian Thomas Aquinas.

In the nineteenth century, therefore, the Roman Catholic Church was firmly resisting the influence of modernism on religious thought while Protestantism was adjusting to it. Pope Pius VI had strongly condemned the manifesto of the French Revolution, which was one of the more violent signs of the coming of modern age. The church continued to resist all social and cultural change throughout the nineteenth and early twentieth centuries. In 1832 Pope Gregory XVI (followed by Pope Pius IX) declared that it was insane to teach that 'the liberty of conscience and of worship is the peculiar right of every man . . . and that citizens have the right to all kinds of liberty . . . by which they may be enabled to manifest openly and publicly their ideas, by word of mouth, through the press or by any other means'.[4] In 1864 Pope Pius IX proceeded to draw up a list of the principal errors of the age which were to be condemned. There were 80 of these, of which the last read: 'It is an error to claim that the Roman Pontiff can, and ought to, reconcile himself and come to terms with progress, liberalism and modern civilisation.'[5] Thus modernism was not to be permitted to penetrate Catholic theological doctrine, and the idea of evolution was strongly condemned. The First Vatican Council (1869–1870) was held in part to strengthen the church against the onslaught of modern thinking, and did so by promulgating the Dogma of Papal Infallibility.

Nonetheless, modern thought took root in Catholicism. When Leo XIII came to the papal chair, he announced his intention of reconciling the church with modern civilisation. His most famous encyclical, *Rerum Novarum* (1891), was directed to 'The Condition of the Working Classes', and it has been hailed as one of the most important modern pronouncements on social justice. This gave encouragement to a group of Catholics who soon became known as the Modernists and who reached the height of their influence in the opening years of the twentieth century. The Catholic Modernists believed that Catholic teaching should be brought into harmony with the modern outlook in philosophy, history and science. They contended that the biblical writers were conditioned by the times in which they lived, and that biblical religion, like all religion, was subject to historical development.

Alfred Loisy (1857–1940) was a French priest and a very able biblical scholar, who published *The Gospel and the Church* (1902) for the express purpose of defending Catholicism against the influence of Protestant Liberalism, particularly as expounded in Harnack's *What is Christianity?* ('the essence of Christianity', in German). Loisy denied that Christianity possessed any permanent and absolute essence; rather he saw it as a living and ever-changing process. He contended that it was quite legitimate for Christianity to evolve, as it had done, into the fully fledged form of Catholicism, and believed Harnack to be mistaken in thinking that, by stripping away what had developed over many centuries, he would find a solid and primitive kernel of essential Christianity. As Loisy saw it, the Gospel was not a message set in unchangeable words which were equally applicable to people of all centuries. Christianity, he claimed, was a living faith which, though always linked to the historical circumstances of its birth, had to be perpetually reshaped and given fresh verbal expression in order to remain a genuine path of faith in later ages.

Loisy was paving the way for an essential reform – in the interpretation of the Bible, in the whole of theology and even in Catholicism itself. His book was welcomed by other liberal-minded Catholics, but the author soon found himself facing the full wrath of the Catholic hierarchy. He was charged with denying the inspiration of Scripture, denying that Jesus was the revealer of infallible truths, denying the bodily resurrection of Jesus by regarding it as myth, and undermining the authority of the papacy. Loisy and other liberal Catholic thinkers had been tolerated and even encouraged during the reign of Pope Leo XIII (1878–1903), who had real respect for academic scholarship. But his successor, Pius X (1903–1914), distrusted this liberal movement from the beginning.

In 1907 Modernism as led by Loisy was condemned by Pope Pius X as 'the synthesis of all heresies'. In an encyclical (*Lamentabili*) and a decree (*Pascendi*) he set out the 65 errors of Modernism, one of which was that 'Scientific progress demands that the concepts of Christian doctrine concerning God, creation, revelation, the Person of the Incarnate Word and Redemption be readjusted'.[6] Loisy was excommunicated in 1908, but in 1909 was appointed to the chair of the History of Religions at the Collège de France, from which position he continued to write about Christian origins for the next 20 years.

The leading Catholic Modernist in England was George Tyrrell (1861–1909). Reared as an evangelical Protestant in Dublin, Tyrrell was attracted to High Church Anglicanism. By 1879 he had become a Roman Catholic and in 1880 he entered the Jesuit novitiate. Remaining strongly attracted to the devotional aspects of Catholicism, he became increasingly hostile to the orthodox scholasticism, and began to publish his views with some vigour, contrasting living faith with dead theology. He was dismissed from the Jesuit order in 1907 for refusing to repudiate his more provocative statements. When the Pope issued his encyclical condemning Modernism, Tyrrell wrote letters to the London *Times* accusing the Pope of heresy. He was immediately excommunicated. He died in 1909 and was refused Catholic burial.

Tyrrell's views were set forth in *Christianity at the Cross-roads*, published posthumously in 1910. There he defined a Modernist as 'a churchman who believes in the possibility of a synthesis between the essential truth of his religion and the essential truth of modernity'.[7] Like Loisy, he was critical of the Protestant Liberals, making the much-quoted remark that the Christ that Harnack saw, looking back through nineteen centuries of Catholic darkness, was only the reflection of a Liberal Protestant face seen at the bottom of a deep well. He believed that, whereas Protestant Liberals were putting the emphasis on historical records and on the moral teaching of Jesus, Catholic Modernism was calling for changes of such a radical nature that it might be necessary for Catholicism to die, in order that it might rise again in a grander form, more appropriate to the age.

Pope Pius X was determined to root out all elements of Modernism from Catholicism. In 1910 he required all priests to swear an anti-modernist oath in which they were to offer complete submission to his earlier condemnations of Modernism. Only 40 priests refused. All ordinands were thereafter required to make a vow renouncing all Modernist tendencies. At that point the Modernist movement was almost completely crushed by papal authority.

In 1898, just as Catholic Modernism was raising its profile in both England and France, an Anglican Society was founded, entitled the Churchmen's Union, later to be called the Modern Churchmen's Union. Its aim was to reformulate Christian thought in ways that would make it more consistent with the modern age. Anglican Modernism had much sympathy with both Protestant Liberalism and Catholic Modernism but, at the same time, remained critical of them both.

The leader and chief organiser of Anglican Modernism was Henry D.A. Major, who was reared, educated and ordained in New Zealand before he returned to his native Britain. In 1911 he founded a monthly journal, *The Modern Churchman*, which he edited until 1956. In 1919 Major was appointed principal of Ripon Hall after it was transferred to Oxford, where it became the centre for Anglican Modernism.

Major defined Modernism as the claim of the modern mind to determine what is true in the light of its own experience, even though its conclusions might contradict those of tradition. He believed this to be a mode of human consciousness that would dominate in the future. The dogmas of the past were to be valued and studied historically, but were not to be taken as infallible and binding. All this he set forth in *English Modernism* (1927), first delivered as lectures in Harvard in 1925–1926.

Major denied that religion was dying. He claimed, rather, that it was being rationalised, moralised and spiritualised. He was convinced that, unless modernised, the church would be a declining influence in shaping the world of the future. He believed that Anglican Modernism would not suffer the same fate as Roman Catholic Modernism since Anglicanism, unlike Catholicism, was a tradition comprehensive enough to have contained many differing schools of thought. However, by the early 1960s, when Major died, Anglican Modernism was already losing ground. By this time Protestant Liberalism was also less vigorous and was being successfully countered by a strong reactionary movement which came to be known as fundamentalism.

In 1909, just one year after the Pope had crushed the rise of Modernism in the Catholic Church, a series of 12 booklets entitled *The Fundamentals* began to appear.[8] Between 1909 and 1915 they were distributed free of charge to every Protestant minister in the English-speaking world. Their intention was to counter the spread of liberal religious thought commonly known as Christian Modernism. They identified it with secular humanism, and condemned it as the cause of all current cultural ills, including the decline in Christian allegiance. They believed the only solution was to return to the fundamental certainties and the supernaturalist thought forms of pre-modern times. The booklets reaffirmed belief in a personal God, the infallibility of the Bible, the deity of Christ, the Virgin Birth, miracles, the bodily resurrection of Jesus, and the substitutionary view of the Atonement. They attacked not only the new biblical criticism and Darwinism, but also Roman Catholicism and the new sects of Mormonism, Jehovah's Witnesses and Christian Science.

Although the publication of the series failed initially to check the spread of Modernism, it led to fierce theological battles between fundamentalists and liberals in seminaries and churches. The theological battle received great publicity during the famous Scopes Trial of 1925, when school teacher John Scopes was tried and convicted for teaching biological evolution in a Tennessee school. Fundamentalists still found themselves in a minority; for example, Presbyterian fundamentalists chose to withdraw from Princeton Theological Seminary and form their own (conservative) Westminster Seminary.

In 1925 Kirsopp Lake, a New Testament scholar of international repute and an Anglican Modernist, wrote a book called *The Religion of Yesterday and To-morrow* in which he asserted that the denominational divisions of the church had already become obsolete. The real divisions, which cut right across the denominations, divided church people into what he called the Fundamentalists (conservatives), the Institutionalists (liberal traditionalists) and the Experimentalists (radicals). He said it had become 'necessary to distinguish the future of the churches from the future of religion'.[9] The future of Christianity he believed to be with the experimentalists but, with regard to the churches, he made this striking prophecy: 'The Fundamentalists will eventually triumph. They will drive the Experimentalists out of the churches and then reabsorb the Institutionalists who, under pressure, will become more orthodox. The Church will shrink from left to right.'[10] This prophecy has largely been fulfilled in the Protestant churches. Fundamentalist or traditionalist Christians tend to dominate the ecclesiastical institutions throughout the world today. The liberals, particularly after the failure of Modernism, have largely ceased to be active in the mainline churches, leaving these to become increasingly conservative.

In Roman Catholicism, liberalism began to resurface for a time from the

1940s onwards, particularly in Catholic biblical scholarship. It came to a head when the Vatican II Council (1962–1965), with its theme of *aggiornamento*, was called by Pope John XXIII as a means of bringing the Roman Catholic Church into the modern world. Although the term Modernist was strictly avoided, the Vatican II Council did initiate a number of moves to which the earlier Modernists would have given hearty approval. For a decade or two the face of Catholicism began to change much more rapidly than that of Protestantism. Then the impetus faltered in the final years of Pope Paul VI, and traditional conservatism returned under Pope John Paul II.

Protestant Liberalism, Anglican Modernism and Roman Catholic Modernism all responded to the advent of the modern age in a positive and constructive way. They set out to show that Christian faith and practice had nothing to fear from modernity. They firmly believed that, though some changes in the expression of Christian doctrine were needed, the essential truth of Christianity would stand firm and would be expressed again in new and more appropriate forms. But they have not succeeded in taking the main body of the churches with them. A few instances of even more radical thought have surfaced within the mainline churches (such as John Robinson's *Honest to God* in 1963, Don Cupitt's *Taking Leave of God* and later books), but these have largely been rejected by Christian officialdom, and the churches have become more attached than ever to one or other of the orthodox forms of the past. The gulf between the church and the world outside it grows ever wider.

Is this because Christianity is unable to be modernised, or does it point to some basic flaws in modernity itself? There is some truth in each of these views. As we look back, we cannot fail to compare the widespread optimism with which the western world was greeting modernism a century ago with today's more ambivalent experience. At the beginning of the century science was being hailed as the new and infallible source of truth. 'Science teaches that . . .' was rapidly replacing 'The church teaches that . . .'; science and religion came to be popularly viewed as polar opposites and mutual enemies. If the body of divinely revealed knowledge contained in the Bible and guarded by the church was the basis of the Christian era, so the body of knowledge being accumulated by science was seen to be the foundation of modernity, fuelling human confidence in an ever better future. This is no longer so.

Many of the events of the twentieth century have eroded the human self-confidence and belief in progress that fuelled modernity. And modernity itself is now held responsible by some for the current ills in society, and for the uncertain and fragile future which we now face. H. Richard Niebuhr wrote just before his death in 1962:

> We see the possibility that human history will come to its end neither in a brotherhood of man nor in universal death under the blows of natural or man-made catastrophe, but in the gangrenous corruption of a social life in which every promise, contract, treaty and 'word of honour' is given and accepted in deception and distrust. If men no longer have faith in each other, can they exist as men?[11]

At the end of the twentieth century science and technology still enjoy approval and inspire confidence in human endeavour, but they no longer go unquestioned. Modernism, as a name for putting one's faith in all things modern, is no longer universally espoused. Indeed, the scientific enterprise is itself entering a more fluid state. The world we find ourselves living in seems not wholly to be determined by the laws of nature which modernism set out to uncover. Rather, the universe appears to be a mystifying mixture of both necessity and chance. Perhaps we have come to the end of modernism, whether Christian or secular.

This ambivalence towards modernity is reflected in two extreme attitudes. Some, such as the fundamentalists, see modernity as the cause of all our ills; they wish wholeheartedly to reject much of it and to return to the supposed security of pre-modern times. At the other extreme there are those who call themselves post-modernists (to be discussed in Chapter 7); they also are strongly critical of much that has characterised modernity but, knowing there can be no turning back, they advocate various ways of moving into a less structured future. Most people could perhaps still be described as lukewarm modernists, in the sense that we are grateful for the comforts and pleasures modernity offers and are prepared to accept as inevitable the problems and disadvantages that come in its train.

And where does this leave Christianity? Is it to be even further marginalised? Is it to become a museum piece? Or is there something about Christianity which we have not yet fully understood?

CHAPTER 5

The Christian Stream of Influence

If Christian civilisation is no more, if Christian orthodoxy is disintegrating and if Christian Modernism has failed to rescue it, where does this leave Christianity? Is it also facing its demise? This depends on what we understand by Christianity – a question which, rather problematically, cannot be answered in the same way for all who call themselves Christian.

Many assume Christianity to be identified with what became the classical Christian doctrines (orthodoxy), yet it was several centuries before these were explicitly enunciated in the creeds by the ecumenical councils. Christianity is older than the orthodoxy it later produced. (In any case, since the Reformation, there have emerged several 'orthodoxies', each claiming to be the true one). Something which might be called Christianity clearly existed from the time the first followers of Jesus proclaimed him to be the Christ and found themselves referred to as Christians (Acts 11:26). Yet the study of Christian history shows there has never been a time when all Christians have agreed on what it is to be a Christian. The first sharp difference of opinion is documented in the New Testament – it was the difference between the original (or Jewish) form of Christian allegiance to Jesus Christ and the Pauline (or Gentile) form. That rift was never healed. The ecumenical councils later achieved the only true form of Christian teaching only by declaring to be heretical all who failed to accept their definitions. But those 'heretical' movements also claimed to be Christian. Thus, over two millennia, there have been innumerable different ways of understanding what it means to be a Christian and during the last 500 years they have been multiplying.

Today, some think of Christianity as a matter of holding certain beliefs, while others think of it as a particular lifestyle. Some regard Christianity as a set of values to be honoured as a guide to living; others experience it as a conversion in which one accepts Jesus Christ as one's personal Lord and Saviour. Some see themselves as incorporated into the church as the body of Christ; others believe everything in the Bible and call themselves bible-believing Christians. The Christian path of faith has been walked in many different ways by innumerable people through the centuries. What links them together is their common respect for the Bible (though they interpret it in different ways) and their desire to give their allegiance to Jesus as the Christ (albeit in many different forms). To avoid adopting a sectarian viewpoint, it is necessary to include in the broad stream of Christianity not only what has been at the centre but also what has been on the margins – and that includes what some have judged to be heresies. We should remember also that what has been heretical to one age has sometimes been approved by another, and vice-versa.

A precise answer to the question 'what is Christianity?' thus remains elusive. However, W. Cantwell Smith in his book *The Meaning and End of Religion* (1964) opened up other ways of apprehending the Christian experience. Objective names such as Christianity, Hinduism, and Buddhism have only come into use in recent centuries; this phenomenon, implying that religions are 'things', is described as 'reification'. Instead of using the term Christianity, Cantwell Smith suggested that we would do better to focus on two quite different components present throughout Christian history – the first he calls the Christian cumulative tradition and the second is the personal faith and commitment of people who think of themselves as Christians.

By the Christian cumulative tradition is meant the sum of all the objective data that has marked the complex path of Christian faith through the centuries. They are, for example, the Bible, creeds, confessions, theological systems, deviant heresies, moral codes, myths, buildings, social institutions – everything that has been left as an extant deposit within the developing Christian culture, and which can be studied by the historian. It is not the historian's place to prefer one set of Christian data to another, or to side with the orthodox over the heretics but only to decide whether the datum is definitely linked with the cumulative Christian tradition as a whole.

Faith is something quite different. It is the attitude of trust and hope with which humans can face the future and all the challenges life brings. Faith is an attitudinal response of the whole person, involving the emotions and the will as well as the mind. It is not therefore to be identified just with beliefs, for these are solely cognitive. Being personal and subjective, faith is not open to historical and objective study as the cumulative tradition is, yet without such faith there would have been no such tradition.

Faith is not the sole prerogative of any one cultural tradition, though Christians have often shown a tendency to think faith was exclusively a Christian phenomenon. Faith is a potential universal to the human species and is to be found in people of every cultural tradition. That is why it has become common to speak of the various traditions as 'paths of faith'. Each particular culture fosters and shapes the faith of those within it by the way it provides a world-view and helps them to understand life. The religious dimension of a culture promotes particular qualities and aspirations which give that culture its identity and even a name. There is no one path of faith which is ideal or exclusively true. Moreover, in the life of an individual or a community the experience of faith may be found to ebb and flow according to changing circumstances.

Long before the modern term 'Christianity' came into use, people used to speak rather of 'the Christian faith'. This term acknowledges (at least tacitly) that there are many different ways of experiencing faith (or trust). The qualifying epithet 'Christian' was used to denote the particular qualities this path of faith was believed to possess, namely, that it drew inspiration and strength from the one known as Jesus Christ.

While faith is so personal and subjective that it is not open to objective study, the religious observance which stems from faith is observable. Instead of asking about the fate of Christianity in the modern world, we can more usefully ask what is happening to Christian observance.

Widespread Christian observance within Christendom not only survived the fragmentation of the church at the Reformation but even seemed to show a new burst of vitality. This was because the focus shifted from participation in Christendom (by virtue of birth) to personal experience and belief (by active choice). Instead of being baptised into 'the one and holy catholic church' as a matter of universal practice, people were being challenged to make a personal choice between the Catholic and the various other Protestant forms of Christian allegiance. This had the effect of intensifying devotion and commitment. Unfortunately it often led to bitter animosity between Protestant and Catholic and even between various forms of Protestantism. What, in theory, should have been allegiance to a common Lord Jesus Christ, often turned out in practice to be sectarian allegiance to a particular confession or denomination. After the rather grudging truce between Catholic and Protestant was entered into at the 1648 Peace of Westphalia, the resurgence of active 'Christian' commitment initiated by the Reformation began to ebb.

Yet there was still no question of abandoning Christian affiliation. This even survived the corrosive effect of the Enlightenment. In doing so, however, Christian allegiance became even more personal, inward and subjective. Protestantism, in particular, survived the rationalism of the

Enlightenment through a shift of emphasis from doctrines (products of the mind) to inner experience (feelings of the heart). The Pietistic movements, initiated by such people as Philipp Spener and Count von Zinzendorf, and spread by the Moravian Brethren, did much to revitalise Protestant church life. These movements, followed by Methodism and the evangelical revival, focused on inner subjective experience, just as the charismatic movements have been doing in the late twentieth century.

Personal religious experience and inner feeling, therefore, began to take precedence over religious thought and dogma at the very time when traditional Christian doctrines were becoming increasingly out of kilter with the new ideas and advancing human knowledge of the last two centuries. Even so, the number of people with serious doubts about the basic Christian concepts and doctrines was still extremely small in the eighteenth century. This did not increase until the nineteenth century, by which time the leading edge of western thought was moving beyond the limits of doctrinal orthodoxy. A great gulf began to open up between what intelligent people were thinking and saying on the one hand, and what the church continued to teach on the other.

At first all these changes were quite gradual. Even the decline of Christendom was hardly noticed until after the end of the nineteenth century. In 1900 it would have been absurd to suggest that Christian allegiance was in any decline, for the opposite appeared to be true. It has been only in the second half of the twentieth century that people of the Christian west have abandoned affiliation to Christianity in some numbers, openly confessing they are no longer Christian. Even when church attendance was becoming more irregular, between 1850–1950, people did not think of themselves as abandoning Christianity but only (what they called) 'churchianity'. Since the end of World War II, however, there have been alarming signs that it is not just Christendom that is vanishing and not just Christian orthodoxy which is disintegrating. Christian allegiance is itself suffering from a deep *malaise*. The proclamation of the age-old Christian message is no longer bringing forth a firm response of Christian commitment. Since the beginning, the Christian message has been boldly presented as the Gospel – 'good news'. Today it is no longer widely heard as any sort of news at all, good or bad.

This first became noticeable in Protestant areas, but predominantly Catholic countries now appear to be affected too. In 1982 the World Christian Encyclopaedia noted the number of white westerners practising Christianity was dropping at a rate of 7,600 per day; in 1986 the Roman

Catholic theologian Hans Küng observed that, of the some five billion inhabitants of the earth, only 950 million were nominally Christian and only a fraction of those took any active part in the church. Although this decline in Christian allegiance, occurring mainly in one century, is quite sudden relative to the length of the Christian era, it has been sufficiently slow and unspectacular relative to a person's lifetime that most churches have, until recently, been hardly aware of it. Many church leaders have flatly refused to acknowledge any decline at all in Christian allegiance.

People born in recent decades have no first-hand experience of what active Christian allegiance was like at the beginning of the twentieth century, when practically everybody in the western world other than Jews claimed to be Christian. Churches were full; Christian festivals dominated the calendar; there was strict sabbath observance; and the various patterns of Christian morality were enforced by peer pressure, even more than they were by law or from the pulpit. Christendom may not have existed at the beginning of this century, but the Christian practice was still very much alive.

At the end of this century things are very different. In Europe, and in countries to which European culture has been transplanted, there is evidence everywhere of decline in outward Christian observance. Many churches now have very small congregations; some churches have closed altogether. Congregations are commonly made up of people aged 50 and over; young people rarely participate. Seminaries for the training of clergy and priests have been closing down. Roman Catholic monastic orders have very few novices and often consist of a few elderly nuns or monks. The great cathedrals have become historic monuments to a past age, chiefly of interest to tourists.

Church-going remains more common in the United States and in some of the African countries; the charismatic and fundamentalist groups are the most active of all the churches. Fundamentalist Christians regard themselves as the last bastions of orthodoxy because of their commitment to the literal text of the Bible, and this meets the needs of people looking for certainty in a time of rapid change. The attraction of the charismatic churches is their emphasis on inner feeling and their ability to foster a sense of emotional fulfilment; there is little critical examination of what the Christian doctrines really mean in a world very different from that in which they were first formulated.

To many, of course, this evidence of decline in Christian allegiance is only too obvious. But there has been a strange reluctance within the churches to acknowledge it. Some insist on interpreting the twentieth century as a period of unfortunate but temporary setback in Christian advance, comparable to those which occurred prior to the Reformation and to the Evangelical Revival. They confidently predict that this decline too will be followed by a renewal. Some claim that this is already happening in the rapid spread of the charismatic movement, while others, like Keith Ward in *The Turn of the Tide*, express optimistic hopes for the future of Christianity. Yet others are sure that radical measures could be taken to reverse the current decline, if only the church were of a mind to adopt them.[1]

The belief that the classical form of Christianity will come through every crisis in the long run is, of course, an essential component of the Christian faith. Over the centuries Christians have said of their church founded by God, 'not even the gates of Hell shall prevail against it', so to contemplate the possible demise of Christianity we have to suspend Christian faith and step outside it, at least temporarily. When we do this the traditional expectations of Christianity's future look very much like wishful thinking.

Already by the end of the nineteenth century, theology was losing credibility as an academic discipline, often finding no place in the new secular universities in the twentieth century. It has sometimes been replaced now by the historical study of all religion as a human phenomenon. The Christian churches have been reluctant to follow the lead of even their own liberal scholars. John Cobb has gone so far as to say: 'The church has lost the ability to think. Unless it recognises that its healthy survival depends on the recovery and exercise of that ability and acts on that recognition, talk of renewal or transformation is idle.'[2]

Modern historical, philosophical and scientific thought has come into conflict at so many points with traditional Christian teaching that the latter has been losing its power to convince ordinary people (to say nothing of the intelligentsia). While most people still affirm what they call 'Christian values', an increasing number at all educational levels find themselves quite unable to embrace traditional Christian beliefs. The Christian views of history, of the nature of the universe and of the human condition are no longer consistent with the understanding that most people have through experience and general education. Many who have tried to remain faithful to the church feel guilty that they are unable to reconcile their personal views or convictions with Christian teaching; they live a kind of schizophrenic religious existence. Others have resolved the tension by distancing themselves and openly saying they are not Christian. During the twentieth century the *mainline* churches have become the *oldline* churches and now find themselves to be the *sidelined* churches (to use John Cobb's words).

We have seen that Christian faith can be described only in very general terms. There is no such thing as *the* Christian faith, but there have been countless people through the ages who have found that their capacity for faith has been nourished and strengthened by drawing on various elements of the now extensive Christian cumulative tradition. In the course of 2,000 years this has not only spread around the world geographically but, like a river fanning out into a delta with streams and tributaries, it has diversified its forms and expression. Its organisational manifestation is to be found in a great variety of churches, denominations, sects, associations, movements and house groups. It has gradually penetrated into different cultures, so shaping and colouring them, that even when the ecclesiastical organisations begin to decay, its influence leaves behind a more permanent deposit. This may not be recognisable as any form of conventional Christianity; yet it is there because of the influence of the Christian cumulative tradition and remains part of that tradition.

To illustrate this, let us look at another religious tradition, that of Zoroastrianism. Zoroaster's teaching also developed into a civilisation. It had two main periods of flowering, one about 540–330 BCE in the time of the Achaemenian rulers, and the second about 225–650 CE in the time of the Sassanian rulers. Zoroastrian civilisation has now long since disappeared, yet Zoroastrianism still lives, in two quite different ways. It is preserved and practised in one form by the descendants of the earlier Zoroastrians, the Parsis, who now number only about 100,000. More remarkably, however, Zoroastrianism continues today in the ideas, values and mythical themes transmitted to the Jews and through them, to Christianity and Islam. Some of the Zoroastrian influences were described briefly in Chapter 1; they include, as noted, our current concern with 'the millennium'.

The components of Zoroastrianism which survive in the three monotheistic traditions of the Middle East are, of course, no longer known as Zoroastrian, nor are they usually acknowledged to have a pre-Jewish source. But today we are much more aware that no religious tradition evolves in complete isolation. Most, on examination, reveal more influence from other traditions than they are usually ready to acknowledge. Some gems of wisdom travel from one culture to another, yet each regards them as its own. This interplay between cultures and between religious traditions means that few, if any, of the great cultures ever wholly disappear;

they leave deposits of their most compelling ideas and themes. In our clocks and watches we still observe the long-term influence of the culture of ancient Babylonia, for it was the ancient Babylonians who began to use the number base of 60 for counting time and for measuring angles.

The modern secular world cannot be properly understood without acknowledging all it owes to the many human cultures which have preceded it – in particular, the culture of western Christendom. Indeed western Christianity, however unintentionally, was chiefly instrumental in bringing the modern world into existence. Thus, just as parts of Zoroastrianism may be said to have survived in Christianity, so much of the Christian cumulative tradition lives on in the secularised modern world, and will continue to do so. It would be almost impossible to stamp out that influence.

What survives of the classical form of Christianity appears thin when compared with the substantial body of teaching in its heyday. Yet it has gained enormously in breadth. The cumulative Christian tradition is now spreading out so widely, both geographically and in shape, that it is coming to include a variety of forms which are inconsistent with others. One cannot today define 'a Christian' without cutting out people who, quite legitimately, wish to count themselves as Christians, or including some who wish to deny any allegiance to the Christian tradition.

The question of whether we are facing the demise of Christianity does not, therefore, admit of any straightforward answer. We are certainly coming to the end of orthodox or conventional Christianity – that is, the Christianity which is Bible-based, and which affirms God as a divine personal being and Jesus Christ as the only Saviour of the world. But the cumulative tradition still goes on. Just as the ancients used the terms 'wind' and 'breath' metaphorically to refer to the invisible 'spiritual' forces that operate in human societies and motivate their cultures, so we may need to draw upon such vague and indefinite terms in order to understand what is happening in this tradition. Viktor von Strauss, the first to notice the ancient cultural change that was later named the Axial Period, described what he observed as 'a strange movement of the spirit [which] passed through all civilised peoples'.[3] Such 'movements of the spirit' may be the key to our understanding of the next phase.

Instead of thinking of Christianity as something which has an unchangeable essence we should view it as a continuing, yet changing, stream of cultural influence. The history and culture of ancient Israel was the chief source from which this stream issued but there were many other tributaries, such as Persian Zoroastrianism and Hellenistic philosophy. Through the centuries were added the thoughts, feelings and personal experiences of countless generations of people who were both shaped by the stream and contributed to it. The development of the mediaeval church, the Renaissance, the Reformation, the Enlightenment, the Evangelical Revival and the advent of modernity have all been significant features of the stream itself, sometimes strengthening it, sometimes modifying it, and always changing it.

As change has taken place, some have accepted it readily, while others have resisted change as inconsistent with some immutable essence. Today such people commonly speak of the danger of 'throwing out the baby with the bath water'. The metaphor is misleading. There is no 'baby', no eternal essence of Christianity. Christianity is the stream itself. The stream is continuous in its flow but ever changing, with new elements entering and others falling out of sight. As Heraclitus noted, one cannot step twice into the same stream.

The stance on human rights is an excellent example of the way radical change can take place in this cultural stream. Many in Christian circles now see it as their duty to give strong support to human rights, yet for nearly 2,000 years the concept of human rights was never acknowledged as a Christian value. There is no explicit mention of such rights in the Bible, nor do they figure in traditional theology and Christian ethics. Even in Emil Brunner's weighty volume on Christian ethics, *The Divine Imperative* (1937), there is no discussion of human rights as such. In pre-modern times the emphasis was always on the duties and responsibilities that lie with us humans – duties to God, duties to the monarch, duties to our fellows. Conventional Christianity asserted that, as sinful creatures in a fallen world ruled by an Almighty God, humans had no rights at all but were at the mercy of a gracious God.

And so the papal encyclicals did not speak about human rights until 1963. In 1864 Pope Pius IX declared that it was insane to teach that citizens had rights to all kinds of liberty,[4] but in 1963 Pope John XXIII, in his encyclical *Pacem in Terris*, said:

> Every man has the *right to life*, to bodily integrity and to the means which are necessary and suitable for the proper development of life. These are primarily food, clothing, shelter, rest, medical care and, finally, the necessary social services. Therefore a human being also has the *right to security* in cases of sickness, inability to work, widowhood, old age, unemployment, or in any case in

which he is deprived of the means of subsistence through no fault of his own . . . *right to respect, right to freedom* in searching for truth, *right to share* in the benefits of culture . . . *the right to choose the state of life which they prefer.*'5

Within 100 years the Roman Catholic Church had completely reversed its position. If such a radical shift can occur in the most conservative bastion of Christian orthodoxy, how much more change is likely in the more indefinable stream of influence, referred to in the past as Christianity? The Catholic Modernist Loisy, argued against Harnack, as we have seen, that Christianity has no permanent and absolute essence. It is free to evolve where the spirit leads it. Thus, if it is true, as has been claimed, that the idea of Christendom and the doctrines of Christian orthodoxy, were not at all what the historical Jesus had in mind when he spoke of the Kingdom of God, we should not be surprised if the continuing stream of cultural influence which he was so instrumental in re-directing should in the future manifest itself in ways very different from the conventional Christianity it later became for a period.

The modern world is definitely not Christian in any traditional sense, but neither is it anti-Christian, as many traditional Christians assert. What was once the 'Christian west' may be legitimately described as post-Christian, a term which acknowledges its continuity with its Christian past. This ongoing 'Christian' stream of cultural influence6 is once again in a fluid state, has widened considerably, and is changing quite radically. It is now becoming part of a larger stream, as all the cultural streams of the past begin to mingle in a global sea.

The Christian presence in the emerging global culture may not always be readily identifiable, but the new global sea of faith cannot help but be continuous with the Christian past. Just how the Christian stream is to relate to the other streams flowing into the global sea may become clearer when, in the next chapter, we acknowledge the phenomenon of relativity.

CHAPTER 6

The Discovery of Relativity

There is a book in the Bible not much loved by Christian preachers, even though it is called 'The Preacher', or by its Greek title, 'Ecclesiastes'. It starts off: '"Vanity of vanities," says the preacher, "Everything is vanity."' The word translated as vanity literally means 'thin air', and it was used to describe whatever is 'vapour-like', 'insubstantial', 'having no solidity or permanence'. The unknown author of this book was writing at time when his Jewish heritage was encountering challenges from Greek critical thought, and he expressed here his sense of uncertainty. In today's fast-changing world, many might share his sense of 'vanity', of impermanence, of the ground shifting beneath their feet. But our equivalent word might be 'relativity' – and how often do we hear the phrase 'everything is relative'?

The phenomenon of relativity has been one of the epoch-making discoveries of this last century of the second millennium. We mostly associate the term with Albert Einstein (1879–1955) and his two famous cosmological theories of relativity. But these simply brought to a surprising climax a thread of thought which began much earlier, and which applies to much more than our understanding of the physical universe. Indeed, the word 'relativity' had already been used in 1890 to refer to the reciprocal interdependence of the individual and society.

Briefly, the concept of relativity means that everything exists in relation to something else and is in some way dependent on something else for its being. No thing in the universe can be fully understood in isolation; everything we previously took to be absolute and final is now relativised. To understand this, we will start with Einstein's cosmic relativity.

Perhaps the first glimpse of cosmic relativity came when Copernicus (1473–1543) proposed that the sun and not the earth is the centre of the universe. This was disturbing at the time because the suggestion that the earth was moving around in space threatened the dependable certainty of the ground beneath our feet (then called *terra firma*). The mental picture of the earth revolving around the sun suggested that, at any time, we might drop into free fall in outer space.

Isaac Newton (1642–1727) was able to bring some reassurance: his theory of gravity meant that we were firmly attached to the earth. But Newton retained the idea of absolutes. The sun, rather than the earth, became the centre of the universe, and the solar system operated within the two basic absolutes of space and time. Indeed, Newton invented these terms, saying, 'Absolute space, in its own nature, without regard to anything external, remains always similar and immovable.' This seemed as self-evident to him as it still does to us; three-dimensional space appears to be just there; objects like planets and falling apples move within space, but space itself does not move.

Similarly, Newton believed that objects can move in space because of the existence of another absolute – time. So Newton said, 'Absolute, true and mathematical time, of itself and by its own nature, flows uniformly, without regard to anything external.' Again, not only does this appear to be common sense, but our clocks also appear to prove it. It was to be another 300 years before these two absolutes were questioned by Albert Einstein.

In 1905 Einstein published his Special Theory of Relativity, in which he questioned the very notion of absolute space, showing that nothing is ever absolutely at rest or absolutely in motion. The idea of rest and motion are valid concepts only when used in relation to something else. In the second century Ptolemy had accurately described the paths of the planets relative to the earth, and very curious paths they were. But when Johann Kepler and Newton measured the movements of the planets relative to the sun, their orbits were seen to be ellipses. These were beautifully simple orbits compared with Ptolemy's complex ones. In Einstein's view, however, Ptolemy was not wholly wrong, and neither were Galileo, Kepler and Newton wholly right: there is no fixed or central point in space to which everything else must be related. That is the first important consequence of Einstein's theory of relativity. All motion that we observe is relative to us. All rest, too, is relative. Of course, for practical purposes we regard the position from which we make an observation as a fixed point, but this is an arbitrary choice on our part.

Now let us turn to time. To measure the orbit of a planet we must record not only the position of the planet relative to us but also the exact time we observe the planet. In other words we are recording a series of events. We can accurately measure cosmic events – say, the 'distance' or 'interval' between any two sightings of a planet – only by means of *a combination of space and time*, and not by either of these separately. This led Einstein to speak of the universe as a space-time continuum. The word 'continuum' means a continuous thing, all of whose elements flow into one another. The universe is a continuum, said Einstein, in which the three dimensions of space and the one dimension of time flow into one another to form an indivisible whole.

Our traditional units of time illustrate how all measurement of time is relative to something else. Our hours and days derive from the time it takes the earth to revolve on its axis; our months from the time it takes the moon to revolve around the earth; and the year from the time of the revolution of the earth around the sun. Thus, just as it is necessary to surrender the notion of absolute space because there is no fixed point in space, so we must now surrender the notion of absolute time.

Every measurement of time is also relative to the place where the observation is made. We used to assume that, when we were observing a planet or star, the time on the star was the same as ours. That is not so. There is no absolute present moment which can be experienced or observed simultaneously throughout the universe. There is no absolute point in time, any more than there is an absolute point in space. Just as the observed position of a heavenly body is relative to us, so the time when we make the observation is also relative to us. It is *our* time. This is not at first easy to grasp, and it comes as a certain shock when we do so. Time and space have been around us for so long that we have taken them for granted. Even around the surface of the planet we can still take them for granted – there is only a momentary delay when we telephone someone on the other side of the earth. But when we move out into celestial space the problem is magnified and the time we measure is clearly our time, not universal time or absolute time.

Or to put it another way, when we look up at the starry sky we are not only looking out into space, we are also looking back into time. The heavenly bodies we see are not there at our present moment but were out there at some time in the past, depending on the time it has taken the light to travel from them to us. This varies tremendously all around the sky. One star we observe may be taking us back a thousand years. But in the same area of sky we may be looking at a star that is taking us back a million years. For the distant nebulae, as seen through the telescope, we are looking back through hundreds of millions of years.

In 1915 Einstein developed the General Theory of Relativity, to explain apparent conflicts between his Special Theory of Relativity and Newton's law of gravity. Why do objects fall to the ground? Newton explained this in terms of the force he called gravity, which causes any two objects to be attracted to each other. The immense mass of the earth attracts the relatively minute mass of our bodies, and so we stay on the surface of the planet even though it is whirling us around its centre at about 1,600 kilometres per hour. Objects feel heavy in our hands because we have to counter the force of gravity pulling them to the earth. But why, when we are going up in a fast elevator, does the parcel we are carrying suddenly feel heavier as we set off? We say that this is because of the acceleration or change of speed of the elevator. Why does acceleration give us the same feeling as gravity gives us? To Einstein, acceleration and gravity are essentially the same force. In the four-dimensional space–time continuum (of Einstein's universe), every object is subject to acceleration along what he called its world line; this curves when it is in the vicinity of any other object with mass, such as the earth or the sun. Thus the path followed by light coming from a distant star curves in the vicinity of the sun. This led Einstein to speak of the curvature of space.

Einstein's theories of relativity opened the way for a new and quite different understanding of the universe. It is, in the first place, billions of times bigger and more complex than people had previously thought. Our sun is one medium-sized star among the billion or more which make up our galaxy and our galaxy in turn is one of more than a billion such galaxies. The planet earth is but the tiniest speck within a vast cosmic sea of nebulae. This planet is of supreme importance to us, but to the rest of the universe it is largely irrelevant.

As a result of Einstein's theories, the static model of the universe was abandoned, and replaced with the dynamic model of an expanding universe. Even Einstein found this difficult to accept and, to avoid this surprising conclusion, he proposed a cosmological constant. But when the astronomer Hubble produced strong evidence that the universe is indeed expanding and that the further away a nebula is, the faster it is receding from us in space, Einstein confessed that his cosmological constant was the biggest blunder of his life.

Einstein's theories of relativity may be wonderful and puzzling, but what is their relevance in this book? J.B.S. Haldane pointed out in *The Philosophy of Humanism* (1922) that Einstein's theory of relativity is a scientific and exact illustration of a much wider principle: all our knowledge is relative to the human mind that produced it. Or to put it in another way, we humans have evolved in a symbiotic relationship with the culture created by the countless generations before us; we are dependent on the culture into which we have been born, not only for what we think and believe we know, but also for our very humanity. In other words, we humans are subject to cultural relativity. The phenomenon of relativity not only denies the absoluteness of time and space; it also undermines the certainty of our knowledge and the absoluteness of the values and purposes by which we live.

Consistent with the new model of an expanding universe in constant flux is that of an ever-changing planet. In its earliest geological history the earth's surface was bubbling with activity – with exploding volcanoes, boiling lakes, massive earthquakes, great gulfs opening and closing, whole continents appearing and disappearing. Even now the continental plates are always moving, albeit slowly, and mountain ranges are rising and wearing away. Nothing is permanent, not even the mountains, which the ancient psalmists used to regard as symbols of enduring stability. On planet earth nothing stays the same for ever.

On the surface of the earth, on the boundary where the atmosphere meets the hydrosphere, evolved the thin film of life we call the biosphere, in which change has been particularly fast and dramatic. Life of some kind on this planet stretches back through more than three billion years. It has been manifesting itself in a variety of species, bewilderingly rich and numerous. Planetary life started with the simplest living cells and amoeba-like creatures, yet out of them, through increasing complexity, our own species eventually evolved. Humans used to think until only last century that all species including our own had been here from the beginning. Now we know that, on the time scale of the earth, we emerged on this planet very late indeed.

Just as scientists from Galileo to Einstein 'relativised' the planet earth from its once central position to a tiny and impermanent fragment of a much vaster space–time continuum, so Darwin and his successors have relativised the centrality of the human species to simply being one species in a continuum of planetary life in which all species past and present are genetically related. The new story of all life on this planet has undermined the permanence of any species, including humans. This is the first consequence of relativity in relation to the planet, to which we have to become adjusted.

It is not surprising that Darwin caused a stir commensurate with that raised by Galileo. People had previously held what is called an anthropocentric view of the universe. In most respects we still do. Our forebears not only saw themselves as a race quite apart from all other animal species, but thought also that the universe was especially made for their benefit.

Many people, on first encountering Darwin's theory of biological evolution, feel deeply affronted and refuse to accept it. That is understandable. Our dignity is hurt when we find ourselves described as animals. We have come to think of ourselves as rational creatures, not only intellectual but also spiritual in character, and made in the image of God.

We belong to the total stream of life on this planet, and all other creatures are our genetic relatives. Physiologically humans differ only in degree but not in kind from other earthly creatures. Our human DNA is said to be 98 percent the same as that of the gorilla. We cannot escape our animal form – to which everything we do and think remains connected. We humans have appeared right at the tail end of earth's history – relative, of course, to the present moment. Many other types of creatures have been here before us, including the dinosaurs who roamed the planet for nearly 200 million years. And just as there is no immortality for any member of a species, so there is no guarantee of permanence for any species itself, even though it may last through countless generations. The time will probably come when humans are extinct on this changing planet, like so many species before them.

There *is*, however, a great gulf separating humans from all other living species. It is not a physiological but a cultural one. We share with all the other higher animals the same vital functions of breathing, eating and reproducing. But that is only half the truth. We are *sociocultural* animals. What is most distinctive about us as an animal species is that all of our vital functions have been qualified and transformed by patterns of behaviour we have learned from the culture into which we were born.

Within the continuum of planetary life there have evolved many interconnected systems, each of them in symbiotic relationship with its environment. In the case of the human species, we have evolved not only in a symbiotic relationship with the physical environment of the earth but with another kind of environment, known as human culture. By this is meant everything we humans have constructed with our hands, performed by our actions and thought with our minds. The basis of all human culture is language. As Don Cupitt has said: 'Language is the medium in which we live and move and have our being. In it we act, we structure the world and order every aspect of our social life. Only Language stands between us and the Void. It shapes everything.'[1]

Language enabled our human forebears to reach a heightened form of consciousness; they came to depend less and less on biological drives and animal instincts, and organised their lives with an increasing awareness of their emotional, intellectual and spiritual needs. Consciousness began to evolve into the critical self-consciousness we are capable of today. So as our species gradually became human, we ceased to live an exclusively animal existence and developed, in addition, a cultural existence. It is by means of language that we have developed human culture and it is by being immersed in culture that each new generation becomes human.

Whether there was ever a time in the past with only one human culture, however primitive, we do not know. But we do know that over time a bewildering plurality of human cultures has evolved, as the Tower of Babel myth symbolically describes. And so we can ask: if it is by being nurtured by a culture that we become human, does this mean that there are many different ways of being human? Yes, it does! There has been a Maori way of being human, a European way of being human, a Chinese way of being human. Cultural differences do turn us into different types of human being.

Until recently each culture assumed itself to be greatly superior to others, and to constitute the norm or truest type of humanity. It was common in the ancient world, for example, to distinguish between the barbarians and those who were civilised. Even as recently as last century, Europeans tended to regard tribal peoples as savages. For Christians, being a Christian was the ideal way of being a human; for Muslims, being a Muslim was. Today such judgements are seen as cultural chauvinism: we are becoming aware of cultural relativity. Just as there is no centre to the universe and no earthly species that is biologically superior to all others, so no human culture provides the norm to which all cultures should conform. All human cultures are relative to time, place and experience.

The evolution of human culture has taken place in a much shorter time than biological evolution. Human culture also changes much faster. No culture stands completely still, even though some change more slowly than others. Each culture is a living, changing phenomenon, and it changes as a result of human thought and decision-making. Each new generation inherits the cultural deposit of the past and adds something of its own. Today human culture is changing much faster than at any previous time. This is all the more reason for us to understand the shifting and relative character of every culture.

What we learn from cultural relativity is firstly this: our cultural convictions and practices are always relative, relative to the time in which we live, the position we choose to take, and the cultural inheritance which has shaped us. Nothing about them is absolute or unchangeable. This book, indeed, is simply one person's thoughts, reflecting a standpoint in western culture and trying to take into account what appear to be dominant global trends. Just as we humans are earth-bound and time-bound, we are also culture-bound. We can no more escape from cultural relativity than we can defy gravity.

Secondly, no culture stays the same. Every attempt to preserve a culture by human effort is doomed. The very fact that people set out to try to preserve it is a sure sign that a culture is already changing fast and perhaps dying. That is true of great religious cultures like Christendom and Islam, even though their respective fundamentalists think otherwise. It is also true of indigenous ethnic cultures, in spite of the best efforts to preserve them. No culture can be made absolute or permanent.

The chief substance or identity of any culture is to be found in its morality and its religion. By morality (literally, the customs or mores) is meant the patterns of behaviour which are deemed by a society to be ideal or at the least permissible. The definition of religion is much more difficult and hence debatable. 'To be religious,' said theologian Paul Tillich, 'is to be grasped by an ultimate concern, a concern which qualifies all other concerns as preliminary and which itself contains the answer to the question of the meaning of life.'[2] Carlo Della Casa said, 'Religion is a total mode of the interpreting and living of life.'[3] These descriptions allow for the many and diverse forms of religion.[4]

Indeed, it is the relativity of religion that makes its definition difficult. Just as there is no one absolute culture and no one absolute morality, so there is no one absolute religion, despite the fact that some religions, particularly the monotheistic ones such as Christianity and Islam, have claimed that they alone possess the absolute truth and that all other religions are false or inferior. There are many forms of devotion, many modes of interpreting life and living; each of them is central for the people who practise it, but that is a relative and subjective judgement.

Every human culture has evolved on the basis of a particular way of interpreting human existence. Tillich suggested that religion is that which gives culture its depth and its strength. Without the religious dimension a culture has no staying power and no clear identity. Whatever provides a culture with its goals, values, motivation and creative energy is its religion (irrespective of whether that term or its equivalent is used).

Religion and culture are so closely interwoven that, though they are not one and the same, neither can exist without the other. In a healthy homogeneous society, culture and religion are deeply blended. That is why the pre-Axial cultures were not even aware they had a religion and hence had no name for it. We still refer to their religions by the ethnic group to which they belong. We speak, for example, of the religion of the Babylonians, of the Greeks, or of pre-European Maori.

Because religion arises out of the quest for meaning, and is a mode of interpreting life, it is dependent upon language. In fact most great religions have never become completely divorced from the particular language in which they came into being. Judaism is closely tied to the Hebrew language. Hinduism goes back to Sanskrit for the study of its founding scriptures. Buddhism, though a little more universal, still sets great store on the Pali texts. Until the last two centuries Christianity was largely tied to Greek and Latin, the languages within which it first evolved. Islam so honours Arabic that it does not officially permit the Qur'an to be translated into any other language. Each of the great religions has also developed its own symbolic language as its interpretation of human existence within the world. Religions have even been defined as symbol-systems. Each symbolic language is a kind of super-language which has to be learned and understood by those who embrace that religion as their way of life. These symbolic terms all cohere and relate together, depending upon one another for their full meaning and often being defined in terms of one another. They formed what the philosopher Wittgenstein called a 'language-game'. Just as a game consists of a set of rules that we have to learn and honour if we are to play it, so a religion consists of a system of symbols that we have to understand as a whole. Each symbol-system forms a religious language, a language of meaning for interpreting the meaning of life (or, more correctly, creating a meaning for life).

Modern scholarship has revealed not only how much our capacity to be human depends on language and culture but also the extent to which all language (and particularly religious language) is symbolic. To many it has been an unwelcome shock to hear basic religious terms such as God, Christ and resurrection referred to as symbols when these terms have previously been used as literal descriptions of unseen reality. Even worse is the idea that these symbols, along with the whole cultural tradition which uses them, have been humanly created.

Yet that is exactly what has been slowly coming to light as the advent of modernity has unfolded to us a new story of human origins. We have seen that all human cultures are human creations, each of them being the collective creation of an ongoing ethnic group. Each of these cultures has produced a human-created morality and each has created its own set of symbols for the interpreting and living of life. The word 'God' is a symbolic term which is no less a human creation than the class of beings called 'gods', which 'God' came to replace at the Axial Period.

Until the modern period humans remained unaware of just how creative they really were. It seemed natural to assume that every new thought or vision came from outside. We still reflect this tendency in such simple expressions as 'I was struck by a brilliant idea', as if it came from somewhere else. Psychology has helped us during the twentieth century to understand the creativity of the human psyche so that we have now a quite natural explanation for, say, the voices heard by Joan of Arc and the vision of John in the Book of Revelation.

Even more important, we now have an explanation for the types of religious experience that led people to attribute their thoughts to divine revelation. What has been claimed as revelation from a divine source of knowledge is in fact the product of human creativity, stretching back over a very long time and involving countless people. For example, the Islamic world accepted from the outset that the words of the Qur'an, expressed in beautiful Arabic poetry, could not have been composed by Muhammad, but must have originated with Allah and been transmitted to Muhammad by way of divine revelation. Muhammad's own account of this was of course perfectly sincere, for he would have been unaware that his own creative psyche was the source of that remarkable outpouring that became the Qur'an.

No traditional Muslim would accept this natural explanation, any more than an orthodox Christian would accept that the long-held revelations of the Christian tradition are the product of human psychic creativity. Each religious tradition has exempted itself from natural explanations, while applying them to all the other traditions. In today's global world, this will no longer do. We land ourselves in this inconsistency by not acknowledging relativity. If Christians use logical or natural explanations to explain the rise of other traditions, such as the foundation of Mormonism on the visions of Joseph Smith, these explanations must be applied to the Judeo-Christian tradition as well.

The new understanding of how the human mind works in creating human culture has shown more clearly the relative nature of all religious traditions. Those who have set much store by the belief in divine revelation feel, at first, a great sense of loss, comparable to that felt when the earth ceased to be the centre of the universe. The loss of divine revelation has left each religious tradition bereft of its supposedly firm foundation.

Yet it has not been all loss. Belief in divine revelation has had its negative side. People have been inspired by revelation, and had great confidence in their beliefs, but they have also been motivated to impose these on others, for the latter's own 'good'. When we attribute to a divine source what are really our own thoughts, visions and aspirations, the consequences are serious. People who adamantly declare they know what is the will of God for society at large, are unconsciously projecting onto an objective deity their own ideals and aspirations, including their prejudices. In this way we become enslaved to our own thinking. It is even more damaging when we treat the words of holy scripture as divine revelation, for then we are enslaved to the thinking of ancient humans, whose ideas may be long outmoded. Any religious tradition claiming to be the absolute truth in a universe so marked by relativity leads not to the salvation of humankind but to its enslavement.

In the last 200 years we have become increasingly aware of the relativity of culture, morality and now of religion. It means that all religious traditions are of human origin – none is exempt.

It means also that all religious ideas, concepts, symbols and traditions are human in origin, however valuable they may remain. Just as there is no one culture which is the norm for all other cultures, no one morality which is the norm for all other moralities, so there is no one religion which is the norm for all others. None of them is absolute and final, and those which claim to be must surrender those claims if they are to continue to be a viable means of the interpreting and living of life.

As theologian Tom Driver put it: 'Christianity has been compelled to see itself as a religion *relative* to other religions and *relative* to the history of the world. Christianity does this reluctantly . . . The gap between Christianity and modern theories of relativity is widening so much that the church's teaching about Christ is in danger of losing both its intellectual and its moral credibility.'[5] Driver then showed that our understanding of relativity has made necessary a radical redrafting of the whole of Christian thought:

> To think of Christ as the centre, model and norm of humanity made a certain sense in the Ptolemaic universe, which had the Earth as its centre. It continued to make some sense, however strained, in the Copernican universe, which had the sun as its centre. Today, christocentrism cannot make sense in the Einsteinian universe, which has no centre and in which every structure is a dynamic relationality of moving parts . . . The ethical theological task of the churches today is to find a Christology which can be liberating in a world of relativity.[6]

Let us return to the words of Ecclesiastes, for this ancient preacher caught something of the spirit of relativity – a word that probably translates the original Hebrew word better than 'vanity'. Vanity implies futility but relativity does not. And Ecclesiastes remained positive in the face of impermanence. He was able to say, 'Go ahead and enjoy life with your partner. Eat your meals and drink your wine with a merry heart. And whatever your hands find to do for your daily toil, do it with zeal'.[7]

Relativity tells us that there is a mysterious elasticity about time and space, that all physical reality is in a state of flux, and that the cosmos was not made for any obvious purpose. But it is just *because* nothing lasts for ever and there *is* continual change that life has been able to evolve and that humanity has developed as it has. There was nothing necessary in this. Each of us exists as the result of an almost infinite number of accidents or chance events. We find ourselves living in an otherwise meaningless universe where there are no absolutes and nothing is certain. Within the changing conditions and evolving life on this planet, and out of the various developing cultures that have shaped us, we humans can and do create meaning for ourselves. Even though our efforts remain subject to relativity, they need not be futile and vain. Since all sense of purpose and human fulfilment resulted from human creation in the past, we can continue to create a purpose for living in the future. It is with that kind of faith and hope that we can enter the new millennium as we come to the end of the Christian era.

PART 2

The Beginning
of the Global Era

CHAPTER 7

A Post-Christian Future

Whatever our future in the western world, it has already been partly shaped by the Christian tradition. Indeed, the post-Christian age we are now entering owes its very existence to the Christian civilisation of the last two thousand years. The structures of the Christian church may have little or no part to play in the years ahead, but the world we live in will remain deeply influenced by Christianity, its beliefs, customs, and culture. This means, first, that the post-Christian age is to be clearly distinguished from the pre-Christian age (which Christians often referred to as pagan). Secondly, it means that the post-Christian era is not necessarily anti-Christian (as many Christians are inclined to judge it), and we can legitimately speak of a Christian 'stream of influence' continuing within it.[1] But how does this influence manifest itself? First we shall discuss the future of conventional Christianity in the post-Christian world.

Organised Christianity in the form of an ecclesiastical institution has already been greatly fragmented. Church structures will continue to multiply in number and to become smaller. There is no longer any place for a national church or an international ecclesiastical organisation which is monolithic and authoritarian. The coming decades may well see the sudden disintegration of the Roman Catholic Church which, because of the central power wielded by the Vatican, has been described as the last great absolutist empire. The pronouncements of the Pope no longer receive from all Catholics the unquestioning and obedient response they traditionally did.

Yet the mainline churches, including Roman Catholicism, will be active for quite some time, carried along by the momentum of past centuries. These churches will increasingly depend on their inherited capital and real estate, until these resources are exhausted. More seminaries will close their doors, and it will be hard to meet any residual demand for a properly trained, professional clergy.

Ultimately there will be no need for a priesthood or ordained ministry. In the post-Christian era divine revelation is no longer seen as a source of knowledge, and the traditional organs of religious authority have become obsolete. The Word of God in the Bible, the voice of the Pope or the decisions of ecclesiastical assemblies – all will fall more and more on deaf ears. The authority of religious leaders, like that of civil and political leaders, will depend on the emotional or intellectual appeal of what they say and not on any special gifts supposedly conferred on them by ordination. The once clear line between priesthood and laity is already blurred and will soon count for little. People no longer seek professional spiritual advice from a supposed authoritative source as they once did.

This all comes from the growth of human autonomy – the freedom of people to think for themselves and to make their own decisions. It is not only the traditional religious institutions that are affected; there has been a rapid multiplication of social groups one may choose to join. Anecdotal evidence suggests, further, that people today are more reluctant to commit themselves *permanently* to any form of association – be it a club, society, political party, church or marriage partner. Taking life-long vows was once regarded as highly virtuous. Now it may be seen as precarious and even unethical: the person one is at the present moment may not have the moral right to bind the person one has yet to become. In this age of rapid change, and with our modern understanding of the human condition, we can see how much alters in a person's lifetime; we must remain open to what may come, and free to respond to new circumstances.

Yet, because humans are social creatures, we shall continue to value opportunities for fellowship and interpersonal activities, whether in sport, culture or spirituality. The institutions best suited for spiritual needs are those that are fluid, informal, inclusive and open to change. They must provide the fullest opportunities for people to be themselves, to participate actively and to share in decision-making. As sociologist Robert Bellah said: 'Each individual must work out their own ultimate solutions and the most the church can do is to provide a favourable environment for doing so, without imposing on him a prefabricated set of answers.'[2] But because such groups have no firm structure, they will always be more vulnerable to passing moods and fashions and will have an uncertain duration.

So what place does conventional Christianity have, in the post-Christian era we are now entering? It is no longer a community-held faith which shapes and motivates society. Instead, in its multiple forms, it is becoming one set of personal options among numerous others, including New Age religions and secular ideologies. Together they form a vast religious supermarket to which people may go when they are looking for a philosophy or way of life, and in which they are free to choose one tailored to their needs.

The more traditional practising Christians will form part of the fundamentalist reactionary movement to be discussed further in Chapter 9. They will even grow in numbers, for their strong convictions are infectious and appear to offer some security in an otherwise frightening world. But, like the remnants of the great churches, they too will become marginalised from society and its chief decision-makers.

For most of the post-Christian world, the Bible will no longer be regarded as the Word of God, but it will continue to be of value as an historical testimony to Judeo-Christian origins and as an essential resource for the understanding of past western culture. It will take its place alongside other great religious classics from the various cultures of the past. Jesus will no longer be hailed as the saviour of the world, or as a divine figure. He will stand among the great pioneering figures of the past, and his sayings and parables will continue to inspire those who take the trouble to search them out.

God will no longer be conceived widely as an objective spiritual being – one who personally hears and answers prayers, and who guides human history from behind the scenes. God language, if used at all, will be treated as symbolic. Spiritual practices may take the form of meditation but will not be understood as conversation with an external personal being. Life in this world will be acknowledged as the only form of human existence. The expectation of conscious personal existence beyond death will gradually be abandoned.

If there is ultimately to be no authoritative ecclesiastical institution, no definitive set of doctrines and no clearly definable personal figure to hold Christianity together and promote it, it may at first appear that Christianity will simply disappear. This might well alarm even nominal Christians – that large group who regard themselves as Christian though no longer active in the church. And this concern would be justified, for when a religious tradition ebbs away from the culture it has inspired, a spiritual vacuum is likely to emerge, leaving the society vulnerable to forces that threaten its survival.

But Christianity will not disappear without a trace. When it is understood as a 'stream of cultural influence', Christianity can be seen as something that already stretches far beyond its ecclesiastical institutions, and is likely to last longer than any of them. The Christian stream of influence may not be clearly identifiable as Christianity and certainly not as conventional Christianity. The Christ figure may continue as a symbol embodying various important values, such as compassion, love, and caring for one's neighbour. The symbols, concepts, images, stories and myths of Christian origin, which remain deeply embedded in the fabric of western culture, will continue to offer the raw material from which people form their understanding of life, develop their capacity for spirituality and experience satisfaction at the deepest levels. From time to time, individuals and groups will receive fresh inspiration, and experience great delight, as they rediscover in the Bible and elsewhere the cultural treasures of the Christian past.

The decline of the old religious institutions, however, will not just open the door to a life of joyful freedom in some secular Paradise, as some are inclined to think. The great traditions of Buddhism, Christianity and Islam were, at their best, long-term civilising forces. They were able to curb personal violence and anti-social behaviour by providing value systems and goals which were accepted widely enough to bring stability and cohesion to the societies they permeated. When these traditions recede – as they are almost everywhere in the face of globalisation – we shall see the re-emergence of the more brutal capacities of the human condition, which have long survived beneath the veneer of civilisation.

Thus social unrest and anti-social behaviour will increase in the coming decades. There will be heightened calls for a return to the religious or ethnic cultures of the past and for the re-introduction of stricter controls backed up by force from a higher authority. Considerable criticism will be directed towards all forms of liberalism. The Enlightenment, which opened the way to secularisation, will be blamed for our current predicament. There is some truth in pointing to the Enlightenment as the door to the modern world and its freedoms, but, as with the opening of Pandora's box, there can be no return to the pre-Enlightenment conditions, except by harsh and repressive measures.

As conventional Christianity is ending, I have chosen to look first at its place in our post-Christian future and to differentiate it from the continuing stream of Christian influence. But what happens to Christianity is no longer the primary question. Far more crucial is the future of the world itself. (Perhaps the church should never have become concerned with its own future or that of Christianity, for it was the imminent future of the world that concerned the first Christians.) No nation, religion or culture can contemplate its future in isolation: as the west leaves Christendom behind, the whole world is entering a new age. All of humankind is being forced to think and act globally. The most important issues before us now (or one could refer to them as the chief religious questions) are these: what is to be the future of humankind in the post-Christian world? What is to be the future of planet earth?

The shape of the coming post-Christian world is therefore important not only to Christians. It is too often assumed (even by many who no longer have any explicit allegiance to the Christian tradition) that the values and social institutions of our cultural past will continue into the future in much the same form. This is very unlikely. As the west emerges out of Christendom, countries across the world are moving into a more unstable and unpredictable situation. The new cultural forces which have emanated from the west and which are causing the decay of traditional Christianity also threaten the future of the other great post-Axial traditions.

We are now aware, as never before, that human history has no predetermined plan. The beliefs that the earth was created especially for humankind, and that human history is providentially controlled by a divine planner, are obsolete (even though they are stoutly defended in some quarters). For all practical purposes, we humans are alone in the universe, and face an unknown and uncertain future. Further, while each of us has some small degree of choice within the tiny micro-world of our personal life, the changes going on in the human mega-world around us are not being planned or controlled even by humans. The ongoing process of planetary life and of cultural change is rushing on like a driverless juggernaut.

All this is clearly reflected in the contemporary school of thought known as post-modernism, which stands at the opposite end of the spectrum from the fundamentalists and anti-modernists. While the term 'post-modernity' is sometimes used as a non-judgemental description of today's intellectual climate, post-modernism refers broadly to the ideological rejection of modernism as the way forward. Some forms of post-modernism are destructive of all unified world views; they deconstruct, or eliminate altogether, such basic terms as God, self, purpose, meaning, reality. Other kinds of postmodernism attempt to be more constructive. But all varieties of postmodernism share a critical distrust of modernity, and a conviction that the deficiencies in modernity cannot be rectified by reviving the premodern age. They see modernism as the legacy of the Enlightenment, with its absolute faith in human reason and its supreme confidence that human endeavour can steadily make progress towards an ultimate goal which promises final knowledge and complete human fulfilment. Post-modernists have become disillusioned with modernism and believe it now to be necessary to go beyond the individualism, scientism, mechanisation, consumerism and militarism which have been the fruits of modernity.

Post-modernism rejects the modernist goal of building a new world on the basis of science, reason and human endeavour. In this, it is the anti-ideology of our time, announcing the end of ideology and even the end of history. There is no one true and absolute human history; there is no one definitive Universe Story which can unite all humankind into one global society. Literary critic Terry Eagleton wrote in 1987: 'Post-modernism signals the death of "meta-narratives". Science and philosophy must jettison their grandiose metaphysical claims and view themselves more modestly as just another set of narratives.'[3]

Post-modernism signals the triumph of the subjective over the objective. Modernism, having celebrated the end of the eternal cosmic order, now finds itself unstable and impermanent as a working philosophy. Some see the emergence of post-modernism as a shift in human consciousness just as radical as the shift from mediaevalism to modernism. It is reflected in the way we use language and the new use we give to older words – talking, for example, about spirituality instead of religion. Instead of being self-confident explorers of a mysterious external world, we first set out to find ourselves: that is, to find out who we are. Post-modernism is indifferent to consistency and continuity. It questions whether we can have strong beliefs in anything at all, for nothing lasts for ever. All our social structures, like so many of our artefacts, are here today and gone tomorrow.

Nowhere is the transition from modernism to post-modernism more visible than in the evolution of physics during the twentieth century. Modernism developed on the basis of the Newtonian universe, conceived as a complex inanimate machine, operating in absolute space and absolute time according to its own internal laws, which were also believed to be eternal and absolute.[4] Understanding this 'natural world' was the key to everything; physicists set about uncovering the laws by which the physical world operates; Adam Smith looked for the natural laws by which the economy operates; Darwin thought he had discovered, in the law of natural selection, the origin of species. Later scientists such as Stephen Hawking are still hoping to arrive at what they call a unified 'Theory of Everything'.

The end of the Newtonian view of reality may be said to date from 1900, when Max Planck laid the foundations of quantum physics, the concepts that introduced us to indeterminism, uncertainty and human subjectivity. No one had any idea at the time of the far-reaching significance of this, and its role in the end of modernity. The discovery of quantum physics led in turn to Einstein's theories, sub-atomic physics and a new way of understanding reality. For example, quantum physicist David Bohm speculated in his 1954 textbook that there may be some relationship between quantum processes and thought processes.[5] He later became convinced of what he called the 'unbroken wholeness' of reality, asserting: 'The primary emphasis is now on undivided wholeness, in which the observing instrument is not separable from what is observed.'[6] He believed that our way of seeing reality as fragmented bits with their own independent existence is an illusion, and he coined the term 'implicate order' to refer to this undivided wholeness. Claiming that we falsify reality if we divide it into mind and matter, into living and non-living, he said: 'consciousness (which we take to include thought, feeling, desire, will etc.) is to be comprehended in terms of the implicate order, along with reality as a whole'.[7] Thus the randomness of sub-atomic elements may be linked with the creative freedom exercised by human consciousness.

Today we are being forced to rethink the nature and origin of the universe, the nature of the human condition and the nature of scientific enterprise. Only by excluding ourselves and our consciousness from the universe can we think of it as a lifeless thing. Once we acknowledge that we are not just *in* the universe but a *part* of the universe, then the universe itself must be conceived of as alive – as we are. And because we are part of the universe and think, the universe has the capacity for thought.

One hundred years ago there was such confidence in science that it seemed set to uncover the last secrets of the universe. Today the mood of the scientific community is much more modest. Indeed, each addition to reliable knowledge has tended to uncover more mystery and complexity. The influential philosopher of science, Karl Popper (1902–1994), has convincingly argued that science does not prove to us what is true: its real strength is to show us what is false. Even Stephen Hawking has conceded that if we did work out a Theory of Everything there would be no way of proving that it were true.

Thus science is no longer the objective activity we took it to be, uncovering the hidden eternal truth of the universe (an idea which goes back to Plato). Science is a human enterprise, which is never free from human limitation. Physics is increasingly dependent on such skills as mathematics, itself a human creation. What we assumed to be the laws of nature, which we humans cleverly discovered, turn out to be human judgements based on observation, experiment and measurement. They are continually open to revision and must be regarded as probabilities rather than as certainties.

Thanks to Max Planck, Albert Einstein, Ernest Rutherford and many others, we now find that physical matter is not the static, inanimate and stable stuff we had assumed it to be. The stuff of which the real world is composed is dynamic in the extreme. Every atom is a fuzzy little cloud of incredible energy and movement. And just as matter is not solid and indestructible, so our knowledge of physical reality is not certain and infallible. Even about quantum physics itself there is no finality. Already there is some theoretical difficulty in reconciling quantum physics with chaos theory, which began to develop rapidly in the 1980s.

Of one thing we can be sure: the absolute laws of nature on which modernism was based are no more. We continue to observe the regularities of cause and effect, which the humanly constructed laws of nature were intended to encapsulate; but we are also much more aware of how many natural events seem to occur through sheer chance. The universe in which we find ourselves appears to be a mystifying mixture of both chance and necessity, to use the words of Jacques Monod.[8]

The way we now apprehend the world (and understand our uncertainty in it), though based on western thought, has an impact far beyond the geographic boundaries of western civilisation. This is why the post-Christian and post-modern future is relevant to the world at large and not just to the west. Over the last 400 years the western world has influenced the rest of humankind (either to its advantage or disadvantage) more than any other civilisation. As Samuel Huntington has said: 'The West inaugurated the processes of modernisation and industrialisation that have become worldwide, and as a result societies in all other civilisations have been attempting to catch up with the West in wealth and modernity.'[9] Today the old western assumption that Christendom would eventually envelop the world is no more likely than the idea of global Islam or Buddhism. However, in its spread around the world, the west did much to bring the modern global world into being. Thus the demise of Christendom, followed by the dissipation of the Christian tradition, will have a direct effect on the whole globe.

Trying to see what the future holds has become such a feature of twentieth century thought that it has earned a title of its own. The earliest form of futurology was science fiction, which usually anticipated the future with pleasurable amazement. This literature has been more than just a new form of entertainment. Like the apocalyptic writings of New Testament times, it has stretched the imagination and inspired great confidence in the future. But, whereas in ancient times the apocalyptic writers expected God to usher in the new world, the first science fiction authors described a future created by human invention. Readers were encouraged to believe in the power of human ingenuity, a power that repeatedly overcame all future problems by scientific discovery and technological expertise. Some of the best examples, such as H.G. Well's *Time Machine* (1895) and *War of the Worlds* (1898), became classics. The genre has continued in cinema and video with such popular epics as *Star Wars*. Not all science fiction, however, is optimistic. Some writers, such as Aldous Huxley in *Brave New World* (1932) and George Orwell in *Nineteen Eighty-four* (1949), struck an early cautionary note.

Futurology has now grown into a widespread industry for more practical purposes: looking into the future has become an essential part of social and economic planning. Some notable books have been written in this field: *The Coming of Post-Industrial Society* (1973) by Daniel Bell, *The Third Wave* (1980) by Alvin Toffler, *The Fate of the Earth* (1982) by Jonathan Schell, and *The Green Machines* (1986) by Nigel Calder. But the attempt to forecast the shape of the future and the post-Christian world is fraught with difficulty. Chaos theory now helps us to understand how small and unknown factors can be instrumental in causing significant change in natural phenomena. Weather forecasting can be seriously astray even 24 hours ahead. Economic forecasting is even more problematic, for it is dependent on the uncertain factors of human choice and idiosyncrasy. How much harder it is, therefore, to look into the general human future when events and trends reflect countless billions of personal choices.

Let no one think that the coming century will present a utopia unfolding smoothly before us. Just as the great religious traditions emerged from their ethnic origins only through confusion, conflict, controversy and even violence, so it will be in the century to come. This has the potential to be the most creative and glorious century yet in human culture. But it also has the potential to be the most violent and destructive period in the long history of humankind.

The human species currently consists of some six billion individuals spread around the globe in millions of groups large and small, all focused on their own affairs without much concept of any ultimate goal, or the value of their contribution. No wonder human expectations about the shape of the future have been considerably shaken during the twentieth century.

The best we can do, in attempting to imagine the twenty-first century, is to assess the current trends in the fast-changing human cultures. As John Naisbitt has observed in *Megatrends* (1982), most trends are found to be interconnected and part of a worldwide process; most also occur over a period and without fanfare. If they do produce an obvious crisis (for example, the French Revolution), we usually find that the forces at work have been present for some time. Cultural change normally creeps up on us relatively unnoticed. Only when we look back can we identify patterns and turning points. That is the case with the end-times discussed in the early part of this book, and it is why so many are still unaware of what has been happening. So what matters in the coming century is not what occurs (or fails to occur) on 1 January 2000 but how the years unfold thereafter.

The most dominant trend today, and the one we must look at first, is globalisation. This will not be experienced everywhere as an unqualified blessing, and it may well lead to a testing period for the human species.

CHAPTER 8

Globalisation

Globalisation is a word that has only recently entered our dictionaries. First used to refer to the new global economy, it now encompasses the great new phenomenon of our time – the process by which all scientific, cultural, religious and economic human activity is being integrated into one worldwide network. Humans of all ethnic groups, all nations, all cultures and all religious traditions are being drawn together into one global community. Without exercising much individual choice, we are becoming part of a global interchange of news, knowledge and ideas; we are increasingly dependent on one global economy, and influenced by a developing global culture. This is in spite of our diversity, our frequent mutual animosity and our all too common fear and distrust of all things foreign.

But if the term globalisation is new, the phenomenon which it names has been around for quite some time. With hindsight we can readily discern several causes, all present in the emergence of western modernity during the last 500 years. Familiar as these trends and developments have been, we have not seen where they were leading us.

Technology is perhaps the most obvious cause of globalisation, particularly the technology that so rapidly advanced travel and communication across geographical and ethnic barriers. For many thousands of years, humans lived in relative isolation from one another on the different parts of the earth's surface, areas to which they had slowly dispersed during long period of human biological and cultural evolution. Then, in the fifteenth century, Europeans invented the ocean-going vessels which gave them access to what they named the 'new world'. (Such terms as 'voyages of discovery', 'the new world' and 'the far east' express a specifically western perspective.) Only after these voyages were humans able to draw a reasonably reliable map of the planet's surface, showing how the various continents and islands each form part of one global world. Gradually it became clear (though this was all too slowly appreciated) that the surface of the earth is finite; eventually we reached the end of new 'worlds' to explore, at least on this planet.

From the sixteenth century onwards, and particularly in the nineteenth century, ocean travel led to the European colonisation of the Americas, Africa and Oceania. This enabled the European nations to export their surplus population and thus begin the global intermingling of races that has continued ever since. At first, globalisation seemed perilously close to being Europeanisation, but in the latter half of the twentieth century European supremacy has been modified, partly by the spread of Indian, Chinese and Japanese people, and partly because some of the colonised peoples took the opportunity of their imperial citizenship to settle in Europe.

In the nineteenth century land travel was speeded up by the invention of steam locomotion and the development of railways. Coupled with the industrialisation of production in factories, this brought a radical shift in people's lives, from a predominantly rural existence to a predominantly urban one, first in Europe and later elsewhere. Whereas families had often stayed in their own village for centuries, people now began to move about in search of work or advancement. With the twentieth-century invention of the motor car, then the aeroplane, families and individuals were even less likely to be anchored to one place for life. When Europeans first began to migrate to Australia and New Zealand in the early 1800s, for example, they faced a three-month sea journey, and many never returned to the land of their birth. Now the journey takes 24 hours. Long-distance travel has become an everyday affair, and is for many young people simply a part of their general education. Even those who cannot afford travel are familiar with the experiences it offers, and often benefit indirectly. Long-distance travel has, most of all, hastened the meeting of races and cultures, and nurtured the incipient global culture.

New technology made another huge contribution to globalisation by intensifying the communication of news, the spread of ideas and the transfer of information. It started with the invention of the printing press by Gutenberg in 1437. The Protestant Reformation would not have spread so successfully had it not been for the ability to print propaganda pamphlets and multiply copies of the Bible in the vernacular. Previously the Bible had to be painstakingly copied by hand and, being in Latin (the Vulgate), was accessible only to scholars. Making the Bible available in all Protestant parish churches in the language of the people increased the desire of ordinary people to become literate so that they could read it for themselves. The idea of universal education took root at that time.

In the seventeenth century the first regular newspapers were published, thus spreading further afield the news and current opinions which were otherwise only locally known. The collection of world news and its dissemination through newsprint flourishes to this day in spite of new technological rivals. The distribution of information was greatly assisted by the invention of the telegraph by Samuel Morse in 1837. Then came the invention of the telephone in 1876: now the human voice could be transmitted across ever longer distances, and communication itself became much more personal.

The discovery of radio in the late nineteenth century led to the establishment of radio broadcasting in the 1920s. Owning a radio started as a privilege but was soon seen as a necessity, and is now almost universal, even in Third World countries. Broadcasting was extended to television by the middle of the century, and has become an enormous industry. Television exerts a powerful cultural influence, not only by sending almost instant visual news all over the globe but also by fostering cultural change. Currently it is one of the chief instruments by which globalisation is being advanced.

One of the twentieth century inventions with an impact reaching far into the future is the electronic computer, which has the capacity to speed up many forms of written communication. As we are still at the beginning of the computer revolution, its consequences are hard to foretell, even within the next decade. We do know, however, that the speed of change in communications technology is such that each innovation is rendered obsolete within a few years.

The last two decades have witnessed the introduction of the internet, offering a new way of sending information almost instantaneously around the world. Electronic mail via the internet provides fast and cheap personal intercommunication on a global scale. It is bringing together different networks of people from all around the world, many of whom may never have any other contact. The computer has also made a huge difference to the collection and storage of information. All the great libraries of the world are now linked together; immense databanks for all sorts of subjects are accumulating. Computer systems and the internet now provide access to an unbelievable amount of information, both good and bad. The industrial age, only 300 years old, has now been superseded by the information age.

This has sometimes been called a knowledge explosion. However, we need to distinguish between information and knowledge. Having access to information is not the same as being knowledgeable, just as the possession of knowledge does not necessarily produce wisdom. To be knowledgeable we need to absorb and master the information. But the time has long passed since any one person could absorb more than the tiniest fragment of the total body of available, reliable information. One can now be a specialist only in a very confined area.

All this has meant that geographical distance is no longer a barrier separating individuals or groups. We may now have more regular and personal contact with someone on the other side of the world than we do with the person living next door. On the one hand, the boundary lines which separate ethnic and national groups (which were mostly geographical in origin) are now becoming blurred, indistinct and sometimes irrelevant. On the other hand, global pressures often serve to intensify ethnic identity and become the cause of conflict. Both types of response illustrate how the world is fast becoming one global city.

Speed of travel, the intensification of communication and the rise in the average level of education have also meant that the various aspects of western modernity have spread quickly around the globe. We are beginning to be aware that, no matter where we were born and whatever our culture, we share a common story – the story of human origins within the more complex story of the evolution of life on the planet. As the once separate cultures meet and cross-fertilise one another, humankind is beginning to share more and more values – such as the concern for human rights and personal freedom.

Today many cultures acknowledge (at least superficially) the supreme value of personal freedom and of human rights, but this dates only from the Declaration of Human Rights during the French Revolution of the late eighteenth century. 'Liberty, Equality, Fraternity' are commonplace ideas today. Yet the same words struck fear into most thinking Europeans of the day, including religious leaders; they appeared then to threaten the very fabric of society.

In the following 200 years, the revolutionary ideas of freedom, equality, brotherhood and human rights for all have spread further and further, inspiring a series of emancipations. First came the emancipation from absolute monarchy and its replacement by democracy. Then came the emancipation from slavery; humans had the right to personal freedom. Then came the emancipation of women from male domination; women initially claimed the right to hold property and to vote, and more recently their right to social equality and career opportunity. During the twentieth century indigenous peoples have sought emancipation from foreign imperialism, and coloured races emancipation from white domination. The emancipation of homosexuals from heterosexual domination is being vigorously debated today. In all cases, the struggle for emancipation has met fierce resistance, which still continues in many quarters.

Globalisation has also meant that we are moving from what may be called the closed society – that is, one surrounded by a clear boundary – to the open society. In a closed society, one's freedom is significantly restricted, for one is deeply involved in the duties (or morality) of that society. Anyone outside the closed society is an outcast, an excommunicate or a foreigner: that which is outside is unknown and potentially dangerous. The closed society has a strong sense of its own identity, from which members draw their sense of security; it is held together as a social organism largely by authority, exercised from above but also supplemented by peer pressure. And it depends on such qualities in its members as loyalty, trust and an absolute respect for authority. Until the rise of the modern world, all societies, whether tribal, ethnic, national or religious, were closed societies, to a greater or lesser degree.

The open society has been emerging in the modern world along with the globalisation. It is a society in which boundary lines are less distinct, so that people can leave or join with relative ease. The open society permits and fosters the growth of individualism; people enjoy greater personal freedom and, by the same token, more responsibility. Whereas membership of a closed society helped to provide personal identity ('I'm a Scotsman', for example, or 'I'm a Presbyterian'), individuals in the open society are both freer and have more responsibility to establish their own identity. Closed societies, by the authority they exert, effectively cushion their members from the exercise of responsibility; decisions are largely made for people, not by them. In the open society, where external authority is greatly reduced, much more responsibility rests with each individual to promote the welfare of the society. Where that responsibility is lacking, the society either disintegrates or is forced to return to the rigid authoritarianism of the closed society.

Many of our current social problems arise from the fact that, as our culture shifts from the closed to the open society, people often struggle with their new social responsibilities. And this is occurring on a grand scale, as a large number of former closed societies find themselves part of one vast, complex and (as yet) embryonic open society. The open society also has some inherent difficulties. Any vigorous human society draws its identity from a shared tradition of common beliefs, values and practices. The growth of individualism and personal freedom can damage such traditions, and this in turn endangers social cohesion. Thus globalisation and the advent of the open society, while bringing great benefit to the individual, can have serious consequences for human society. These consequences are the more serious if we remember that our very humanity, as individuals, relies upon human society and what we receive from it.

Language, so essential to our culture and humanity, remains the basis of a human society. Without it there can be no social cohesion. Nonetheless, language has been (and still is) one of the main causes of humankind's division into separate closed societies. Globalisation is now throwing the spotlight on this phenomenon. If there is to be one global community, clearly it would be easier for all humankind to have one language (though that would be no guarantee of peace and unity). There are still over 6,000 living languages, but many have disappeared already, and it has been estimated that another 80 percent will die out during the twenty-first century.

But language is not solely a form of communication; it also provides an essential means of identifying our particular kind of humanity. Diversity of language among humans has provided a richness in human culture not to be undervalued. If all languages but one were to die, the rich cultural heritage of the past would be lost to all but a small scholarly elite. Already the prospect of losing of their mother tongue represents a profound loss of identity to many cultures and many peoples. The practical need for a common language in a global society has already assisted the spread of the most widely-used languages, such as English and Spanish. Yet David Crystal, an acknowledged authority in linguistics, has warned that the survival of English as the only language left in 500 years' time would be a great intellectual disaster.

In various places and at different times in the past, a particular language has emerged as a *lingua franca* alongside a local language. The ideal future would be one in which everybody could converse in at least two languages – a mother tongue sustaining their own cultural heritage, and a *lingua franca* providing access to other people and cultures around the globe. The creation of Esperanto was an artificial attempt to achieve this but it is unlikely to succeed. Yet something like a universal language is being provided by empirical science (for example, in mathematics), this being one of the important areas of commonality in the new global culture.

Globalisation is further exemplified by the great increase in international commerce and trade. Less and less do countries live solely off the products they themselves produce; more and more, they are engaged together in a complex global economy. Production of goods, marketing, financial backing and promotion are all increasingly planned at a transnational level, with the result that national governments have less economic power (especially smaller states, or those in the so-called developing world). Globalisation strategies by the major transnational organisations now dominate the corporate scene, leading to a narrow specialisation in key sectors. It is widely claimed that the globalisation of production helps to cut costs, and that (as long as gains are not outweighed by transport costs) everybody benefits; the truth of such claims is also strenuously challenged, and there is strong evidence that the real beneficiaries are powerful, wealthy, western countries, and the transnational companies they support. Organisations such as the International Monetary Fund and the World Bank have been formed by the powerful nation states to foster globalisation. Initially started by the United States and Britain during World War II to assist postwar international financial and economic co-operation, these have been joined by others such as the World Trade Organisation, and act as brokers for the free market. We are moving by stages to a single global economy, operating on free market principles. (The negative and possibly destructive consequences of a free market global economy will be discussed in the next chapter.)

In drawing the nations of the world into one arena, globalisation can also lead to serious conflict, as the twentieth century has already demonstrated. Paradoxically, though they threatened to tear humanity apart, the two world wars led to the foundation of international organisations that may be seen as the first steps towards some global form of world government. The League of Nations was established by the victorious Allied powers at the end of World War I for the purpose of preventing another destructive global conflict. It promoted the principle of collective security, arbitration of international disputes, and reduction of armaments; it also set up a Permanent Court of International Justice. But while the League of Nations did assist with minor international disputes, it had little real power for dealing with issues such as the Japanese invasion of Asia, Italian expansion in Africa and German aggression in Europe. In 1946 it was replaced by the United Nations, which inherited many of the League's goals. According to its charter, the United Nations aims to save succeeding generations from the scourge of war, to reaffirm faith in fundamental human rights, to promote worldwide co-operation in the solving of international economic, social, cultural and humanitarian problems, and to maintain international peace and security. Beginning with 51 nations, membership had grown to 80 by 1956 and to more than 180 by 1996.

Parallel to these international organisations in government and commerce are many international societies of religious, cultural, humanitarian and sporting interests. No sooner does some new enterprise begin than, within a short time, it spreads around the world and takes root in other areas. All major sports are now linked on a global level, and world cup tournaments are the order of the day. Most notable are the Olympic Games, rejuvenated in 1896. Originally a product of Greek culture, the Olympics ran for over 1,000 years as a series of contests including music and poetry along with sport, before being abolished in 393 CE. Today their success is emulated in localised events such as the Commonwealth Games.

The phenomenon of globalisation has already begun to generate what may be called global consciousness. This new and developing form of human consciousness is still far from universal, but the world that we each create in our heads[1] (our mental picture of reality) is now being constructed rather differently, by absorbing innumerable bits of knowledge and information from all over the world, not just from our own small locality. In particular, as Thomas Berry has observed, the discovery of the evolutionary process is making a profound impact on human consciousness.[2]

In global consciousness we know that, if we go far enough back in time, we share a common origin not only with people from very different cultural and religious backgrounds, but also with all forms of life on the planet. Moreover, we now face a common planetary future with all other humans and all other creatures. Our forebears, whose lives were contained by cultural and geographical horizons, had only the haziest knowledge of people who lived in other countries, and could afford to ignore them completely – as we can no longer do. An emerging global awareness has (as we saw in Chapter 6) forced us to see all cultures, including our own, in relative terms.

We understand too that our earthly home is a tiny planet spinning in space, and that it is strictly finite and limited. We know that if we go far enough around the world in one direction we come back to where we started. For the first time in human history we have, in the twentieth century, been able to construct a fairly clear picture of the whole globe in our mind. Space exploration and satellite photography allows us to see even what the earth looks like from outer space. Into our mental picture we slot the various bits of news we see each night on television.

Global consciousness is causing us to discover and acknowledge both cultural diversity and cultural relativity. It is making us more aware of our own cultural identity (or lack of it). Only a few years ago people never used the word 'culture' in the way we do today, and never thought of themselves as belonging to a particular culture. Today we continually hear discussions about cultural identity, cultural autonomy and cultural diversity. People of different cultures are meeting personally, reading about each other's lives, or seeing one another on television. Few of us live any longer within the boundaries of only one culture, and new terms, such as bi-cultural and multi-cultural, are emerging.

All this is evidence of a massive and far-reaching change reshaping the sort of creatures we humans are. We are now conscious of the ways in which our social, cultural, economic and even our mental life is being interwoven with that of others. We are becoming more interdependent, and are having to learn how to become one global society whether we wish to or not.

Although globalisation is a modern phenomenon, the idea of a global consciousness and society goes back a very long way, and originated as a religious vision. The prophets and psalmists of ancient Israel envisaged a time when the people of all languages and nations would come from the four corners of the earth and be gathered together into a re-united family. This vision was intensified in the Christian and Islamic traditions to which Judaism unwittingly gave birth. Each of these monotheistic religious traditions had, at its best, the capacity to unite humanity. Each set out with a vision of binding humankind into one community of nations. Christianity looked forward to the time when 'all nations shall come and worship' the one deity; Christians spoke of the Kingdom of God, which would supersede the kingdoms of this world. Islam affirmed that people of all nations are brothers one to the other. The Muslims saw it as the culmination of human brotherhood, a concept symbolised magnificently in the ceremony of the annual Hajj to Mecca. Although these visions led to two great multiethnic civilisations – Christendom and the Islamic world – neither of these has succeeded in becoming the new global society, partly because each encountered within itself a continual resurgence of pre-Axial ethnic tribalism, and partly because each developed an intolerant exclusiveness which turned it into another closed society, this time of a religious kind. It has been difficult to resolve the uneasy tension between loyalty to the local community, whether ethnic or religious, and that to the larger human community, which globalisation requires.

Perhaps the first to grasp the full significance of globalisation, and to experience global consciousness intensively, was the Jesuit priest-scientist Pierre Teilhard de Chardin (1881–1955), whose seminal book *The Phenomenon of Man* was written before 1940 but not published until after his death. Writing at a time when the signs of globalisation were not nearly as obvious as they are today, he foresaw a process he called 'planetisation', by which 'peoples and civilisations reach such a degree either of frontier contact or economic interdependence or psychic communion that they can no longer develop save by the interpenetration of one another'.[3] Teilhard de Chardin wholly identified with the traditions of the Christian west, yet his visionary mind was able to lift the Christian themes and symbols out of their traditional usage and re-interpret them. In his breathtaking conceptualisation of planetary life, he saw the emergence of the human species and the subsequent globalisation of the planet not in terms of the conquest of the globe by Christianity but as the logical consequence of an ongoing evolutionary process.

He identified one aspect of evolution as divergence. Divergence can be seen not only in the multiplication of species over a long period of time, but also in the multiplication and diversification of languages, cultures and nations within the human species. This phenomenon of divergence functions rather like the lines of longitude on the surface of the planet, growing further apart as they move away from their point of origin at the earth's pole. At the equator, however, the lines of longitude start to come closer together. This other aspect of evolution Teilhard de Chardin called convergence; he saw it, like divergence, as an integral part of the evolving process as it moved from the point of origin he called Alpha to the end point he called Omega. From the time the species *Homo sapiens* consolidated itself to become the only survivor of the various hominoid species that had evolved as a result of divergence, humankind slowly spread over the earth, moving into previously uninhabited areas.

But what was to happen when there were no more places into which to spread on this finite planet? That very point, said Teilhard de Chardin, would mark the transition in humankind from divergence to convergence. The human species would fold back upon itself, merging all ethnic groups and cultures into one unified species, one global culture. This would then produce a new, higher form of human consciousness. He foresaw the rise of global consciousness, and dared to call it super-consciousness. Teilhard de Chardin believed that the twentieth century marked the coming of that crucial time in the planet's history.

What we have described as globalisation is remarkably close to Teilhard de Chardin's planetisation, in which '[m]ankind, born on this planet and spread over its entire surface, come[s] gradually to form round its earthly matrix, a single, major, organic unity, enclosed upon itself'.[4] Thus the globalisation of humankind could lead to the formation of a new kind of living entity – a social organism – on the same cosmic principle as that by which atoms join to form molecules, molecules join to form mega-molecules, mega-molecules unite to form living cells, and innumerable cells constitute an organism. Within this social organism there would arise 'a spiritual centre, a supreme pole of consciousness, upon which all the separate consciousnesses of the world may converge and within which they may love one another'.[5] This super-consciousness would evolve in the same way that personal consciousness does within the complex physiology of the human organism.

Of course Teilhard de Chardin's vision of the evolutionary process need not be taken too literally. It was severely criticised on publication – by many scientists for not being truly scientific and by many theologians for not being truly Christian. Some of its details are now dated. Yet, as a total vision of the story of the planet and of the future of humanity, it is still inspiring, and shows remarkable insight.

But is such a scenario even possible, let alone probable? A tenuous global culture is now emerging, though it is still embryonic. It is relativising all the earlier cultures, just as the trans-ethnic cultures created by Christianity and Islam each relativised the ethnic cultures of the countries into which they spread. Motivating this global culture is the growing global consciousness which we have just described. Is this anything like Teilhard de Chardin's super-consciousness? It is far too early to say. Possibly the human species, by successfully responding to current challenges, *could* become so united in love and goodwill that there would be some kind of spiritual centre linking all humans together in a commonality of consciousness. Martin Buber in his spiritual classic *I and Thou* maintained that where people are drawn together by deep personal relationships to form a true community, there emerges in their midst a spiritual centre, which both reflects and continues to foster the unique quality of their relationships. Such a centre could constitute a super-consciousness.

It must be conceded, however, that Teilhard de Chardin was working within an exclusively Christian framework. He was thinking very much in terms of the church as the supra-national society with Christ as the spiritual centre. While globalisation has been largely made possible by the Christian west, with its rapidly expanding technology and imperialistic ambitions, this does not make globalisation necessarily welcome in non-Christian cultures. They welcome the new technology but often regard the associated cultural challenges not as aspects of globalisation but as westernisation – and this they wish to reject. The resulting conflicts and difficulties now surfacing in the international arena were not part of Teilhard de Chardin's planetisation.

In addition, it needs to be remembered that the globalising process, advanced by western science and technology, also gave rise to today's secular culture. This is a product of the west, yet it was not planned by those proclaiming and defending Christianity; indeed, traditional Christian preachers often treat secularism as one of their chief enemies. Yet secularity became so much a part of western culture that the mission of bringing Christianity to the rest of the world has spread secularity as well. Today's embryonic global culture is secular in nature, however much it may draw its values from the Christian and other cultures which have preceded it.

Globalisation means that all kinds of allegiances – personal, family, religious and national – are increasingly subject to global concerns. We can still value, and feel some loyalty to, our own personal circle and cultural background, but these loyalties are now becoming subject to the imperatives laid upon us by globalisation. The citizenship of each particular nationality must take its place alongside global citizenship, our current cultures and our religious allegiance alongside an emerging global culture. But what will be the character of this culture and will it come at all? I would venture that any coming global culture will need to be humanistic (rather than traditionally religious), naturalistic (rather than supernaturalistic) and ecological (designed to promote the health of all planetary life). But as we shall see in the next two chapters, there are strong forces – economic, political and religious – which will seek to prevent the coming of such a culture. Have we the wisdom, courage and motivation to become global citizens and to welcome a global culture?

An important aspect of globalisation is that no human problem of any size exists in isolation. It therefore does not lend itself to any simple solution. What happens in one geographical area and/or in one aspect of life is quickly reflected elsewhere. Human life on this planet has the capacity to become a complex social organism with the kind of super-consciousness foreseen by Teilhard de Chardin. But there are also divisive and destructive forces present in the humanisation of the globe.

Globalisation is currently rolling along without any one person, organisation or nation controlling it. Like the march of time, it is going on its way relentlessly. There is very little possibility of holding it back or of directing it. As we arrive at the year 2000 CE, the process of globalisation has reached a turning point. It could lead to a form of human existence more wonderful and exciting than we can possibly imagine – a veritable heaven on earth. Or some of the trends that have been encouraging globalisation may have disastrous consequences far beyond human control.

Whichever way the future unfolds – and this we shall tentatively explore

– the year 2000 CE in the Christian calendar may well prove a milestone in human history after all. Calendars are built around such milestones, for, as we have seen, Dionysius Exiguus changed the year 753 of the ancient Roman calendar into the year 1 CE. The year 2000 CE marks not merely the end of the second Christian millennium; it may well mark the end of Christianity as a clearly definable tradition. Globalisation is bringing us into such a profoundly different era that some future generation may well be moved to discard the Christian calendar entirely, and rename the year 2000 AD as 1 GE, the first year of the Global Era.

CHAPTER 9

*Humanity at War
with Itself*

Among the biblical myths of human origin, two are particularly relevant to the problems raised by globalisation. One tells the story of Cain, the first child of Adam (humankind), who killed his brother Abel; when asked to explain what had happened to Abel, Cain made the well-known reply, 'I do not know. Am I my brother's keeper?'[1] This story symbolically describes the extremes to which the anti-social tendencies in the human condition can go, and indicates that humanity has been at war with itself from the very beginning. The other myth describes a time when all human beings lived in one harmonious society; 'the whole earth had one language and the same words,' says the story of the Tower of Babel.[2] The myth then explains why, in historical time, there have always been many languages, many cultures and many societies. They are the result of divine punishment for the blatant hubris of humankind.

Whether there ever was a time when humans were so few in number that they constituted only one society and spoke only one language we cannot say. It remains possible that all belonging to the species of *Homo sapiens* are descended from the same two parents, such as the Adam and Eve of the biblical myth of Eden. In that case, their descendants would have formed the first extended human family or tribe, united genetically and linguistically. All that we can say with confidence, however, is that our earliest knowledge of humankind takes us back only to the point where humans were already scattered into groups, living a tribal existence, each with its own language and culture.

The oldest and most basic form of the human social group is the family – not the nuclear family (which is largely a modern phenomenon) but the extended family. The family is bound genetically by blood ties and by a closely knit culture arising out of its common life. The family unit evolved in the far distant past into the dominant type of human society, the tribe. For a long time, most likely, the extended family and the tribe were indistinguishable, though gradually (it may be conjectured) the tribe grew to become a society of families.

The tribe is held together largely by a commonality of blood and culture. The bonds of the tribe started with blood ties and are instinctive in origin (as they are with all non-human gregarious mammals). This genetic base of tribalism remains strong even today, for 'blood is thicker than water', as we say. In the case of humans, however, the genetic ties have been supplemented by the bonding power of an ever-evolving culture. Each culture (or civilisation) contains a common language, a shared view of reality, a shared set of values and goals, and common patterns of behaviour, both moral and ritualistic.

The strength of tribalism lies in the personal bonds of mutual loyalty which hold the tribe together, give it an identity, endow it with strength and courage to overcome threats, and enable it to survive from generation to generation. So strong are the bonds of the tribe that its members vigorously defend its vitality and may even be prepared to die to ensure its preservation. There is much that is commendable in tribalism and it has been essential to human survival, at least until the present. The negative side of tribalism is that, manifesting the mark of Cain, it fosters distrust and antagonism to those outside the tribe, who are seen as a threat.

To this day the tribe remains the social base of the later forms of society which began to evolve less than 10,000 years ago, when the agricultural 'revolution' brought a more settled existence. This cultural change led to the establishment of walled cities, the cultivation of the various arts which city life makes possible, and hence what was called civilisation. From that time on, the city, the nation and even a whole civilisation have manifested themselves as particular forms of tribalism, and each has to some degree retained the loyalties and sense of social identity that constitute tribalism.

From the far distant past right up until the twentieth century, humankind showed a tendency to divide and diversify into ever more ethnic groups, all of them retaining the tribal type of social life. As we saw in the last chapter, it was this tendency to divide that Teilhard de Chardin labelled divergence. However, after the rise of the first civilisations some 5,000 years ago, powerful conquerors have forced a number of different social groups to enter into a compulsory form of unity. Because these empires were dependent upon the use of force, they had no great permanence and, in time, the original tribal or ethnic entities usually regained their independence. That process is still occurring; the twentieth century saw the British and other European empires gradually disbanding, and it has ended with the break-up of communist Yugoslavia after the death of Tito.

From the Axial Period onwards, a different and more permanent form of inter-ethnic social cohesion evolved. The strong commitment to ethnic or blood-related social groups came to be superseded by or subordinated to the formation of a multi-ethnic society of a religious kind. As noted in the previous chapter, Christianity and Islam each hoped to eliminate the negative aspects of ethnic tribalism by incorporating all of humankind into a new trans-ethnic community.

Out of the original Christian hope for the imminent coming of the Kingdom of God evolved the institution of the church (in which there was to be 'neither Jew nor Greek, neither slave nor free, neither male nor female');[3] this eventually developed into Christendom. The Muslims called it the brotherhood or Umma Muslima (Muslim people), and Islam dates its calendar from the establishment of the first Islamic state or society – that at Medina. At their height, Christendom and the Islamic world were both impressive in overcoming tribal and ethnic animosity and establishing a form of international society. However, even these religiously based super-societies have been subject to divergence, tending either to fragment (as in denominational divisions) or to give way to the resurgence of ethnic tribalism.

Ethnic divergence, or the dispersion of humanity into ever more tribes, cultures, nations and languages, was possible because there was, until recently, always more land to which they could go. The Pilgrim Fathers set sail for what they thought was the relatively empty 'new world'. The Quakers found freedom in Pennsylvania. The nations of Europe exported to their new colonies the surplus population that followed the industrial revolution. But this avenue for dealing with increased population no longer exists.

Because humans have not only spread to the limits of the earth but have also started to multiply at an alarming rate, the mythical story of the Tower of Babel is now being reversed. The whole earth has been reduced to the vicinity of the Tower; there is no more land to which we may scatter. Further divergence into more tribes and races is no longer possible, and is being replaced by what Teilhard de Chardin called convergence. Human societies of all kinds now find themselves being pushed more closely together. Minor languages are dying fast and major languages are in competition to become the one global language.

We are beginning to feel the birth pangs of what could be a new form of human society – global society. But will it emerge successfully? Will we humans now form ourselves into one global society, or will we simply slide into social chaos and end up destroying one another? The truth in the myth of Cain and Abel still remains: the mark of Cain is upon us. Will our anti-social tendencies prevent us from becoming one global society? That is the question globalisation is forcing us now to answer.

We humans are becoming a danger to ourselves, simply because of our natural capacity to multiply indefinitely on a finite planet. Globalisation has been partly promoted by the population explosion. The basic instinct to procreate has always been essential for the survival of humankind, as it is for any species. That is why, in the biblical tradition, humankind was commanded to 'be fruitful, multiply and fill the earth'. We are now filling the earth abundantly, even to overflowing, but we find it difficult to stop multiplying. The procreative instinct has become not only an asset for humankind but also a liability. It is tragically ironic that the very capacity required for survival is now that which threatens the well-being (even the future) of the species.

At the beginning of the Christian era (it has been estimated) the human population of the earth was approximately 300 million. Population growth remained relatively slow, so that by 1750 it had reached only about 800 million. Disease, epidemics, famine and high mortality among children took their toll. (Only about half of newborn babies survived to the age of five years.) Disease and early mortality, which were understandably judged to be evil, nonetheless kept in check the natural increase in human population. All that has been drastically changed by such otherwise beneficial developments as medical science, education in personal hygiene, better sanitation, and the improved economic conditions brought about by the industrial revolution. These factors reduced infant mortality, cured diseases, and prevented some plagues; the average length of life was gradually extended, and the population began to increase.

Population growth began to accelerate from 1750 onwards. As early as 1790 a Venetian monk, Gianmaria Ortis, declared that the human population could not continue to grow indefinitely. In 1798 Thomas Malthus (1766–1834), an Anglican clergyman and economist, published his seminal *Essay on the Principle of Population*, in which he argued that the human population has a natural tendency to multiply faster than the increase in food supply. Natural causes had long kept the population growth within sustainable limits; if these were removed, special efforts would be required to reduce the birthrate, either by self-restraint or by compulsory birth control.

By 1800 the world population had reached one billion, and it had taken some two million years to do so. But by only 1930 it had doubled to two billion. Then, partly as a result of the comparative peace and prosperity following World War II, a third billion was added by 1960, a fourth by 1974, the fifth before 1990 and the sixth by 1998. It has been projected that, on present rates of fertility, mortality and migration, the global population will have reached eight billion people by 2025. Since the size of the planet remains the same, the increase in human population will force people to live more closely together, as well as be more dependent on one another.

Until the 1950s the debate about human numbers remained largely academic. When artificial forms of contraception were coming into common use in the first half of the twentieth century, they were vigorously opposed by some on religious grounds. The debate was pursued purely on the basis of personal morality. Now that global population is reaching the limits of sustainability on the earth, contraception has become a social concern as well as a personal one. The traditional morality surrounding procreation and sexual relationships in the so-called free world is sadly out of touch with present reality: witness the Roman Catholic rejection of all artificial forms of contraception and the still widespread moral condemnation of clinical abortion.

However, drastic attempts to curb the population explosion, such as very strict forms of birth control and clinical abortion, do not offer any simple solution, for they have alarming social consequences. Any sudden decrease in the birth rate brings serious dislocation to the age composition of human society, so that (for example) too few working people have to provide for the material needs of too many old people. Programmes of enforced birth control also come into conflict with long-standing cultural customs and religious convictions, cause considerable anguish and are often strenuously opposed. Harsh and rigid methods of birth control, such as those instituted in China, can seriously upset the gender balance.

The population explosion has also changed patterns of land occupation and, in latter years, brought a dramatic increase in urban density. It was not until about 10,000 years ago that humans began to live in permanent settlements. Even up to 5,000 years ago such settlements were small, consisting of semi-permanent villages of peasant farmers. Only during the great empires of Mesopotamia, Egypt, Greece and Rome did cities have more than 100,000 inhabitants. Even then, and for a long time thereafter, human existence was still predominantly rural and village-like. In 1800, less than 3 per cent of the world's population were living in cities of 20,000 or more.

This percentage has rapidly increased, in line with the population explosion; it reached 25 per cent by the mid-1960s and 40 percent by 1980. In the year 2000 about half the world's population will be living an urban existence. What has been called the 'global village' is turning out to be one global city.

How will life in the global city be different from earlier human experience?

First of all, as Harvey Cox pointed out in *The Secular City*, in the modern city human existence is becoming more rootless and mobile on the one hand and more anonymous on the other. Our neighbours may remain strangers and our closest friends may be found in various scattered networks or sub-societies that we have chosen. Cities spring up like mushrooms, flourish, then show signs of decay. A flourishing suburb may, a generation later, turn into a slum.

Secondly, human existence will no longer be lived exclusively within one culture with its own identity and language. The embryonic global culture is already relativising both the trans-ethnic cultures (such as Christendom and the Islamic world) and the many ethnic cultures. The global mix will not necessarily destroy the values and goals found in these cultures, but it deprives them of their absolute status, and makes them closer to personal options.

The global city could provide exciting new possibilities for humankind, but it also presents challenges far exceeding any that the human species has yet faced. Not only is there the pressure of the population explosion and its increased needs, but there is also the fact that the various nations (with their burgeoning populations and their diverse cultures) are being pushed together rather like the continental plates on the earth's surface. Just as the clash of these geological plates causes earthquakes, so we can expect massive cultural earthquakes as the great cultures are forced into closer contact. The recent troubles in the Balkans, the Holy land and East Timor, to name but a few, may be small compared with what is yet to come.

In 1996 Samuel Huntington, director of the Harvard Institute of Strategic Studies, published *The Clash of Civilizations and the Remaking of World Order*. He argued that the phenomenon of globalisation is bringing new pressures of such magnitude that they could easily result in disastrous human conflicts, and that a global war of civilisations can be avoided only if world leaders accept the multi-civilisational character of global politics, and learn to co-operate. Among the factors contributing to global instability he cited the following:

- For the first time in history, politics have become global, being both multi-polar and multi-civilisational.
- The influence of the west is declining.
- The patronising superiority of the west is bringing it into conflict with other civilisations, particularly Islam and China.
- Asian civilisations are expanding, economically and politically. Islam is exploding demographically and destabilising Muslim countries and their neighbours.
- Modernisation is not currently producing a universal civilisation.

Huntington sees major fault lines appearing between what we may call the earth's 'civilisation plates' – between the Muslim and Asian societies on the one hand and the West on the other. These fault lines are being exacerbated by 'Western arrogance, Islamic intolerance and Chinese assertiveness'.[4] As Huntington writes:

> The West . . . believe[s] that the non-Western peoples should commit themselves to the Western values of democracy, free markets, limited government, human rights, individualism, the rule of law and embody these values in their institutions . . . What is universalism to the West is imperialism to the rest . . . The West is, for instance, attempting to integrate the economies of the non-Western societies into a global economic system which it dominates.[5]

This impending civilisational conflict indicates the fact that tribalism is so deeply entrenched in human behavioural patterns that it not only refuses to wither away but, in times of mounting tension in the face of threatening world crises, it is likely to intensify.

Tribalism was an asset for human societies before globalisation, but its persistence now constitutes a threat to the future race, if it prevents the evolution of one global society. We have reached that point in the evolution of the human species where traditional tribalism must be superseded by the acceptance of the essential unity of all human society. The distinctive strengths of tribalism need to be transferred to the whole human race; tribalism needs to be transformed into globalism.

Yet, in spite of encouraging signs in international and global activity (as described in Chapter 8), we are also witnessing an alarming resurgence of tribalism. In Europe during the last four centuries the disintegration of Christendom has led to the rise of nationalism, a modern form of tribalism. On the global scale, however, tribalism can operate in whole civilisations. As Huntington has stated: 'Civilizations are the ultimate human tribes and the clash of civilizations is tribal conflict on a global scale.'[6] And he predicts: 'Cold peace, cold war, trade war, quasi war, uneasy peace, troubled relations, intense rivalry, competitive co-existence, arms races: these phrases are the most probable descriptions of relations between entities from different civilizations. Trust and friendship will be rare.'[7]

It is much the same, if not worse, when we turn to the conservative defenders of the various religious traditions. An original goal of those traditions was, among other things, to overcome tribalism. But the old tribalism dies hard. Not only did ethnic tribalism spring to life again with the fragmentation of Christendom, but Christianity and Islam have each tended to develop further forms of tribalism – religious tribalism. Christian tribalism took the form of denominationalism. During the twentieth century, as denominationalism has lost its vitality, religious tribalism has taken the form of animosity and unco-operativeness among the conservative, liberal and radical wings of the ecclesiastical organisations, with the conservative wing being particularly militant.

In 1993 there appeared two books with a similar theme, *Out of Control: Global Turmoil on the Eve of the Twenty-first Century* by Zbigniew Brzezinski and *Pandaemonium: Ethnicity in International Politics* by Daniel Moynihan, who had had a distinguished career as a Harvard professor, US ambassador to the UN, president of the Security Council and then senior US senator. They both argue that the world is heading for chaos as a result of the break-up of nation states; the intensification of tribal, ethnic and religious loyalties; the spread of international terrorism; and the proliferation of weapons of mass destruction. Senator Moynihan rightly concedes that one's ethnicity or nationality can be a legitimate source of pride, but warns, using the words of the Christian ethicist Reinhold Niebuhr, that it can also be a form of collective egotism, potentially very destructive.[8]

Brzezinski, who was formerly national security adviser to US President Jimmy Carter, published a book in 1989 called *The Grand Failure*, in which he prophesied the collapse of communism. In *Out of Control* he suggests that the world today is 'like a plane on automatic pilot, with its speed continuously accelerating but with no defined destination'.[9] The idea that humankind is in control of the various forces promoting change is an illusion:

> Man does not control or even determine the basic directions of his ever-expanding physical powers. The plunge into space, the acquisition of new weapons, the breakthroughs in medical and

other sciences are shaped largely by their own internal dynamics
. . . The human being, while being the inventor, is simultaneously
the prisoner of the process of invention.[10]

In the same year, 1993, Alvin and Heidi Toffler published *War and Anti-war: Survival at the Dawn of the 21st Century*, in which they said:

> For the past three centuries the basic unit of the world system
> has been the nation-state. But this building block of the global
> system is itself changing . . . Many of today's states are going to
> splinter or transform, and the resultant units may not be inte-
> grated nations at all, in the modern sense, but a variety of other
> entities from tribal federations to Third Wave city-states.[11]

Many have noted that while globalisation has been drawing people
together into worldwide unions and federations, opposite forces have been
focusing attention on individualism and on small, tightly knit groups and
movements. There is therefore a strange ambivalence present in globalisation. On the one hand, it is drawing all nations and cultures into one
global conglomeration which has the capacity to formulate some common
moral standards that might enable us to eliminate the wars of the past and
establish a stable global society. On the other hand, it has stimulated a
resurgence of both ethnic and religious tribalism, which is causing new
pressures, and their accompanying tensions and hostilities, to emerge.

Religious tribalism is exemplified in the twentieth century by the rise of
fundamentalism. Although the term fundamentalist originated in
Christians circles (see Chapter 4), it is now used to refer to any person who
tries to hold at bay the impact of cultural change on their traditional beliefs
and practices. So today there are Muslim fundamentalists, Jewish fundamentalists, Hindu fundamentalists and ethnic fundamentalists, each trying
to preserve and revive their traditional rites, practices and beliefs. All of
these reject some or all of the various values which we have earlier sketched
as modernity. Modernity is for them a blind road; and while they are not
necessarily wholly opposed to entering a global society, they are adamant
that they alone hold the key that will enable that society to eventuate.

Gilles Kepel, after studying the rise of fundamentalism in Islam,
Christianity and Judaism, particularly from the 1970s onward, warned of its
dangers in his book *The Revenge of God*. All fundamentalists have much in
common, according to Kepel. They all reject secularism, which they attribute to the influence of the western Enlightenment. This secular rejection
of the traditional form of religious faith they see as the reason for the rise

of both Nazism and communism. They reject what they see as the immoral mode of life in the modern secular city. But, by the same token, they also diverge sharply from one another. Each looks for the reorganisation of society in accordance with its own specific set of holy scriptures. That is, they aim to re-Islamise, of re-Judaise, or re-Christianise society, and so their ideals clash. Thus fundamentalists are not only at odds with the more liberal sections of their own religious or ethnic community but they disagree also with fundamentalists of other persuasians, although they share a similar mind set.

Fundamentalism, in its various forms, is a force that can no longer be ignored, for it constitutes one of the most serious obstacles to the evolution of a global society. Global society calls for flexibility of thought and practice, for empathy with those who differ, for compromise in a spirit of goodwill; it requires mutual co-operation for the common good. Fundamentalism, by contrast, is socially divisive, calling for absolute (and even) blind loyalty to a holy book or a set of fixed principles. Fundamentalism leads readily to fanaticism, for fundamentalists are so sure of the truth that they are not open to dialogue or other human reasoning. Fundamentalists insist on remaining loyal to the fundamentals, even if this leads to their own death or the death of others. Indeed, Muslim fundamentalists sometimes see martyrdom as the fast road to eternal bliss. Such fanaticism soon leads to terrorism and suicide bombings, as in the Muslim Hizbollah and the Jewish Gush Emunim. Fundamentalism is an intense form of religious tribalism which can lead to social chaos in today's world.

Alternative to the road to social chaos is the evolution of a global society. Globalisation offers the opportunity for the rise of a new kind of human society, an open society on a global scale. The global economy, which is already emerging, will form a natural part of this. The dominant part played by the global economy in globalisation is, however, no guarantee of a secure future. By virtue of its very size and complexity, the global economy is also unstable and vulnerable. Most of us know from personal experience that the more complex the technological gadget, the greater the consequences when it breaks down. So it is with the global economy. A sudden change or disaster in one place sends shockwaves around the world. A rapid economic success story in one country may put thousands of people out of work on the other side of the globe. The stockmarkets around the world respond within moments of hearing a particular item of news.

Another reason for regarding the global economy as unstable is the expanding gulf between rich and poor nations. Immediately after World

War II, the acknowledged disparity in the wealth of nations led to the establishment of the World Bank and the International Monetary Fund; it was then widely assumed that the so-called developing countries could be brought up to some sort of parity with the developed countries by lending money and promoting economic growth. Indeed, economic growth has become the chief goal of most national economies; governments use it as a barometer for their political policies. Yet even Adam Smith, whose book *The Wealth of Nations* (1776) has become the bible of today's protagonists of free trade, conceded that his theory of economic growth broke down at the point where human expansion reached the limits of the Earth's resources. Writing more than 200 years ago, he believed this point to be only hypothetical; we know that we have now reached it.

In 1972 the Club of Rome, an international assembly of business leaders, published *The Limits to Growth*. Just as Thomas Malthus had shown how population had the capacity to increase faster than the food supply, so this computer-based report concluded that world order would collapse if population growth, industrial expansion, increased pollution and the depletion of natural resources were to continue at current rates. The Club of Rome called for 'a Copernican revolution of the mind', which abandoned the commitment to endless economic growth and set instead as its goals zero population growth, a levelling-off of industrial production, increased pollution control, and a shift from consumerism to a more service-based economy. The recommendations of the Club of Rome were heavily criticised by business interests who had most to lose, but their claims served only to illustrate how much political and economic ideology is driven by self-interest.

The promotion of economic growth has not reduced the economic gap between the developing and the developed countries, as the World Bank and the International Monetary Fund assumed it would. In 1960 the wealthiest 20 per cent of the world's population had a per capita income 30 times that of the poorest 20 per cent. By 1989 the disparity had doubled to 60 times more. Third World countries now find themselves so heavily in debt that they have become economically enslaved to the developed nations. The old colonialism has gone, only to be replaced by a new kind: economic colonialism.

What we should be aiming for today is not economic growth but greater social cohesion. Between about 1870 and 1970 many countries of the western world did focus their attention on economic policies that promoted social cohesion at the national level. They did this by means of social welfare schemes, and by making education and health resources freely avail-

able. These welfare state economies are now mostly in disarray or are under
great strain, particularly since the collapse of communism. The move to a
global economy is partly responsible; globalisation has intensified the interdependence of economics, health, education, culture and religion.
Increased pressure in one area soon causes tension in the others, both
nationally and globally. Any attempt to plan the future of one area (such
as health or education) in isolation from the others, soon encounters insuperable difficulties.

What we need – and what we lack – is the vision of an ultimate goal, such
as the promotion of social cohesion on a global scale and the realisation of
a global society. Globalisation is challenging us to exercise a greatly
increased sense of responsibility to our fellow humans. Today's answer to
the rhetorical question 'Am I my brother's keeper?' has to be a resounding
'*Yes*'. We humans must learn how to live together in harmony, goodwill
and mutual responsibility.

The vitality of human society has always rested on bonds of loyalty that
were both genetic and cultural; now both need to widen their framework.
The genetic bonds of globalism are to be found in our common humanity,
irrespective of tribe, nationality, culture and religion. For we humans are
all genetically linked; we share nearly all of the DNA formula peculiar to
our species, and we are already bonded as blood brothers and sisters. Our
cultural bonds must now become global rather than regional. Our common humanity has been acknowledged, for example, in a declaration of
human rights and a growing recognition of racism as an immoral attitude.
What separates us and makes us all different is our cultural conditioning,
which still strongly reflects the diversities and tribalism of the past. We
have yet to evolve a common human culture, and this will be essential if
there is to be a global society.

Yet some faint outlines of a global human culture are already appearing.
The recognition of our common humanity is leading us, if haltingly, to a
set of common, humanly based values, which arise out of the human condition we all share. We increasingly feel a moral obligation to treat all fellow humans as equally as possible.

One of these common values is personal freedom. For the first time in
human history, people are being encouraged to think for themselves, and
to challenge any beliefs and way of life imposed upon them. This freedom
to think for oneself, to make personal judgements and decisions, good
though it may be at the local and individual level, can unfortunately prove
a liability at the global level. Individual autonomy places on human shoul-

ders much greater responsibilities than the majority of people have had to bear before. It may well be asked whether, as a species, we are ready to shoulder that responsibility.

Thus what has emerged as a great human gain at the individual level may well prove to be a further threat at the collective level. It is entirely possible that, at a time when very important decisions have to be made and acted upon for the good of humankind and the planet as a whole, far too many people will focus their attention on their own immediate vicinity and insist on claiming their individual right to act within it as they wish. They may end up going in different and conflicting directions, thus producing anarchy and social chaos. Huntington, for example, contends that 'far more significant than the global issues of economics and demography are problems of moral decline', an 'increase in antisocial behaviour', decay of family structures, weakening of the 'work ethic', and decreasing commitment to intellectual activity.[12] Similarly Brzezinski refers to a current global crisis of spirit which has to be overcome if the human race is to regain some control over its destiny.

This dilemma is far more important as we enter the twenty-first century than economic theories of how to achieve economic growth. Either we learn how to live in harmony with one another and in harmony with the earth or else the human species goes the way of the dinosaurs. The twenty-first century will be a severe test of the human species. Instead of finding our enemies in other ethnic groups or in spiritual principalities and powers such as the Devil, we humans are just beginning to realise that we are becoming our own worst enemies. We are at war with ourselves.

After a long period of dispersion over the whole earth the human race is now being pushed together, whether we are ready for it or not. We find that, with millennia of civilisation behind us, there is much primitive tribalism still beneath that veneer. We live in a global world and we have a common destiny on this planet, but our decisions are hampered by narrow-mindedness and short-sightedness. The majority of us are so immersed in our personal affairs in our own small part of the world that we are unaware of the sword of Damocles now suspended over our heads – a sword that hovers because of the continuing tribalism which keeps us in a state of war with other humans, and because the very earth on which we live is now issuing its own a set of warnings about the limitations on a human future.

CHAPTER 10

Humanity at War
with the Planet

Ever since humans began to emerge from their pre-human ancestry (maybe around two million years ago), the species learned to accommodate itself to the natural environment. Humans, like all other earthly creatures, evolved in a symbiotic relationship with the world around them, living at the mercy of natural forces. In their slowly developing, language-based culture, our far distant ancestors gained some understanding of the ways of nature and they developed beliefs, myths and rituals to acknowledge their absolute dependence on the earth, which supplied all the essentials of life.

As our forebears came to name the particular forces of nature as unseen spirits and/or gods, they showed them the utmost respect. The gods of nature were the chief objects of their worship and veneration. Dependent upon these 'spiritual forces', the early humans knew they were not free to do whatever they liked on the earth. On the contrary, they developed practices to protect and sustain the various sources of their food supply. To early humans, the earth was revered in personal terms, and often regarded as their Mother.

This relationship between humans and nature lasted for many centuries, until the Axial Period[1] introduced some radical changes. These were most pronounced in the monotheistic culture which arose in ancient Israel and which diverged eventually into Judaism, Christianity and Islam. As polytheism turned to monotheism, the focus of attention shifted from the earth to the sky. In mythological terms it was a shift in worship from the Earth Mother to the Sky Father. The Israelite prophet Hosea reflected this when he portrayed the divine Heavenly Father complaining that the people of Israel 'did not know that it was I who gave them the grain and the wine and the oil and lavished upon them the silver and the gold' – gifts which they in their ignorance attributed to Baal (one of the Canaanite gods of nature).[2]

The monotheistic cultural traditions have long interpreted this ancient struggle between the old nature religions and the worship of the One who ruled from the heavens as a struggle between idolatry and the truth, in which the latter ultimately prevailed. But banishing the gods of nature had the effect of desacralising the earth. Christians, even more than Jews and Muslims, came to regard the earth as a fallen world and contrasted it with the wholly spiritual world of heaven. Christian monasticism encouraged the faithful to withdraw from the materialistic world with its earthly attractions and prepare themselves for their ultimate destiny in the heavenly realms.

Western culture has been slowly relinquishing this dualistic view of reality and learning to value the physical world – the only world of which we have first-hand experience. Yet that traditional dualism left a deposit of attitudes which we have yet to overcome, and whose consequences we have only begun to acknowledge in the twentieth century. For one thing, monotheism's rejection of the gods of nature badly upset the prevailing gender balance. In polytheism, the Sky Father was a somewhat distant figure, complemented by the Earth Mother, with whom humans had the closer relationship. When the one and only deity affirmed by Israel banished the Earth Mother and the other gods of nature (both male and female), the Sky Father was left supreme. As the term Heavenly Father suggests, this God inherited many of the characteristics of the primitive Sky Father, such as unlimited power and the male macho image – manifested in storms and thunderbolts. The elimination of the Earth Mother effectively downgraded the earth in favour of heaven. And as a result, women and female characteristics were downgraded, and a superior place for men was established in society. When the divine male gender reigns supreme in the heavenly places as the Almighty, so the human male gender dominates the earth. Thus the monotheistic traditions became strongly patriarchal and the feminine virtues were devalued.

The first expression of pure monotheism in Israelite thought is found as late as the sixth century BCE, in the words of an unknown prophet. In the latter part of the Book of Isaiah he wrote: 'I am the Lord and there is no other. Apart from me there is no god.'3 About the same time (according to most modern scholars) the opening chapter of Genesis was composed in its present form. In this creation story, humankind was made in the image of this all-powerful Creator, able likewise to subdue the earth and exercise dominion over every living creature that lives upon it. Although this later biblical myth specifically stated, 'God created mankind in his own image . . . male and female he created them,'4 God continued to be described in male terms. It was natural, therefore, for the mediaeval theologian Aquinas to conclude that women are simply unfinished males.

This biblical tradition went deep into the collective consciousness of the western world, causing people to believe that the earth was expressly made for the use of humankind, with the male gender in authority. People felt free to exploit the earth and its resources for their own ends. In no century more than the twentieth has this exploitation been so widespread. James Gaius Watt, a committed Christian and Ronald Reagan's Secretary of the Interior, argued that developers should have access to controlled parks and natural resources, with this reasoning:

> The earth is merely a temporary way station on the road to eternal life. It is unimportant except as a place of testing to get into heaven. In this evil and dangerous world, one's duty is to pass through unspotted by the surrounding corruption. The earth was put here by the Lord for his people to subdue and to use for profitable purposes on the way to the hereafter.

While this view may be considered extreme, it was nevertheless consistent with traditional Christian teaching – and indeed expressed popular (although ill-considered) Christian thought. As recently as 1952, a theologian of world renown, Emil Brunner (1889–1966), wrote:

> Because man, and man alone, has been created in the image of God, and for communion with the Creator, *therefore he may and should make the earth subject to himself, and should have dominion over all other creatures . . . Man is only capable of realizing his divine destiny when he rises above Nature and looks at it from a distance* [emphasis added].'5

This attitude towards the natural world is now facing strong criticism. However, this same attitude may well be the reason why empirical science first evolved in western civilisation. Some philosophers and scientists have claimed that empirical science could only develop where there was nothing sacred about the earth, leaving humans free to experiment with it. In Christian teaching, not only were there no gods of nature to take vengeance on humans who interfered with their domain, but also humans already had dominion over the earth, granted by the one and only God.

Empirical science gave rise to modern technology, and this has been not only a justified source of pride but also welcomed by people in many different cultures. Few are willing to dispense with the technology on which human life has now come to depend. But from the far distant past, when primitive humans discovered how to make fire and invent tools, up until the recent present, nothing that humans did through their technology made much difference to the forces of nature. It is only in the twentieth century that human forces have become sufficiently magnified as to be comparable with natural forces. We may not yet be able to control the weather, but our collective activities now have subtle but serious effects on weather patterns. Our extravagant use of the earth's resources is now turning to wasteful exploitation, and our human activities are causing many other species to become extinct.

During the last two decades an ever-increasing number of books have been published, warning that a frightening nemesis is now appearing on the horizon as a result of our changing relationship with the earth. They started with Rachel Carson's *Silent Spring* (1966); later came titles such as *The Fate of the Earth* by Jonathan Schell (1982), *The Dream of the Earth* by Thomas Berry (1988), *Earth in the Balance* by Al Gore (1993), and *The Sacred Balance* by David Suzuki (1997). We are being awakened to the fact that not all of our technological and other achievements necessarily promote the long-term well-being of the human race. We find that the rise of modern culture in the Christian west, followed by its rapid spread around the world, has been both a blessing and a curse.

The Christian west, including monotheism, is now meeting moral criticism, from within the western culture. Arnold Toynbee in 1973 wrote:

> Some of the major maladies of the present day world – in partic-ular the recklessly extravagant consumption of nature's irreplace-able treasures, and the pollution of those of them that man has not already devoured – can be traced back to a religious cause, and this cause is the rise of monotheism . . . Monotheism, as enunciated in the book of Genesis, has removed the age-old restraint that was once placed on man's greed by his awe. Man's greedy impulse to exploit nature used to be held in check by his pious worship of nature.[6]

Similarly the Lutheran theologian Jürgen Moltmann said:

> It was the Western 'religion of modern times' that freed the way for the secularisation of nature. At the end of civilisation's long history, the ancient view about the harmony between the forces of nature has been destroyed – destroyed by modern monothe-ism on the one hand, and by scientific mechanism on the other. Modern monotheism has robbed nature of its divine mystery and has broken its spell.[7]

Toynbee's growing concern about the future of humankind led him, after spending a lifetime studying human history, to devote the last book of his career to *Mankind and Mother Earth*. As he observed: 'We now stand at a turning-point in the history of the biosphere and in the shorter history of one of its products, mankind . . . Man is the first species of living being in our biosphere that has acquired the power to wreck the biosphere and, in wrecking it, to liquidate himself.'[8]

The word biosphere has come into common use only in the twentieth century. It was coined by Austrian scientist Edouard Suess in 1875 to refer to the thin film of life around the earth between the hydrosphere and the atmosphere, and penetrating them both; in this are found all earthly living creatures, great and small. Teilhard de Chardin used the word to draw attention to the unity of all planetary life, and to the complex and awe-inspiring ways in which the myriad living species within the biosphere interrelate both with one another and with their environment.

The increasing use of such terms as biosphere illustrates a radical shift taking place in our understanding of the world, a shift which may be described as a move from atomism to holism. Atomism (which goes all the way back to Democritus, who coined the term atom) assumes that physical reality consists of tiny indestructible parts or atoms, and that by analysing an object into smaller and smaller parts one can learn all there is to know about it. Analysis of this kind has been very fruitful in modern chemistry and physics. But there is much that this sort of analysis misses, and may even destroy, in the search for knowledge. The term 'holism' was coined in 1926 by J.C. Smuts to refer to the tendency of nature to produce wholes from ordered groups of units. We now know that, in the phenomenon of life, the whole is more than the sum of its parts. To understand life in general, including the many particular forms of it within the biosphere, we must study it holistically.

All living creatures are organisms or living systems, the essential components of which are carbon, hydrogen, nitrogen and oxygen. These are, in themselves, lifeless and inert. A system is alive if it obtains energy and other substances from its environment, returns wastes to that environment, and maintains the conditions necessary for the process to continue. All living organisms not only possess an internal living system but also constitute with their environment a larger living system, which could be called a 'life field'. The holistic approach, which examines physical reality in ever-greater wholes, has thus told us that all forms of life are dependent on systems. Even the biosphere of the earth itself is dependent on the energy drawn from the sun.

The continuing life of each species depends upon the preservation of a delicate balance between the organism and the environment which supports it. Each organism contains self-regulating mechanisms which help to preserve that balance. We can understand this best by thinking of the organism we know best – the human being. We have long been used to thinking of ourselves as wholes rather than as aggregations of parts. Indeed, it is only modern physiology that has fully identified the various organs or sub-systems which exist within the human body. When one or more of those systems has its balance disturbed and can no longer function (as, say, in diabetes) our health (literally, our 'wholeness') suffers. We become ill and, if the balance cannot be restored, we die.

The earth has provided certain basic conditions which must be met by all earthly creatures if they are to survive as a species. Humans have evolved within those parameters. Our respiratory system fits both the nature and the proportions of the gases found in the atmosphere. Our bodies, which are 80 per cent water, fit the earth's water supply. The ozone layer protects us from the sun's harmful radioactivity. Our muscles and bone structure have evolved to meet the conditions of the earth's mass. For humans to be healthy they must be able to breathe fresh air, drink clean water, eat adequate food, and live in an environment not too different from that in which they became human. The more the environment changes from that in which a species has evolved, the more the health and behaviour of that species will show maladjustment. Its health will deteriorate and then it will die. We humans will always be earthlings, along with all other earthly creatures. Our existence remains earth-related.

To acknowledge the reality of living systems, and especially the ultimate system which links all systems of earthly life, the word eco-sphere is now often preferred to the earlier word biosphere. A full appreciation of the whole eco-system has led some, such as James Lovelock with the Gaia hypothesis, to describe the earth itself in terms of an organism, of which the biosphere is the living skin in the same way as bark is the living skin of the tree. His term Gaia is the name for Mother Earth derived from ancient Greek mythology.[9]

At the very time we humans have been learning more about the ecology of all planetary life, we have been discovering to our horror how much we are now upsetting the delicate balances in the living systems of the eco-sphere. Humanity has had no intention of 'wrecking the biosphere', to use Toynbee's words. While there is an unfortunate streak in the human psyche that delights in destruction (as vandalism ancient and modern shows), the current damage to the eco-sphere is quite unintentional and occurs partly out of ignorance. The eco-sphere is suffering chiefly through our sudden expansion in numbers and our rapidly growing technology – and the first of these is serving to exacerbate the second.

The impact of the population explosion on a finite world has already been discussed in Chapter 9. It is also shifting balances within humanity itself. The racial composition of the world's population is altering rapidly, for the population increase is occurring mainly among the non-white races. For example, in 1950 the population of Africa was only half that of Europe, but by 2025 it could be three times that of Europe. In the 30 years before 2025, Nigeria's population could jump from 113 to 301 million, Kenya's from 25 to 77 million, Tanzania's from 27 to 84 million and Zaire's from 36 to 99 million. The population explosion is also changing the economic balances, for it is the nations that are already economically poor, and in many cases saddled with massive international debt, that will bear the burden of feeding between two and three times as many more mouths than they do at present.

The fast-increasing population also upsets the ecological balance between various species and their source of sustenance, by putting added strain on the natural resources of the earth. Humans, in order to live, are interfering with the food chains which have evolved over time, and are depriving many other creatures as well as ourselves of sustenance. All food for human consumption, and for many other species as well comes either directly or indirectly from four biological systems: croplands, grasslands, forests and fisheries. Each of these is being seriously depleted at the same time as the human population is rapidly growing. It was estimated in the 1970s that, from the time human agriculture began to develop some 10,000 years ago, one half of the earth's food-producing soil had disappeared and a third of the remainder would be lost in the last quarter of the twentieth century. Because of the clearing of pasture and forest lands for agriculture, vast amounts of topsoil are being swept down into the ocean and lost for the future. The United States alone is said to lose four to six billion tonnes annually.

Further, and even more seriously for the eco-sphere, the human population explosion is upsetting the balance which has long existed among earthly creatures. All species have evolved in a state of interdependence with one another and with their total environment. Humans now dominate the surface of the earth as never before. Human expansion into previously uninhabited areas has disturbed, and in many cases already destroyed, the natural habitat of other species. Species are becoming extinct much more rapidly.

The delicate balances in the planetary eco-system are also being upset by technology, much of which has been specifically developed to meet the needs of a greatly increased population. Human technology began, of course, many thousands of years ago and took a great step forward with the rise of agriculture. Yet, for a very long period, human technology was basically of the same order as (and not greatly more advanced than) the simple technology which other higher animals had developed and operated largely by instinct. The difference between the spinning of a spider's web (for example) and human technology is that the latter came to depend increasingly on human thought – or what Teilhard de Chardin called the evolution of the noosphere. This he saw as the thin sphere of creative and self-conscious human thought within the biosphere. Teilhard de Chardin identified the arrival of the noosphere as a transition in the evolutionary process just as far-reaching as the evolution of life out of a non-living planet. The philosopher Karl Popper, using a different model, referred to the total product of noogenesis as World 3, a non-physical but very real world of objective knowledge created by human thought.[10]

Human knowledge has been slowly accumulating over many millennia and has been transmitted from generation to generation; its practical application constitutes human technology. In the last 200 years there has been an explosion in (World 3) knowledge. This partly contributed to population growth, in that we had a better understanding of human health. But it has also greatly expanded human technology. The ratio between the forces of nature and human forces has significantly changed.

Population pressures and human technology are together adversely affecting the natural conditions of the surface of the planet in the following ways:

- We are polluting air and water, the two most basic commodities on which human existence depends.
- We are increasing the amount of carbon dioxide in the air, causing changing climatic conditions and global warming. This in turn raises ocean levels sufficiently to endanger the habitation of those living near sea-level.
- We are depleting the ozone layer, which protects us from the harmful effects of the sun's radiation. This not only increases the incidence of malignant cancers but can also bring about unforeseen genetic changes.
- We are destroying the rainforests, increasing the deserts and, as noted above, washing the topsoil into the sea. (The earth's forests are shrinking by 17 million hectares per year.)
- We are making massive demands on the earth's natural resources and rapidly exhausting many of its non-renewable deposits.

- Our increasing competition for the fruits of the earth, coupled with the quite unequal use of the earth's limited resources, is building up explosive tensions within the human species.
- The complexity of our growing interdependence in the global village makes the global economy exceedingly fragile.

Modern secular prophets (such as the writers referred to above) are telling us about the early warning signals of a living earth feeling the pressure of the activities of one species. What has evolved over millions of years we are now in the act of destroying in a few decades, either knowingly or unknowingly. And this is the result of what may be called the humanisation of the earth. Some of these prophets are so pessimistic that they ask whether it is possible for some five to eight billion people to change the direction of our global life in the relatively short time available.

Others are more hopeful and see no reason why, with human ingenuity and further technology, we should not be able to reverse the dangerous policies we have set in motion. We have, for example, already taken some measures to deal with one of the probable causes of the growing holes in the ozone layer, and to reverse the destruction of European forests by acid rain. Thus, the more optimistic of the modern prophets (like their ancient counterparts) are far from saying that doom is inevitable. Jonathan Schell ends his book *The Fate of the Earth* by pointing to the choice humankind must make between the path that leads to death and the path that leads to life. His words are reminiscent of the words of Moses: 'I have set before you this day life and good, death and evil . . . Therefore choose life.'

But do enough people even see this choice between life and death? Plenty of critics dismiss these prophetic voices as 'doom merchants', who grossly exaggerate the warning signs and too readily ignore the capacity of human ingenuity to cope with threats. When Rachel Carson dared to suggest in *Silent Spring* that synthetic pesticides did more harm than good, her book was dismissed as so much hogwash. Carson's allegations have since been confirmed as legitimate, with the result that many pesticides are now banned and organic farming is expanding fast.

It is not difficult to discover that the critics are usually people in the affluent west whose wealth, business interests and economic policies are dependent upon the technology doing the damage. Those who flatly dismiss the warning bells appear to be largely driven by self-interest, and so they shut their eyes to the consequences of their commitments just as surely as the Christian fundamentalists turn from the evidence that points to the end of the Christian era.

Even more serious is the fact that resistance to environmental issues is built into the economic policy underlying capitalism itself – an economic policy which, since the fall of communism in Eastern Europe, has been widely adopted around the globe. Its first maxim is that a nation's well-being depends upon the wealth produced by its industry, technology and economic development. The second maxim is that this wealth can be measured by its per capita Gross National Product (GNP). The third maxim is that to maximise a nation's well-being it must maximise its economic growth. Thus annual economic growth is commonly being used as a criterion to measure the success or failure of political policies. Modern economic orthodoxy regards these maxims not only as basic to capitalism but also as normal for the way humans relate to the natural world. As Edward Goldsmith says:

> The modern discipline of economics is based on the assumption that the destructive economic system which is operative today is normal . . . it does not occur to many academics that what they take to be normal is highly atypical of humanity's total experience on this planet . . . They are like biologists who have only seen cancerous tissue and understandably mistake it for a healthy tissue.[11]

It is not surprising therefore that these maxims are coming under attack. Herman Daly, one-time economist with the World Bank, collaborated with theologian John Cobb to publish in 1989 *For the Common Good: Redirecting the Economy toward Community, the Environment and a Sustainable Future.* They argued that the standard system of profit-and-loss accounting used by economists is deeply flawed. For example, many solar-powered energy systems are currently considered uneconomic when compared with those dependent on coal, oil or uranium; but if the full costs of production, consumption of a non-renewable resource, waste disposal and damage to environment are all taken into account, they could begin to look relatively inexpensive. Similarly, they argue, the accounting system used for the calculation of GNP can seriously mislead. However useful GNP may be for short-term planning, it gives false expectations about the long term, because it regards a national economy as a self-contained system which can be divorced from its surroundings. A national economy needs to be treated as a sub-system of the larger eco-system on which it is dependent, for it is drawing upon raw materials (some of which are irreplaceable), it is producing waste products (which have to be deposited somewhere) and it may be causing some damage to the eco-system. Thus any calculation of GNP is false if it does not subtract the negative impact caused by these other factors. When these subtractions are made, 'positive' economic growth may well turn out to be negative in fact.

Daly and Cobb argued that, to get a balanced picture of the current state of human well-being on the planet, we need to see that state in terms of the whole eco-system and not just in terms of one of its sub-systems. They set about constructing an alternative way of measuring economic growth, one that took account of the whole system. They called it the Index of Sustainable Economic Welfare (ISEW). Then they applied it to the American economy. Judged by the standard GNP statistics, the US per capita income had increased in real value by 25 per cent since 1976; but, using the ISEW, they found that over the same period the economic well-being of Americans had actually declined by 10 per cent.

At a time when humans have become emancipated from the many social and religious restrictions of the past, including what our forebears thought to be the dictates of the Heavenly Father, we find ourselves becoming increasingly dependent on another set of forces. The eco-sphere itself has now become the God 'in whom we live and move and have our being' (to use the words of Acts 17:28), and the warning voices referred to above are its prophets. Indeed, the giving of our full attention to the needs of the eco-system (call it Mother Earth, Gaia or Nature, if you wish) is in many ways replacing the dutiful obedience which humans were expected to show to the Heavenly Father in traditional monotheism. The basic Christian doctrine of sin, which stressed that humanity exists in a tragic state of alienation from the God who created it in his own image, is being replaced by the discovery that humanity is currently in a state of war with the planet which has brought it forth.

Leading theologian Jürgen Moltmann has said:

> What we need above all [if modern society is to have any future] is a new respect for nature, and a new reverence for the life of all created things . . . for it was the Western 'religion of modern times' that freed the way for the secularisation of nature. At the end of civilisation's long history, the ancient view about the harmony between the forces of nature has been destroyed – destroyed by modern monotheism on the one hand, and by scientific mechanism on the other.[12]

The question of how humans are to return to a state of harmony with the forces of nature is a daunting one. Those in the affluent countries who are in a position to appreciate the whole picture and respond positively are often blinded to the consequences of their countries' policies because everything around them seems to be in good heart. Most of them have never been so well off financially and materially. It is very tempting, and much more reassuring, simply to dismiss today's prophets of doom as scaremongers. This negative response has been likened to the refusal of the passengers on the Titanic to take seriously the announcement that the boat would sink within an hour and a half. The people in undeveloped countries who are already suffering the results of the imminent nemesis are often powerless to obtain information, or to act on it. In any case, their immediate concern is often where the next meal is coming from.

Thus an appreciation of the damage we are doing to the earth has been slow to surface in modern human consciousness. Most people are so taken up with personal and local affairs of the moment that they are almost completely unaware of the larger picture. It is for such reasons that the more pessimistic prophets believe we have collectively, but unintentionally, set in motion a global movement that we have no means of stopping. To surrender in despair to what may appear to be inevitable will simply hasten the possible disasters. Yet some of these may have to occur before we are jolted out of our complacency. Just what these may be, we shall now explore.

CHAPTER II

Scenarios
of the Future

It is rather ironic that we can forecast the far distant future of this planet more clearly than we can foresee the immediate human future on its surface. As a result of twentieth-century science, we can say with some confidence that the earth will eventually become uninhabitable; the sun will finally exhaust its nuclear fuel and swell out to be a giant red ball that will swallow up the earth. This devastating scenario, however, is likely to occur some four billion years away. It may raise theoretical questions as to whether the universe as a whole, along with the phenomenon of life on this planet, has any ultimate significance, but otherwise this macro-future of the planet does not have any direct impact upon us.

What matters is our imminent future, particularly in the light of the 'end-times' outlined in Chapters 2–6, and the rise of the global problems discussed in Chapters 8–10. Predicting the human future is, however, more problematic than foretelling the future of the solar system. The story of the physical universe is wholly determined by its own inherent structures, which we commonly refer to as the laws of physics. Human history, by contrast, is not a mechanical process. More rigid forms of monotheism, it is true, have tended to regard our history as predetermined, as part of a divine plan.[1] Where God was conceived as creating the universe for a purpose, then, since he is also Almighty, his plan could not possibly fail. In the biblical tradition, God was thought to possess full knowledge of human history, past and present; and from time to time he chose to reveal the future to certain select people, such as Joseph, Daniel and John of Patmos. The belief that human history was the working out of the will of an all-powerful, all-knowing God led to a somewhat fatalistic attitude in popular Islam and to the doctrine of predestination in Christianity.

The difficulty with such rigid forms of monotheism, as with philosophical determinism, is that they deny the reality of human freedom and choice. In the end they make a mockery of all morality, for if one has no real power to choose one cannot be held responsible for one's actions. However, acknowledging the reality of human choice also suggests that the human future is open-ended and indeterminable. And the reason that we cannot predict the forthcoming events of human history is that the human future is quite unknowable (even by any presumed God!): it is yet to be shaped by an almost infinite number of human choices, most of them relatively unimportant.

Moving from the purely physical universe to the biosphere, we must allow for chance and choice as well as cause and effect. All living creatures have some power of choice. Even the sparrow, with its little bird brain, has to make tiny choices about the sticks to pick up to construct its nest. It is in the human species, however, that the capacity to choose becomes greatly magnified, so that considered decisions begin to replace instinct. The existence of human choice will always prevent the human sciences from predicting the future with the accuracy available to the physical sciences. The study of humans and their future is more appropriately called an art, for it can never really be a science.

In our attempt to look into the twenty-first century we can, however, sketch possibilities and probabilities, based on past events and present trends. We get some idea of the scale of potential change if we glance back at what the future looked like to westerners at the beginning of the twentieth century. The European empires had spread right around the globe. Every area of the so-called dark continent of Africa had at last been penetrated by Europeans. Many countries of the Islamic world had become subject to European imperialism. The British people proudly claimed that the sun never set on their empire. The United States had emerged from the civil war and was welcoming a bright and expanding future. Only the countries of what westerners called the Far East – such as China, Tibet, Japan and Korea – were still bound by tradition and hardly touched by the waves of cultural change from the west. Christian missionaries, moving out on those waves, fully expected to evangelise the whole world in their generation. Science and technology were growing so fast that there seemed to be no limit to what humans would eventually achieve.

In 1900, therefore, westerners looked into the future with extreme optimism. They welcomed the twentieth century with great expectations. They may have been surprised, but excitedly so, if they had been told of the full extent of the technological advance that was to take place, such as television, the computer revolution and space travel. But how shocked they would have been by the world wars, the 'great depression', the spread of communism, the rise of fascist totalitarian states, the construction of nuclear weapons, and genocide, to say nothing of the dramatic changes in social customs. Brzezinski has called the twentieth century the 'Century of Megadeath'. It has been reckoned that, in addition to the 87 million lives taken in the wars of this century, an additional 80 million were deliberately killed or starved to death in Hitler's death camps, Stalin's labour camps, Mao's cultural revolution and the 'killing-fields' of Cambodia.[2] So much for the advanced civilisation of the twentieth century.

All of these things, good and bad, have occurred in only 100 years. With this experience of what we humans are capable of doing to one another, and with the decline of belief in a providential God, there is far less confidence about the human future among informed people today than there was at the beginning of the twentieth century.

What will occur in the next 100 years? Social change is still accelerating and on a global scale; the population is expanding exponentially; technology is ever more powerful; the environment is under acute pressure. So we need to prepare ourselves for more drastic events and changes than we have known before. However, some things we expect to change or even to disappear may surprisingly survive as they are. The future is truly unknowable.

An important difference between the twenty-first century and those that preceded it is that the western world as a whole can no longer seek comfort and security in the certainties of a century ago. As late as the 1940s King George VI could still seek divine help against the enemy in World War II by calling for a national 'Day of Prayer' (though the enemy was making similar appeals to the same God). With the end of Christian orthodoxy, we have to come to terms with the fact that we humans are on our own in the world. Humanity has 'come of age', as theologian Dietrich Bonhoeffer observed from his prison cell.[3]

Thus we have to take more responsibility for the future of our species than we have in the past. We do not live, as our forebears thought, in a permanent, earthly home where our security is assured by the watchful eye and guiding hand of a parental God. Rather, we are on a spaceship hurtling into the unknown, just like the solitary passenger in Stanley Kubrick's *2001: A Space Odyssey* after he had tried to regain control by dismantling his spaceship's computer.

Our planet home is a giant spaceship, and it is vulnerable to all the objects wandering aimlessly about in space. Small ones are hitting us daily but do no harm; they are usually burnt up in the atmosphere. Large ones hit us occasionally, like the one thought to have brought an end to the dinosaurs some 60 million years ago. That a similar one will hit the earth in the future is probable rather than possible; the chance that it will occur in the next century may be slight but it cannot be ruled out.

For these and other reasons, humanity in the twentieth century has been forced to contemplate an end to human existence on the planet. In 1954

Harrison Brown said in *The Challenge of Man's Future*: 'Just as we know rationally that the time will come when each of us as individuals will perish, so we know that our country, our culture and our species cannot exist for ever. Sometime there must be an end.'[4]

The chief reasons for looking into the twenty-first century with grave concern are to be found not in outer space but on the surface of the planet and within humankind itself. As we have seen in the last two chapters, we are now receiving alarming signals about what we are doing both to ourselves and to all life on the planet. Some prophetic voices tell us that we have only a few years to make vital and far-reaching decisions – or else human existence on this planet will come to a tragic end long before the earth is swallowed by a dying sun. Even within the coming century, they say, we could be facing the end of human existence as we know it. Such an end would cause to pale into insignificance the end-times we considered in the earlier chapters.

Let us now survey some scenarios of the global human future. None of these is certain but all are possible; some are probable. None are alternatives; they nearly all impinge on one another. Each can exacerbate the others, so that the cumulative effect could be worse than we can contemplate. We start with the most catastrophic scenarios. The cautionary voices warning us of these are the modern equivalent of the ancient prophets.

SCENARIO I *A Thermonuclear Holocaust*

During the twentieth century this scenario became uncomfortably close as a result of the cold war between the capitalist west and the socialist east. When the danger of an all-out nuclear war seemed imminent, fictional documentaries appeared on our television screens, showing the results. All sane and responsible people are agreed that no one could really win a nuclear war and that such an event would be a disaster of the first magnitude. But this threat has not been eliminated with the end of the cold war. Now that we possess the knowledge of how to construct nuclear warheads there can be no return to the relative safety of the pre-nuclear age.

Nuclear weapons have already been used once. About eight or nine nations now possess nuclear warheads, many of them a great deal more destructive than the atomic bombs used at Hiroshima and Nagasaki. The number of nuclear-capable nations is likely to increase. Further, we have to reckon with the sheer stupidity of which humans are capable, especially in a position of authority. People like Hitler, Stalin, Mao and Saddam Hussein do not hesitate to bring the whole world down with them if their own power is threatened.

As terrorist activities spread, it would be possible for nuclear war to be triggered by the irresponsible behaviour of a relatively small group or nation, and for it quickly to escalate as the more responsible nations resorted to their nuclear arsenals to end the conflict. But a nuclear war would do such irreparable damage to both humanity and the ecology of the planet that it could bring an end not to specific acts of aggression but to all the higher forms of life on the planet.

SCENARIO 2 *World War III*

Even if the use of nuclear warheads were avoided, the outbreak of an international conflict using more conventional but highly sophisticated weapons remains possible. This could arise from the 'clash of civilisations' (as contemplated by Huntington) or from the attempt of nations to extend their possession of land, both for living space and to gain control over resources.

The very finiteness of the earth and its resources means that there is increasing competition among nations and international corporates for possession. During the twentieth century it was the oil crisis that shook the world economy. Control of the oil deposits rather than the sovereignty of Kuwait was the key to the Gulf War. Not only oil, but also many other minerals and even pure water are going to be in short supply in the twenty-first century. The natural resources of the earth are also unequally shared. It has been estimated that, if the whole world enjoyed a standard of living and energy consumption equal to the US average, the world's fossil fuel reserves would last only 20 years. Brzezinski has said: 'The world can be seen as divided into two mankinds, living in two distinct cultures: the rich minority and poor majority. By the end of the century, the first might number somewhere round 1 billion and the second account for the remaining 5 billion.'5

The gap between the rich and the poor nations is growing, and this inequality is already building up explosive tensions. Thus the factors leading to past international hostilities have been intensified through globalisation; the risk of armed conflict grows greater. There are smouldering hot-spots all around the world and any one of them could escalate with little warning. World War III could leave the earth much more impoverished than World War II, even if the finality of a thermonuclear catastrophe was avoided.

SCENARIO 3 *The Rise of Authoritarian Dictatorships*

Wherever there are signs of widespread social discontent and/or the fear of war, we have the conditions in which people are ready to give their blind allegiance to a charismatic, authoritarian leader in the belief that he or she will be able to restore a more ordered and secure environment and save them from a much worse fate.

With the decline of hereditary monarchies over the last two centuries, dictatorship and constitutional democracy have become the two principal forms of government around the world. Democracy is not proving to be as steady and permanent as expected: powerful lobby groups and financial interests can too easily destabilise it. When this happens a totalitarian government often takes over. Rule by dictators has taken several different forms. During the twentieth century we have seen dictatorships arise not only in Germany, Italy, Russia and China but also in South American countries and in the new states of Africa and Asia.

There is every sign that this form of twentieth-century government will continue to occur, and possibly on a much larger scale. During times of domestic or foreign crisis, most constitutional governments have conferred emergency powers on the chief executive. These can easily provide the opportunity for democratically elected leaders to overthrow democracy and rule dictatorially thereafter. Because of globalisation, the twenty-first century may see dictators ruling over unions of nations and even over the whole world. There has already been a swing to the political right in many democracies, and a call for more rigid social controls. The island state of Singapore is even held up by some as a model of the firm, if somewhat repressive, government. Just as population and other pressures brought stricter social control to Singapore, so the same problems on a global scale are likely to lead us to this dilemna: face social chaos following the breakdown of law and order, or accept more authoritarian government with the subsequent loss of some recently gained personal freedoms.

SCENARIO 4 *Mass Starvation*

Starvation on a colossal scale is one of the more probable global catastrophes. People are already starving in large numbers; between 500 million and a billion people are currently estimated to be already severely undernourished. The factors causing these famines show every sign of accelerating rather than diminishing. The human population has quadrupled during the twentieth century and is likely to increase by up to 50 per cent by 2025. Of the eight or nine billion people then living, some six and a half billion will be in the poorer states; it is estimated that Bangladesh will have grown from 115 to 235 million, Egypt from 50 to 125 million, India from 855 to 1440 million. Even if the total population does not go beyond eight billion (as some claim), mass starvation cannot be avoided.

There are two chief reasons for the probability of mass starvation in the future: the inability of the poorer nations to grow enough food, owing to loss of arable land, droughts and a rapidly growing population; and the fact that our monetary system militates against the redistribution of food from the richer countries with surpluses to poorer nations with starving populations (see Scenario 7).

SCENARIO 5 *Pandemics*

Expanding populations used to be held in check by plagues and epidemics. Some see these as nature's way of restoring ecological balance when the numbers of one species increase beyond the capacity of the environment to support it. Fatal diseases are far from being the ideal way of reducing the human population, yet they are likely to recur in spite of modern medical knowledge.

The Black Death of 1346–1349 killed a third of the inhabitants in many of the areas to which it spread. More died from the Spanish Influenza epidemic of 1918–1919 than were killed in World War I. This was the most severe influenza outbreak of the twentieth century and, in terms of total numbers of deaths, possibly the most devastating epidemic in human history. Populations throughout the world were affected, by three successive waves of the pandemic (as it is more appropriately called). It spread to nearly every inhabited part of the world, causing an estimated 30 million deaths.

New diseases can break out at any time. For example, in the last quarter of the twentieth century there suddenly emerged the frightening new disease of AIDS (Acquired Immune Deficiency Syndrome). Caused by a virus called HIV, it has the capacity to attack and destroy the human immune system, leaving the individual vulnerable to the infections that eventually cause death. The first cases of AIDS were identified in 1981 in Los Angeles, and HIV was isolated in 1983. By December 1996 more than eight million cases of AIDS were known worldwide and these led to six million deaths. By then about 23 million individuals throughout the world were thought to be infected with HIV, more than 90 per cent of them in developing countries.

In the future, not only will more virulent strains of the older diseases probably evolve, but also entirely new diseases will appear. Medical science, remarkable though its achievements have been, is engaged in a touch-and-go struggle to retain its ascendancy over disease.[6] New surgical skills, treatments and medicines are often outstripping our capacity to afford them. In developing countries there has always been a substantial gap (now widening) between what medical science can do and what the vast majority of people can afford to have done for them. This gap is now surfacing in the affluent countries, where public health systems are under severe financial pressure.

In addition to organic disease (bacterial and viral illness), the human organism is being exposed to multiple changes to its environment, mostly through modern technology. Radiation waves, genetic alteration of food and drastic changes in the traditional diet may have a cumulative effect. Cancerous conditions are increasing fairly rapidly, and this may be the result of environmental factors. Widespread fear about the long-term consequences of these environmental changes seems entirely justified.

Thus over-population, starvation and malnutrition in the poorer countries; worsening sanitation in large urban areas; and the unintended effects of advancing technology – all have the potential to bring new and deadly diseases, and pandemics on a colossal scale.

SCENARIO 6 *Destruction of the Ecological Balance*
In 1989 a report from the United Nations Environment Programme issued this warning:

> If the world continues to accept disappearing tree-cover, land degradation, the expansion of deserts, the loss of plant and animal species, air and water pollution, and the changing chemistry of the atmosphere it will also have to accept economic decline and social disintegration . . . such disintegration would bring human suffering on a scale that has no precedent . . .'[7]

Many governments now have ministries of the environment (or similar agencies), but they often pay only lip-service to the grave issues raised by the endangered eco-system. Governments and their officials usually give low priority to problems in the environment; in any case, they argue, there is no unanimity among the experts about the dangers and/or their causes. And when the changes in the environment are not readily perceived as catastrophic, there is no sense of urgency.

For example, who really notices that the amount of carbon dioxide in the atmosphere has increased by 25 per cent since the middle of the nineteenth century (as a result of the burning of fossil fuels, along with destruction of rainforests)? And can the ordinary person really be expected to notice that the earth's average temperature has risen by $0.5°C$ in the last 80 years? It is only when scientists describe the future consequences of these trends that alarm bells begin to ring. There is a direct connection between the current changes in the world's atmosphere and the rise in average temperature; this is known as global warming or the 'greenhouse effect'. A growing number of scientists have predicted that, if present trends continue, there will be significant alterations in climate patterns from the beginning of the twenty-first century onward. Global average temperatures could increase by as much as 5°C by the middle of the century. The rise in global temperature would produce new weather patterns and extremes of drought and rainfall. This would seriously disrupt food production in many regions and reduce even further the amount of food available to deal with growing starvation. Many believe there has been strong evidence of these changes during the 1990s.

Global warming would also cause the polar ice caps and mountain glaciers to melt rapidly. This, coupled with the fact that seawater expands when warmed, could cause sea levels to rise by up to half a metre. Low-lying regions such as Bangladesh, Holland, the Nile Delta and some Polynesian islands would be flooded and whole populations would have to be relocated.

A large number of scientists support some or all of these predictions, although others maintain that they are overstated. The potential problems are of such magnitude, however, that if we wait for irrefutable evidence before taking steps to halt the emission of gases and the destruction of rainforests, it will be too late (quite literally) to 'stem the tide'.

It is even more difficult to provide convincing evidence of the dangers to life caused by the rapid extinction of species and by other forms of ecological damage. Because our knowledge of the many delicate balances in the ecology of the planet is still in its infancy, and because what is known is not widely understood, the consequences of what the human race is (in its ignorance) doing to the earth may turn out to be even more serious than global warming.

SCENARIO 7 *Collapse of the Global Economy*

The emerging global economy is fragile and vulnerable, simply because of its size and complexity. The increasing global population will add further pressures. Rapid population growth requires heavier investment in education, health and transport merely to maintain these services at their present levels. The countries of the developed world already find it difficult to provide national services in these areas. There is now increased competition for a fair share of these services, not only within a country but also between countries. Even more serious is the competition for an equal share of such basic natural resources as food and water. In a competitive environment, the powerful will gain and retain control, refusing to share with the weak and the disadvantaged, except in the most miserly fashion.

For these and other reasons, the global economy will be subject to unpredictable fluctuations. Moreover, since the global economy already affects most if not all of the regional economies, it will be difficult for national governments to do any long-term planning. If the global economy collapses, it will lead to widespread economic and social chaos far greater than that caused by the 1929 Wall Street crash – which led to the great depression in the western world.

Some suggest that the international monetary system of western capitalism may suffer the same sudden collapse as state socialism did in Russia and its satellite countries. In 1998 international financier George Soros startled some people with his book *The Crisis of Global Capitalism*. He argued that we are already in the early stages of a global bear market which will lead to a global recession, a worldwide depression and the disintegration of the capitalist system. Some economists and commentators are warning that it is no longer a case of *if* the global economy crashes, but *when*.

The collapse of the global economy would raise serious questions about the future of capitalism. As William Greider has pointed out: 'Capitalism, for all its wondrous creativity and wealth, has not yet found a way to clothe the poor and feed the hungry unless they pay for it.'[8] It allows unused foodstuffs to pile up in the producing nations while millions go hungry elsewhere, and is powerless to use these surpluses constructively. Neither has capitalism found a way to keep all able-bodied people usefully employed and contributing to the common good. Unemployment has been a continual problem ever since the industrial revolution, and it is getting worse.

The already noticeable gap in per capita income between the rich and the poor (whether nations or individuals) will continue to widen. Even among the affluent nations of the western world, the rich are getting richer and the poor are getting the poorer. The economic gap is now widening, rather than lessening, between the developed nations and the developing nations. So Greider believes that global capitalism, since it not only allows but actually causes the rich to get richer and the poor to get poorer, 'will probably experience a series of terrible events – wrenching calamities which are economic, or social or environmental in nature – before common sense can prevail'.[9]

SCENARIO 8 *The Global Spread of Terrorism*
Terrorism has been practised throughout history and throughout the world. In the twentieth century we have witnessed a resurgence of terror-

ism in spite of the new emphasis on human rights. Some governments have resorted to terrorist tactics – arbitrary arrest, indefinite imprisonment, torture, and execution – in order to create a climate of fear and so force submission to their rule. But we more commonly associate the term terrorism with individuals, political organisations, racist and other groups attempting to destabilise or overthrow existing situations. The issue may be a dispute over land possession (Palestinians and Israelis), conflicts over religion (Catholics and Protestants in Northern Ireland), or the failure of protesters to achieve any success (assassination of doctors who perform clinical abortions). The victims of modern terrorism (unlike those of the past) are often innocent civilians who are picked at random or who merely happen to be in the wrong place at the wrong time. Whenever people become frustrated and desperate, either because the future is frightening or because they have failed to achieve their ends by other means, they are tempted to resort to unpredictable violence in order to publicise their cause or provoke a response. Since any act of violence is certain to attract television coverage and give exposure to the terrorists' goals, the electronic media have (unintentionally) greatly magnified the effectiveness of terrorist acts.

The growing tensions and frustrations that will probably arise in the twenty-first century are likely to increase terrorism, both on the part of governments and on the part of sectional groups. The preservation of law and order and the guarantee of personal security will become increasingly difficult.

SCENARIO 9 *Sliding into Social Chaos*
Less dramatic than the scenarios outlined above would be the gradual decline of social order. Ultimately this is as alarming as any sudden catastrophe. Every new generation has of course been inclined to look back through rose-coloured spectacles and lament the fact that society is experiencing a moral decline. However, there are good reasons for believing that anti-social behaviour is on the increase, not only because we have statistics to show it, but also because we can see the reasons for it. Human society almost everywhere is undergoing the transition from being a predominantly closed society to a more open society (as discussed in Chapter 8). In an open society there is much less pressure, either from one's peers or from the governing authority, to conform to mutually accepted standards of behaviour; it is even less clear what those common standards are.

If any one of the above scenarios comes to pass, even partially, the delicate and complex set of human relationships that constitute a healthy human society will be disturbed. Social order can descend into social chaos very quickly, with its own disastrous consequences for the future of humanity. In this age of individualism there is all too little appreciation of how much our humanity depends on being nurtured within a stable, cohesive society. Only because our species evolved within such societies do we now have, each of us, the capacity to experience reflective self-consciousness and develop an individual identity. This process took place over millions of years, as language and culture evolved. When the fabric of a society begins to decay, the resulting problems tend to multiply at an alarming rate.

In the transition from traditional tribalism to globalism, there will be a delicate period of social instability. Freed from the restraints of tribalism and religious orthodoxies, and not yet aware of the imperatives of globalism and the eco-system, modern individualism can manifest itself in massively self-centred behaviour. Until we achieve a more stable form of global society, there is real danger of descent into social chaos. Even if we muddle our way through by crises, as we have done before, it will not be without widespread pain and anguish.

SCENARIO 10 *Saving Ourselves and the Planet*

Of one thing we can be sure: future catastrophes will not occur because they have been sent as a divine punishment. Now we do not have to 'contend with spiritual hosts of wickedness in heavenly places',[10] but with the dark side of the human condition. If there are alarming problems ahead, we will have brought them upon ourselves, either through ignorance or wilfulness. Carl Jung once said in a television interview: 'Man himself is the origin of all coming evil.' It is because humanity is at war both with itself and with the planet that we now face an uncertain future.

We humans have created these global problems; it is only we who can solve them. The final scenario, therefore, is the one in which we manage to avert the worst of the catastrophic scenarios and save both ourselves and the planet. Is this possible? Can we do it in time? Do we have the wisdom, ingenuity and skill? The optimists are sure that we have; the pessimists doubt it.

The optimists acknowledge that we face global problems but believe that talk of a coming nemesis has been grossly overstated. Such could even be dangerous, they claim, since it might become a self-fulfilling prophecy. They see many encouraging signs – for example, in the way we are already coping with some of the problems. They believe we are sufficiently intelligent and knowledgeable to overcome all coming crises. John Naisbitt and Patricia Aburdene in their book *Megatrends 2000* spoke derogatorily of the prophets of doom. When they surveyed current cultural trends in 1990, they came to a very positive view of globalisation. They predicted for the 1990s a booming global economy, a renaissance in the arts, the privatisation of the welfare state, the triumph of the individual, the emergence of global lifestyles, and the rise of women to positions of leadership. Some of these predictions have been at least partially fulfilled, though some have not.

The pessimists however point out that the problems of the new era are often far advanced before we become aware of them, and that they frequently turn out to be worse than at first thought. Moreover, individuals and governments are equally reluctant to take the stern measures required, when these interfere with our personal interests. Take, for example, the question of world peace, for which the United Nations was originally established. Brzezinski rightly says: 'The UN's time has finally come. It is only within the framework of that global organisation that the common problems of mankind can be collectively addressed.'[11] But here we face an obstacle. The five permanent members of the Security Council hold the power of veto over UN decisions because they are unwilling to let power slip out of their hands. This has hampered the power of the UN from the beginning, and reflects our reluctance to surrender personal interests in favour of the common good. This reluctance could be the undoing of the human race.

So who are we to believe – the prophets of doom or the optimists? As the future is unknowable, we cannot be sure who is right. Perhaps that in itself is important. As Moltmann wisely points out:

> We cannot know [whether modern society has any future] and we must not know. If we knew that humanity is not going to survive we should not do anything more for our children but would say 'after us, the deluge'. If we knew that humanity is going to survive, we should not do anything either . . . Because we cannot know whether humanity is going to survive or not, we have to act today as if the future of the whole of humanity were dependent on us.[12]

It is interesting to observe that even the more optimistic voices refer to the need for some radical change of a vaguely spiritual kind. The authors of *Megatrends 2000* wrote:

> The most exciting breakthroughs of the 21st century will occur not because of technology, but because of an expanding concept of what it means to be human . . . Humanity will probably not

be rescued by a *deus ex machina* either in the form of a literal Second Coming (the fundamentalist expectation) or by friendly spaceships (the New Age version). Though we will be guided by a revived spirituality, the answers will have to come from us. Apocalypse or Golden Age. The choice is ours'.[13]

Some even predicted a religious revival in the new millennium. Alvin and Heidi Toffler, in their book *War and Anti-war, Survival at the Dawn of the 21st Century* said:

> We are witnessing the sudden eruption of a new civilization on the planet, carrying with it a knowledge-intensive way of creating wealth that is trisecting and transforming the entire global system today. Everything in that system is now mutating, from its basic components . . . to the way they interrelate . . . to the speed of their interaction . . . to the interests over which countries contend . . . to the kinds of wars that may result and which need to be prevented.[14]

William Greider, strongly critical of global capitalism in his book *One World Ready or Not*, still believed there were remedies available if we were prepared to face up to them boldly. He sensed 'a new ideology struggling to be born – a new global consciousness'.[15] It would share some of the ideals that led to the socialist experiments of the twentieth century but it would also embrace the ecological imperatives.

What sort of 'revived spirituality', 'new global consciousness', 'new civilisation' could possibly occur? There are Muslims, Buddhists and Christians (to name but a few) who, while fully acknowledging the reality of the threats discussed in the above scenarios, still believe their own tradition contains the answers. Howard Snyder, for example, in his book *Earth Currents*, offers a clear and balanced cultural analysis of the chief global trends he sees operating in the period 1900–2030. He agrees that 'Earth is experiencing an unprecedented global struggle. Powerful trends point to a possible global crisis around the year 2020.'[16] He acknowledges that for any world view to be adequate it must be ecological. He then concludes by commending, as the solution, a return to a fairly traditional form of the Christian story, even suggesting that 'Jesus embodies and transcends the post-modern sensibility'.[17]

The reasons conventional Christianity cannot possibly supply the answers to our global problems have been fully discussed in Part 1. We have come to the end of the Christian era and have entered the post-Christian world. Moreover, this global, post-Christian world is, for better or for worse, largely the product of the Christian west. The problems that have resulted can be solved only within the context of an embryonic global society. If the global society emerges, it will require humanity to develop a new consciousness and a new form of spirituality.

CHAPTER 12

A Faith for the Future

Globalisation is a process that cannot now be held back. With it come, however, extremely serious threats, both to the well-being of the human species and to the future of planetary life. The human species may bring about its own demise by warring with its own kind and with the planet. In this highly sophisticated, industrialised, technological civilisation we possess a great deal more knowledge than the tribal cultures of the pre-Axial Period. Yet perhaps we possess less real wisdom, relative to our time. As T.S. Eliot wrote:

> All our knowledge brings us nearer to our ignorance,
> All our ignorance brings us nearer to death,
> But nearness to death no nearer to GOD.
> Where is the Life we have lost in living?
> Where is the wisdom we have lost in knowledge?
> Where is the knowledge we have lost in information?[1]

As ancient humanity slowly accumulated its knowledge, the early cultures learned to accommodate themselves to the forces and pressures of the natural environment. Contemporary humankind has now to relearn this – on a global scale, and with the benefit of immense scientific knowledge. We also have to counter the momentum of destructive forces which, unknowingly, we have set in motion.

By the same token, globalisation also offers great opportunities. If the human species is not to self-destruct (be it with a 'bang' or 'whimper' to use T.S. Eliot's phrase),[2] it must develop into a global society which will find cohesion in its own distinctive life, in what may be called a global human culture. The very idea of a global society is, of course, a religious vision which has already had a long history. The Israelite prophets looked hopefully towards it. Christians spoke of it as the coming of the Kingdom of God. Muslims expected it when Islam embraced all peoples in a brotherhood. Karl Marx hailed the coming of the classless society. What now follows is simply my personal vision and hope for a global society in the world to come.

Humans currently exist in a large number of societies, each with its own identity and culture. These each retain aspects of tribalism, which is showing more vigorous tendencies as people fear that the globalising process will destroy their cultural identity. Different cultures need not be obliterated by the formation of any global society, but they do need to be relativised. Regional tribalism must give way, where necessary, to globalism. Just as in tribalism the destiny of the tribe is more important than that of the individual, so the destiny and well-being of humanity as a whole must now take precedence over that of any tribe, nation or regional culture.

The culture in which the global society finds its cohesion needs to be able to draw all human groups and individuals into some form of shared life, a degree of commonality that allows for harmony between peoples and also with the planetary environment. This global culture need not replace existing cultures but it should provide an umbrella to cover them. Each human culture needs to continue with some independence in its own locality, in a way that enables it to relate to the whole. This global culture will rest on a shared view of the universe, a common story of human origins, a shared set of values and goals, and a basic set of behavioural patterns to be practised in common.

A future global culture will need to evolve of its own accord. It will not be achieved simply by implementing a grandiose plan designed by a body such as the United Nations; even less can it be imposed by the dictates of one or more strong leaders. Repressive measures taken by powerful human authorities, however well intentioned, can do no more than delay global disasters, and may instead exacerbate them. A global culture implies a widespread recognition that the coming crises threaten all humans equally, and requires an urgent collective response to the imminent threats to human survival. For this new culture to emerge, there must be a willingness for most cultures and most people in the world to work together to achieve a common global goal.

The global culture will evolve, if it evolves at all, out of the spread of global consciousness (as described in Chapter 8) – a consciousness of the human predicament, an appreciation of humanity's dependence on the earth, and a willingness to act jointly in response. These are the very things which may be said to constitute the raw material of the spirituality of the coming global culture. For like all earlier cultures, global culture will depend for its goals, values, motivation and creative energy on the possession of a religious dimension.

Emile Durkheim, one of the founding fathers of sociology, wrote in 1915:

> There is something eternal in religion which is destined to surive all the particular symbols in which religious thought has successively enveloped itself. There can be no society which does not feel the need of upholding and reaffirming at regular intervals the collective sentiments and the collective ideas which make its unity and its personality.[3]

Historian Arnold Toynbee agreed, understanding religion to be 'an intrinsic and distinctive trait of human nature. It is a human being's necessary response to the challenge of mysteriousness of the phenomena that he encounters in virtue of his uniquely human faculty of consciousness.'[4] In his late work, *Mankind and Mother Earth*, he foresaw that the present threat to humankind's survival could be removed only by a revolutionary change of heart in individual human beings, and that only religion could generate the willpower needed for such a task. Toynbee observed that since the dawn of civilisation there has been a growing 'morality gap' between humankind's physical power over nature and the level of its spirituality – a gap that has increased rapidly in the last 200 years. So he closed his book with the alarming question: 'Will mankind murder Mother Earth or will he redeem her?'

Can there be some global form of spirituality which does for the whole of humankind what the previous religions did for their cultures? And if it is possible, how will it arise? It will not be based on any one race or ethnic tradition, as religion was in the pre-Axial age; it must arise from and involve the whole human race. Nor will it emerge from some new divine revelation, like the post-Axial religions; it will need to be naturalistic and humanistic in origin and form. It is unlikely to originate with one charismatic person and then spread to different parts of the world, as Buddhism, Christianity and Islam did. It will not be built on some external authority, since people live today more by internalised authority. The vision, goals and values to be found in any global religion must possess their own inherent power to win conviction; they must appear to be self-evidently true to all humans irrespective of their cultural past.

Whereas the religious traditions from the Axial Period onwards each arose at one point and then radiated outwards, the global religion (if it comes at all) will probably arise more or less spontaneously out of the common human predicament. It will arise simply because its time has come. Just as the cultural change of the Axial Period occurred more or less simultaneously and independently at several points on the earth's surface, so the new global form of spirituality may well germinate at many different points and then take more visible form as those points form a network. In other words, the coming global religion may evolve out of the diversity of the past, as more and more people become alert to the common threats and dangers ahead. Out of a growing shared experience, human creativity may collectively rise to the occasion. However, none of these things is certain, and the future remains an open question.

In the evolution of culture there are often crises and radical changes, but there are never complete breaks. There will be both continuity and discontinuity with the religious past. Whatever evolves (or is collectively created) in response to the new global situation will grow partly from past traditions. It will not be simply a new and more extensive version of an earlier religion; the exclusive claims so dominant in Christianity and Islam, for example, have become inappropriate for the pluralistic future and may well be judged offensive. All religious traditions will contribute to the future, and those that can respond most flexibly and freely to the current challenges are likely to offer the most.

Each religious tradition must be left free to work out the best way to share in the new global future. Speaking from within the Christian tradition, Harvard theologian Gordon Kaufman in 1993 said something like this: since we are moving very rapidly toward one world, and a global consciousness is already beginning to enter into us, our religious practices and thinking must reflect this great historical fact; all the particular religious traditions have become outmoded and can no longer meet the needs of our new cultural situation in their traditional form.[5]

Similarly, Jürgen Moltmann has proposed that the great task for the religions of the world, and above all for the Christian church, is to be reformed so profoundly that they can contribute to the 'religion of modern times'.[6] Although we are not in a position to predict, let alone prescribe, the shape of the global religion, we can say that it will evolve out of preceding cultural traditions. Since death and resurrection have long been central Christian themes, Christianity is well prepared for the task of letting its old conventional self die, in order to rise again as a facet of a new global religion.[7]

The introduction noted that some of those who were silenced or marginalised by orthodoxy in the past now seem prophetic. Feuerbach, for example, was one of the first to understand the positive value of religion in society, even when religion is understood as a human creation and expressed in naturalistic terms. He led us back to the old nature religions as the base from which religion must start once again. Feuerbach agreed with his theological teacher, Schleiermacher, that '[t]he basis of religion is the feeling of dependency', but went on to assert that 'that upon which human beings are fully dependent is originally, nothing other than Nature. Nature is the first, original object of religion'.[8]

Our dependence upon nature is very basic. We share with the other animals the need for air, drink, food, shelter, survival and the regeneration of the species. Built into every species, including the human species, are the instincts to survive and to procreate. These simple needs and animal instincts were the starting point from which our primitive human ancestors set out slowly and unconsciously to create human culture and all the various forms in which they expressed their devotion.

We too must go back to that simplicity. The need for pure air, clean water, healthy food, adequate shelter, the regeneration of the species and the overcoming of all threats to human survival – these have once again become the central issues to which we must 'devote' ourselves. They are genuinely 'religious' issues. In spite of all our modern sophistication, scientific knowledge, technological expertise, philosophical wisdom and traditional forms of spirituality, it is from these basic instincts for survival and regeneration that the new path of faith will come. Thus the new global religion will draw not only from the more ideological and intellectualised faiths of the Axial Period but from the preceding nature religions. These not only survived until modern times in many indigenous cultures, such as those of the New Zealand Maori and the North American Indians, but they often continued beneath the surface of the post-Axial faiths, despite strenuous efforts over the centuries to destroy them.

Our ancient forebears stood in such awe of the forces of nature that they created concepts, symbols and a language by which to understand them. These concepts and symbols constituted the raw material not only of their religion but also of their 'science' (or knowledge). The basic realities they conceptualised in order to explain the phenomena and natural events of their world they spoke of as gods and spirits. Cycles of stories or myths told how the gods came to be and what they controlled. The Maori creation myth, for example, related how Rangi the sky-god was forced out of his embrace of Papa the earth-mother by the gods of nature whom they had procreated. Maori religion, as everywhere in pre-Axial times, consisted of showing proper devotion to these forces of nature, of acknowledging their obligations to the gods. Our ancestors did this by devising and performing the appropriate rituals.

We now understand the natural world differently and we have developed a different set of concepts. Where they talked about spirit, we talk about physical energy. Where they explained the phenomena in terms of gods and spirits, we do so in terms of electrons and quarks, gravity and nuclear forces, DNA and chromosomes, immune systems and amino acids, neurones and synapses. For us these are the components of reality that explain the nature of the world, the phenomenon of life within it, and even how we human organisms think through our brains. Even Feuerbach defined nature as 'everything which man . . . experiences directly and sensuously as the ground and substance of his life. Nature is light, electricity, magnetism, air, water, fire, earth, animals, plants; nature is man, insofar as he is a being who acts instinctively and unconsciously.'[9]

In the last two or three centuries, this new way of understanding the natural world has been emerging alongside the traditional religious superstructure. For many the traditional religious perspective continued to provide a meaning for human life. For others the competing claims of science and religion led to profound inner conflict. Some abandoned traditional religion altogether, only to find that scientific knowledge of the natural world does not in itself provide answers to the meaning and purpose of life.

Those who practised the earlier nature religions saw the natural world operating with some meaning and purpose because they unconsciously projected their own thoughts and feelings into the supposed gods of nature, including Mother Earth and the Sky Father. Our modern understanding leads us to see the natural world as lacking any ultimate purpose. It operates according to both chance and necessity.[10] The only area in which we find any real evidence of purposeful behaviour is human activity. One of the great mysteries of the natural world is that out of it has evolved the human species, which has the capacity to think, to ask questions, to look for meaning and to be creative. It was part of the genius of Teilhard de Chardin, in *The Phenomenon of Man*, to relocate the chief mystery of nature in humankind itself.

There are now signs that we are beginning to recover some of the awe our ancestors felt towards the natural world. We are regaining some of their sense of dependence on the forces of nature. We are learning to appreciate the positive value in the nature religion of indigenous peoples; we see it as a genuine form of spirituality, no longer to be arrogantly dismissed as primitive magic. In addition, however, we also recognise *ourselves* as a part of nature in all its complexity and mystery. It is in the human species and its many cultures that meaning and purpose have become explicit aspects of nature. As some have already observed, it is through humankind that the universe has become conscious of itself.

Thus there are differences between us and the ancient worshippers of the gods of nature. We, including modern indigenous peoples, treat the gods of nature as symbolic rather than as objective realities. Whereas the ancients simply had to obey the dictates of their gods (as known within their traditions), we now find that, as a very important part of nature ourselves, an increasing measure of responsibility lies upon our species for the future of all planetary life.

All this has led us to question the brash, domineering attitude towards nature which characterised western thought increasingly in the twentieth century. Some suggest that we should resymbolise, as Mother Earth, the mystery and complexity of nature on which we depend; and that this should replace the way monotheism related all forces, natural and super-natural, to the Sky Father. Mother Earth would not now be some external spiritual being (as Gaia was in an earlier religion); rather, Mother Earth would be a consciously chosen symbol referring to everything about the earth's eco-system at which we can marvel and on which we depend.

Many of the particular aspects of nature, as we have seen, which ancient humans found awesome can be readily explained now in quite mundane ways, but our new picture of the universe is, in other ways, just as awe-inspiring. While the world we inhabit is confined to planet earth, we know that this is only the tiniest speck in a universe so vast that our minds can barely imagine it. We know very little indeed about what takes place in the rest of this universe. We may never know whether there is life in any other part of it. Life on our planet has apparently evolved over some three bil-lion years; our human species emerged only very recently, relative to the story of the earth, and more by accident than by any design. There is no obvious reason why we have evolved as we have, nor why there should be any life at all on this planet, since none of our planetary neighbours shows signs of life. The origin and purpose of human existence is itself a mystery.

In the religion of the coming global society, the forces of nature, the process of evolution and the existence of life itself will be the objects of respect and veneration. Thomas Berry, an American Catholic priest, wrote:

> Our new sense of the universe is itself a type of revelatory experi-ence. Presently we are moving beyond any religious expression so far known to the human into a meta-religious age, that seems

to be a new comprehensive context for all religions . . . The natural world itself is the primary economic reality, the primary edu-
cator, the primary governance, the primary technologist, the
primary healer, the primary presence of the sacred, the primary
moral value . . . The primary sacred community is the earth community. The human community becomes sacred through its participation in the larger planetary community.[11]

Some steps towards acknowledging the sacred character of the earth have
already been taken. We no longer restrict the concept of 'sanctuary' to the
church building or temple but are giving it back to the earth, in bird sanctuaries, fish sanctuaries and so on. The eco-sphere itself is gradually being
resanctified. The loving care of Mother Earth is in many quarters replacing
the former sense of obedience to the Heavenly Father. In her book *The
Body of God*, theologian Sallie McFague goes further, suggesting that the
combined influence of post-modern science and Christian faith requires
the construction of a new model in which we see the universe as the body
of God.[12]

The universe is itself so vast and mysterious that it is more than enough
to induce the sense of awe and joyful gratitude that characterised earlier
religious experience. The religious rituals of the future will celebrate the
wonder of the universe and the mystery of life. They will revolve around
the natural processes which have brought life into being and continue to
sustain it. It is salutary to remember that the great annual Christian festivals (mostly inherited from Judaism) all originated as festivals for the
changing seasons. The Jewish festivals of Passover and Unleavened Bread,
which later became the Christian Easter, originated as early spring festivals
celebrating the resurrection of nature to new life after the death of winter.[13] The Feast of Pentecost began as the early harvest festival, the Jewish
Feast of Booths as the vintage festival, Christmas as a New Year festival to
mark the passing of the shortest day and the return of the sun. As
humankind begins to appreciate again how much our earthly life depends
upon the conditions and processes of the earth itself, we will re-create the
appropriate festivals to celebrate the earth's role in our lives.

The new religious rituals will be based not only on our relationship to
the natural world, they will also celebrate everything we have come to value
in human existence, such as the importance of healthy human relationships, and the rich inheritance of human culture. This can already be seen
in the way Christians celebrate their chief ritual, known variously as Holy
Communion, the Lord's Supper or the Eucharist. For some time this has

been interpreted less as the commemoration of a sacrifice offered on an altar to God and more as the sharing of a common meal around a table to celebrate the rich and sacred character of human fellowship. That indeed is how it began.

Christmas, which is just as popular as ever, is already changing from being a commemoration of the birthday of a supposed saviour to a celebration of family life. Much to the chagrin of traditional Christian clergy, the widespread celebration of Easter survives primarily in the form of Easter eggs and Easter bunnies, which point back to a very ancient spring festival long before the Jewish Passover and the Christian commemoration of the death and resurrection of Jesus. Perhaps the new institutions of Mother's Day and Father's Day should not be dismissed as commercial gimmicks but interpreted as a more spontaneous desire to acknowledge specific roles in family relationships. Indeed, our new practice of devoting a particular day of the year, whether nationally or internationally, to some special feature of human society indicates a trend towards the making of new and appropriate rituals.

What then will this new faith, the religion of the future, look like? It is far too early to tell, but some broad outlines can be seen. I suggest that being religious in the global era will be:

- to be devoted to maximising the future for all living creatures whose destiny is increasingly in our hands;
- to place the needs of the coming global society before those of our own immediate family, tribe or nation;
- to develop a lifestyle consistent with preserving the balance of the planetary eco-system on which all living creatures depend;
- to refrain from all activities which endanger the future of all species;
- to set a high value on the total cultural legacy we have received from the past and which enables us to develop our potential to become human;
- to value the importance of the human relationships which bind us together into social groups and which enable us to become fully human;
- to promote the virtues of love, goodwill and peacefulness.

These general principles do no more than set the parameters of a global spirituality. For its detail, the new faith will need to draw on the cultures of the past, allowing for both the universality and the diversity of a rich global culture. There will not be 'only one way' of being religious (as Christian exclusivists love to assert) but a great variety of ways. There will not be one religious organisation operating globally, but rather a host of relatively small and somewhat diverse social groups, in which the members are bonded to one another on a personal basis. But if religion is to flourish in the global era, these groups must learn to be inclusive; they must be ready to welcome anyone wishing to join them and, even in their diversity, they will need to acknowledge a broad set of common goals and values, such as concern for the earth's future. Exclusivity, whether religious or ethnic, will be damaging to the future of the human race.

How much or how little of the traditional religious ritual and terminology is retained in new, transformed religious forms we cannot predict. That will depend on how ready people are to reshape their spiritual inheritance in response to the new global culture, for in the coming global era, new terms and concepts will be created, along with new rituals and patterns of social behaviour. As Don Cupitt says: 'We do not yet have any global religious vocabulary.'[14] In a future that draws on the diversity and richness of our past cultures, we should not expect one set of symbols and concepts to provide the 'religiously correct' language of a global religion. Each culture must be free to draw from its own tradition, but always in such a way as to direct it towards the needs of an ecologically sensitive global society. There is no one religious symbol or concept from the past which it is essential to retain for the spirituality of the global society, any more than the language of the whole world ought to be English, Arabic, Chinese or Latin. All languages and all symbols are humanly created. They have no permanence. They come and go, and change continually. So it is with religious symbols and concepts.

The word 'God', for example, may or may not continue to be used – though it has been so central to the Christian and other monotheistic traditions. If it does remain a significant religious symbol, it will no longer refer to an objective spiritual being. Theologian Gordon Kaufman has suggested that the function of this symbolic word 'God' is to serve as 'an ultimate point of reference'. It enables us to unify and order our experience of reality in our mental world. This leads him to say in *In Face of Mystery*: 'To believe in God is to commit oneself to a particular way of ordering one's life and action. It is to devote oneself to working towards a fully humane world within the ecological restraints here on planet Earth, while standing in piety and awe before the profound mysteries of existence.'[15]

That is why the word God is likely to continue for at least some time in the societies of the Christian west. It will symbolise the values we find com-

pelling, the goals we aspire to, and the meaning we seek in human existence. From the New Testament we have learned to say that 'God is love'.
Mahatma Gandhi taught us to say that 'God is truth'. To these we can readily add that 'God is life'. (In everyday English speech, evidence suggests
that the word 'life' is already replacing the word 'God'.)[16] 'God' sums up,
symbolises and unifies all that we value. That is why we can readily speak
of the 'God within us', as well as the 'God in our neighbour' and the 'God
in the mystery of the universe'. The God-symbol refers to the sum total of
all that concerns us most; it can call forth the same gamut of emotions of
awe, wonder, gratitude and obligation as it did in the past, when our forebears had a very different view of reality.

To worship God in the global era would mean, among other things, that
we stand in awe of this self-evolving universe, continually marvelling at the
living eco-sphere of this planet. We would be able to acknowledge the ines-
timable value of life in ourselves and in all other creatures, and express
gratitude to the successive generations of our human ancestors who have
slowly created our inheritance – the rich variety of human culture which
has enabled us to become the human beings we are. We would possess the
capacity to feel, to love and be loved, to show compassion and selfless sacrifice, to think and to be engaged in the quest for what is true and mean-
ingful. We would be strong enough to accept in a selfless fashion the
burden of responsibility now laid upon us for the future of our world and
all its planetary life.

Just as important as the attempt of each tradition to reinterpret their
symbols and rituals to meet the needs of the new spiritual parameters will
be the cross-fertilisation of cultures which takes place in the globalising
process. This has already been going on for some time, and is most likely
to accelerate, in spite of strong resistance by defenders of the traditional
forms of spirituality. Many in the Christian west have been attracted to the
non-theistic and more humanistic character of the Buddhist tradition, or
to the deep mystical spirituality of the Hindu tradition; others have been
attracted to the more physical practice of spirituality to be found in
Chinese tradition.

Within this complex, global pot-pourri of religious symbols and interchange of ideas, concepts and values, individuals will easily feel lost and
bewildered. This is a time when we must relearn the value of personal relationships, initially in our own family and then in society at large. We
humans are essentially social creatures and human society is an intricate
network of personal relationhips, experienced though not visible. Just as
we depend for physical existence on the forces of the natural world, so to

find meaning, fulfilment and purpose in life, we depend on the culture which continues to shape us, on what we receive from one another and on what we are able to give back in return. We do not live by bread alone but by the love, compassion and goodwill which we can show to one another.

We are coming to the end of the Christian era and find ourselves standing on the threshold of the global era. We are living through a fragile stage of social, cultural and religious transition, as we move from being primarily members of tribal society to learning how to find our place in a new kind of society, the global society. In the world to come we humans find we are dependent wholly on our own inner resources, yet not so much individually as collectively. The challenges which lie ahead cannot be overcome by any one person or group working on their own but only by the human species working as a whole. Whether the global society will ever be fully realised, we cannot say. What we can do individually is to hope for it, try to visualise it, and do our utmost to bring it to pass. As I have tried to show in this book, unless we humans are strongly motivated to become a global society, we are likely in the imminent future to suffer horrendous catastrophes which will be of our own making. The realisation of the global society will require from the whole of humanity creative thinking, self-sacrificing endeavour of the highest order, and all the mutual goodwill of which we are capable.

NOTES

Introduction

1. Isaiah 2:1–4.
2. Jeremiah 4:23–26.
3. Condensed from Matthew 24:29–39 and 2 Timothy 3:1–3.
4. Revelation 21:1
5. 1 Thessalonians 4:16–7
6. 2 Corinthians 5:17.
7. Grace Halsell, *Prophecy and Politics: Militant Evangelists on the Road to Nuclear War*.
8. See Chapter 6.
9. There is a fuller discussion in the author's *Tomorrow's God*, Chapter 7.
10. Robert W. Funk, *Honest to Jesus*, p. 70.
11. Ewert Cousins, *Christ of the 21st Century*, p. 135.
12. For a fuller account of the work of Ludwig Feuerbach see the author's *Faith's New Age*, Chapter 7.
13. Ludwig Feuerbach, *Lectures on the Essence of Religion*, p. 172.

CHAPTER 1 *The End of the Millennium*

1. Marcus J. Borg (ed.), *Jesus at 2000*.
2. Norman Cohn, *Cosmos, Chaos and the World to Come: The Ancient Roots of Apocalyptic Faith*, Foreword.
3. Ibid., p. 227
4. D.S. Russell, *Between the Testaments*, p. 22.
5. R.C. Zaehner, *The Dawn and Twilight of Zoroastrianism*, p. 58.
6. Cohn, op. cit., p. 222.
7. Ibid., pp. 227–28.
8. Ibid., p. 198.

CHAPTER 2 *The Decline of Christian Civilisation*

1. John Baillie, *What is Christian Civilization?*, p. 44.
2. Christopher Dawson, *The Making of Europe*, pp. vii–viii.
3. Christopher Dawson, *The Formation of Christendom*, p. 35.
4. Wilfred Cantwell Smith, *The Meaning and End of Religion*.
5. Ronald Gregor Smith, *Secular Christianity*, p. 138
6. Jacob Burckhardt, *The Civilization of the Renaissance in Italy*, p. 185.
7. See also Chapter 4.
8. Johann-Baptist Metz and Jürgen Moltmann, *Faith and the Future*, p. 31.
9. Dietrich Bonhoeffer, *Letters & Papers from Prison*, pp. 325–27.
10. Alvin and Heidi Toffler, *War and Anti-war: Survival at the Dawn of the 21st Century*, p. 242.

CHAPTER 3 *The Disintegration of Orthodoxy*

1. K.S. Latourette, *A History of Christianity,* p. 1063.
2. W.H. van de Pol, *The End of Conventional Christianity,* p. 12.
3. See the author's *Faith's New Age,* Chapter 6.
4. Stephen Neill, *The Interpretation of the New Testament 1861–1961,* p. 12.
5. Peter de Rosa, *Jesus who Became the Christ.*
6. Albert Schweitzer, *The Quest of the Historical Jesus,* p. 396.
7. Ibid., p. 399.
8. Martin Kähler, *The So-called Historical Jesus and the Historic Biblical Christ,* p. 65. For a fuller account, see pp. 42–71.
9. Ibid., p. 63 (italics added).
10. Ibid., p. 68.
11. Hans Werner Bartsch (ed.), trans. Reginald Fuller, *Kerygma and Myth.*
12. James M. Robinson, *A New Quest of the Historical Jesus.*
13. Marcus J. Borg (ed.), *Jesus at 2000.*
14. Robert Funk, *Honest to Jesus, The Five Gospels: The Search for the Authentic Words of Jesus,* and *The Acts of Jesus: The Search for the Authentic Deeds of Jesus.*
15. John Calvin, *Institutions of the Christian Religion,* Book 1, Chapter 3, para. 1.
16. Paul Tillich, *Systematic Theology,* Vol. 1, pp. 17, 181, and other writings.
17. Paul Tillich, *The Courage to Be,* p. 176.
18. Don Cupitt, *Taking Leave of God,* p. 166.
19. Gordon Kaufman, *In Face of Mystery,* p. 311.
20. Johann-Baptist Metz and Jürgen Moltmann, *Faith and the Future,* p. 31.

CHAPTER 4 *The Failure of Christian Modernism*

1. R.G. Collingwood, *The Idea of History,* pp. 144–46.
2. *Essays and Reviews,* sixth edition, p. 139.
3. Charles Gore (ed.), *Lux Mundi,* p. 132.
4. Anne Freemantle (ed.), *The Papal Encyclicals,* p. 137.
5. Ibid., pp. 143–52.
6. Ibid., p. 207.
7. G. Tyrrell, *Christianity at the Cross-roads,* p. 26.
8. Issued by the Testimony Publishing Company, Chicago, and distributed with the 'compliments of two Christian laymen'.
9. Kirsopp Lake, *The Religion of Yesterday and To-morrow,* p. 159.
10. Ibid., p. 163.
11. H. Richard Niebuhr, *Faith on Earth,* p. 1.

CHAPTER 5 *The Christian Stream of Influence*

1. See John Shelby Spong in such books as *Rescuing the Bible from Fundamentalism* and *Why Christianity Must Change or Die;* John Cobb, *Reclaiming the Church.*
2. Cobb, op. cit., p. 56.
3. Karl Jaspers, *The Origin and Goal of History,* p. 8.
4. See Chapter 4 for quote from Pius IX.
5. Anne Freemantle (ed.), *The Papal Encyclicals,* pp. 393 ff. (italics added).

6. This loose but useful term will be taken up again in the last chapter.

CHAPTER 6 *The Discovery of Relativity*

1. Don Cupitt, *Creation out of Nothing*, pp. 4–5.
2. Paul Tillich, *Christianity and the Encounter of World Religions*, p. 3.
3. C. Jouko Bleeker and Geo Widengreen (eds.), *Historia Religionum*, Vol. 2, p. 355.
4. There is a fuller discussion in the author's *Tomorrow's God*, Chapter 7.
5. Tom Driver, *Christ in a Changing World*, pp. 69, 66.
6. Ibid., p. 56.
7. Ecclesiastes 9:7, 10 (author's translation).

CHAPTER 7 *A Post-Christian Future*

1. See Chapter 5.
2. Robert Bellah, *Beyond Belief*, pp. 43–44.
3. Quoted in David Harvey, *The Condition of Post-modernity*, p. 9.
4. See Chapter 6.
5. David Bohm, *Quantum Theory*.
6. David Bohm, *Wholeness and the Implicate Order*, p. 134.
7. Ibid., p. 196.
8. See Jacques Monod, *Chance and Necessity*.
9. Samuel p. Huntington, *The Clash of Civilizations and the Remaking of World Order*, p. 302.

CHAPTER 8 *Globalisation*

1. See the author's *Tomorrow's God*, Part I.
2. Thomas Berry, *The Dream of the Earth*, p. 117.
3. Pierre Teilhard de Chardin, *The Phenomenon of Man*, p. 277.
4. Pierre Teilhard de Chardin, *The Future of Man*, p. 120.
5. Ibid., p. 124.

CHAPTER 9 *Humanity at War with Itself*

1. Genesis 4:1–16.
2. Genesis 11:1–9.
3. Galatians 3:28.
4. Samuel p. Huntington, *The Clash of Civilizations and the Remaking of World Order*, p. 183.
5. Ibid., p. 184.
6. Ibid., p. 207.
7. Ibid.
8. Daniel p. Moynihan, *Pandaemonium: Ethnicity in International Politics*, pp. 146, 173
9. Zbigniew Brzezinski, *Out of Control*, p. xiv.
10. Ibid., pp. 204–5.
11. Alvin and Heidi Toffler, *War and Anti-war*, p. 242.
12. Huntington, op. cit., p. 304.

CHAPTER 10 *Humanity at War with the Planet*

1. See Preface
2. Hosea 2:11.
3. Isaiah 45:5, 6, 14, 18, 23.
4. Genesis 1:27. The priestly creation myth Genesis 1–2:4a is now commonly regarded as reflecting a later cultural period than the Yahwistic creation myth, Genesis 2:4b–3:24, which the ancient compilers of the Pentateuch placed after it. .
5. Emil Brunner, *The Christian Doctrine of Creation and Redemption*, pp. 67–68.
6. Arnold Toynbee, 'The Genesis of Pollution', *Horizon* (New York, American Heritage), Summer 1973, p. 7.
7. Johann-Baptist Metz and Jürgen Moltmann , *Faith and the Future*, p. 71.
8. Arnold Toynbee, *Mankind and Mother Earth*, p. 17.
9. James Lovelock, *The Ages of Gaia: A Biography of Our Living Earth*.
10. For a fuller description of World 3, see the author's *Tomorrow's God*, pp. 63–71.
11. Edward Goldsmith, *The Way: An Ecological World-View*, p. xiii.
12. Metz and Moltmann, op. cit., p. 176.

CHAPTER 11 *Scenarios of the Future*

1. See Chapter 1.
2. For fuller details, see Zbigniew Brzezinski, *Out of Control: Global Turmoil on the Eve of the 21st Century*, pp. 8–18.
3. Dietrich Bonhoeffer, *Letters and Papers from Prison*, pp. 325–29.
4. Harrison Brown, *The Challenge of Man's Future*, p. x.
5. Brzezinski, op. cit., p. 227.
6. See Michio Kaku, *Visions*, pp. 183–92, for a sketch of this struggle.
7. United Nations, *The State of the World Environment*, p. 16.
8. William Greider, *One World Ready or Not*, p. 468.
9. Ibid., p. 473.
10. Ephesians 6:12.
11. Brzezinski, op. cit., p. 225.
12. Johann-Baptist Metz and Jürgen Moltmann, *Faith and the Future*, p. 176.
13. John Naisbitt and Patricia Aburdene, *Megatrends 2000*, pp. 161–67.
14. Alvin and Heidi Toffler, *War and Anti-war: Survival at the Dawn of the 21st Century*, p. 242.
15. Greider, op. cit., p. 468.
16. Howard Snyder, *Earth Currents: The Struggle for the World's Soul*, p. 291.
17. Ibid., p. 297.

CHAPTER 12 *A Faith for the Future*

1. T.S. Eliot, *Collected Poems*, Faber & Faber, 1936, p. 157.
2. Ibid., p. 90.
3. Emile Durkheim, *The Elementary Forms of the Religious Life*, p. 427.
4. Arnold Toynbee, *Mankind and Mother Earth*, p. 4.
5. Gordon D. Kaufman, *In Face of Mystery*, pp. 120–33.
6. Johann-Baptist Metz and Jürgen Moltmann, *Faith and the Future*, p. 176.

7. Compare John 12:24.
8. See Van A. Harvey, *Feuerbach and the Interpretation of Religion*, p. 164.
9. Ibid., p. 166.
10. Jacques Monod, *Chance and Necessity*.
11. Brian Swimme and Thomas Berry, *The Universe Story*, pp. 255–57.
12. Sallie McFague, *The Body of God*, p. 83.
13. See the author's *Resurrection – A Symbol of Hope*.
14. Don Cupitt, *After God*, p. 127.
15. Kaufman, op. cit., p. 347.
16. Don Cupitt, *The New Religion of Life in Everyday Speech*.

SELECT BIBLIOGRAPHY

Anderson, Walter Truett (ed.), *The Fontana Post-modernism Reader*, Fontana, 1996

Baillie, John, *What is Christian Civilization?*, Oxford University Press, 1945

Bartsch, Hans Werner (ed.), *Kerygma and Myth*, Harper & Row, 1961

Bellah, Robert, *Beyond Belief*, Harper & Row, 1970

Berger, Peter, *The Heretical Imperative*, Anchor Press, 1979

Berry, Thomas, *The Dream of the Earth*, Sierra Club Books, 1988

Bleeker, C. Jouko, and Geo Widengren (eds), *Historia Religionum*, Vol. 2, E.J. Brill, 1971

Bloom, Harold, *Omens of Millennium*, Fourth Estate, 1996

Bohm, David, *Wholeness and the Implicate Order*, Routledge and Kegan Paul, 1980

Bohm, David, *Quantum Theory*, Constable, 1954

Bonhoeffer, Dietrich, *Letters & Papers from Prison*, The Enlarged Edition, SCM Press, 1971

Borg, Marcus J. (ed.), *Jesus at 2000*, Westview Press, 1997

Brown, Harrison, *The Challenge of Man's Future*, Westview Press, 1954

Brown, Lester R. *et al.*, *Saving the Planet*, W. W. Norton & Co., 1991

Brunner, Emil, *The Christian Doctrine of Creation and Redemption*, Lutterworth Press, 1952

Brzezinski, Zbigniew, *Out of Control: Global Turmoil on the Eve of the 21st Century*, Macmillan, 1993

Burckhardt, Jacob, *The Civilization of the Renaissance in Italy*, George Allen & Unwin, 1951

Calvin, John, *Institutions of the Christian Religion*, Calvin Translation Society, 1895

Campion, Norman, *The Great Year*, Arkana, 1994

Capra, Fritjof, *The Tao of Physics*, Flamingo, 1992

Capra, Fritjof, *The Turning Point*, Flamingo, 1982

Capra, Fritjof, *The Web of Life*, HarperCollins, 1996

Cobb, John, *Reclaiming the Church*, Westminster John Knox Press, 1997

Clifford, Paula, *A Brief History of End-Time*, Lion Publishing Company, 1997

Cohn, Norman, *The Pursuit of the Millennium*, Secker & Warburg, 1957

Cohn, Norman, *Cosmos, Chaos and the World to Come: The Ancient Roots of Apocalyptic Faith*, Yale University Press, 1993

Collingwood, R.G., *The Idea of History*, Oxford University Press, 1946

Cooper, Tim, *Green Christianity*, Hodder & Stoughton, 1990

Cox, Harvey, *The Secular City*, SCM Press, 1965

Cousins, Ewert, *Christ of the 21st Century*, Element, 1992

Crystal, David, *English as a Global Language*, Cambridge University Press, 1997

Cupitt, Don, *Taking Leave of God*, SCM Press, 1980

Cupitt, Don, *Creation out of Nothing*, SCM Press, 1990

Cupitt, Don, *After God: The Future of Religion*, BasicBooks, 1997

Cupitt, Don, *The New Religion of Life in Everyday Speech*, SCM Press, 1999

Daly, Hermann E., and John B.Cobb, *For the Common Good,* Beacon Press, 1989

Daly, Hermann E. (ed.), *Economics, Ecology, Ethics,* W. H. Freeman & Co., 1980

Dawson, Christopher, *The Making of Europe,* Sheed & Ward, 1948

Dawson, Christopher, *The Formation of Christendom,* Sheed & Ward, 1967

Dawson, Christopher, *The Dividing of Christendom,* Sidgwick & Jackson, 1971

de Rosa, Peter, *Jesus who Became the Christ,* Collins, 1975

Driver, Tom, *Christ in a Changing World,* SCM Press, 1981

Duncan, David Ewing, *The Calendar,* Fourth Estate, 1998

Durkheim, Emile, *The Elementary Forms of the Religious Life,* George, Allen & Unwin, 1915, 1976

Edwards, David L., *The Futures of Christianity,* Hodder & Stoughton, 1987

Feuerbach, Ludwig, *The Essence of Christianity,* [1841], translated by George Eliot, Harper & Row, 1957

Feuerbach, Ludwig, *Lectures on the Essence of Religion,* translated by Ralph Mannheim, Harper & Row, 1967

Freemantle, Anne (ed.), *The Papal Encyclicals,* Mentor Omega, 1963

Fukuyama, Francis, *The End of History and the Last Man,* Avon Books, 1992

Funk, Robert W., *Honest to Jesus,* HarperSanFrancisco, 1996

Funk, Robert W., Roy W. Hoover and the Jesus Seminar, *The Five Gospels,* HarperSanFrancisco, 1997

Funk, Robert W., and the Jesus Seminar, *The Acts of Jesus,* HarperSanFrancisco, 1998

Geering, Lloyd, *Faith's New Age,* Collins, 1980

Geering, Lloyd, *Tomorrow's God,* Bridget Williams Books, 1994

Geering, Lloyd, *Relativity: the Key to Human Understanding,* St. Andrew's Trust, 1997

Geering, Lloyd, *Does Society Need Religion?,* St. Andrew's Trust, 1998

Goldsmith, Edward, *The Way: An Ecological World-View,* The University of Georgia Press, 1992, 1998

Gore, Charles (ed.), *Lux Mundi,* John Murray, 1891

Gould, Stephen Jay, *Questioning the Millennium: A Rationalist's Guide to a Precisely Arbitrary Countdown,* Cape, 1997

Greider, Williams, *One World, Ready or Not,* Simon and Schuster, 1997

Griffin, David Ray, *God and Religion in the Postmodern World,* State University of New York Press, 1989

Griffin, David Ray, William A. Beardslee and Joe Holland, *Varieties of Postmodern Theology,* State University of New York Press, 1989

Hall, Douglas John, *The End of Christendom and the Future of Christianity,* Trinity Press International, 1997

Halsell, Grace, *Prophecy and Politics: Militant Evangelists on the Road to Nuclear War,* Lawrence Hill & Co., 1986

Harnack, Adolf, *What is Christianity?,* Harper & Brothers, 1957

Harvey, David, *The Condition of Post-modernity,* Blackwell, 1989

Harvey, Van A., *Feuerbach and the Interpretation of Religion,* Cambridge University Press, 1997

Heilbroner, Robert, and William Milberg, *The Crisis of Vision in Modern Economic Thought,* Cambridge University Press, 1995

Hopper, Stanley Romaine, *The Crisis of Faith,* Hodder & Stoughton, 1947

Horgan, John, *The End of Science,* Abacus, 1998

Huntington, Samuel P., *The Clash of Civilizations and the Remaking of World Order*, Simon & Schuster, 1996

Jaspers, Karl, *The Origin and Goal of History*, Routledge and Kegan Paul, 1953

Jencks, Charles, *What is Post-modernism?*, 4th ed., Academy Editions, 1996

Kähler, Martin, *The So-called Historical Jesus and the Historic Biblical Christ*, Fortress Press, 1964

Kaku, Michio, *Visions, How Science will Revolutionize the Twenty-first Century*, Oxford University Press, 1998

Kaufman, Gordon D., *In Face of Mystery*, Harvard University Press, 1993

Kennedy, Paul, *Preparing for the Twenty-first Century*, Vintage Books, 1994

Lake, Kirsopp, *The Religion of Yesterday and To-morrow*, Christophers, 1925

Kepel, Gilles, *The Revenge of God*, Pennsylvania State University Press, 1994

Lakeland, Paul, *Postmodernity*, Fortress Press, 1977

Latourette, Kenneth Scott, *A History of Christianity*, Eyre & Spottiswoode Limited, 1964

Lovelock, James, *The Ages of Gaia: A Biography of Our Living Earth*, W. W. Norton & Co., 1988.

McDaniel, Jay B., *Earth, Sky, Gods & Mortals*, Twenty-third Publications, 1990

McFague, Sallie, *The Body of God*, SCM Press, 1993

Metz, Johann-Baptist, and Jürgen Moltmann, *Faith and the Future*, Orbis Books, 1995

Meadows, Donella H. *et al.*, *Beyond the Limits*, Earthscan Publications, 1992

Monod, Jacques, *Chance and Necessity*, Collins, 1972

Moynihan, Daniel Patrick, *Pandaemonium: Ethnicity in International Politics*, Oxford University Press, 1993

Naisbitt, John and Patricia Aburdene, *Megatrends 2000*, William & Co., 1990

Neill, Stephen, *The Interpretation of the New Testament 1861-1961*, Oxford University Press, 1964

Niebuhr, H. Richard [ed. by his son Richard R. Niebuhr], *Faith on Earth*, Yale University Press, 1989

Robinson, James M., *A New Quest of the Historical Jesus*, SCM Press, 1959

Russell, D.S., *Between the Testaments*, SCM Press, 1960

Schell, Jonathan, *The Fate of the Earth*, Avon Books, 1982

Schweitzer, Albert, *The Quest of the Historical Jesus*, Adam and Charles Black, 1906

Smith, Ronald Gregor, *Secular Christianity*, Collins, 1966

Smith, Wilfred Cantwell, *The Meaning and End of Religion*, Mentor Books, 1964

Smith, Wilfred Cantwell, *Faith and Belief*, Princeton University Press, 1979

Smith, Wilfred Cantwell, *Towards a World Theology*, Macmillan Press, 1981

Snyder, Howard A., *Earth Currents: The Struggle for the World's Soul*, Abingdon Press, 1995

Soros, George, *The Crisis of Global Capitalism*, Public Affairs, 1998

Spong, John Shelby, *Rescuing the Bible from Fundamentalism*, HarperSanFrancisco, 1991

Spong, John Shelby, *Why Christianity Must Change or Die*, HarperSanFrancisco, 1998

Strauss, D.F., *The Life of Jesus Critically Examined*, SCM Press, 1973

Suzuki David, *The Sacred Balance*, Allen & Unwin, 1997

Suzuki, David, *Earth Time,* Allen & Unwin, 1998

Swimme, Brian, and Thomas Berry, *The Universe Story,* Arkana Penguin, 1992

Teilhard de Chardin, Pierre, *The Phenomenon of Man,* Fontana, 1965

Teilhard de Chardin, Pierre, *The Future of Man,* Fontana, 1969

Thompson, Damian, *The End of Time,* Minerva, 1997

Tillich, Paul, *Systematic Theology,* 3 vols., Nisbet & Co, 1953–64

Tillich, Paul, *The Courage to Be,* Collins, 1962

Tillich, Paul, *Christianity and the Encounter of World Religions,* Columbia University Press, 1964

Toffler, Alvin, *Future Shock,* Random House, 1970

Toffler, Alvin and Heidi, *War and Anti-war: Survival at the dawn of the 21st Century,* Little, Brown & Co., 1993

Toynbee, Arnold, *Surviving the Future,* Oxford University Press, 1971

Toynbee, Arnold, *Mankind and Mother Earth,* Oxford University Press, 1976

Tyrrell, George, *Christianity at the Cross-roads,* Longmans Green & Co, 1910

United Nations, *The State of the World Environment,* Nairobi, 1989

van de Pol, W. H., *The End of Conventional Christianity,* Newman Press, 1968

Veitch, James (ed.), *Can Humanity Survive? The World's Religions and the Environment,* Awareness Book Company, New Zealand, 1996

Wilson, Bryan, *Magic and the Millennium,* Paladin, 1975

Zaehner, R.C., *The Dawn and Twilight of Zoroastrianism,* Weidenfeld & Nicolson, 1961

INDEX